A Comparative Guide to the Asian Infrastructure Investment Bank

A Comparative Guide to the Asian Infrastructure Investment Bank

Second Edition

NATALIE LICHTENSTEIN

OXFORD
UNIVERSITY PRESS

OXFORD
UNIVERSITY PRESS

Oxford University Press is a department of the University of Oxford.
It furthers the University's objective of excellence in research, scholarship,
and education by publishing worldwide. Oxford is a registered trade mark of
Oxford University Press in the UK and certain other countries.

Published in the United States of America by Oxford University Press
198 Madison Avenue, New York, NY 10016, United States of America.

First Edition published in 2018
Second Edition published in 2025

Library of Congress Cataloging-in-Publication Data
Names: Lichtenstein, Natalie author
Title: A comparative guide to the Asian Infrastructure Investment Bank / Natalie Lichtenstein.
Description: New York : Oxford University Press, 2025.
Identifiers: LCCN 2025042280 (print) | LCCN 2025042281 (ebook) |
ISBN 9780197823088 hardback | ISBN 9780197823101 UPDF | ISBN 9780197823095 epub |
ISBN 9780197823118 Law Pro
Subjects: LCSH: Asian Infrastructure Investment Bank | Development banks—Law and legislation—Asia | Infrastructure (Economics)—Finance—Law and legislation—Asia | Investment banking—Asia | Asia—Foreign economic relations
Classification: LCC KM909.A835 L53 2026 (print) | LCC KM909.A835 (ebook) |
DDC 332.1/53095—dc23/eng/20250910
LC record available at https://lccn.loc.gov/2025042280
LC ebook record available at https://lccn.loc.gov/2025042281

DOI: 10.1093/law/9780197823088.001.0001

The manufacturer's authorized representative in the EU for product safety is
Oxford University Press España S.A. of Parque Empresarial San Fernando de Henares,
Avenida de Castilla, 2 – 28830 Madrid (www.oup.es/en or product.safety@oup.com).
OUP España S.A. also acts as importer into Spain of products made by the manufacturer.

Note to Readers

This publication is designed to provide accurate and authoritative information in regard to the subject matter covered. It is based upon sources believed to be accurate and reliable and is intended to be current as of the time it was written. It is sold with the understanding that the publisher is not engaged in rendering legal, accounting, or other professional services. If legal advice or other expert assistance is required, the services of a competent professional person should be sought. Also, to confirm that the information has not been affected or changed by recent developments, traditional legal research techniques should be used, including checking primary sources where appropriate.

(Based on the Declaration of Principles jointly adopted by a Committee of the American Bar Association and a Committee of Publishers and Associations.)

FOREWORD TO THE FIRST EDITION

Her name came to mind the moment I was appointed Secretary General of the Multilateral Interim Secretariat tasked to create a new multilateral development bank (MDB). None better than Natalie Lichtenstein to be Chief Counsel, I thought. Her long legal service experience in the public sector, government and the World Bank complemented her knowledge about and deep attachment to Asia.

Some questioned my choice of an American for such an important job, given the United States' stance on the MDB's creation at that time. Instead, a strong underlying message was delivered to the world: inclusiveness, merit-based recruitment and gender balance would be deeply embedded in this new institution. So, she joined the preparatory team of diverse nationalities and expertise that I quickly assembled for the Asian Infrastructure Investment Bank (AIIB). The Secretariat team worked well with the Chief Negotiators of the initial twenty-two prospective founding members that had signed the 2014 Memorandum of Understanding, soon joined by other regional and non-regional countries, boosting the number to fifty-seven.

The variety of items on the agenda matched the variety of meeting venues. We began the first meeting in Kunming, then moved to Mumbai, Almaty, Beijing, Singapore, Tbilisi, Frankfurt and Jakarta. The sense of the importance of connectivity was enhanced by the host countries' eagerness to develop infrastructure and their overwhelming support for the AIIB concept. I envisioned a caravan along the ancient silk road, its company continuously swelling as it moved forward. China's leader had planted the seed, yet what made it grow was the shared vision and concerted effort of all shareholders.

Reaching consensus on the Articles of Agreement was surprisingly smooth, showing the stakeholders' shared vision and commitment to creating a new MDB for the twenty-first century. The Chief Negotiators kept AIIB's mission and mandate in the crosshairs, focusing on major issues to bring the negotiation to a conclusion without lengthy debate and bargaining. Our discussions were intense yet collegial because the vision and need were clear to everyone.

It was time, we thought. Asia needed a new development institution. Success has bred new challenges, and decades of fast growth have led to serious infrastructure bottlenecks—roadblocks waiting to be removed. Nations have benefited from globalization in varying levels of success, yet those benefits were not equally shared, leaving some behind. A new way forward based on the ideals of shared benefits and collaborative participation was needed. Inspiration came from the experiences of Asian nations such as China, the Republic of Korea and Japan which had successfully demonstrated how infrastructure investments can drive economic growth and lift hundreds of millions out of poverty. Embracing collaboration and connectivity, we welcomed the idea of a new MDB that would develop a new way of doing things and would actively participate in the shaping of Asia.

AIIB's reason for being is reflected in its special governance structure and operating style, among other innovative features. It is remarkable that we all embraced the new concept of the institution we were creating. Together, we agreed on its signature combination of a non-resident Board, the Board's delegation of project approval authority to Management and an organizational structure for cost-effectiveness and efficiency, with commitments to transparency and Asian development thinking embedded in the bank's philosophy. A striking new element was the introduction of the Compliance, Effectiveness and Integrity Unit, which works independently of Management and reports directly to the Board of Directors.

From the outset, the core principles could not have been clearer: We were not aiming for a bank that would be dominated by one or a few members. Rather, the bank would rest upon multilateralism and international cooperation. It would be inclusive, innovative, efficient and cost-effective. It would be built on trust and partnership. It should remain in the gene pool of the MDB family, but by no means should it become a clone of the existing members. The youngest child of the multilaterals should represent the new century while closely collaborating with its well-established siblings. Thus AIIB was born expeditiously, carrying the DNA of its founders.

It was humbling for all of us to have contributed to the creation of this new investment bank with an Asian identity, with the benefit of the experience of other MDBs that came before it. Among us, Ms Lichtenstein's role cannot be overstated. She was the lynchpin and realist who translated the Chief Negotiators' vision into a pragmatic and well-defined legal framework that became the foundation of AIIB. She was exceptionally resourceful and always ready to take out a legal phrase from her toolkit to work out a disputed provision, thereby bridging gaps in understanding. Her deep expertise, wise counsel and diligence won the respect of all, generously expressed by the Chief Negotiators and Secretariat staff.

I join them in gratitude and appreciation for her dedication. This book is a testament to her contributions. AIIB will forever bear her fingerprints.

Many publications about AIIB are sure to come out in the years to come. Ms Lichtenstein is here to take the lead.

Jin Liqun
President, Asian Infrastructure Investment Bank

FOREWORD TO THE SECOND EDITION

As AIIB has just concluded its Tenth Annual Meeting and approaches its tenth anniversary on January 16, 2026, much has changed since the Bank first became operational. A question that is frequently asked—by those pleasantly surprised and curious about the secret of its success—is: *"What do you think is the greatest achievement in the first decade of this Bank?"*

What AIIB has become appears to exceed even the most optimistic expectations.

For a development bank, the most important measure of success is its development impact. Since the Charter was negotiated and institutional arrangements finalized, AIIB has established itself as a fully operational multilateral development bank (MDB). With more than 320 operations across thirty-eight members and over US$61 billion in financing, AIIB has much to recommend itself.

From a start-up with 57 founding members, the Bank now counts 110 members, representing over 80% of the global population and more than 65% of global GDP. Its staff of 700 comes from over 70 economies. While AIIB's mandate is focused on Asia, its financing extends beyond the region, recognizing that Asia's sustainable development depends on strong trade and investment ties with the rest of the world.

AIIB's mandate is to foster broad-based economic and social development through investment in infrastructure and other productive sectors. We define infrastructure in a broad sense, going well beyond traditional concepts. Renewable energy and climate financing are at the forefront of our operations, helping countries grow and green their economies. In 2024, nearly all projects incorporated climate components, surpassing the goal of allocating at least 50% of total financing to climate mitigation and adaptation. That same year, one-third of AIIB's financing supported cross-border connectivity.

Investments in digital infrastructure—data centers, connectivity platforms, and digital public goods—help bridge the digital divide and enable inclusive growth. Social infrastructure such as education and health care remains important, even if its share is relatively smaller. During the pandemic, AIIB launched a Crisis Recovery Facility that provided timely financial support totaling US$18.5 billion to members. Our lending modalities emphasize adaptability and responsiveness.

AIIB has also established a strong financial foundation. With its AAA ratings well maintained, the Bank has raised over US$54 billion in twenty currencies. Since 2022, operating income has covered administrative expenses, and in 2024, the Bank reported a profit of US$1.1 billion. This strong position enables us to raise funds at the lowest possible cost, benefiting our clients directly.

Behind these numbers is a consistent commitment to multilateralism, high governance standards, and international best practices. In the early days, doubts and questions swirled about the intent behind the creation of this new development institution. But over time, AIIB has proven its credibility as an apolitical, high-standard multilateral development bank.

I believe the Bank's greatest success lies in this very credibility. Its founding principle—to be "lean, clean, and green"—has become its defining ethos. Over the past decade, we have earned the trust of the international community. AIIB's commitment to multilateralism is unwavering and reflected in its growing network of partnerships, including MDBs, international financial institutions, bilateral agencies, development finance institutions, philanthropic organizations, multilateral funds and platforms, knowledge institutions, the UN, and technical assistance providers. This inclusivity amplifies our development impact across systems.

The geopolitical storms of the past decade have tested AIIB's resilience and integrity. We have remained steadfast through turbulent times. To quote Shakespeare, "[W]hen the sea was calm, all boats alike [s]howed mastery in floating." The sea has not always been calm—and it never will be. Yet, AIIB has held its course.

AIIB's multilateral foundations are further explored in this second edition of Ms. Lichtenstein's book. The first edition helped global audiences understand how AIIB fit into the existing MDB landscape, and where it brought new ideas and approaches. This second edition enriches that understanding, offering new chapters on the history of MDB Charters and examining AIIB's heritage and innovations in practice.

I am confident that Ms. Lichtenstein's work will support AIIB as it enters its second decade and continues to evolve as a trusted multilateral partner.

Jin Liqun
President, Asian Infrastructure Investment Bank

PREFACE TO THE FIRST EDITION

This book began with another book.

When I flew to Beijing in the autumn of 2014 to begin discussions on drafting the Asian Infrastructure Investment Bank (AIIB) Charter, I had with me a concise and seminal work: *The European Bank for Reconstruction and Development—A Comparative Analysis of the Constituent Instrument*, published in 1990 by Ibrahim F.I. Shihata (World Bank General Counsel, 1983–98). As I retrieved it from my bookshelf in preparation for the trip, I discovered that my copy was inscribed to me with his appreciation for my small contribution, a quarter of a century earlier. Now that AIIB has been set up and my own book is ready, the appreciation is mine.

My appreciation for the breadth and depth of the issues that confront a drafter and a General Counsel was already deep as a result of my work at the World Bank, where a Shihata legal opinion was worth its weight in gold. (My copy of his classic compilation, *The World Bank Legal Papers*, is both inscribed and well-worn.) In preparing the AIIB Charter, though, I came to realize just how useful "Shihata on EBRD" had been. In consulting multilateral development bank (MDB) lawyers from around the world for insights on various MDB Charters, so many people mentioned that book, saying it was one of the most used volumes on their office shelves. What they found useful went beyond the description of the EBRD Charter: it was what Dr Shihata himself called "a much needed source for a ready comparison of the texts of the agreements establishing various multilateral development institutions . . ."[1]

Written as soon as the EBRD Charter was finalized, and published the year before EBRD was formally established, *The European Bank for Reconstruction and Development* focused primarily on the legal provisions. In updating and expanding these earlier references to other MDB Charters,[2] I found myself drawn even more to the origin stories of various MDB Charters. With appreciation gained from the drafting of the AIIB Charter, I began to wonder why particular clauses were in some (or, occasionally, all) of the other Charters. Full research into each one is well beyond the scope of this book on AIIB. Some early findings are tucked into

[1] Shihata (1990) at xi.

[2] Many aspects of the 1990 comparative survey of MDB Charters were updated in the lectures given by Dr Andres Rigo Sureda at the Hague Academy of International Law in 2004, on the Law Applicable to the Activities of International Development Banks. These were published in Rigo Sureda (2004), which I also kept handy for my AIIB work.

the footnotes where relevant, and some cross-cutting observations can be found in Chapter 10's Reflections (Chapter 13, Reflections Revisited, in the Second Edition).

The book before you draws heavily on what I learned in preparing and negotiating the AIIB Charter. One of the most rewarding aspects of that process was the multitude of conversations with lawyers experienced in a wide range of international financial institutions. They told me what they would have liked to have seen (and not seen) in other Charters, which pillars to preserve and what pitfalls to avoid. Some were retired, looking back on long careers in different places and times, offering perspectives removed from day-to-day pressures; others were grappling with the issues of the day. I treasured the insights from them all. Many found their way into AIIB's Charter, and still others illuminate the pages of this book. Among those many advisors, let me thank first Jeremy Hovland, Elizabeth Hunt, Daud Ilyas, Emmanuel Maurice, Andres Rigo Sureda and James Spinner—collectively, they provided viewpoints from the Asian Development Bank (AsDB), Black Sea Trade and Development Bank (BSTDB), EBRD, Inter-American Development Bank (IADB), International Fund for Agricultural Development (IFAD), the World Bank and the Global Fund, to name a few. I'm also grateful to several of my former World Bank colleagues who shared their advice in that formative period (Abel Caamano, Anna Chytla, Clifford Frazier, David Rivero, and especially Adam Shayne and Jaap van Opstal), along with Heikki Cantell, Damien Eastman and Gerard Sanders, and Professors William Alford and Edith Brown Weiss.

My role in drafting the AIIB Charter was not to invent AIIB's requirements, but rather to translate into long-lasting and nuanced legal structures the plans of others. Lest I leave the impression that the drafter created the content of the Charter, let me emphasize that the substantive directions came from the AIIB Multilateral Interim Secretariat, led by Jin Liqun as Secretary-General. At the Secretariat, I also benefited from working closely with many colleagues from around the world. Ultimately, it was the Chief Negotiators from many countries who gave us all guidance, and the final blessing.

Eventually, it came time to leave behind my AIIB work, and my monthly commutes to Beijing from my home in Washington, DC. A non-resident Board of Directors will have its benefits for AIIB, I believe, but a non-resident General Counsel is not a long-term solution for a fully operating and active MDB. In the autumn of 2016, I then turned to preparing this book, to share what I had learned and, as it turned out, to learn more. I was extremely fortunate that several people, knowledgeable and generous, read earlier drafts of this manuscript, and offered helpful suggestions and critiques. For these most valuable contributions, I am deeply grateful to Philip Daltrop, Nicolette DeWitt, Jeremy Hovland, Daud Ilyas, Elie Raimond, Andres Rigo Sureda and Jaap van Opstal. Others took time to review relevant sections, and shared their expertise in different areas (Nancy Jacklin, Lance Liebman, Stephen Lintner, Eva Meigher, Russell Munk, Ian Nightingale, Joan Powers and Gerard

Sanders). Still others helped educate me about the publishing world (Antonio Parra and Scott Seligman). Vikram Ragahavan at the World Bank is an unmatched repository of World Bank history, which he graciously shared. Charles Hobbs helped immeasurably as a diligent and thoughtful research assistant in the final stages of preparation.

Throughout this period, I've benefited enormously from the collegiality and support of the China Studies team at SAIS (Johns Hopkins School of Advanced International Studies), where I have been teaching Law and Society in China as an adjunct professor. The assistance from SAIS was essential, as were the thoughtful interactions with Professors David Lampton, Pieter Bottelier and Carla Freeman, and Zhaojin Ji.

At Oxford University Press, I wish to thank Merel Alstein, who saw merit in the book proposal and shepherded it expeditiously, as well as Natasha Flemming and James Baird, who saw to the book's timely production.

It is traditional to thank my family here. It is also insufficient. They had every reason to expect that my retirement from the World Bank in 2010 would serve to re-right the balance between home and professional pursuits, in their favor. When AIIB came into my life four years later, their hopes were largely dashed. By the time I took an extra year after AIIB to write this book, I suppose they had become resigned to my preoccupation—and were unstintingly supportive and occasionally enthusiastic about this project!

For their loving forbearance, I dedicate my everlasting appreciation—and this book—to my beloved husband, Willard Tom, and our most wonderful sons, Alexander Lichtenstein Tom and Joshua Lichtenstein Tom; my dear brother, Jonathan Lichtenstein, and his family (Deann, Nathaniel and Samuel Lichtenstein); and my proud parents, Cecile and the late Abba Lichtenstein. It was Abba who insisted, at my World Bank retirement, that the MDB world was not done with me yet—how prescient he proved to be.

The advice and support from all these good people and others notwithstanding, any errors are all mine.

Washington, DC
December 2017

AUTHOR'S PREFACE TO THE SECOND EDITION

This second edition of *A Comparative Guide to the Asian Infrastructure Investment Bank* took me in two intriguing directions: the Asian Infrastructure Investment Bank (AIIB) in action and the Charters of multilateral development banks (MDBs) in history.

Updating the first edition text and tables from end 2017 to mid-2025 gave me a detailed appreciation of the development of AIIB in the intervening years. I looked at the latest information for every chapter: mandate, investment operations, membership, finance, governance, and institutional matters. Having helped to establish AIIB's legal framework in these areas, I found it quite interesting to see how it has been utilized in reality. That exercise inspired Chapter 12 in the new edition (Innovative Practice: AIIB's First Decade), which looks at some of the key innovative aspects of AIIB's first decade. Topics such as the non-resident Board of Directors, delegation and accountability, oversight, and COVID-19 response are the highlights.

Delving into the origins of MDB Charters was more unusual. They are certainly unique as a class. As I drafted the AIIB Charter in 2014–2015, I had a wealth of MDB Charters as handy resources. I realized afterwards that I didn't know where my path-breaking predecessors had looked, seventy years earlier, in drafting the first of the MDB Charters, the Articles of Agreement of the International Bank for Reconstruction and Development (IBRD).

Preliminary study for the first edition had yielded the short answer. The earliest ancestor was the Bank for International Settlements (BIS, 1930), itself the first international financial institution (IFI). Even closer connections exist between IBRD and a never-established Inter-American Bank (IAB, 1940), a precursor to the Inter-American Development Bank (IADB). This time around, I looked deeply into how the BIS and IAB Charters were put together, and how they can be traced in the IBRD Charter. Many articles, a few books and oral histories, and some fascinating stories later, I have recorded my speculations in Chapter 2 (Legal Origins: IBRD).

From there, I went on to trace this MDB legal structure through the major MDBs that followed IBRD, and to retrace my steps in creating the latest Charter in the MDB chain. This background proved useful for describing the continuities in the AIIB Charter as well as the innovations. Chapter 3 provides this second piece in the legal origins story (Legal Origins: From IBRD to AIIB). New insights from

AIIB's first decade and MDB history are melded into the concluding Chapter 13 (Reflections Revisited).

I had not expected to produce a second edition. The response to the first edition was truly gratifying. I was pleased to hear from IFI colleagues around the world who swore by the detailed content of the first edition. I was glad to see that experts in many fields around the web used it as a resource for their own works. Especially after the pandemic turned my attention to family health and genealogy, and curtailed my international travel, I didn't envision a return to the world of MDBs. The occasion of AIIB's 10th anniversary in 2025 and the intricacies of MDB history brought me back.

The interconnections seemed predestined when I read more about the British banker who played a leading role on the draft BIS Statutes in 1929. Sir Charles Addis, a leader of the Hong Kong and Shanghai Bank and a Director of the Bank of England, spent much of his career in finance related to China, including infrastructure financing for Chinese railways. He began his Asian assignments with Singapore and Hong Kong, and was one of the first Western bankers living in Beijing in 1886, later assigned to Tianjin, Shanghai, Calcutta, and elsewhere. As I read of his 19th century appreciation for the beauty of Beijing's Western Hills, my mind was instantly filled with an image of those same hills—on January 17, 2016, as we celebrated the conclusion of the Inaugural Meeting of the AIIB Board of Directors.

AIIB has evolved in its ten years, as you will read. So, too, has the circle of friends, former colleagues, and advisors evolved from the first edition, wise and generous folks who took the time to read and make suggestions on different parts of this edition, and to help me find sources I couldn't reach as a desk-chair detective. The more senior folks have aged along with me, growing more distant from our professional pursuits yet gaining new perspectives. At the same time, it has been immensely rewarding to watch the younger team move into more senior and demanding roles in their institutions—less time to catch my errors, more insights to share. I thank many of them below:

- Friends who encouraged me to pursue my BIS and IAB research: Wendy Krasner, Diane Pierce Williams.
- Those well-versed in the realm of MDBs and IFIs: Nancy Jacklin, Vikram Raghavan, Andres Rigo Sureda, Edith Brown Weiss.
- Those who helped update me about MDBs today: Nicolette DeWitt, Alberto Ninio, Ranjini Ramakrishnan, Christopher Smith, Tingying Wang (AIIB); Diana Wilson Patrick (Caribbean Development Bank); Tom Edmonston-Low, Elie Raimond (European Bank for Reconstruction and Development); and Dominique Bichara, Duncan Kiara, Sajjad Ali Shah (World Bank).
- Those who shared wisdom from the academic world: William Alford, Tamar Gutner, Rosa Lastra, Gerald Sanders.
- Those who offered insights on MDB reforms: Chris Humphrey, Kyle Peters.

I am especially grateful to Prachi Tadsare, who was an invaluable and adept partner in discovering the history of MDB Charters and presenting the results for current-day MDBs. Similarly, I had the benefit of suggestions from Gustavo Mathias Alves Pinto, who brought to bear his experience across several IFIs and a wide breadth of resources.

My explorations into BIS history would not have gotten far without advice from Pierre Panchaud (thanks to Joan Powers) and without the essential assistance of Piet Clement in accessing BIS Archives remotely. For BIS-related documents from the Federal Reserve Bank of New York archives, I have to thank Joseph Komljenovich. For IAB documents from the OAS Library, I have to thank Rocio Suarez.

My experience with Oxford University Press (OUP) as an author has been stellar the second time around. For this, I have to thank Fay Gibbons, acquisitions editor; Lisa Butts, development editor; and the OUP teams.

My association as a Fellow with the China Global Research Center at Johns Hopkins School of Advanced International Studies (SAIS) was invaluable for my research on this book.

As I did for the first edition, I have reserved the biggest thanks for my family. It was doubtless foolhardy of me to think I could pull this together in six months, but with their forbearance, I came close. My husband, Will Tom, read far more of this edition, and it is far better for it. My sons, Alex Tom and Joshua Tom, were unfailingly supportive and interested in this project. My brother, Jon Lichtenstein, always had good advice on research and governance in our frequent calls.

Now, I can turn back to the family genealogy that I put aside to work on this book, researching previous generations of the Lichtenstein, Geffen, Jacobus, Chun, and Tom families instead of the family of MDBs. In that vein, let me simply dedicate this second edition: To My Grandchildren.

Chevy Chase, Maryland
August 2025

CONTENTS

FIGURES

ABBREVIATIONS AND TERMS

AfDB means the African Development Bank, and **AfDB Charter** means the Agreement Establishing the African Development Bank, August 4, 1963, 510 UNTS 546, as amended through July 5, 2002.

AIIB means the Asian Infrastructure Investment Bank, and **AIIB Charter** means the Articles of Agreement of the Asian Infrastructure Investment Bank, dated June 29, 2015.

AsDB means the Asian Development Bank, and **AsDB Charter** means the Agreement Establishing the Asian Development Bank, December 4, 1965, 571 UNTS 123.

BIS means the Bank for International Settlements, **BIS Statutes** means the Statutes of the Bank for International Settlement (of January 20, 1930 *unless updated version is cited*) and **BIS Constituent Charter** means the Constituent Charter of the Bank for International Settlements, all incorporated in the Convention Respecting the Bank for International Settlements, found R 104 League of Nations Treaty Series (LNTS) 441.

BRICS means Brazil, Russia, India, China, and South Africa, all founding members of NDB.

BSTDB means the Black Sea Trade and Development Bank, and **BSTDB Charter** means the Agreement Establishing the Black Sea Trade and Development Bank, dated June 30, 1994, as amended through 2013.

CAF means the Andean Development Corporation (Corporación Andina de Fomento), and **CAF Charter** means the Agreement Establishing the Andean Development Corporation, as amended through 2022, now known as Development Bank for Latin America and the Caribbean.

CDB means the Caribbean Development Bank, and **CDB Charter** means the Articles of Agreement of the Caribbean Development Bank, dated January 26, 1970, as amended through 2007.

CEIU means the Complaints-resolution, Evaluation and Integrity Unit of AIIB.

Charter means the Charters as defined under each of the MDBs, and references to MDB Articles are to Articles of the respective Charter, unless otherwise specified.

Chief Negotiators' Report means Report on the Articles of Agreement of the Asian Infrastructure Investment Bank, agreed by the Chief Negotiators for Establishing the Asian Infrastructure Investment Bank in Singapore on May 22, 2015, when they agreed on the final text of the AIIB Charter.

CNM means the Chief Negotiators' Meeting, the forum for negotiations on the AIIB Charter and the establishment of AIIB.

EBRD means the European Bank for Reconstruction and Development, and **EBRD Charter** means the Agreement Establishing the European Bank for Reconstruction and Development, May 29, 1990, 1646 UNTS 97, as amended through July 22, 2025.

ECAFE and **ESCAP** mean the United Nations Economic Commission for Asia and the Far East and then its successor, the Economic and Social Commission for Asia and the Pacific.

EIB means the European Investment Bank, and **EIB Charter** means the Statute of the European Investment Bank, version dated March 15, 2025.

EU means the European Union.

IADB means the Inter-American Development Bank, and **IADB Charter** means the Agreement Establishing the Inter-American Development Bank, April 8, 1959, 389 UNTS 69, as amended through 1995.

IBRD means the International Bank for Reconstruction and Development, and **IBRD Charter** means the Articles of Agreement of the International Bank for Reconstruction and Development, December 27, 1945, 2 UNTS 134, as amended through June 27, 2012.

IDA means the International Development Association, and **IDA Charter** means the Articles of Agreement of the International Development Association, January 26, 1960, 439 UNTS 249.

IFC means the International Finance Corporation, and **IFC Charter** means the Articles of Agreement of the International Finance Corporation, May 25, 1955, 264 UNTS 117, as amended through June 27, 2012.

IMF means the International Monetary Fund, and **IMF Charter** means the Articles of Agreement of the International Monetary Fund, December 27, 1945, 2 UNTS 40, as amended through January 26, 2016.

ISDB means the Islamic Development Bank, and **ISDB Charter** means the Articles of Agreement of the Islamic Development Bank, August 12, 1974.

MDB means generally, a multilateral development bank such as AfDB, AsDB, EBRD, EIB, IADB and IBRD, among others.

MOU means generally a Memorandum of Understanding, and "the MOU" in this book refers to the Memorandum of Understanding on Establishing the Asian Infrastructure Investment Bank among Prospective Founding Members, dated October 24, 2014.

NDB means the New Development Bank, and **NDB Charter** means the Articles of Agreement of the New Development Bank, annexed to the Agreement on the New Development Bank, dated July 15, 2014.

NIB means the Nordic Investment Bank, and **NIB Charter** means the Statutes of the Nordic Investment Bank, as amended through July 29, 2020.

OAS means the Organization of American States.

PFM means a Prospective Founding Member of AIIB, as defined in the MOU.

Special Majority means a decision of the AIIB Board of Governors by an affirmative vote of a majority of the total number of Governors, representing not less than a majority of the total voting power of the members, under AIIB Article 28-2 (iii).

Super Majority means a decision of the AIIB Board of Governors by an affirmative vote of two-thirds of the total number of Governors, representing not less than three-fourths of the total voting power of the members, under AIIB Article 28-2 (ii).

UN means the United Nations.

US dollar and **US$** mean the currency of the United States of America.

NOTE: In line with AIIB Article 36-2, all references in this book to a specific gender are equally applicable to any gender.

1
BEGINNINGS

On a warm May day in Singapore in 2015, the final text of the draft Articles of Agreement of the Asian Infrastructure Investment Bank (AIIB) was accepted by representatives of fifty-seven countries, mostly from Asia and Europe, concluding a whirlwind four-month negotiation. On a hot June day in Beijing a month later, that multilateral treaty (the AIIB Charter) was formally signed on behalf of fifty countries; the other seven countries signed later that year. Finally, on one very cold day in Beijing in January 2016, AIIB's Board of Governors met for their Inaugural Meeting, declaring AIIB officially open—just one year after the first discussions on the draft AIIB Charter began in balmy Mumbai. **1.01**

And so AIIB came to be: a US$100 billion multilateral development bank (MDB) financing infrastructure for the development of Asia, from the Pacific to the Mediterranean. AIIB's investments in infrastructure in its first ten years totaled more than US$60 billion. As an international organization, AIIB counts among its 110 approved members countries in East Asia, South Asia, Central Asia, Western Asia and Oceania, as well as in Europe, Africa, Latin America and North America. As an international financial institution, AIIB enjoys a AAA rating in international capital markets. AIIB's multinational management and staff have taken root in its headquarters in Beijing, home of its initiator and largest shareholder, the People's Republic of China. **1.02**

This outcome was hardly predetermined: at conception, no one knew what precise shape AIIB would take, nor who would actually join in its founding. From a general concept circulating in Asian financial circles in the 2000s, a concrete AIIB proposal by China attracted initial support from twenty-one Asian countries in 2014. Some other countries, within and outside Asia, developed and developing, were initially cautious or opposed, raising questions common for new MDBs: Why set up a new organization instead of expanding or reforming existing ones? Will a potential rival be created for current MDBs and their major shareholders? With a new major shareholder in the lead (China), will this new MDB follow the traditions and standards of the older ones? **1.03**

Charter negotiations could well have concluded among the first twenty-six Asian countries gathered around the table in Mumbai. They might have agreed on a smaller organization, with a smaller scope and footprint. After all, the largest player in MDBs, the United States, was publicly negative about the AIIB proposal; the **1.04** largest MDB shareholder in Asia, Japan, was also reluctant. Nonetheless, when final agreement was reached that day in Singapore, AIIB's Asian founders had grown to thirty-seven, joined by twenty non-Asian founders, with a mix of developed and developing countries in each group.

1.05 The history of past MDB initiatives also might have suggested a smaller beginning. The first MDB, the International Bank for Reconstruction and Development (IBRD, or World Bank), was initiated with a global reach by forty-four countries at the Bretton Woods Conference in 1944, alongside the International Monetary Fund (IMF). Negotiated during World War II, IBRD was to provide finance for both reconstruction and development in the post-war world. Today, IBRD has 189 members; IMF has 191. Other MDBs launched in the following decades had a regional focus under their Charters, and far fewer members than is the case nowadays. These include the major MDBs whose Charters provided the closest models for AIIB:

- The European Investment Bank (EIB), with six European countries in 1957 (now twenty-seven), set up to contribute to the development of the European internal market.
- The Inter-American Development Bank (IADB), with the United States and twenty Latin American countries in 1959 (now forty-eight), set up to contribute to the economic and social development of regional member countries.
- The African Development Bank (AfDB), with thirty-three African countries in 1963 (now eighty-one), set up to contribute to the economic development and social progress of its regional members.
- The Asian Development Bank (AsDB), with twenty-one Asian countries and twelve non-regional countries, focused on Asian development, economic growth, and cooperation, set up in 1965 (now sixty-nine members).
- The European Bank for Reconstruction and Development (EBRD), with thirty-one European countries and nine non-European countries (and two European institutions), focused on Central and Eastern European development and transformation, set up in 1990 (now seventy-seven countries).

Subregional MDBs established in these years, such as the Caribbean Development Bank (CDB), the Black Sea Trade and Development Bank (BSTDB), and the Nordic Investment Bank (NIB), have had a more limited focus. Some MDBs provide mostly public sector loans and guarantees for projects in member countries, as is the case with IBRD; others also provide private sector loans, guarantees and equity investments, or have affiliates that do so. In short, history suggests that AIIB could have taken on different forms, sizes, and objectives, all within the MDB model.

1.06 What are the key features of AIIB that emerged? How indeed does AIIB's framework compare to these other MDBs? This book answers these questions through the lens of the AIIB Charter, the constituent document that these fifty-seven founders put in place as AIIB's legal foundation.

Uniquely, this book introduces the AIIB Charter from the perspective of the lawyer who prepared its many drafts and advised the founders during their discussions. Truly, I was most fortunate to have the most extraordinary seat at the table for AIIB's establishment. As Chief Counsel for the Multilateral Interim Secretariat for Establishing the Asian Infrastructure Investment Bank from November 2014 onwards, I was responsible for the legal work in drafting the AIIB Charter and preparing for AIIB's life as an MDB. After AIIB's Inaugural Meeting in January 2016, I continued as AIIB's Inaugural General Counsel until my successor could take up the position in Beijing in August 2016. For me, it was the opportunity of a lifetime, a chance to translate three decades of experience as a lawyer at the oldest MDB (IBRD) into the setup of the newest MDB (AIIB). My work on AIIB's founding drew on deep knowledge of MDB legal and governance issues as well as long involvement with MDB operations in China and with the development of the Chinese legal system. What was surprising to many was my American passport, considering the US absence from the scene; others took this as an early indication of AIIB's preference for technical skills and recruitment regardless of nationality. **1.07**

Befitting my background and function at AIIB, this book is rich in legal detail about AIIB and its principal MDB comparators. But it is not just for lawyers. Anyone interested in AIIB will have the same basic questions: Why set up AIIB? What will it do? Who are its members? How will it be funded? How will it be governed? How will its organization work? **1.08**

The main part of this book is organized into chapters that present the answers in the context of the AIIB Charter: Mandate (Chapter 4); Investment Operations (Chapter 5); Membership (Chapter 6); Capital and Finance (Chapter 7); Governance: Framework (Chapter 8) and Governance: Decision-Making (Chapter 9); and Institutional Matters (Chapter 11). AIIB's transition from draft Charter to full-fledged organization is chronicled in Chapter 10 (Transitions), laying out the interim governance arrangements and processes in that period. That story may be informative for those initiating future intergovernmental organizations, whether MDBs or other types. **1.09**

In each chapter, there is an introduction for the general reader new to MDBs. Then, I lay out the related legal provisions in the AIIB Charter (found at Appendix 1), and offer comparisons with the Charters of AIIB's closest counterparts in the MDB world—AfDB, AsDB, EBRD, IADB, and IBRD, among others. Extensive footnotes are designed to provide more background for the experts, especially my fellow legal counsel in sister international financial institutions, many of whom offered invaluable insights in the drafting process and beyond. Throughout, the AIIB Charter provisions are supplemented by summaries of AIIB's key documents and policies adopted and actions taken, through June 2025. **1.10**

What the reader will not find here are the ins and outs of the negotiations of the AIIB Charter nor an expose of the motivations of those who proposed AIIB or **1.11** joined in the effort along the way. Those are stories for others to tell, presumably respecting the bounds of confidentiality. What this book does offer is an unparalleled window into the sources and choices for the legal text.

1.12 There is another dimension to the focus here on the results of the negotiations rather than the discussions themselves. A singular theme throughout the AIIB Charter is the legal flexibility offered for AIIB to carry out the mandate its members have given it and to develop and adjust to future changes in the world, as its members see fit. What will matter most as the Charter shapes AIIB in the years to come are the legal provisions that the negotiators agreed upon, not the recollections of their drafter.

1.13 Coming ten years after the AIIB Charter was signed, this second edition updates the areas of focus from the first edition: mandate; investment operations; membership; capital and finance; governance; and institutional matters. The second edition begins, however, with an historical question: where did MDB Charters come from?

1.14 Chapter 2 (Legal Origins: IBRD) explains the roots of the IBRD Charter, drawing lines back to the establishment of the Bank for International Settlements (BIS) in 1930 and agreement on an Inter-American Bank (IAB) in 1940 (never established). Chapter 3 (Legal Origins: From IBRD to AIIB) examines the evolution of MDB Charters from IBRD to AIIB, and discusses AIIB's establishment, with an overview of the inherited as well as unique features of the AIIB Charter in comparison with its predecessors. Both chapters present detailed research into the Charter provisions that rarely sees the light of day.

1.15 Bringing the book up to date in 2025, Chapter 12 (Innovations in Practice: AIIB's First Decade) highlights some of AIIB's experience in its first decade, with a focus on how the legal framework has been fleshed out. Chapter 13 (Reflections Revisited) offers a personal overview of the key trends in MDB development that may affect AIIB in the future, taking into account its recent past.

2
LEGAL ORIGINS: IBRD

For three weeks in July 1944 in Bretton Woods, New Hampshire, the final texts of the Articles of Agreement of the International Bank for Reconstruction and Development (IBRD) and of the International Monetary Fund (IMF) were hammered out by representatives of forty-four countries from around a world at war. The chief proponents were the United States and the United Kingdom; detailed plans dating to 1942 had been discussed between them, and with allies. They were joined in the final negotiations by allies and associated nations from Europe, Latin America, Asia, Africa, and the Union of Soviet Socialist Republics. By December 27, 1945, the requisite number of countries had signed and ratified the Articles for them to come into legal effect. The inaugural meeting of the Board of Governors took place in Savannah, Georgia in March 1946 and IBRD opened its doors in Washington, DC in June 1946.[1] **2.01**

Seven decades later, the Asian Infrastructure Investment Bank (AIIB) followed a similar path to establishment. Multilateral consultations took place in 2014 among more than twenty Asian countries, organized by China, AIIB's chief proponent. Negotiations on AIIB's establishment and its Charter took place in the first half of 2015 among a larger group, fifty-seven countries from Asia writ large, Europe, Latin America, and Africa. By the end of 2015, all fifty-seven negotiating countries had signed the Charter, which became effective on December 25, 2015. AIIB opened its doors in Beijing following the Inaugural Meetings of its Boards in January 2016.[2] **2.02**

The IBRD Charter was seminal for the multilateral development bank (MDB) Charters that followed, including the AIIB Charter. This chapter explores the legal origins of the IBRD Charter itself, which was the first MDB charter. While the history of IBRD has been written many times from many perspectives over the past eighty years, few accounts highlight the legal drafting history reviewed in this chapter. Here, the main focus is on the legal dimensions of two institutions that predated IBRD: the Bank for International Settlements (BIS) in 1930 and the Inter-American Bank (IAB) of 1940 (a precursor of the 1959 Inter-American Development Bank, IADB). **2.03**

[1] *See* Oliver (1996) at 224–8.
[2] Paragraphs 3.19–3.30 provide details.

2.04 The origins of BIS and IAB are recounted, followed by a look at the drafting of the IBRD Charter itself. The chapter concludes by tracing the lineage of legal concepts and clauses from the BIS and IAB Charters into the IBRD Charter. Chapter 3, Legal Origins: From IBRD to AIIB, provides additional insight into the evolution of MDB Charters that followed the IBRD Charter, and shows how AIIB fits into this development process.

A. Overview of MDB Charters

2.05 AIIB's creators and drafters could draw on IBRD's legal and financial structure and seven decades of institutional life, as well as the many permutations found in similar MDBs established in the decades since 1944. The AIIB Charter drew from the IBRD Charter, as it had evolved through the charters of the Inter-American Development Bank (IADB, 1959), the African Development Bank (AfDB, 1963) and the Asian Development Bank (AsDB, 1965), and the European Bank for Reconstruction and Development (EBRD, 1990). There were other examples from the more than twenty other international financial organizations of different mandates that are also considered MDBs, most with charters that resemble in large or small part those of IBRD and these others.[3]

2.06 IBRD was the first MDB, an unusual hybrid model: an international financial institution structured along the lines of a joint-stock bank or company with the principal goal of financing loans to or with the guarantee of a member country for projects that support economic development. Countries become members by subscribing to shares of IBRD capital, paying in 20% of the share value and committing to pay the remaining 80% when called upon by IBRD to do so. Relying on its financial strength, including this callable capital, IBRD raises funds for its operations in international financial markets, maintaining a AAA credit rating to keep down the cost of loans for its members.

2.07 Decisions by the membership are made through weighted voting, with each country's voting power dependent primarily on its subscribed capital shares. Key major decisions are made by a Board of Governors, with one Governor for each member, along the lines of an annual shareholders' assembly in some company structures. Most decisions are made by a Board of Directors—for IBRD, the now

[3] In addition to these principal comparator MDBs, other counterparts for AIIB included Caribbean Development (CDB), European Investment Bank (EIB), Islamic Development Bank (IsDB), and New Development Bank (NDB), as well as sub-regional development banks such as Black Sea Trade and Development Bank (BSTDB), Nordic Investment Bank (NIB), and Development Bank of Latin America and the Caribbean (Corporación Andina de Fomento, CAF). Humphrey (2022) counts thirty MDBs at 1. *See* Humphrey's opening chapter, "Multilateral Development Banks in a Fast-Changing World," for a discussion of MDB characteristics and comparisons to other types of institutions.

Sanders (2022) provides an overview of how the MDBs (and international financial institutions generally) fit into the history of international organizations.

twenty-five resident Executive Directors (Board of Directors) each represent one or more member countries, and are reminiscent of an executive board in some companies. The management is led by a President, also the Chairman of the Board of Directors.

IBRD is not simply a multinational bank in corporate form, however. IBRD's broad purposes are aimed at economic development,[4] not generating profit as a commercial bank would.[5] It is an international organization whose members are countries, with specific supranational privileges and immunities under its Charter and international law. Member countries may benefit from access to its loans and guarantees, while economically developed countries may find that their own contributions to global development go further when combined with the contributions of other countries through Bank financing.[6] Indeed, it was the potential benefits to recipients that made the Bank proposal more attractive to some than the Fund proposal, at least in the eyes of the US Treasury planners.[7] **2.08**

Where were the models for IBRD? Even today, there are few international organizations that resemble the MDBs. In the early 1940s, there were but two similar institutions that planners could look to for inspiration: one was BIS, the first international financial institution, established in 1930; and the other was IAB, an institution that drew on BIS for its 1940 Convention, yet was never established. **2.09**

B. BIS

BIS was founded in 1930 as part of the "so-called final settlement" of First World War reparations.[8] German reparations to the Allied governments, stipulated under the Treaty of Versailles, were set in April 1921, and revised under the Dawes Plan in 1924. By 1928, economic developments were affecting Germany's ability to pay, and **2.10**

[4] Among the purposes listed in IBRD Article I are:

"(i) To assist in the reconstruction and development of territories of members by facilitating the investment of capital for productive purposes, including the restoration of economies destroyed or disrupted by war, the reconversion of productive facilities to peacetime needs and the encouragement of the development of productive facilities and resources in less developed countries.

(ii) To promote private foreign investment by means of guarantees or participations in loans and other investments made by private investors; and when private capital is not available on reasonable terms, to supplement private investment by providing, on suitable conditions, finance for productive purposes out of its own capital, funds raised by it and its other resources."

[5] Humphrey (2022) at 7. *See also* Gutner (2025) for another overview of MDBs.

[6] *See* Morris (2016) at 2: "the United States has long benefited from the work of a core group of MDBs in the developing world, led by the World Bank, which is active globally, and including four regionally focused MDBs [IADB, EBRD, AfDB, AsDB] . . . The United States has also benefited from the financial leverage associated with its contributions to the MDBs ($2 billion in annual U.S. contributions to the MDBs leverages $120 billion in financing in developing countries), their financing instruments and modes of operation (providing large-scale loans alongside technical expertise), and their involvement across a larger number of countries and economic sectors than the United States can provide alone . . ."

[7] *See* paragraph 2.30.

[8] Clement (2023) at 84–6 summarizes the final deliberations for the establishment of BIS.

politically, it was becoming untenable for Germany to be under the direct supervision of a foreign supervisory agency, the Reparations Commission.[9] The inflow of foreign (mostly American) private capital to Germany was vital for the country to meet its international obligations and domestic needs,[10] so that American financiers had a keen interest in the reparations situation, while the official United States government position sought to separate the repayment of World War I debts from its allies from the German reparations payments to the same allies. A number of factors were at play:

> The 1926 agreement between France and the United States for settlement of war debts had to be ratified by the French Parliament before August 1929. Failure to do so would compel France to pay the whole debt principal. The French were therefore interested in a settlement of reparations entailing a so-called commercialisation, whereby the German debt (or part of it) would be issued in the form of long-term bonds to be subscribed by private international banks and financial houses. The scheme seemed attractive not only because it would make fresh cash available but also because it seemed to promise to take much of the political heat off the reparations issue by turning it into a normal financial transaction. American financial firms were obviously interested, while depoliticization looked appealing to Washington. The Germans were also keen to reopen negotiations with a view both to alleviating the burden of reparations and to speeding up an early evacuation of the Rhineland by allied troops.[11]

In late 1928, the six powers (Belgium, France, Germany, Italy, Japan, and the United Kingdom), agreed to convene a conference of experts to study the commercialization of the German debt.[12]

2.11 The committee of their experts began meeting in February 1929 to develop a solution.[13] The committee also included unofficial experts from the United States;[14] its final output was known as the Young Plan, after the American committee chairman, Owen Young.[15] In the Young Committee discussions, several plans were proposed, leading to the emergence of a 'brand-new idea':

[9] Toniolo (2005) has a thorough discussion of the historical background at 24–33. *See also* Simmons (1993) at 376–7. The German reparations and the Reparations Commission were provided for under Part VIII of the Treaty of Versailles (1919).

[10] Toniolo (2005) at 31.

[11] Toniolo (2005) at 32. Notes omitted.

[12] Agreement to convene the committee of experts was reached during a session of the Council of the League of Nations in Geneva in September 1928, illustrating the international organization background of BIS. Toniolo (2005) at 33.

[13] Committee of Experts (1929) at 81. Dulles (1932) at 4–5.

[14] Oliver (1996) at 53 notes: "Because of the official American position that there was no connection between war debts and reparations, the government of the United States forbade any Federal Reserve Bank to participate in the B.I.S." Nonetheless, Federal Reserve staff and officials were deeply involved in the formative process. *See* Figure 2.1.

[15] Owen Young was Chairman of the General Electric Company, and a Director of the Federal Reserve Bank of New York. Baffi (2002) at 11.

a nonpolitical institution that would liquidate the foreign-controlled reparations machinery, receive and distribute reparations, serve as a trustee for Germany's official creditors, and oversee the problem of commercializing German obligations by selling bonds to private investors. As it emerged in June 1929, the Young Plan contained the broad outlines of the proposed BIS, with the suggestion that it expand credit, enhance central bank cooperation in monetary affairs, and facilitate payment of Germany's reparations debt in a way compatible with the servicing of its massive debts to private lenders.[16]

That new institution would need to undertake a range of financial and commercial transactions from a suitable financial position, enjoy the expectation of political neutrality among countries, and foster central bank cooperation. Neither international nor domestic organizational forms were a precise fit.

International organizations were becoming more common at the time,[17] yet international organizations of that day such as international administrative unions or river commissions would not have readily accommodated the financial functions and standing anticipated for BIS.[18] The main intergovernmental organization, the League of Nations, was perceived as political.[19] The officials and bankers in the Young Committee were doubtless aware of these international organizations.[20] They were even more familiar with proposals for solutions to the international financial and economic crises that had been plentiful in the 1920s, notably at international conferences,[21] including suggestions for some kind of international bank and for other forms for central bank cooperation.[22] **2.12**

[16] Simmons (1993) at 381–2. Toniolo (2005) provides a detailed description of the work of the Young Committee and subsequent steps to BIS establishment, at 33–48. The idea of establishing a bank was put forth early in the discussions first by Emile Franqui from Belgium, and a different proposal was made by Hjalmar Schacht, head of the German central bank. Neither one was accepted.

[17] As a contemporaneous observer noted: "There would have been nothing new in the spring of 1929 in a proposal to establish in the international world a right-and-duty bearing institution which was not a State." Williams (1930) at 666–7.

[18] Howland (2015) at 164 notes that the international administrative unions and river commissions were treaty-based international associations of governments. Functionally, the international unions such as the International Telegraph Union (ITU) and the Universal Postal Union (UPU) were administrative in nature, although the Bureau of the UPU did oversee financial matters. Howland (2015) at 168–9. *See also* Karns, Johnson and Karns, Johnson, and Mingst (2024) at 76–7. One seminal figure in the field of central bank cooperation, Luigi Luzzatti, drew a parallel with these unions, however, recognizing that setting up a mechanism for central bank cooperation was a similar response to common interests, in a technical, apolitical way. Toniolo (2005) at 22.

[19] Dulles (1932) at 52.

[20] The Chairman of the BIS Organization Committee, Jackson Reynolds, mentioned as examples the International Copyright Union, International Association of the Congo, the Pan-American Union, the European Commission of the Danube, the Reparation Commission, and the League of Nations. He concluded that "it required the complexities of the World War with its aftermath of reparations difficulties to produce the unique entity under consideration." Reynolds (1933) at 289. *See also* Williams (1930) at 666, listing the same institutions. Sir John Fischer Williams was formerly British Legal Representative on the Reparations Commission.

[21] Conferences included the 1920 International Financial Conference in Brussels under League of Nations' auspices and the 1922 Genoa Conference. Eichengreen (1992) at 153–62 describes this period in detail.

[22] *See* Oliver (1996) at 27–58 (Chapter II, "Proposals for International Economic Cooperation"), for detailed descriptions. The proposal by Belgian Prime Minister Leon Delacroix for an "International Bank of Issue" had some features later seen in IBRD, such as a share structure and weighted voting; it did not gain traction. Oliver (1996) at 28–32. *See also* Toniolo (2005) at 20–3. Eichengreen notes that the United States was

2.13 Under national law, setting up BIS as a joint stock bank would not have been unusual. Joint stock banks were numerous in the United States at the time.[23] Several of the European central banks involved had that form (with public functions), notably the central banks of Belgium and Switzerland, and the Bank of England.[24] The close relationship with national corporate law for these central banks is illustrated in the 1905 Swiss Banking Act which makes the civil code provisions relating to joint stock companies the default mode for the Swiss National Bank, the central bank.[25]

2.14 The BIS, a company limited by shares per Article 1 of its Statutes, went beyond a joint stock bank with public functions, created as a new type of international institution. (Figure 2.1 speculates about BIS legal origins.)

BIS had three core purposes (promoting central bank cooperation, providing additional facilities for international financial operations, and handling of German reparations)[26] and a novel dual personality.[27] Set up as a corporate entity and chartered under Swiss law, BIS was given immunities and tax exemptions under national law.[28] In the view of the Chair of the BIS Organization Committee:

> the intricate mechanism of its creation and the extraordinary privileges it is granted will demonstrate its hybrid character. It stems from international treaties but is chartered by a single State. It functions very like any bank and is subject to municipal law in its commercial dealings; but under the Hague Agreement it moves almost as an equal among sovereign states and can hale them before the bar of justice. It has no fellow in the legal firmament and is certainly *sui generis*.[29]

opposed to the establishment of another free-standing international institution. Eichengreen (1992) at 156. That opposition is a theme repeated time and again in the history of the establishment of MDBs after IBRD, such as IADB, AsDB, and EBRD (*see* paragraphs 3.08–3.09, 3.14, and 3.16).

[23] For the United States, *see* Wright, Robert. "Origins of Commercial Banking in the United States, 1781–1830." *EH.Net Encyclopedia*, edited by Robert Whaples. March 26, 2008. https://eh.net/encyclopedia/origins-of-commercial-banking-in-the-united-states-1781-1830/ (last visited July 14, 2025).

[24] Giovanoli (1989) at 845. Historically, the Swedish Riksbank was the first institution recognized as a central bank, established in 1668 as a joint stock bank. The most famous central bank of that era, the Bank of England, was founded as a joint stock company in 1694. Bordo (2007) at 2. The National Bank of Belgium, established in 1850, served as a model for the central banks of the Netherlands and Japan. Conant (1910) at 12–13.

[25] The 1905 Swiss Banking Act provides in Article 14: "The provisions of chapter 26 of the Swiss Civil Code relating to joint stock companies apply to the National Bank in so far as special provisions for its organization and administration are not contained in the present act." Landmann (1910) at 208.

[26] BIS Statutes Article 3: "The objects of the Bank are: to promote the cooperation of central banks and to provide additional facilities for international financial operations; and to act as trustee or agent in regard to international financial settlements entrusted to it under agreements with the parties concerned."

[27] Mario Giovanoli, a BIS General Counsel, summed it up: "On the one hand, the Bank is unquestionably an international organization, possessing the international legal personality and the privileges and immunities customarily conferred on intergovernmental organizations. On the other hand, the BIS is a banking institution established in the form of a company limited by shares, although its legal structure deviates in many respects from that found in ordinary company law and, above all, is de facto and de jure controlled by its member central banks." Giovanoli (1989) at 845.

[28] Reynolds (1933) at 292–3. The exemptions and immunities are listed in paragraphs 6–11 of the BIS Constituent Charter, annexed to the Convention Respecting the Bank for International Settlements, January 20, 1930 and resolution of disputes is addressed in BIS Statutes Article 56–7. *See* paragraph 2.42.

[29] Reynolds (1933) at 289.

Where could the creators of the BIS plan have found inspiration in setting up this novel legal entity?

- In the preceding decades of discussions on central bank cooperations, there had been proposals for some kind of international bank or association. For instance, a 1920 proposal by Belgian Prime Minister Leon Delacroix for an "International Bank of Issue" had a share structure and weighted voting. *(Oliver (1996) at 28–32.)*
- Montagu Norman, governor of the Bank of England, worked toward convening international conferences of central banks in the 1920s. A 1927 proposal for an Association of European Central Banks from Pierre Quesnay at Banque de France and Harry Siepmann at Bank of England was very close to the BIS in concept. *(Yago (2012) at 3.)*
- As the Young Committee began discussions in February 1929, two proposals were made:
  - o Belgian Emile Franqui, looking back to the 1920 Brussels conference, proposed a private bank that would attend to reparations and the economic recovery of Europe generally, as well as providing a venue for European financial leaders to discuss mutual problems. The bank would be managed like a commercial organization. *(Toniolo (2005) at 35; Dulles (1932) at 6.)*
  - o German Hjalmar Schacht proposed an international clearing house created by the seven central banks that would provide credit to central banks, governments, and others with government guarantee, which he renamed the International Settlements Bank. *(Toniolo (2005) at 36.)*
- Chairman Owen Young made a compromise proposal for what became BIS, putting together a corporate structure with international characteristics. (Chairman Young tasked a working group to prepare initial plans (Randolph Burgess, Walter Stewart, Shepherd Morgan (with Federal Reserve ties), and US investment banker Ferdinand Eberstadt, in consultation with European members of the expert committee). *(Toniolo (2005) at 36; Baffi (2002) at 18.)*
- Sir Charles Addis (Bank of England) submitted "draft statutes" on behalf of the UK. This so-called "Addis draft" was incorporated into a general plan drawn up by Sir Josiah Stamp on the basis of the discussions and approved in committee on March 18 and 19. (*Baffi (2002) at 22–3.*) Earlier theories and plans at the Bank of England had an important bearing on the proposal. (*Dulles (1932) at 10.*)
- The final report of the Young Committee in June 1929 had a detailed Annex I, Suggested Outline for the Organization of the Bank for International Settlements. Annex I provided the structure and powers of the proposed BIS, without indicating its legal status and detailed provisions. Annex I stipulated that the Organization Committee would subsequently draw up statutes for such matters as are usual in banking organization. (*Report of the Committee of Experts (1929) at 110 and following.*)
- During the Organization Committee deliberations in October–November 1929, the British, French, and Belgian central banks each prepared draft statutes. *(Toniolo (2005) at 40.)* All of the proposed drafts specified that BIS would be a company limited by shares. ("*Synoptic table of Statutes in French and English," in BIS Archives, BISA 7.16.1.2.4 – BIS Organisation Committee (COBRI), 1929.) (See also Toniolo (2005) note 122, at 497.)*
- Article I of the BIS Statutes as agreed provides: "There is constituted under the name of the Bank for International Settlements (hereinafter referred to as the Bank) a company limited by shares." The international privileges and immunities for BIS are provided in its Constituent Charter.

Figure 2.1 BIS Legal Origins

A key reason for this duality was "a concern on the part of the Bank's founding fathers to ensure that the BIS should, as far as possible, be free from direct governmental influence, both at the institutional and financial level."[30] Independence from political interference was considered essential for BIS to fulfil its new role in solving the reparations problems that had arisen in the 1920s.[31]

2.15 The agreement to establish BIS involved the central banks of Belgium, England, France, Germany, Italy, and Japan along with unofficial representatives from the United States, and in the final stages, Switzerland, where BIS was to be chartered and located; the legal foundation took the form of an integrated Convention, Constituent Charter, and Statutes.[32] One analysis concludes that the private American financiers were key to the agreement;[33] another identifies BIS as the brainchild of directors of the founder central banks.[34] Whatever the driving impetus, the reparations-related functions of BIS ended in 1931,[35] while BIS continues to this day as a forum for central bank cooperation and more.[36]

2.16 This combination of a financial institution that could function commercially with the international rights and obligations of an international organization was the invention that set BIS apart.[37] The BIS model provided inspiration for IAB, whose

[30] Giovanoli (1989) at 845.

[31] As recounted by Jackson Reynolds, the BIS Statutes manifested "a clear intent to insulate the Bank from all government meddling . . . The League of Nations made an abortive gesture to modify this principle by transmitting to the interested governments the League's deliberations on the subject at the Tenth Ordinary Session of the Assembly held in September, 1929. These in turn were transmitted to the Organization Committee the following month. It was contended in these deliberations that the Bank would exercise an exceptional influence upon the economic life of the world, might pursue a policy in conflict with the efforts of the League, or might exert too powerful an influence over individual states. On these grounds an official liaison between the League and the Bank was suggested. The Organization Committee did not, however, adopt the idea and the suggestion was never renewed." Reynolds (1933) at 290–1.

[32] The Convention Respecting the Bank for International Settlements (January 20, 1930) was agreed among the governments of Belgium, France, Germany, United Kingdom, Italy, and Japan, on one part, and the government of Switzerland, on the other part. Annexed to the Convention, the BIS Constituent Charter refers to "the founding by the central banks of Belgium, France, Germany, Great Britain, Italy and Japan and by a financial institution of the United States of America of an international bank to be called the Bank for International Settlements [and that] . . . the said central banks and a banking group including Messrs. J. P. Morgan & Company of New York, the First National Bank of New York, New York and the First National Bank of Chicago, Chicago have undertaken to found the said Bank." BIS Constituent Charter, whereas clauses, Gr.Brit. TS No. 6 (1931) (Cmd.3766) at 3. Basle, Switzerland was agreed as the location in the Organization Committee on November 9, 1929. Baffi (2002) at 58.

[33] Simmons (1993) at 400–1: "In its crudest form, then, the deal between financiers and creditor governments was reduced reparations for commercialization. But the only way in which the American bankers were willing to hold up their end of the bargain was through international cooperation, which would improve the chances of collecting reparations and protect individual firms from the risky business of managing the German debt . . . The price of private cooperation was the Bank for International Settlements. It was a price the creditor governments were not averse to paying, since it also improved the expected value of reparations."

[34] Clement (2023) at 84, 86, 92.

[35] Oliver (1996) at 52–3, citing the moratorium on war-debt and reparations payments in 1931 and the defaults on those payments the following year.

[36] *See* "About BIS" on the BIS website, https://www.bis.org/ (last visited July 14 2025): "Our mission is to support central banks' pursuit of monetary and financial stability through international cooperation, and to act as a bank for central banks."

[37] Simmons (1993) at 363. Simmons also notes an earlier piece that is largely historical but makes the same connection, Frank Costigliola, "The Other Side of Isolation: Establishment of the First World Bank, 1929-30," Journal of American History 61 (December 1972). Simmons (1993) at 364 note 6.

Latin American proponents were influenced by the Young Plan that spawned BIS;[38] IAB, in turn, had a direct influence on IBRD. BIS itself was also known to many of the bankers and economic officials negotiating the agreement on IBRD, especially the European BIS members and some US participants (e.g., the Federal Reserve).

C. IAB

The idea of a bank to facilitate economic relations between Latin American countries and the United States predated the BIS discussions by several decades. The First Pan-American Conference (1889–1890) was convened in Washington by the United States, joined by seventeen Latin American countries. Among its proposals was the chartering of an International American Bank. This Bank would have been a private entity, with powers of commercial and investment banks, chartered by the United States. However, the law necessary for its establishment failed to pass the United States Congress in 1898, and thus this International American Bank never came to be.[39] **2.17**

The idea of an Inter-American banking institution continued to be discussed in the 1930s, taking on "renewed urgency after the credit contraction that followed the crash of 1929, and Mexico became the Inter-American Bank's strongest and most consistent advocate."[40] In a 1931 study, Mexican experts surveyed many of the same proposals for central bank cooperation that laid the foundation for BIS, and, indeed: **2.18**

> The Mexican national section was most interested, however, in the Bank for International Settlements (BIS), founded just a year earlier, in 1930. The BIS had been created to coordinate German reparations payments, but also to provide "an increasingly close and valuable link in the cooperation of central banking institutions" of Europe, which the founders deemed "essential to the continuing stability of the world's credit structure." The Mexican representatives on the High Commission had Germany and the BIS at the forefront of their minds when they began to outline the project for what they were now calling the International American Bank.[41]

By 1933, a resolution at the Seventh Inter-American Conference in Montevideo recommended consideration of an agency for economic and financial cooperation

[38] Thornton (2018) at 266–7 (note 10) mentions a 1931 study by the Mexican section of the Inter-American High Commission. *See* paragraph 2.18.
[39] Díaz-Bonilla and del Campo (2010) at 4–9. *See also* Sanders (2022) at 8–9 on the International American Bank.
[40] Thornton (2017) at 151.
[41] Thornton (2021) at 60. Later in the decade, the idea of a Latin American Bank for International Settlements also surfaces in the US Treasury files. *See* Figure 2.2.

in the region, including an inter-American bank, that would have functioned as a continental central bank.[42] The United States remained wary.[43] In 1938, at the Eighth Inter-American Conference in Lima, the idea was recommended for further study.[44]

2.19 With war beginning in Europe, the Foreign Ministers of the Americas met in Panama in September 1939 where another proposal for a new multilateral financial institution was discussed; a draft was presented under the leadership of the Mexican delegation.[45] That proposal outlined a range of functions for the proposed bank.[46] With the United States reluctant to support the proposal, the meeting agreed to create the Inter-American Financial and Economic Advisory Committee (IAFEAC) that would, inter alia, study the need, form, and conditions for an inter-American banking institution.[47] The Finance Ministers of the American Republics met in Guatemala in November 1939, agreeing to ask the IAFEAC to study the proposed regional financial institution urgently.[48]

2.20 The IAFEAC started work in Washington on November 15, 1939, with delegates from twenty-one American countries, assisted by a group of experts from the United States State Department, Treasury Department, Federal Reserve Board of Governors, and the Federal Loan Agency. A draft was prepared by the finance subcommittee, chaired by the United States and including delegates from Argentina, Bolivia, Colombia, Ecuador, Mexico, and Peru, and forwarded to the full IAFEAC on November 28, 1939.[49] Texts of the international Convention, Charter and By-Laws, a legal foundation similar to BIS, were finalized in February 1940 and were approved by IAFEAC on April 16, 1940.[50] (Figure 2.2 speculates about IAB's legal origins.)

[42] Díaz-Bonilla and del Campo (2010) at 27 and Helleiner (2014) at 54. Proposals for an international bank at the Montevideo Conference came from Mexico, as well as Peru and Uruguay. Thornton (2018) at 269–70.

[43] Helleiner (2014) at 55. Helleiner (2014) at 55, note 13, quotes the United States delegate, Spruille Braden, as reporting that it "seemed unwise for the American delegation to openly oppose these projects, particularly as it is conceivable that at some future time a central bank comparable to [BIS] . . . may prove advantageous to the Americas."

[44] Díaz-Bonilla and del Campo (2010) at 27 and Helleiner (2014) at 55.

[45] Díaz-Bonilla and del Campo (2010) at 32.

[46] These functions included that the bank (1) act as an inter-American clearing house; (2) serve as financial agent of central banks in international capital markets; (3) assist central banks in stabilizing the internal and external value of currencies; (4) study trade, exchange, and other problems; and (5) contract with the US government to accept not just gold but also silver in settlement of international balances owed by any country. Helleiner (2014) at 55.

[47] Díaz-Bonilla and del Campo (2010) at 33.

[48] Díaz-Bonilla and del Campo (2010) at 33. Mexico's Eduardo Villasenor offered a detailed six-point proposal for the immediate establishment of a Pan-American Central Bank. Thornton (2017) at 151.

[49] Helleiner (2014) at 59 notes that "US policymakers took the lead role because the United States was to be the largest contributor." Díaz-Bonilla and del Campo note, however, that "the large presence of U.S. officials participating in the deliberations and in the drafting of documents generated uneasiness among some LAC delegates, who felt outnumbered and, at times, marginalized in the negotiations." Díaz-Bonilla and del Campo (2010) at 34, note 25.

[50] Díaz-Bonilla and del Campo (2010) at 34.

The IAB process brought together a variety of sources, many later connected to the development of the IBRD Charter.

- The IAB proposal was presented by the Mexican delegation. As early as 1931, Mexican experts had been studying BIS. (*Paragraph 2.18.*)
- The draft IAB convention was prepared by Esteban Jaramillo Gutiérrez (former Colombian finance minister) and Antonio Espinosa de los Monteros (head of the Mexican industrial development bank Nacional Financiera). (*Helleiner (2014) at 62–3.*) The structure of Convention, Charter, and By-Laws mirrored the Convention, Constituent Charter, and Statutes of BIS.
- The draft IAB By-Laws were worked out at the IAFEAC subcommittee with the United States team taking the lead (primarily from the State Department, Treasury Department, and Federal Reserve Board). Active participation in the discussions and contributions from the Latin American participants were recognized by the US team. (*Helleiner (2014) at 59–63.*) The IAFAEC records (in the OAS Library) show active participation and proposals from a number of countries.
- Comparison to BIS. A review of relevant US records reveals comparisons to BIS, as the team considered whether IAB would become a Latin American BIS. Benefits of BIS were noted, chief among them the frequent meetings of European Central Bank Governors, as well as the BIS economic and financial section. (*Cochran to White, December 4, 1939, US Department of Treasury Records.*)
- IBRD Features. The internal discussions about IAB also presage integral features of IBRD (such as representative groups for an executive body, the importance of market acceptance of the Bank's debentures, and a technical review of loan proposals). (*Hanson to Glasser, Organization of the Inter-American Bank, January 3, 1940, US Department of Treasury Records.*)
- Continuity with IBRD Preparations. Among the US officials, Emilio Collado, Assistant Chief of the State Department's Division of the American Republics, was a principal architect of IAB, assisting Adolf Berle, Assistant Secretary of State for Latin American Affairs. (Oliver (1996) at 92.) (Collado was later the first US Executive Director at the IBRD.) Berle gave Harry Dexter White, then Director of Treasury's Division of Monetary Research, the principal credit for IAB drafting, as much of the final text came from his January 1940 draft of the By-Laws. (*Helleiner (2014) at 61.*) White was also assisted by his team and Treasury lawyers. (*Oliver (1996) at 357 note 39 also credits legal work by Ansel Luxford, later Chief Legal Adviser at Bretton Woods.*)

Figure 2.2 IAB Legal Origins

The Convention for IAB's establishment was signed by the United States and seven other countries in May 1940,[51] yet still required treaty approvals for the Bank to begin operations. Six months of intensive collaboration after many years of discussion brought IAB to the brink of establishment. However, continued opposition in the United States, especially from the banking community, prevented IAB from 2.21

[51] Convention for the Establishment of An Inter-American Bank, Department of State Bulletin, May 11, 1940, at 512–25. The Convention was deposited at the Pan American Union on May 10, 1940, and signed on behalf of Bolivia, Colombia, Dominican Republic, Ecuador, Mexico, Nicaragua, Paraguay, and the United States. Attached to the Convention were a proposed Charter and By-Laws.

coming to life: the IAB Convention was never ratified by the United States Senate, and never came into effect.[52]

2.22 Several IAB innovations contributed to the MDB model: its wide multilateral membership; its character as a public intergovernmental institution;[53] and its mandate to provide public international loans to achieve development objectives.[54] Other elements of the MDB model were present in the IAB setup, and some functions carried through to IBRD, such as extending loans and guarantees and issuance of securities and other obligations. The potential mechanism of IAB's borrowing against its capital to finance loans presaged IBRD's operating mechanism.[55] Strikingly, governance similarities foreshadowed the MDB structure:

> The shares of the Bank [IAB] were to be held by the member governments, which would appoint their directors. Voting was to be weighted by stock ownership plus a minimum of twenty "country votes," but no member could have more than half of the votes. Certain actions, including loan transactions, required a four-fifths vote, which would, in practice, have given the United States a veto power since it was expected to provide $25 million of the total share capital of $100 million.[56]

2.23 Even so, the IAB model was "a strange halfway station between the BIS governance model and that of the Bretton Woods institutions" in that IAB would be chartered as a corporation by an act of the United States Congress, and it would have accepted private deposits and dealt with private customers in other ways.[57] Like BIS before it, IAB was unique in its design:

> Although an association of governments, the I.A.B. takes the form of a private corporation. Naturally it does not conform strictly to any known type but is sui generis. It may be described as a cross between a share company and a co-operative society.[58]

While IAB never came into operation, it nonetheless paved the way for another set of unique international institutions, IMF[59] and IBRD, and later the family of

[52] Helleiner (2014) at 74–6.

[53] Helleiner (2017) at 68–9, noting that all twenty-one republics of the Americas were to be members of IAB and had input into its creation. The IAB legal foundation as proposed was similar to that of BIS: established under a multilateral convention, chartered by one state, and governed by detailed By-Laws.

[54] Helleiner (2014) at 63.

[55] Oliver (1996) at 96 notes that IAB's authorized capital of $100 million would have been 50% paid-in, "operations would have depended substantially on the Bank's ability to borrow by selling its own bonds in its member countries."

[56] Bittermann (1971) at 61. Helleiner (2017a) at 20 observes: "The IAB's decision-making rules also anticipated those of the Bretton Woods institutions: its board was to use a weighted voting scheme with super-majority voting rules that guaranteed the USA a veto over important decisions. In internal discussions, US officials also raised the idea of a possible constituency system for representation within the IAB, an idea later incorporated into the IMF and IBRD." *See also* Sanders (2022) at 9–13, with a different perspective on the US role in IAB.

[57] Helleiner (2014) at 72.

[58] Helleiner (2014) at 72, quoting a BIS official at note 95.

[59] Horsefield (1969) at 11, suggests that three of IAB's purposes were relevant to the eventual IMF (currency stabilization, clearinghouse, and research), but otherwise saw little resemblance. What he termed incidental features of IAB were part of the background against which White drafted his plans.

MDBs. Indeed, IAB has been referred to as the first draft for the IBRD, echoing the comments made by members of the American teams for Bretton Woods themselves,[60] many of whom had been involved in the IAB process.[61]

D. IBRD

While US participation in IAB was still pending in Congress, the first proposals that led to IBRD had already begun to circulate, first among the economists and policymakers in the United States Treasury, and then within the departments of the United States government concerned with postwar economic planning. The first complete draft was prepared during 1941 by Harry White in combination with his plan for an international stabilization fund, and available to others within the government early in 1942; the road to the IBRD was started with this plan for "A Bank for Reconstruction and Development of the United and Associated Nations."[62] Much of the next year featured intense discussions with the United Kingdom and consultations with other countries on the Fund plan; it was later in 1943 that interagency considerations within the United States government turned to focus on the Bank plan.[63] **2.24**

A complete draft of the Bank plan was published by Treasury in November 1943.[64] The evolving drafts by the United States and a subsequent explanatory document[65] were the focus of the ongoing multilateral discussions that included comments and **2.25**

[60] Oliver (1996) at 99; Mason and Asher (1973) at 15–16. For instance, Adolf Berle and Emilio Collado from the State Department team took note of the IAB precedent. Helleiner (2014) at 77. One of the Treasury economists involved, Henry Bittermann, also noted IAB as precedent. Bittermann (1971) at 61.

[61] Helleiner observes: "it is striking how many of the US officials involved in IAB's drafting went on to participate in various ways in the discussions surrounding the Bretton Woods agreements, including not just [Adolf] Berle and [Emilio] Collado but also [Treasury Secretary Henry] Morgenthau, [Harry Dexter] White, [Edward] Bernstein, [Will] Clayton, [Walter] Gardner, [Emanuel] Goldenweiser, [Winfield] Riefler, [Orvis] Schmidt, and [Jacob] Viner." Helleiner (2014) at 77. Mexican officials who had played leading roles in IAB preparation were also later participants in the Bretton Woods discussions, such as Eduardo Villasenor (head of Bank of Mexico) and Antonio Espinosa de los Monteros (head of the Mexican industrial development bank, Nacional Financiera). Helleiner (2014) at 58, 77.

Among the lawyers, Oliver (1996) at 357 note 39 also credits "the law firm of Luxford and Paley" in the drafting of the Inter-American Bank. This is most likely a reference to Ansel Luxford, then briefly in private law practice in the midst of a long Treasury and later World Bank career, as John Pehle was still at Treasury in early 1940. Luxford became the senior lawyer in the Treasury work on IMF and IBRD, and the Chief Legal Adviser for the United States at Bretton Woods. He later practiced law with Pehle in a law firm that bore their names, after he stepped down as Associate General Counsel at IBRD.

[62] Oliver (1996) includes as Appendix A the entire "Suggested Plan for a United and Associated Nations Stabilization Fund and a Bank for Reconstruction and Development of the United and Associated Nations" at 279–322. This plan was far broader than what eventually became the IBRD, as Oliver details at 114–27.

[63] Oliver (1996) notes that the American Technical Committee took up the Bank plans in August 1943, and that plans from the State Department were circulated in September 1943. Oliver (1996) at 142–50.

[64] Preliminary Draft Outline Of a Proposal for A Bank for Reconstruction and Development of the United and Associated Nations, U.S. Treasury, November 24, 1943 (BWC1289-01), included in Schuler and Canning (2019) at 67–76.

[65] Questions and Answers on the Bank for Reconstruction and Development, issued by the United States Treasury in February 1944 [later version June 1944]. *See* U.S. Department of Treasury (1944).

The archived drafts of the Articles of Agreement (IMF and IBRD) are in the Bretton Woods Collection (BWC) in IMF Archives (available online). Few are dated, but one can deduce their order. These were clearly working documents of the drafters, as they are filled with marginal handwritten notes.

IMF Drafts:
Draft #1. A document titled Convention (BWC594-09) is marked as #1 in pencil on the hard copy in IMF Archives. Most likely, this is the April 25, 1944 draft.

Draft #2. The next full draft in the files—identified as "2d" in pencil on the IMF Archives' hard copy—is attached to a routing slip from Mr. Luxford to a large group of Treasury officials (BWC594-08).

Draft #3. The June 1–2 draft (BWC594-07) is probably #3.

Draft #4. The draft of June 11, 1944 is marked as 4th draft (BWC8318-01).

IBRD Drafts: The earliest drafts of the IBRD Charter in Bretton Woods Collection (BWC) held in IMF Archives are dated in a similar fashion.

Draft #1. An undated draft for the Bank (BWC7823-01) refers to the April 25, 1944 draft of IMF Agreement, so this could be the first draft for the Bank. A May 27, 1944 memo refers to the first drafts of the IMF and IBRD agreements (BWC8349-01), confirming that there was at least one draft for IBRD that predated the June 12, 1944 draft.

Draft #2. There is another draft dated June 12, 1944 from Luxford (BWC8324-08).

Figure 2.3 Early Drafts of the Articles of Agreement (IMF and IBRD)

proposals from many other countries.[66] The draft Bank plan was shared with the British in September 1943, with an exchange of views in April 1944, followed by bilateral discussions in the Atlantic City pre-negotiations in June 1944.[67] It was at the Bretton Woods conference in July 1944 that negotiations on the IBRD Charter were completed, taking the much-modified United States plan as the core.

2.26 While the Bank plans were somewhat legalistic in parts,[68] true legal agreements would eventually be needed to cement the parties' agreement on how to establish, operate, and govern the Bank.[69] The first legal drafts of Articles of Agreement for IMF and IBRD appear in the Bretton Woods Archives in April–June 1944. (See Figure 2.3 listing the early drafts that are available online.[70]) As one can imagine, they are drawn heavily from the plan documents under discussion (especially the

[66] Helleiner (2014) details the background and participation of Latin America (Chapter 6), East Asia (Chapter 7), and Eastern Europe and India (Chapter 9), as well as Britain's perspectives on development (Chapter 8). For the multilateral consultations in March–April 1944, *see* Oliver (1996) at 163–7.

[67] Oliver (1996) at 148–52 (September 1943), 169–74 (April–May 1944), and 174–81 (Atlantic City).

[68] The early plans by Harry Dexter White draw directly from the IAB By-Laws in places, as noted in paragraph 2.30. Some commentators refer to these evolving plans as drafts of the IBRD Charter. *See, e.g.*, Shihata (2000) at 649–52, listing as charter drafts various plans as well as a US Treasury Draft Agreement to Establish a Bank for Reconstruction and Development, US Treasury Department, May 1944.

[69] For AIIB, similarly, the Memorandum of Understanding on Establishing the Asian Infrastructure Investment Bank among Prospective Founding Members (October 24, 2014) had to be translated into draft Articles of Agreement for AIIB's Chief Negotiators to reach agreement on the AIIB Charter. *See* paragraphs 3.24–3.25.

[70] Bretton Woods Conference Collection in the IMF Archives, https://archivescatalog.imf.org/Details/archive/110042780 (last visited July 14, 2025).

Joint Statement of April 1944), yet also from the IAB[71] and other legal charters[72] and instruments.[73]

The drafts appeared at the time when plans were being made for the coming conference, to be held at Bretton Woods, New Hampshire, which was to be preceded by pre-negotiations in Atlantic City.[74] The Chief Legal Adviser for the United States delegation, Ansel Luxford, explained: 2.27

> As we got down to pre-Bretton Woods, it was necessary to come in with drafts. . . when we left for Atlantic City, we had drafts of both documents that embodied our approach, realizing that a lot of these things had to be thrashed out, but if you go back to those drafts you'll see how closely they were followed in terms of so many of the later provisions, if for no other reason than that we had worked through a coherent draft from which we were working, in terms of our negotiations and subsequent drafts.[75]

The American proposal was discussed in the pre-negotiations at Atlantic City in June 1944.[76] At that point, the British brought in a revised draft reflecting discussion among the delegations who travelled there together on board the Queen Mary.[77] Comments on management were taken up in a separate committee based on earlier suggestions from the British.[78] Together, these were

[71] In the first draft (BWC594-09), references to the IAB Charter and By-Laws can be found in:

(a) Article VII (Management), in Section 1 on location of offices (IAB By-Laws I); Section 3A, Directors and Alternates appointed by governments (IAB By-Laws 3); and Section E, miscellaneous power to contract (IAB Charter 6), and incidental powers (IAB Charter 2); and
(b) Article IX (Additional Undertakings), in Section 6, restrictions on taxation of the Fund or its assets (IAB Charter IIC) and Section 7, restrictions on attachments of assets of the Fund (IAB Charter IIA).

[72] In the first draft (BWC594-09), references to the RFC Act (Reconstruction Finance Corporation Act) include the miscellaneous powers of acquisition of property under Article VII, E-7, and employment of officers in E-9 (RFC Act Section 4).

[73] In the first draft (BWC594-09), references to international treaties and agreements include: Article XI (Amendments), request to governments to accept amendment if 4/5 vote (1933 Convention on Sanitary Aerial Navigation, Malloy 5503); and Article XIII (Final Provisions) on ratification (1936 Limitation of Naval Armament, Malloy 5559), notification by U.S. government of receipt of ratification instruments (1928 Kellogg-Briand Peace Pact, Malloy 5132), effectiveness of convention requires the four big powers and 10 others (1930 Limitation of Naval Armament, Malloy 5282) and subsequent deposit of instruments (1929 International Air Transport, Malloy 5259).

[74] Countries represented at Atlantic City: Australia, Belgium, Brazil, Canada, Chile, China, Cuba, Czechoslovakia, France, Greece, India, Mexico, Netherlands, Norway, Union of Soviet Socialist Republics, United Kingdom, United States. Schuler and Canning (2019) at 505–14.

[75] Luxford (1961) at 3–4.

[76] *See* Schuler and Canning (2019) at 305–14 for the notes on discussions of the Formal Agenda Committee on June 29–30, 1944.

[77] *See* Schuler and Canning (2019) at 141–64 for the notes on the on-board discussions, and 448–56 for the resulting document B-1, The Reconstruction Bank [British proposal], June 29, 1944. The countries represented in the shipboard discussions, in addition to the United Kingdom, were Belgium, China, Czechoslovakia, Greece, India, Netherlands, Norway, and Poland. *See* Oliver (1996) at 179–80 for a summary of the proposals, concluding "the European modifications of the November draft . . . made explicit what had been implicit in the American draft all along."

[78] Subcommittee on Management, June 27, 1944, at Schuler and Canning (2019) at 357–65. *See* Schuler and Canning (2019) at 476 (British Report on the International Monetary Fund, Annex E on Management and Inauguration, June 21, 1944).

the basis for the completed draft circulated for discussion at the Bretton Woods Conference.[79]

2.28 The IAB legal instruments were an apparent jumping off point for IBRD, with some clauses repeated word for word in the policy documents and later legal drafts. For instance, in Harry White's April 1942 draft proposal for IBRD, IAB wording can be found for capital structure, governing bodies and their powers, and some operational provisions.[80] In the first draft of the IMF Charter, IAB provisions are listed as the source for certain powers.[81] In that draft, the text of the provision dealing with lawsuits is virtually the same as provided in the IAB By-Laws.[82]

2.29 There were also aspects of IAB where the IBRD planners wanted differences. As the difficulties in getting approval for IAB from the United States Congress became increasingly apparent to the US team after 1941, those difficulties were an indication of concerns to be avoided for IBRD.[83] Notably, both the IMF and IBRD Charters were designed as a single agreement among the parties (Articles of Agreement), differing from the legal package of convention, charter and statutes/by-laws used for BIS and IAB.[84]

2.30 The IBRD Charter also reflected the IMF Charter. Many of the institutional provisions were agreed for IMF and carried over to IBRD.[85] At the core, however, the two organizations are rather dissimilar—fraternal not identical "Bretton Woods Twins" that share DNA while appearances and actions diverge. IBRD as a shareholding entity that would participate in international financial markets and commercial transactions and provide guarantees and loans to members and their entities was quite different from the intergovernmental quota-based backbone of IMF. Less discussion of the IBRD proposal had taken place in the years before Bretton Woods, in part because the United States team believed that the issues on the IBRD proposal would be easier to resolve and in part because many countries were more interested in the IBRD for its benefits than taking on the obligations of IMF membership.[86] IBRD was not an

[79] "Proposal for a Bank for Reconstruction and Development (Bretton Woods Document 169)" in Schuler and Canning (2019) at 480.

[80] "Articles of Agreement Compared with Earlier Proposals," BWC8316-01.

[81] *See* note 71.

[82] In the first draft (BWC594-09), Article VII, Part E (8), Powers of the Board of Directors contains the same text as the IAB Charter, Section 7 on the power to sue and be sued in United States courts, but IAB is not identified as the source. Later drafts do identify IAB as the source. While these early drafts provided for the Fund to be subject to suit as the IAB would have been, the provision was substantially revised at the Atlantic City pre-negotiations to provide for the Fund to be sued only with its consent.

[83] Bittermann (1967) at 7. Mason and Asher (1973) at 16 notes that White "attempted to guard against the objections of the commercial bankers by providing that short-term capital would be offered only where such capital was not available from private sources at reasonable rates."

[84] *See* paragraphs 2.15 and 2.20.

[85] Bittermann (1967) at 38 cites organization, privileges and immunities, and other formal conditions.

[86] Luxford (1961) at 6: "The Fund, as a technical problem, was obviously a far more challenging problem than the Bank. The Fund was pretty much moving out to the periphery of economics, and especially in terms of international operations. The Bank was being formulated along more orthodox lines. And we were

afterthought,[87] but rather part of a strategic approach to multilateral agreement on IMF.

The discussions leading to the establishment of the United Nations itself were also in progress in this period. The Bretton Woods Conference took place in July 1944, ending a few weeks before the Dumbarton Oaks conference in Washington, DC, for the drafting of the United Nations Charter. The UN Charter negotiations took place the next year in San Francisco, in April–June 1945, and the United Nations was established October 24, 1945.[88] That was two months before the IMF and IBRD Charters became effective on December 27, 1945. 2.31

There were other international organizations under discussion among the allied nations in the same time period as the Fund and Bank proposals were being discussed (1942–1944).[89] The United Nations Relief and Rehabilitation Administration (UNRRA) was established in 1943 to provide relief and rehabilitation for war-torn populations.[90] The International Labor Office (ILO), originally established under the League of Nations, was then in transition to a freestanding organization.[91] The United Nations Interim Committee on Food and Agriculture was the precursor to the Food and Agriculture Organization, FAO.[92] Invitations to the Bretton Woods Conference were issued to UNRRA, ILO, and FAO to send observers, which they did.[93] In the area of immunities in particular, governments were looking across 2.32

satisfied in our own hearts that we would have no problem selling the Bank internationally, because this is a simple proposition of, here is a place to get some money, and you didn't have to put very much up in order to get a lot."

[87] Luxford (1961) at 8: "The Bank was not an afterthought. It was started from the word go, the first White document . . . It's a 100-page document and the first part is on the Fund, the last part is on the Bank, or vice versa, but they were always treated as one package. But the complexities of the Bank were not the same as those of the Fund, and the big point in selling had to be the Fund. What was being done structurally within the Fund, in terms of organization and concepts, crept into the Bank. If you look at the provisions on administration and the like, you'll find them almost identical."

Oral histories from State Department officials who were also involved offer a different view, suggesting that Harry Dexter White was not interested in the Bank and that their efforts predominated. Emilio Collado Oral History Interview (July 11, 1974) at 13–17. Harry S. Truman Library https://www.trumanlibrary.gov/library/oral-histories/collado2 (last visited July 14, 2025).

John Parke Young Oral History Interview (February 21, 1974) at 7–8. Young prepared a separate plan for the Bank. Oliver (1996) at 144–8. https://www.trumanlibrary.gov/library/oral-histories/youngjp (last visited July 14, 2025).

[88] Karns, Johnson, and Mingst (2024) at 85–6.

[89] Helleiner (2014) describes the Bretton Woods connections to President Franklin Roosevelt and New Deal values at 119–23.

[90] Fox (1950) at 561.

[91] The International Labor Organization (ILO) had originally been established as the International Labor Office under the League of Nations. Following the transition from the League to the United Nations, the ILO Charter was revised in 1946, after discussions at the Philadelphia Conference in May 1944. "The International Labor Organization," 1 Int'l Org. 117 (1947).

[92] The United Nations Conference on Food and Agriculture had been convened in Hot Springs in May 1943, among the forty-four allied nations, and its Interim Commission was set up in July 1943. P. B. P., "The Interim Commission on Food and Agriculture and the FAO," 38 Am. J. Int'l L. 708, 711 (1944).

[93] US Department of State (1948) at 113 and 1134. As noted shortly afterwards, "What Bretton Woods was to money, what Hot Springs [FAO] was to food, Philadelphia [ILO] was to the 'social question,' i.e., the conditions under which men live and labor." Simpson (1944) at 558.

institutions; in the immunities discussions for the Fund and Bank, these agencies are noted.[94]

E. Legacy Features in the IBRD Charter

2.33 The IBRD Charter reveals legacies from both BIS and, more directly, from IAB. BIS offered a functioning model by its existence as an international intergovernmental financial institution with exemptions and immunities provided to it. BIS offered an example in its joint stock structure (paid-in and callable capital) and corporate statutes with their key provisions on governance (Board of Directors and executive committee, shareholding structure with weighted voting). IAB transmitted these BIS elements through to IBRD, and added relevant functions (long-term development loans), issuance of securities in the markets, and weighted voting by shares with a basic votes component.[95] In other ways, BIS was less relevant for IBRD.[96] IAB had other functions that were beyond what was intended for IBRD, such as acting as a clearing house for international payments, and normal banking functions.

2.34 There are many familiar clauses to be found across the legal instruments for BIS, IAB, and IBRD, like a DNA test revealing the family ties outlined in the preceding sections. These similarities reinforce the view that the drafters worked from precedents where relevant. Most notably, these influences can be seen in: (1) financial structure, (2) governance structure, and (3) management arrangements.

(1) Financial structure

2.35 Both BIS and IAB were designed as financial institutions based on a shareholding structure, as befits the joint-stock company model on which they were based. Each member subscribes to an agreed number of shares, and each share is partially paid-in at subscription: 25% paid-in for BIS and 50% paid-in for IAB. The remaining

[94] The immunities provided for UNRRA, ILO, and FAO are expressly mentioned in the records of the Fund and Bank discussions. A Czech delegate at Atlantic City, Professor Ervin Hexner (later IMF Assistant General Counsel) suggested aligning with the International Labor Organization (ILO) Document No. 1 that had just been discussed at the May 1944 conference in Philadelphia. Schuler and Canning (2019) at 351 (Subcommittee 4 at Atlantic City, June 22, 1944). In a British memorandum submitted at Bretton Woods, it was suggested to seek uniformity as much as feasible with other organizations, specifically "[t]o take account of the experience of the past in connexion with the League of Nations and the I.L.O. and the recent agreements relating to UNRRA and the F.A.O." United Kingdom Delegation Memorandum to Commission I (Document 250) in US Department of State (1948) at 422.

[95] Mason and Asher (1973) at 15–16. They also note that IAB had some functions later incorporated in IMF, as IAB would have combined the functions of an intergovernmental bank, an international stabilization fund, and an ordinary commercial bank.

[96] Bittermann (1967) at 4–5 notes as less relevant for IBRD: BIS functions (management of reparations and central bank cooperation), public shareholding (both central bank shares and privately-owned and traded shares), and voting and control by the founder central banks.

callable capital payments (75% for BIS and 50% for IAB) did not need to be paid until called by the Bank at the discretion of the Board of Directors.[97]

The IBRD Charter similarly provides for a shareholding-based financial institution, with the percentage paid-in at 20%, lowered from the 1942 draft that initially followed IAB in setting the percentage at 50%. An additional limitation under the IBRD Charter is that the 80% callable portion may be called by the Bank only when required to meet obligations of the Bank.[98] The lower paid-in portion and limitations on calls were expected to be helpful to many of the war-torn economies participating in the Bretton Woods conference.[99] The callable capital feature is considered one of the advantages of the MDB model,[100] making this a seminal contribution from IBRD's predecessors. **2.36**

(2) Governance structure

For both BIS and IAB, the institution was to be governed by a Board of Directors representing members, with a general meeting of shareholders in BIS. Again, governance by a Board selected by shareholders is another common feature that harks back to the joint-stock company origins. Both Boards were to meet periodically throughout the year (at least ten times for BIS and at least four times for IAB), but were not resident at headquarters. For actions when the Board was not in session, the Board of Directors was specifically empowered to appoint an Executive Committee of Directors.[101] For BIS, there was debate on the role of an executive committee, but agreement could not be reached on requiring one in the final Statutes.[102] For IAB, the executive committee provision may have reflected a suggestion for "a small operating board made up of officials representing groups of countries" in lieu of an unworkable body with all countries represented.[103] **2.37**

The IBRD Charter provisions in this area were much discussed, and the final structure of a Board of Governors and a resident body called the Executive Directors[104] represents an unusual combination. (See Chapter 12, Section A.) The 1942 Bank Plan looked very much like IAB, with a Board of Directors and optional Executive Committee, in very similar language.[105] By 1943, the plan included a Board of **2.38**

[97] BIS Statutes Article 8; IAB By-Laws Section 2A. For IAB's smaller members, the paid-in portion could be paid in two installments within one year.

[98] IBRD Article II, Sections 5 and 7. For the 1942 Plan, see April 1942 Suggested Plan, quoted in Oliver (1996) at 294.

[99] *See* Bittermann (1971) at 74.

[100] Humphrey (2022) at 11–12.

[101] BIS Statutes Articles 27, 28, 32, 43, 46, 48, and 49; IAB By-Laws Section 3A, 3B, and 3E.

[102] Baffi (2002) at 51.

[103] This was suggested by Walter Gardner of the Federal Reserve staff. Helleiner (2014) at 72, noting the similarity to the constituency system later adopted for the IMF Executive Board (and IBRD Executive Directors).

[104] IBRD Article V, Sections 2 and 4.

[105] Oliver (1996) at 295.

Directors and an Executive Committee continuously available at the Bank.[106] As discussions deepened in 1944, the United Kingdom proposed that the Bank would be governed by a Directorate with a general body of all members called a Governing Council. The British proposal included both a Chairman and a General Manager (akin to BIS) and argued against a resident Board.[107]

2.39 With respect to voting, neither IAB nor IBRD continued the particular arrangements that were necessary for BIS (voting at the Board by number of Directors, voting at the general meeting by number of shares subscribed in each country).[108] Both IAB and IBRD Charters provide for weighted voting, with a combination of share votes and member votes (based on a certain minimum). In IAB, each member would have had twenty votes for its stipulated minimum shares and one vote for each share above that.[109] In IBRD, each member had 250 so-called basic votes plus one vote for each share of stock held; in 2012, the IBRD Charter was amended to replace the 250 votes with basic votes at 5.55% of total votes.[110]

(3) Management

2.40 The clearest echoes in the IBRD Charter from BIS and IAB can be heard in the provisions related to the IBRD President.

- IBRD's President is (1) selected by the Board of Directors (Executive Directors); (2) serves as Chairman of that Board; (3) has no vote except a deciding vote in case of an equal division; (4) serves as chief of the operating staff; and (5) conducts the ordinary business of the Bank under the direction of the Executive Directors. [111]
- IAB's President would have (1) been selected by the Board of Directors; (2) served as ex-officio chairman of the Board of Directors; (3) had a deciding vote; and (4) served as chief of the operating staff. [112]
- BIS had two positions and three titles: a Chairman of the Board selected by the Board from among its members, who would also be President of the Bank, and a General Manager appointed by the Board on proposal of the President. The Chairman had a second or casting vote (being a Board member). The General Manager was responsible to the President for the operations of the Bank, and was chief of the operating staff. [113]

[106] Schuler and Canning (2019) at 75.
[107] Schuler and Canning (2019) at 475–6 (British Report on the International Monetary Fund, Annex E on Management and Inauguration, June 21, 1944).
[108] BIS Statutes Articles 34 and 46.
[109] IAB By-Laws Section 2H.
[110] IBRD Article V, Section 3. *See* paragraphs 9.07–9.08 for a description of basic votes.
[111] IBRD Article V, Section 5 (a) and (b).
[112] IAB By-Laws Section 3C and 3I.
[113] BIS Statutes Articles 34, 39, and 41 (1930 version). Originally, BIS had an arrangement under which there was a Chairman of the Board, who was the President of the bank, as well as a General Manager appointed by the Board and reporting to the President; the current BIS Statutes omit the position of President.

A telltale sign of lineage is the phrase "chief of the[its] operating staff," found in the IAB By-Laws, IBRD Charter, and the IMF Charter.[114]

In addition to these three main areas, two others deserve note. 2.41

Privileges and immunities. BIS pioneered immunities for international financial institutions, including immunity of assets from seizure and restrictions and tax immunities.[115] IAB expanded these immunities with more specificity, including the obligations of members to enact the necessary legislation to provide them.[116] IBRD built upon these provisions.[117] IBRD's position with respect to judicial process also reflects its predecessors.[118] 2.42

Operational provisions. IAB would have been required to ensure the government not object to any loan beyond two years, and also provide a government guarantee; IBRD requires a member guarantee for all loans.[119] For intermediate and short-term loans, IAB would have required a "full written report on the merits" prepared by experts that could include non-bank personnel.[120] This provision can be seen as the forerunner for what was known as the statutory committee report at IBRD, requiring a "careful study of the merits of the proposal" and including an expert on the committee selected by the member concerned.[121] 2.43

A World Bank. The final text of the IBRD Charter should be seen as a multilateral, multidisciplinary product. From the European, American, and Japanese experts who worked out the BIS arrangements,[122] to IAB's Latin American proponents and United States partners,[123] to the American instigators of IBRD and the British and others who revised their drafts[124] and the forty-four delegations that participated 2.44

[114] From IADB onwards, the phrase became "chief of its staff." In the French text of the BIS Statutes, Article 41, it is "chef du personnel."

[115] BIS Constituent Charter, paragraphs 6–10.

[116] IAB Convention, Article II. For IAB, immunity of assets from seizure before final judgment was added.

[117] IBRD's privileges and immunities include immunity of assets from seizure and restriction, and from seizure before final judgment, as well as tax immunities. IBRD Article VII.

[118] IBRD Article VII, Section 3 provides that actions may be brought in a court of competent jurisdiction in certain member territories but no actions can be brought by members. IAB, with commercial bank functions, could sue and be sued under its Charter, Section 7. BIS, as a financial institution established by central banks, could have disputes with members in arbitration at the Hague tribunal, and was otherwise subject to suit, under BIS Statutes Articles 56 and 57. *See* paragraphs 11.19–11.20.

[119] IAB By-Laws Section 5B(1); IBRD Article VIII, Section 4 (i).

[120] IAB By-Laws Section 3H.

[121] IBRD Article III Section 4 (iii) and Article V, Section 7.

[122] The first BIS proposal was drafted by Americans working with Owen Young (Ferdinand Eberstadt, Randolph Burgess, Shepherd Morgan, and Walter Stewart. Baffi (2002) at 18; Toniolo (2005) at 36. A draft of the statutes was prepared by Sir Charles Addis, on behalf of the British delegation, and incorporated into the general plan drawn up by Sir Josiah Stamp; both were Directors of the Bank of England. Baffi (2002) at 11, 22–3. The final draft statutes worked out by the Organization Committee came from drafts presented by the British, French, and Belgian delegations, with discussions focused on the French and British texts. Baffi (2002) at 44.

[123] For IAB, the Convention was prepared by Esteban Jaramillo Gutiérrez (former Colombian finance minister) and Antonio Espinosa de los Monteros (head of the Mexican industrial development bank Nacional Financiera). Helleiner (2014) at 62–3. The United States team, primarily from the State Department, Treasury Department and Federal Reserve, took the lead in drafting the IAB By-Laws, with credit given to Emilio Collado at State and Harry Dexter White at Treasury. Oliver (1996) at 92 and Helleiner (2014) at 61.

[124] The IBRD proposal was the brainchild of Harry Dexter White, and the legal drafts came from the Treasury lawyers, led by Ansel Luxford. Both were vetted by an interagency process to produce the American

in the Bretton Woods Conference,[125] the influences were truly global. How fitting that IBRD's common name became the World Bank. The legal texts represented not just a mix of legal systems (civil law, common law, and international law), but also the collaborations of bankers (many of them with legal training and experience), economists (such as Harry Dexter White, John Maynard Keynes, and their colleagues) and government lawyers. It proved to be a rich resource for the MDBs that came next.

draft. The British team led by Sir John Maynard Keynes worked with other countries in producing the boat draft (note 77 in this chapter).

[125] From a listing prepared later, written proposals on the IBRD draft charter were made by more than a dozen countries, including the United States and United Kingdom as well as Czechoslovakia, El Salvador, Egypt, France, India, Mexico, Netherlands, New Zealand, Norway, Poland, Venezuela and the Union of Soviet Socialist Republics as well as representatives of the International Labor Organization and the precursor to the Food and Agriculture Organization. *See* "Comparison of Alternative Proposals for Articles of Agreement for the International Bank for Reconstruction and Development," Volume I (Articles I–IV, BWC8384-01) and Volume II (Articles V–XI, BWC8385-01).

3

LEGAL ORIGINS: FROM IBRD TO AIIB

In the seventy years between the Bretton Woods Conference in 1944 and the initial discussions on the Asian Infrastructure Investment Bank (AIIB) proposal in 2014, the landscape of multilateral development banks (MDBs) changed dramatically. There were only two examples for the International Bank for Reconstruction and Development (IBRD) drafters, each providing a model that was partial at best (Bank for International Settlement, BIS, and Inter-American Bank, IAB, as discussed in Chapter 2). The AIIB drafters had many more useful models for the AIIB that they envisaged. These models included the major regional development banks, namely, African Development Bank (AfDB), Asian Development Bank (AsDB), Inter-American Development Bank (IADB), and European Bank for Reconstruction and Development (EBRD); close counterparts such as Caribbean Development Bank (CDB), Islamic Development Bank (IsDB), and European Investment Bank (EIB); and sub-regional development banks, including Black Sea Trade and Development Bank (BSTDB), Nordic Investment Bank (NIB), and Development Bank for Latin America and the Caribbean (CAF). 3.01

The strong influence of BIS and IAB on the IBRD Charter demonstrated in Chapter 2 extended primarily to legal provisions and institutional and governance structures, not necessarily to intended aims and operations. The objectives and activities of BIS—handling German reparations and central bank cooperation—were not relevant for IBRD's development loans and guarantees, yet the establishment of BIS as the first international intergovernmental financial institution offered a foundation for IBRD. IAB's potential development lending was relevant for IBRD, but not the full range of its permitted scope (clearing house for international payments, normal banking functions). The IBRD Charter also took on many provisions from the International Monetary Fund (IMF) Charter, despite the differences between the two institutions in objectives, functions, and financial structure. 3.02

For the MDBs that followed IBRD, the borrowing of the model was more extensive. These were institutions that would have similar objectives (tailored to the goals of founders); similar operations (modified to include financing not supported by IBRD); similar governance arrangements; and, as a consequence, similar charters to that of IBRD. Eventually, they would have similar challenges and issues.[1] 3.03

[1] *See* Humphrey (2022) at 11–13 for a summary of the MDB model and its attraction.

Moreover, for existing MDBs themselves, a proposal for another MDB could raise concerns about duplication and competition (when mandates overlap) and fears of different operational and governance standards, amid hopes for complementarity. This was particularly true for the World Bank in earlier decades, when the proposals for the regional development banks (AfDB, AsDB, EIB, and IADB) could be characterized as "at once a tribute and a rebuke."[2]

3.04 Nowadays, inter-MDB collaboration receives considerable attention, as can be seen in AIIB's relations with its counterparts.[3] Today's MDBs collaborate in nearly every sphere of activity, though tensions inevitably remain.

A. AIIB Predecessors

(1) European Investment Bank (EIB)

3.05 EIB grew out of years of discussions within Europe on its post-war development,[4] after IBRD's opening in 1946 and following the announcement of the Marshall Plan in 1947. There had been proposals for a European investment bank in the late 1940s. The proposal for EIB grew from the intention of its six founders (Belgium, France, Germany, Italy, the Netherlands, and the Grand Duchy of Luxembourg) to set up an investment fund, and was realized in the 1957 Treaty of Rome.[5] EIB was established to contribute to the balanced and steady development of the European internal market, through loans and guarantees.[6]

3.06 Reportedly, IBRD was initially opposed to competition from the new institution, in particular because IBRD's private sector arm, International Finance Corporation (IFC), was in the process of being established in 1956.[7] Nonetheless, EIB's first transaction was undertaken jointly with IBRD.[8]

3.07 EIB's overall governance framework was built upon the IBRD Charter, such as its Board of Governors and Board of Directors, while many other governance aspects

[2] Mason and Asher (1973) at 578, explaining: "a tribute in the sense that it could not have happened without the example previously set by the World Bank of probity, technical and economic competence, and ability to raise funds in capital markets and put them to good use in low-income countries; a rebuke in the sense that, had the World Bank been as popular in those countries as it thought it was, their desire for regional banks would have been weaker."

[3] Paragraphs 4.15–4.18 summarize AIIB's collaboration with other MDBs.

[4] For a detailed discussion of EIB's formation, *see* EIB (2008), Chapter 1, "The birth of an institution: from a European investment fund to the European Investment Bank," at 23–35.

[5] EIB (2008) at 23 and 30 (French proposal to the Organization for European Economic Cooperation (OEEC) in 1949).

[6] EIB Article 2, referring to the Treaty on the Functioning of the European Union, Article 309 (ex Article 267, Treaty establishing the European Community).

[7] EIB (2008) at 32–4 and Mason and Asher (1973) at 582–3.

[8] EIB's "History of the EIB" timeline online lists a transaction jointly with IBRD to support three Italian companies in April 1959 as the first transaction. Eib.org.en/about/key-figures/timeline/index (last visited July 14, 2025).

were entirely new, such as the Management Committee and the non-resident status of the Board of Directors.[9] EIB was the first of the MDBs described here to adapt the IBRD model, though EIB's structure and its function as an institution of the European Union (EU) differentiate it from the others. In that sense, it had a more general influence on the governance design at AIIB.

(2) Inter-American Development Bank (IADB)

IADB was founded in 1959, yet its story can be traced through decades of economic and political interactions between Latin America as a region and its northern neighbor, the United States. An "International American Bank" had been proposed in 1890 as a private regional banking institution, and later in 1940, an intergovernmental financial institution, IAB, nearly came to life, as discussed in Chapter 2.[10] Latin American countries renewed the push for a similar institution in the 1950s, when they found that IBRD did not fully meet regional needs in its early years.[11] The proposal for this new regional institution was not initially supported by the United States, likely concerned about competition with IBRD for its support. 3.08

Then, the winds of US foreign policy changed with tensions in the region and brought the United States to the negotiating table, becoming IADB's key funder and largest shareholder.[12] With the United States finally on board, work on the agreements proceeded. Following a ministerial conference in September 1958, charter negotiations took place from January to April 1959, and the IADB Charter became effective on December 30, 1959.[13] 3.09

IADB's purpose is to contribute to the economic and social development of its regional member countries, through loans and guarantees; filling a gap in the 3.10

[9] EIB (2008) at 44–5.

[10] Paragraphs 2.17–2.23. *See* Díaz-Bonilla and del Campo (2010) at 4–11 (International American Bank) and 32–41 (Inter-American Bank).

[11] Díaz-Bonilla and del Campo (2010) at 57–9, noting elements of dissatisfaction with existing international financial institutions, including that IBRD and the US Export-Import Bank did not finance local costs and social projects, and that the level of Latin American representation was low. Dell (1974) at 5–23 also highlights the inability of IBRD to lend to private enterprise without a government guarantee, and the desire for more support for industry, agriculture, and mining.

[12] In earlier times, the United States reportedly was cool to the IADB proposal until US bilateral activities in Latin America met with public outcry. *See* Tussie (1995) at 18–19, citing as a motivating factor for US participation in IADB negotiations the hostility encountered by US Vice President Richard Nixon in his 1958 trip to Latin America. It has also been suggested that final US agreement to join the IADB negotiations was timed days before a public proposal by US President Eisenhower to establish an Arab development institution in the wake of US problems in Lebanon and elsewhere in the Middle East in 1958. *See* Díaz-Bonilla and del Campo (2010) at 68–9. The US share of IADB capital at its inception was 42% and it was the largest funder of the Fund for Special Operations, the soft-loan window.

[13] Herrera (1960) at 217 lays out the steps: August 12, 1958, announcement that the United States was prepared to consider establishment of an Inter-American bank; September 1958, conference of the foreign ministers of the 21 American republics; January–April 1959, Specialized Committee for Negotiations and Drafting of the Instrument of Organization of an Inter-American Financial Institution.

IBRD Charter, technical assistance is also expressly authorized.[14] While IADB's initial governance framework mirrored that of IBRD, later innovations reflected IADB's regional character. Originally, IADB members were all regional countries and only members of the Organization of American States (OAS). Following a decline in US financial support in the late 1960s, the IADB Charter was amended in the 1970s to allow Canada and other non-OAS regional countries to join, and then to bring in non-regional members and their capital (Europe and Japan, initially). To preserve the position of the regional members, IADB led the way with Charter clauses specifying the shareholding level for regional developing members (now 50.005%), the United States (now 30%) and Canada (4%). IADB also pioneered the introduction of specific regional majority requirements for key decisions.[15] Interestingly, IADB members also established a separate entity for private sector and equity investment, the Inter-American Investment Corporation, as EIB had with its European Investment Fund, both parallels to IBRD's addition of IFC.

(3) African Development Bank (AfDB)

3.11 Regional economic history also lay behind the formation of AfDB as an African financial institution in the post-colonial era. The UN Economic Commission for Africa played a seminal role in AfDB's establishment (as its Asian equivalent did for Asian Development Bank and the Economic Commission of Latin America for IADB). Nonetheless, it was the economic and political relations among different groups of African countries that determined the timing and contours of the bank that emerged. Relations with developed countries had an impact regarding decisions to join the bank and on forms of concessional financing (e.g., relations with France and the United States).[16] However, non-regionals were not part of the AfDB membership discussions until much later.

3.12 Established in 1964, AfDB's purpose is to contribute to the sustainable economic development and social progress of its regional members, through loans, guarantees, and equity investment.[17] AfDB's overall governance arrangements were also based on the IBRD model, with adjustments over time in response to its own institutional experience. For instance, the President was originally selected

[14] IADB Article I, Section 1 (purpose); Article III, Section 4 and Article IV, Section 4 (operations); and Article VI (technical assistance).

[15] For IADB regional shareholding requirements, *see* IADB Article VIII, Section 4 (b) and the detailed listing in note 23 in this chapter.

[16] Gardiner and Pickett (1984) at 8–13.

[17] AfDB Article 1 (purpose) and Article 14-1 (methods of operation). Technical assistance is also among AfDB's functions. AfDB Article 2-1 (e). The word "sustainable" was added in 2001. AfDB Board of Governors' Resolution No. B/BG/2001/08, *Amendments to the Agreement Establishing the African Development Bank*, adopted May 29, 2001, entered into force July 5, 2002.

by the Board of Directors, as at IBRD, and later this was changed to election by the Board of Governors, as at IADB and AsDB.[18] From the beginning, the AfDB Charter included detailed provisions on the establishment of special funds, and the separation of special and ordinary resources and operations, building on the singular Fund for Special Operations created in the IADB Charter.[19] Later, AfDB's need for concessional finance led to the innovative African Development Fund, a separate entity jointly owned by AfDB and non-regional donors.[20]

The AfDB Charter has undergone periodic revisions, both to introduce changes in the institution and to revise outdated legal provisions.[21] For example, in the 1980s, AfDB followed the IADB experiment and opened up AfDB itself to non-regional members and their capital contributions, limiting their share (now 40% non-regional and 60% regional).[22] The introduction of non-regional membership in both institutions was enacted in a comprehensive way, including regional majorities related to changes in Board composition, election of the President, suspension of membership, and amendment.[23] **3.13**

[18] AfDB Article 36 (as amended in 1979). The appointment process for Vice-Presidents was also changed in response to AfDB's experience. The AfDB Charter, Article 37-2 empowers the President to appoint Vice-Presidents, "provided that he shall act in consultation with the Board of Directors in the exercise of his powers of appointment and release of Vice-Presidents." Originally, AfDB Vice-Presidents were also appointed by the Board of Directors on the recommendation of the President; the AfDB Charter was amended to the language quoted by AfDB Board of Governors' Resolution B/BG/97/05, *Concerning Measures to Enhance Governance of the African Development Bank and Amending the Agreement Establishing the Bank*, adopted May 29, 1997, entered into force May 2, 1998, paragraph 5.

[19] AfDB Articles 8-11; IADB Articles III and IV.

[20] The African Development Fund (AfDF) was originally set up as an AfDB special fund with AfDB funding, as the response of potential donors was not encouraging. By 1972, the AfDF was established as a separate international institution, by AfDB and non-regional donors. *See* Rigo Sureda (2004) at paragraphs 410–420.

[21] The 2016 publication of the AfDB Charter lists five amendments, in 1982, 1994, 1998, 1999, and 2002. For non-regional membership, *see* AfDB Board of Governors' Resolution 05-79, *Concerning the Amendments of the Agreement Establishing the African Development Bank to Enable Non-African Countries to Become Members Thereof*, approved May 17, 1979, entered into force May 7, 1982, Annex, paragraph 5 (ii). For the most recent changes, *see* AfDB Board of Governors' Resolution B/BG/2001/08, *Amendments to the Agreement Establishing the African Development Bank*, adopted May 29, 2001, entered into force June 5, 2002.

[22] AfDB Article 5-4.

[23] Specific regional majorities were introduced with the advent of non-regional membership in IADB, and later in AfDB. These include:

(1) capital increases (not in AfDB; IADB Charter, Article II, Section 2 (e));
(2) changes in composition of the Board of Directors, with a special regional majority for changes in regional rules (AfDB Charter, Article 33-1; IADB Charter, Article VIII, Section 3 (b) (ii));
(3) election of the President (AfDB Charter, Article 36; IADB Charter, Article VIII, Section 5 (a));
(4) quorum for the Board of Governors and for the Board of Directors (AfDB Charter, Articles 31-2 and 34-2, later amended to delete the regional majority and require 70% of total voting power; IADB Charter, Article VIII, Sections 2 (e) and 3 (f));
(5) suspension of membership (AfDB Charter, Article 44, later amended to delete the regional majority and require 70% of total voting power; IADB Charter, Article IX, Section 2—depending on whether the member is regional or nonregional);
(6) termination and distribution of assets (AfDB Charter, Article 47-1, later amended to delete the regional majority and require 70% of total voting power and Article 49-1 (ii), later amended to delete any qualified majority; IADB Article X, Sections 2 and 4 (a)); and
(7) amendment (AfDB Charter, Article 60-1; IADB Charter, Article XII (a)).

(4) Asian Development Bank (AsDB)

3.14 A proposal for a regional development bank in Asia had been floated by Japan in the early 1960s, without gaining traction. Around the same time, a similar idea was under discussion among other Asian countries through the UN Economic Commission for Asia and the Far East (ECAFE). Like the Latin America countries proposing IADB a decade earlier, they had found the extent of IBRD support for their development less than expected.[24] The United States was also an important player and potential funder in Asia. Yet, the US was also initially cool to the AsDB proposal, not perceiving the depth of the unmet needs, and concerned about competition with IBRD. Again, the winds of American foreign policy shifted (in connection with the US war in Southeast Asia), buoying the AsDB proposal to a successful conclusion with full US support.[25] Japan and the United States have continued since as the two largest shareholders and supporters of AsDB.

3.15 AsDB was established in 1966 to foster economic growth and cooperation in Asia and to contribute to the economic development of developing member countries.[26] The AsDB Charter was the first to include both regional and non-regional members from the outset but, unlike the AfDB and IADB Charters, it does not require specific regional majorities for its qualified majority decisions.[27] Regional shareholding in AsDB is maintained at 60%, preserving the regional character of the institution.[28] The AsDB Charter also permits all types of operations (loans and guarantees for both public and private entities and equity investment) as well as the establishment of special funds (often a mechanism for concessional finance contributed by donors) and provision of technical assistance.[29] The drafting of the AsDB Charter took into account the IBRD, IADB, and AfDB Charters,[30] and served as a foundation for the EBRD Charter and later the AIIB Charter.

[24] At the time, a high proportion of World Bank Group financing for Asia was directed to larger Asian developing countries (65% of IBRD and 95% of IDA financing for Asia went to India and Pakistan). Wilson (1987) at 6. For a detailed history of the proposals and discussions that led to the establishment of AsDB, *see* Huang (1975).

[25] After initial opposition, the United States warmed to the AsDB proposal after the start of the Vietnam War, as the US sought to improve its standing in Southeast Asia. *See* Wilson (1987) at 12–13, citing US President Lyndon Johnson's change of view on AsDB as part of a large commitment of US assistance to Southeast Asia in April 1965.

[26] AsDB Article 1 (purpose) and Article 11 (methods of operation).

[27] *See* note 23 in this chapter.

[28] The regional shareholding minimum is found in AsDB Article 5-1.

[29] AsDB Charter, Article 11 (methods of operation), Article 19 (Special Funds), and Article 21 (vi)(technical assistance).

[30] As part of the process, the UN Commission for Asia and the Far East (ECAFE) Secretariat oversaw the preparation of a draft by Tadao Chino on loan from Japan's Ministry of Finance, who reviewed existing MDB charters, in particular the World Bank and IADB. The provisions on regional control were new. Huang (1975) at 41–2. Mr. Chino later served as AsDB President from 1999–2005.

(5) European Bank for Reconstruction and Development (EBRD)

Following AsDB by some twenty-five years, EBRD began as a regional initiative among Europeans, in response to the newly emerging need for assistance to Central and Eastern Europe. With a longstanding regional investment bank (EIB) already in operation, EBRD was set up with a specialized set of goals: "to foster the transition towards open market-oriented economies and to promote private and entrepreneurial initiative in the Central and Eastern European countries committed to and applying the principles of multiparty democracy, pluralism and market economics."[31] Politics was no less a part of EBRD's creation than for its predecessors, reflecting differing views of key European protagonists (France, Germany, United Kingdom), European institutions (the EU and EIB were original EBRD members), and the United States and Japan.[32] 3.16

To serve its specific purposes, EBRD is authorized to make loans to and invest in the equity capital of private enterprises, and state-owned enterprises that meet certain conditions; guarantees in some circumstances and technical assistance are also expressly authorized.[33] Specifically designed for EBRD is the requirement that not more than 40% of its committed loans, guarantees, and equity investment be provided to the state sector.[34] 3.17

While its operational mandate is unique, EBRD's governance arrangements are closely aligned with its predecessors. For both political and economic reasons, EBRD was established with a combination of regional and non-regional shareholders from the start, and included EIB and the EU as shareholders. EBRD eventually found itself undertaking Charter amendments to expand its countries of operation beyond the geographical confines of Central and Eastern Europe to include Mongolia and the Southern and Eastern Mediterranean.[35] In 2025, EBRD shareholders accepted an amendment intended to enable the expansion of operations to selected countries in sub-Saharan Africa and Iraq.[36] 3.18

[31] EBRD Article 1.

[32] Weber (1994) at 15–16, also pointing out that US skepticism about regional banks was longstanding and deep.

[33] EBRD Article 11-1.

[34] EBRD Article 11-3.

[35] EBRD Board of Governors' Resolution No. 90, *Amendment to the Agreement Establishing the Bank in order to Admit Mongolia as a Country of Operations*, adopted January 30, 2004, entered into force October 15, 2006. EBRD Board of Governors' Resolution No. 137, *Amendment of the Agreement Establishing the Bank in order to Enable the Bank to Operate in Countries of the Southern and Eastern Mediterranean*, adopted September 30, 2011, entered into force September 12, 2013.

[36] "EBRD shareholders take further step towards geographical expansion," EBRD Press Office, April 23, 2025 at https://www.ebrd.com/home/news-and-events/news/2025/ebrd-shareholders-take-further-step-towards-geographical-expansi.html (last visited July 14, 2025). EBRD Board of Governors' Resolution No. 259, *Amendment to Article 1 of the Agreement Establishing the Bank to Enable a Limited and Incremental Expansion of the Geographic Scope of the Bank's Operations to Sub-Saharan Africa and Iraq*, adopted May 18, 2023, entered into force July 22, 2025.

(6) Other MDBs

3.19 Not mentioned here are a number of other MDBs and similar international financial institutions, many subregional and some more specialized, whose charters were available to AIIB drafters.[37] They form part of the MDB family and offer variations in governance and other provisions. CDB, BSTDB, and IsDB operate under charters and governance structures that are largely comparable to the MDBs described above, in their specific geographic areas. The International Fund for Agricultural Development (IFAD) is another source of development finance, as a UN specialized agency with worldwide operations. The New Development Bank (NDB), established just before AIIB, was another example.

B. AIIB Takes Shape

(1) AIIB Proposal

3.20 The specific proposal for an Asian infrastructure investment bank was floated in October 2013 by Chinese President Xi Jinping during a Southeast Asian visit. President Xi's proposal was rooted in the infrastructure needs of Asia:

> At present, Asian countries, especially emerging markets and developing countries, are in great financial needs to develop infrastructure. Particularly in the face of such severe challenges as mounting downward pressure and financial volatility, it is necessary for us to mobilize more funds for infrastructural development to maintain sustained and steady economic growth and promote connectivity and economic integration in the region. To this end, we propose to establish an Asian infrastructure investment bank to help fund the infrastructural development of ASEAN countries and other developing countries in the region. This proposed bank will work together with the existing multilateral development banks in and outside the region and complement one another to fuel the sustained and steady growth of the Asian economy.[38]

This proposal echoed earlier suggestions for a similar institution. In 2005, a report from the UN Economic and Social Commission for Asia and the Pacific (ESCAP) proposed the establishment of an Asian Investment Bank, adapted from the EIB model, to meet the region's infrastructure needs and promote regional

[37] *See* paragraph 3.01.

[38] Xi (2013). The quotation is from President Xi's speech to the APEC CEO Summit, October 7, 2013. The proposal was also mentioned earlier, in his speech to the Indonesian Parliament on October 3, 2013. *See* "China proposes Asian infrastructure investment bank," *China Daily*, October 3, 2013.

development.[39] The Asian Investment Bank idea was floated in regional discussions thereafter.[40]

The idea of a regional development bank led by China was being discussed in China as well.[41] China's 2013 proposal also came in a period when a renewed focus on the need for more investment in infrastructure was increasingly evident in economic development circles.[42] **3.21**

As additional background to the proposal, some observers pointed to the increasing frustration of China and other developing countries with the pace of reforms in other international financial institutions. They noted that governance reforms at IMF and World Bank at the time were not enough for these countries' shares to keep up with their rising ranking in the global economy. In principle, the voting power of member countries in these institutions is expected to correspond to global economic weight. But increasing the voice of new economic powers can only be achieved by reducing the voice of other countries. That inherent conflict kept China and other rapidly growing developing countries from increasing their shares in line with economic growth. For some developing countries, frustration with MDB operating practices has been suggested as another motivation for starting a new institution rather than expanding an existing one.[43] **3.22**

The relationship between voting power and finance also helps to explain the constraints on China and others in directing more MDB finance to Asian infrastructure through existing multilateral institutions. In the World Bank and AsDB, they could only provide additional funds by buying more shares if other key members would be willing to reduce their voting power and influence; otherwise, any contributions to the MDBs would be donor funds, not shares, and would not provide an increase in voting power. China itself could have increased **3.23**

[39] *See* UN ESCAP (2005) at 154: "The possibility of setting up an Asian Investment Bank adapted from the European Investment Bank model to meet the region's infrastructure needs and promote regional integration merits further study. Its mandate could be to raise substantial capital from financial markets and other sources and direct investment capital towards the projects of participating countries. An Asian Investment Bank would be able to address special and urgent needs of the region's weaker countries, particularly LDCs for financing crucial infrastructure development." This report concluded that, just as the Commission had launched preparatory work for the creation of the Asian Development Bank in the 1960s, it could issue a similar mandate to study the feasibility of setting up an Asian Investment Bank. UN ESCAP (2005) at 155.

[40] *See, e.g.*, Bhattacharyay (2012) at 376, mentioning commentary on the proposal and pointing out some disadvantages of setting up a new institution (lengthy establishment process, lower cost-effectiveness compared to using existing institutions, expected lack of AAA rating and thus higher cost of borrowing, time needed to create a knowledge base and expertise).

[41] *See* Gutner (2025) at 32–4 on Chinese discussions starting in 2009.

[42] *See, e.g.*, MDB Working Group on Infrastructure, Infrastructure Action Plan (Submitted to the G20, October 2011), https://documents.worldbank.org/pt/publication/documents-reports/documentdetail/828751468331900533/infrastructure-action-plan (last accessed July 14, 2005), and Gutner (2025) at 34–6.

[43] He (2016), at 3–4, notes: "Indeed, China and other emerging powers have criticized the World Bank and the IMF for their inefficient and over-supervised processes of granting loans. The current gap between the demands for infrastructure investment and available investment from existing international financing organizations in developing countries creates an opportunity for emerging economies to establish a new type of bank with a directed focus in this area."

funding for infrastructure through its bilateral development banks, such as China Development Bank. Like others before it, China's turn to a multilateral approach in proposing AIIB may well recognize some advantages of multilateral leverage and efficiency,[44] and some disadvantages of a bilateral approach (such as higher cost and public relations risks).

3.24 China's proposal reflected the important role that the development of infrastructure has played in China's own economic development. China-watchers also highlight China's economic and political developments at that time, including in foreign economic relations with its neighbors, such as One Belt, One Road, now known as the Belt and Road Initiative (BRI).[45]

(2) AIIB Negotiations

3.25 A few months after the launch of the proposal, China and other interested parties joined in five Multilateral Consultation Meetings held from January 2014 onwards, each no doubt with its own motivating factors at play.[46] These meetings culminated in the Memorandum of Understanding on Establishing the Asian Infrastructure Investment Bank among Prospective Founding Members, dated October 24, 2014 (the MOU). In all, twenty-two countries signed the MOU, becoming the first wave of Prospective Founding Members (PFMs).[47]

3.26 The negotiation stage began shortly after the MOU signing. Each PFM authorized its Chief Negotiator to work with the others to reach agreement on the Charter for AIIB and other matters necessary for AIIB's establishment. These Chief Negotiators launched a forum, known as the Chief Negotiators' Meeting (CNM), which became the main mechanism for the Charter negotiations. Other interested parties could also endorse the MOU and join the CNM as PFMs. A Multilateral

[44] Morris (2016), at 2–3, identifies several benefits for the United States from its leading role and participation in MDBs: furthering an ideological agenda of promoting integrated market economies; leveraging its financial contributions; reaching a larger number of countries and economic sectors than the United States is able to through its own agencies and programs; effectively meeting the needs of developing countries; and serving as effective instruments of US foreign policy by offering or withholding assistance.

[45] Accounts of the background to the AIIB proposal and the motivations behind it include Gutner (2025) at 29–41, Sun (2015), Wang (2015), Wang (2016), and Weiss (2017).

For more on BRI, *see* paragraphs 12.62–12.65.

[46] Xu (2021) at 57–8. As part of the preparatory work, China's Ministry of Finance set up an AIIB preparatory working group under former Vice Minister Jin Liqun in early 2014. *See* "[Lou Jiwei talks about the preparations for the establishment of the Asian Infrastructure Investment Bank] 楼继伟谈亚洲基础设施投资银行筹建情况," Ministry of Finance of the People's Republic of China, Press Release, April 11, 2014 (on file with author).

[47] The MOU signatories were Bangladesh, Brunei Darussalam, Cambodia, China, India, Indonesia, Kazakhstan, Kuwait, Lao PDR, Malaysia, Mongolia, Myanmar, Nepal, Oman, Pakistan, Philippines, Qatar, Singapore, Sri Lanka, Thailand, Uzbekistan, and Vietnam. Twenty-one countries signed the MOU on October 24, 2014 in Beijing. Xu (2021) at 59–60. Indonesia signed the MOU on November 25, 2014. *See* Reuters Staff, "Indonesia's finance ministry signs MOU to join China-backed Asian bank," http://www.reuters.com/article/indonesia-china-infrastructure-bank-idUSL3N0TH1T420141127 (last visited July 14, 2025).

Interim Secretariat responsible for providing technical and professional support and services for AIIB's establishment was set up, with Mr. Jin Liqun appointed as its Secretary-General.[48]

The first CNM, in Kunming, China in late November 2014, laid the groundwork for the AIIB establishment process, and aimed for the signing of the AIIB Charter in June 2015 and AIIB establishment by end-2015. To meet that timetable, newcomers were expected to express formal interest in joining the negotiations on the basis of the MOU by March 31, 2015, so that, if accepted by the CNM, they could join the CNM process as PFMs by April. In that way, the Chief Negotiators for all PFMs could agree on the final text of the AIIB Charter by end-May, and the AIIB Charter could be ready for their signature by end-June. **3.27**

Through this mechanism, the initial twenty-two PFMs were joined by another thirty-five countries during the course of the negotiations, as illustrated in Figure 3.1. An additional four regional PFMs joined the first discussion of the draft AIIB Charter at the second CNM in Mumbai in January 2015; four more PFMs joined the third CNM in Almaty in March 2015, including the first three non-regional countries. Following the March 31 deadline for additional PFMs, a final twenty-seven new PFMs joined the CNM process, in time for the fourth CNM in Beijing in April 2015. In all, fifty-seven PFMs were represented in the CNM when negotiations on the AIIB Charter were concluded at the fifth CNM in Singapore in May 2015.[49] All PFMs were listed in Schedule A in the final text of the AIIB Charter, making them eligible to sign the Charter by end-2015 and become Founding Members of AIIB.[50] **3.28**

The addition of seventeen non-regional PFMs in April brought the balance to thirty-seven regional PFMs and twenty non-regional PFMs, giving a broad range of perspectives to the Charter negotiations. While all of them were IBRD members, many also had extensive experience as members at AsDB, EBRD, and other institutions that could be drawn upon in comparisons—whether as developed country members or as potential and actual recipients. **3.29**

The two largest shareholders in IBRD, AsDB, and EBRD—the United States and Japan—did not join the AIIB negotiations, though many allies in Europe and Asia came on board. Inevitably, this difference of views between the United States and **3.30**

[48] An overall summary of the process can be found in Jin (2014) at 54 and Xu (2021) at 59–62. This author served as Chief Counsel for the Multilateral Interim Secretariat. *See* Foreword to the first edition.

[49] The fifth CNM took place in Singapore on May 20–22, 2015. The actual time frame for the negotiation of the AIIB Charter was remarkably (and unintentionally) similar to the time frame noted for the EBRD Charter in the EBRD Chairman's Report on the Agreement Establishing the EBRD. In 1990, the EBRD negotiations began on January 15–16, and concluded on May 20. In 2015, the AIIB negotiations began on January 15–16 and concluded on May 22. The EBRD Charter was signed soon after negotiations concluded, on May 29, 1990, while its entry into force came on March 28, 1991, about ten months later. The AIIB Charter was signed on June 29, 2015 and entered into force on December 25, 2015, about six months later.

[50] As of June 2025, all PFMs have become AIIB members.

Participants in the AIIB Charter Negotiations

CNM 1 Kunming, China November 28, 2014
Regional: Bangladesh, Brunei Darussalam, Cambodia, China, India, Indonesia, Kazakhstan, Kuwait, Lao PDR, Malaysia, Mongolia, Myanmar, Nepal, Oman, Pakistan, Philippines, Qatar, Singapore, Sri Lanka, Thailand, Uzbekistan, Vietnam (signatories to the Memorandum of Understanding, October 2, 2014) **(22 PFMs)**

CNM 2 Mumbai, India January 15–16, 2015
Regional: joined by Maldives, New Zealand, Saudi Arabia, and Tajikistan **(26 PFMs)**

CNM 3 Almaty, Kazakhstan March 30-31, 2015
Regional: joined by Jordan
Non-Regional: Switzerland, United Kingdom **(30 PFMs)**

CNM 4 Beijing, China April 27–28, 2015
Regional: joined by Australia, Azerbaijan, Iran, Israel, Republic of Korea, Kyrgyz Republic, Russia, Türkiye, United Arab Emirates
Non-Regional: joined by Austria, Brazil, Denmark, Egypt, Finland, France, Germany, Iceland, Italy, Malta, Netherlands, Norway, Poland, Portugal, South Africa, Spain, Sweden **(57 PFMs)**

CNM 5 Singapore May 20–22, 2015
Regional PFMs: Australia, Azerbaijan, Bangladesh, Brunei Darussalam, Cambodia, China, Georgia, India, Indonesia, Iran, Israel, Jordan, Kazakhstan, Republic of Korea, Kuwait, Kyrgyz Republic, Lao PDR, Malaysia, Maldives, Mongolia, Myanmar, Nepal, New Zealand, Oman, Pakistan, Philippines, Qatar, Russia, Saudi Arabia, Singapore, Sri Lanka, Thailand, Türkiye, United Arab Emirates, Uzbekistan, Vietnam
Non-Regional PFMs: Austria, Brazil, Denmark, Egypt, Finland, France, Germany, Iceland, Italy, Luxembourg, Malta, Netherlands, Norway, Poland, Portugal, South Africa, Spain, Sweden, Switzerland, United Kingdom **(57 PFMs)**

Signing of the AIIB Charter Beijing, China June 29, 2015
Fifty countries signed the Articles of Agreement on June 29, 2015; the remaining seven signed later in 2015. (*See* note 1 in Chapter 10.)

Figure 3.1 Participants in the AIIB Charter Negotiations
Source: The AIIB Chief Negotiators' Report (found at Appendix 2) lists attendance at the first five CNMs.

China was featured in commentaries on Sino-American relations. Perhaps more interesting is the parallel with the initial US reluctance to support previous regional MDB initiatives, such as IADB, AsDB, and EBRD,[51] in contrast to the US role as prime initiator for the World Bank. For the creation of these regional MDBs, changes in political and economic relationships eventually led to US participation, creating international financial institutions in which the United States continues to play a leading role.[52]

[51] *See* note 12 (IADB), note 25 (AsDB), and note 32 (EBRD) in this chapter.

[52] In IADB, the United States is the largest shareholder, now with 30% of the total voting power (originally higher). https://www.iadb.org/en/who-we-are/how-we-are-organized/board-governors/capital-stock-and-voting-power (last visited July 14, 2025). In AsDB, the United States and Japan are the largest two shareholders, each with 12.747% of total voting power. AsDB Annual Report 2024 at 69 (Appendix 5). In EBRD, the United States is the largest shareholder, with 9.46% of total voting power; followed by Japan (9.14%); France; Germany; the United Kingdom (8.977%); and Italy (7.913%). https://www.ebrd.com/home/who-we-are/our-organisation/shareholders.html (last visited July 14, 2025).

(3) Establishment

The AIIB Charter was opened for signature at a signing ceremony in Beijing on June 29, 2015. A total of fifty PFMs signed on that day, and the others signed later in the year. Effectiveness of the AIIB Charter required subsequent ratification by at least ten Signatories with a majority of the allocated shareholding. That threshold was met on December 25, 2015, when the AIIB Charter legally entered into force. Entry into force in turn triggered the Inaugural Meeting of the Board of Governors on January 16–17, 2016, when AIIB was declared open for business.[53] **3.31**

(4) Chief Negotiators' Report

The CNM agreement on the text of the AIIB Charter was accompanied by a "Report on the Articles of Agreement of the Asian Infrastructure Investment Bank" by the Chief Negotiators for Establishing the Asian Infrastructure Investment Bank, dated May 22, 2015 (the Chief Negotiators' Report). The Chief Negotiators' Report was agreed along with the final text of the AIIB Charter, and summarizes the understandings of the Chief Negotiators on certain clauses in the AIIB Charter. The Chief Negotiators' Report states that it would form part of AIIB's basic documents for future use in interpreting the AIIB Charter. The Chief Negotiators' Report itself is similar in form and structure to the Chairman's Report on the Agreement Establishing the European Bank for Reconstruction and Development. Relevant references to the AIIB Chief Negotiators' Report are included throughout this book. The text can be found at Appendix 2. **3.32**

In terms of legal structure, the interplay of the legal provisions in the AIIB Charter and the parties' agreements recorded in the Chief Negotiators' Report gives AIIB a firm basis for adjusting to changes in the future. By providing specifics on such matters as GDP as the basic parameter for capital allocation, the Chief Negotiators' Report keeps today's details clear and transparent without enshrining them in the AIIB Charter where they may someday become outdated. **3.33**

C. Tracing Legal Lineage in AIIB's Charter

It is useful to consider the legal lineage of the AIIB Charter itself before turning to the chapters describing the institution it created. The considerable overlap with the Charters of other MDBs is apparent to those who peruse the AIIB Charter. Indeed, the history of the creation of other MDBs shows the same pattern, whether it was using the IBRD framework to design EIB and IADB; the IADB legal experts **3.34**

[53] *See* paragraphs 10.09–10.12.

assisting the AfDB drafters; the AsDB preparatory team melding the IBRD, IADB, and AfDB provisions; or the EBRD drafters building on the AsDB text.[54] For AIIB, there were also several strategic reasons for this overlap.

3.35 First, the parties were seeking to mobilize additional finance for infrastructure in Asia; the establishment of a new financing mechanism was not the primary objective. In setting up a new institution, the parties sought to differentiate AIIB from others by its specialized focus and its operation in practice. They could have chosen different structural models. The choice to build upon an MDB model can be seen as a reflection that this model was considered a useful and valuable one.[55] That choice also reflects the knowledge that the model has been successfully molded in different ways: in the seventy years since the IBRD Charter had been negotiated, the basic model had been adapted to suit the varying goals and needs of twenty or more MDBs and MDB-like institutions.[56] Taking the model as a base still left wide latitude for variation: existing MDBs already amply demonstrate that the same legal text and same structures can lead to very different institutions and ways of operating.

3.36 Second, timing was a major consideration, as AIIB was aimed at meeting pressing financing needs in infrastructure in Asia. Building on existing structures also meant that startup could be quicker. While the model had proved itself to be by and large reliable, there had been much criticism of MDBs and many proposals for their reform over the decades. With room for improvement and updating, alterations would certainly be needed for AIIB, but that would be less time-consuming and complex than starting an entirely new structure from scratch.

3.37 Third, the credibility of a brand-new financial institution was another consideration. Starting with something workable, known, and respected would offer something reliable to governments, financial markets, potential recipients, and contractors. For the lead agency in each PFM government engaging its domestic

[54] The AfDB drafting team consulted the IADB General Counsel (Arnold Weiss). Gardiner and Pickett (1984) at 12. Comments on the draft AfDB charter were also provided from IBRD, as a UN Specialized Agency, including on immunities. Comments and Proposals Received by [from] the International Bank for Reconstruction and Development Concerning the Draft Agreement Establishing an African Development Bank, E/CN.14/FMAB/4/Add.5, July 16, 1963. *See* paragraph 11.21.

The AsDB Charter resembled the IBRD Charter, IADB Charter and AfDB Charter. AsDB preparations included support from the IADB, whose President Felipe Herrera, sent his advisor, Orlando Letelier, to work with the group early on. An IBRD Assistant General Counsel, Ellsworth Clark, was available at negotiations to provide advice for the ECAFE legal consultant, Florentino Feliciano, who undertook most of the legal labors. Huang (1975) at 39, 60, and 87.

For EBRD, *see* comments by former World Bank General Counsel Aron Broches on the EBRD draft's reliance on the AsDB model. Aron Broches Oral History, World Bank History Project, October 20, 1990, at 34.

For AIIB, former General Counsel and Deputy General Counsel from AsDB, BSTDB, EBRD, IADB and IBRD (among others) provided informal advice in the drafting and establishment phases.

[55] Humphrey (2022) at 149–50 notes: "A further reason behind the creation of AIIB and NDB is an implicit recognition of the enduring viability and relevance of the MDB model . . . Creating new MDBs makes sense for EMDCs [emerging market developing countries] in purely pragmatic terms, as the up-front capitalization costs are relatively modest and MDBs mostly pay for themselves going forward. And the potential benefits in terms of development promotion and geopolitical influence are substantial."

[56] Humphrey (2022) at 195 provides an overview of MDBs in chart form.

authorities and public for the necessary approvals to join AIIB, a familiar structure would facilitate discussions and make it easier to draw attention to AIIB's special features. For rating agencies and investors in AIIB securities, it would be beneficial to assess AIIB's financial structure and condition through common MDB frameworks. For potential borrowers and other recipients evaluating AIIB's suitability for their infrastructure finance requirements, recognizable financial products and policies could be more easily compared with other options. Familiar but improved operational processes would be less burdensome than brand-new ones in an age when MDBs have emphasized harmonization of policies and procedures, to the benefit of the developing countries that actually implement MDB-financed projects. Lastly, AIIB would have the ability to draw from the vast and varied experience of other MDBs. That experience could inform not only AIIB's structure but also its future operations, administration, and legal interpretations.

Which MDB Charter would best serve as a model? The MOU, which set the main **3.38**
parameters for the AIIB Charter, was negotiated and signed by regional PFMs, and the participants in the initial CNM discussions were all regional. For many of these PFMs, a regional model, such as the AsDB Charter, had the distinct advantage of familiarity. Moreover, the AsDB Charter (1965) already incorporated some of the structural improvements on the IBRD Charter (1945) that came into play through the Charters of IADB (1959) and AfDB (1963). Its suitability as a model had been demonstrated in the preparation of the Charter for EBRD in 1990, where the AsDB Charter provided the structural foundation.

The AsDB Charter was also the first of the MDB Charters to incorporate provisions **3.39**
for regional and non-regional members from the start, as both IADB and AfDB started out with only regional membership. Thus, using the AsDB Charter as the basic framework for the AIIB Charter brought a wealth of time-tested practice from other MDBs. That framework was then restructured and updated, bringing in concepts and clauses from most of the core MDBs, and introducing new ones to suit AIIB's own circumstances. The similarities between and differences from other Charters will be highlighted in the chapters that follow and are summarized in the following sections, Continuities and Innovations.

(1) Continuities

The interplay of similar provisions in these Charters illustrates the evolutionary **3.40**
process. Some key examples include: (a) Board of Directors, (b) President, and (c) international character of the Bank.

(a) Board of Directors

The origins of the Board of Directors are detailed in Chapters 2 and 12, as the joint- **3.41**
stock model Board of Directors from BIS and IAB went through several iterations

in the development of the IBRD plan.[57] The final version provides IBRD with a Board, known as the Executive Directors, whose role is to be "responsible for the conduct of the general operations of the Bank" exercising all the powers delegated to them by the Board of Governors.[58]

3.42 The general role of the Board in subsequent Charters is almost identical to the provision quoted above from the IBRD Charter. For later MDBs, additional specific powers of the Board are spelled out. The IADB Charter, for instance, adds the determination of the basic organization of the Bank, approval of the budget, and the appointment of an Executive Vice President and other Vice Presidents.[59] The AfDB Charter adds the power to take decisions on investment operations and borrowings; in the current text, the President appoints Vice Presidents (in consultation with the Board) and determines the organization of the Bank.[60] The AsDB Charter echoes the AfDB Charter, providing for the Board to take decisions on investment operations and borrowings (adding decisions on technical assistance and other operations) and budget approval; the AsDB Board appoints Vice Presidents on the recommendation of the President.[61] The EBRD Charter is quite similar to the AsDB Charter with respect to these powers.[62]

3.43 The Board is resident at the Bank's headquarters for all four of these institutions. The Charter provisions are slightly different. The IBRD Charter, IADB Charter, and AfDB Charter provide that the Board "shall function in continuous session at the principal office of the Bank and shall meet as often as the business of the Bank may require."[63] The wording is slightly more flexible in the AsDB Charter and EBRD Charter, providing that the Board "shall normally function at the principal office of the Bank and shall meet as often as the business of the Bank may require."[64]

3.44 The AIIB Charter is similar to the AsDB and EBRD in its provisions for the general role of the Board of Directors, and its specified powers. The AIIB Charter expands the specified powers of the Board, in respect of decisions on policies and investments, on delegation, and on supervision; these AIIB provisions are discussed under the subsection Innovations, at paragraph 3.50.[65] The AIIB Charter is also different in providing for a non-resident Board of Directors that

[57] *See* Shihata (2000) at 649–52 for a discussion of the drafting history. *See also* paragraphs 2.38 and 12.06–12.11.

[58] IBRD Article V, Section 4 (a). The IMF Charter refers to the comparable group as the Executive Board. The IADB Charter used a clearer term, the Board of Executive Directors, and from the AfDB Charter onwards, the term Board of Directors is used.

[59] IADB Article VIII, Section 3 (a) and (i) and Section 5 (b) and (c).

[60] AfDB Articles 32 and 37.

[61] AsDB Articles 31 and 35.

[62] EBRD Articles 27 and 31.

[63] IBRD Article V, Section 4 (e); IADB Article VIII, Section 3 (e); AfDB Article 34.

[64] AsDB Article 32; EBRD Article 28. The Caribbean Development Bank, which has a non-resident Board, has the same Charter provision as AsDB and EBRD. CDB Article 31.

[65] AIIB Article 26. Delegations under policy and of investment decisions require a three-quarters majority of total voting power as do decisions on major operational and financial policies.

meets periodically throughout the year, as often as the business of the Bank may require.[66]

(b) The President

All of these Charters follow the final version of the IBRD Charter by providing for a President of the Bank who presides over Board meetings holding a deciding vote (Chairman of the Board except in IADB), and is chief of the staff of the Bank. These provisions hark back to BIS and IAB.[67] The fluidity of the relationship between the Board and the President that plagued the IBRD in its early years[68] remains visible in the provision for the President to conduct the business of the Bank under the direction of the Board.[69] A bit more legal clarity is offered in subsequent Charters by specifying certain powers of the Board, as outlined in paragraphs 3.42–3.43. **3.45**

(c) International character of the Bank

Another area of continuity across these Charters is ensuring the international character of the Bank. The IBRD Charter began with a prohibition against political activity: **3.46**

> The Bank and its officers shall not interfere in the political affairs of any member; nor shall they be influenced in their decisions by the political character of the member or members concerned. Only economic considerations shall be relevant to their decisions, and these considerations shall be weighed impartially in order to achieve the purposes stated in Article I.[70]

3.1 Furthermore, the President, officers, and staff operate under a mandate of neutrality:

> The President, officers and staff of the Bank, in the discharge of their offices, owe their duty entirely to the Bank and to no other authority. Each member of the Bank shall respect the international character of this duty and shall refrain from all attempts to influence any of them in the discharge of their duties.[71]

These provisions are maintained, in nearly identical language, in the later Charters, including AIIB, with appropriate deletions in the EBRD Charter to reflect its political mandate.[72] An additional provision was initiated in the AfDB Charter,

[66] AIIB Article 27-1. *See* Chapter 12.
[67] BIS Statutes Articles 34, 39, and 41; IAB By-Laws Section 3C and 31. *See* paragraph 2.40.
[68] *See* Shihata (2000) at 646–9.
[69] IBRD Article V, Section 5 (b); IADB Article VIII, Section 5 (a); AfDB Article 37-2; AsDB Article 34; EBRD Article 30.
[70] IBRD Article IV, Section 10.
[71] IBRD Article V, Section 5 (c).
[72] IADB Article VIII, Section 5 (d) and (f); AfDB Article 38; AsDB Article 36; EBRD Article 32; AIIB Article 31. *See* EBRD's political mandate in EBRD Article 1.

constraining the acceptance of loans or assistance that could affect its purposes or functions, which accompanied the first provisions on special funds:

> The Bank shall not accept loans or assistance that could in any way prejudice, limit, deflect or otherwise alter its purpose or functions.[73]

That provision was retained in the later Charters, including AIIB.[74]

(2) Innovations

3.47 AIIB followed its predecessors in another important respect, by innovating as its founders perceived appropriate to bring it into a new age. A few of the innovations in the AIIB Charter are highlighted: (a) Board of Governors, (b) Board of Directors, (c) MDB Voice Reforms, and (d) Flexibility.

(a) Board of Governors

3.48 The reserved powers of the AIIB Board of Governors listed in the AIIB Charter are comparable and often identical to the reserved powers of other MDB Boards of Governors.[75] In addition, the AIIB Charter assigns a number of other powers solely to the Board of Governors, and these cannot be delegated either. Most of these specifically assigned powers are new for AIIB, and they include: variations in the classification of the Asia region; change to the non-resident status of the Board of Directors; variation in the 75% regional shareholding requirement; allocation of net income to other purposes; increase in the lending limit; establishment of subsidiaries; setting a framework for trust funds; allowing financing for non-member recipients; and approving new types of financing.[76]

3.49 At the start, the AIIB Board of Governors indeed delegated to the AIIB Board of Directors all of its powers that are not reserved or specifically assigned, following the practice of the others.[77] One difference in AIIB powers is that the power to approve arrangements for cooperation with other international organizations is

[73] AfDB Article 38-1.

[74] AsDB Article 36-1; EBRD Article 32-1; AIIB Article 31.

[75] *See* AfDB Article 29-2; ADB Article 28-2; EBRD Article 24-2; IADB Article VIII, Section 2 (b); and IBRD Article V, Section 2 (b).

[76] Specifically assigned powers of the AIIB Board of Governors can be found in the AIIB Charter as follows: Asia definition (Article 1-2); exceptions to 75% regional shareholding, and review of capital stock (Articles 5-2 and 5-3); non-par value shares (Article 7-1); non-member recipient (Article 11-1 (b)); new types of financing (Article 11-2 (vi)); increase in lending limit (Article 12-1); trust fund framework (Article 16-7); subsidiaries (Article 16-8); allocation of net income to other purposes (Article 18-1); size or composition of the Board of Directors (Article 25-2); number of constituency members for second Alternate Director (Article 25-3); change in non-residential status of the Board of Directors (Article 27-1); and extension of the final date for Signatories to ratify (Article 58-1). Figure 8.2 also lists these powers.

[77] AIIB By-Laws, Section 6. This section further provides that the Board of Directors shall not take any action pursuant to powers delegated by the Board of Governors which is inconsistent with any action taken by the Board of Governors. This delegation and proviso are also common. *See* AfDB General Regulations Article 4-1; ADB By-Laws Section 8; EBRD By-Laws Section 8 (a); IADB By-Laws Section 4; and IBRD By-Laws Section 14.

directly assigned to the Board of Directors in the AIIB Charter; in others, it is often reserved to the Board of Governors.[78]

(b) Board of Directors

There is considerable continuity in the AIIB Charter provisions regarding the Board of Directors, as has been mentioned. This is also an area of considerable innovation in the AIIB Charter, as several specific powers set AIIB apart.[79] **3.50**

- Policy. The AIIB Board of Directors has the authority to establish the policies of the Bank; this is the practice elsewhere but it is not always explicit. Major operational and financial policies require Board approval by a majority representing not less than three-fourths of total voting power.[80] The Board may, under Bank policies, delegate authority to the President, and decisions on such delegation also require approval of the Board of Directors by the same majority. This higher majority for certain decisions by the Board of Directors on policy matters recalls a provision in the EBRD Charter that requires a two-thirds majority for general policy decisions.[81] Higher majority Board of Directors' decisions are not the practice in other MDBs.
- Decisions on Financing Operations. The AIIB Board of Directors has the authority to take decisions on the financing operations of AIIB, and to delegate that authority to the President.[82] Delegation decisions require the same 75% majority as for delegation under policies. Many MDB Boards exercise this approval authority, but only later Charters make this explicit;[83] rarely do they provide for delegation.[84]
- Strategy, Plan, and Budget. The Board of Directors has the authority to approve AIIB's strategy, annual plan, and budget.[85] How the content of the strategy and annual plan evolves over time is worked out between the Board and management. Other MDBs have similar planning documents without Charter-based

[78] AIIB Article 35. *See* paragraph 8.10. The power to approve general agreements with other international organizations is a reserved power of the Board of Governors in AfDB, ADB, EBRD, IADB, and IBRD, in varying terms. *See* AfDB Article 29-2; ADB Article 28-2; EBRD Article 24-2; IADB Article VIII, Section 2 (b); and IBRD Article V, Section 2 (b).

[79] Other MDB Charter provisions on the powers of the Board of Directors can be found in: AfDB Charter, art 32; ADB Article 31; EBRD Charter, Article 27; IADB Charter, Article VIII, Section 3 (a); and IBRD Charter, Article V, Section 4 (a).

[80] AIIB Charter, Article 26 (ii).

[81] EBRD Charter, Article 29-3. The meaning of this provision at the time negotiations on the EBRD Charter were concluded is set out in the Chairman's Report on the Agreement Establishing the EBRD: "Delegates intended that, in the case of differing views on whether or not issues involved 'general policy', decisions would be made by the Board on the basis of advice from the Legal Counsel. In general, decisions on individual operations would not involve such issues, but 'general policy issues' would include, inter alia, the budget; the annual program of operations; borrowing policy, including borrowing limits; interest rate policy; exchange risk management policy; the drawing down of notes; underwriting policy and the organizational structure of the Bank."

[82] AIIB Article 26 (iii). *See* Chapter 12, Section B, for the delegation to the President under AIIB's Accountability Framework.

[83] *See* AfDB Article 32-2; ADB Article 31 (ii); and EBRD Article 27 (ii).

[84] *See* paragraph 12.22.

[85] AIIB Article 26 (v).

requirements. The annual budgets are also approved by the Board of Directors and generally reported to the Board of Governors in other MDBs.[86]

- Oversight. In a provision unique to the AIIB Charter, the Board of Directors is expressly required to supervise the management and operation of AIIB on a regular basis.[87] This general function is understood to be part of the Board's overall responsibility in other MDB Boards of Directors, so that making it explicit for AIIB adds more definition to the Board's role in the non-residential context, where physical presence is not an element of oversight. Indeed, the AIIB Charter further requires the Board of Directors to establish an oversight mechanism for this purpose, "in line with principles of transparency, openness, independence and accountability."[88]

(c) MDB voice reforms

3.51 Some provisions of the AIIB Charter reflect discussions over the preceding decade about reforms to enhance MDB governance. For example, AIIB's President is limited to two terms. The selection of the President and Vice-Presidents through an open, transparent, and merit-based process sets a new legal standard. The desirability of a greater voice for regional and smaller members is recognized by adding a second Alternate Director for larger Board constituencies, rotation privileges for Founding Members and the 12% weight for basic votes.[89]

(d) Flexibility

3.52 There are some more subtle differences in the AIIB Charter provisions that also balance clarity and flexibility.[90] The IBRD Articles of Agreement can be seen as a hybrid between the specificity of a company charter and the grand principles of a country's constitution. Oftentimes, it can be difficult to operate legally within particular constraints that made sense in 1944 but are no longer relevant. Great creativity and wisdom have been required of IBRD lawyers and decision-makers to keep the Bank relevant over the decades. Moreover, the IBRD Articles of Agreement have rarely been amended, and then only in limited ways, leaving anachronistic clauses in place (e.g., Advisory Council).[91]

3.53 To ameliorate this potential for unwarranted rigidity, the AIIB Charter offers legal avenues that would allow AIIB to evolve with the times and the objectives of its members as a whole. A few charter provisions specifically allow for modifications

[86] AsDB Article 31 (iv); EBRD Article 27 (iv); and IADB Article VIII, Section 3 (i). The requirement to submit the annual budget approved by the Board of Directors to the Board of Governors for information is found in the AIIB By-Laws, Section 5 (c). The approval and reporting requirements are found in the By-Laws for IBRD (Section 18 (b)) and the General Regulations for AfDB (Section 8-1).

[87] AIIB Article 26 (iv).

[88] *See* Chapter 12, Section C.

[89] *See* paragraphs 6.22–6.23, 8.16–8.17 and 9.07–9.08.

[90] A simple example, related to gender: AIIB Article 36-2 provides: "References in this Agreement to a specific gender shall be equally applicable to any gender."

[91] *See* paragraph 11.06.

of a rule, but by a high majority vote of the relevant Board. That way, evolution can take place within the legal structure by clear and conscious decision of the shareholders on the merits of the modification, instead of through a sometimes-tortured legal interpretation. To illustrate:

- Definition of the Asia Region (Article 1-2). The definition of regional can be important in regional MDBs for several reasons.[92] A simple geographical definition in the charter is not so easily achieved for Asia. AIIB's Charter has a general reference, and leaves the power to decide otherwise to the Board of Governors. In addition, AIIB's Chief Negotiators agreed on a UN statistical definition (for Asia and Oceania) and recorded it in the Chief Negotiators' Report for reference for future Boards of Governors. This multilayered approach could make future membership decisions easier, and avoid the necessity of Charter amendments.[93]
- Financing in Non-Member Territory (Article 11-1 (b)). Providing support for entities that are not members has been a difficult issue in other MDBs. Creativity was required to permit World Bank Group support to such entities as the Soviet Union (before Russia's membership), West Bank and Gaza, Kosovo, and East Timor. For AIIB, there is an explicit provision permitting the Board of Governors to agree on financing for recipients that are not members or international and regional entities by a Super Majority vote, after determining that particular type of finance is designed to serve AIIB's purpose and come within AIIB's functions, and is in the interest of AIIB's membership.[94]
- New Types of Financing (Article 11-2 (vi)). Like many MDBs, AIIB's financing instruments include loans and guarantees, equity investments, and technical assistance. Occasionally, there is a new financial structure proposed that would create legal problems to be classified as one of those, such as a loan. Rather than restructuring the deal to look like a loan (or guarantee or equity investment), or declining to finance it, AIIB could proceed with a different structure, by a special majority vote of the Board of Governors.[95]
- Statutory Lending Limit (Article 12-1). AIIB loans, equity investments, guarantees, and other financing are not, as a baseline, to exceed its unimpaired subscribed capital, reserves, and retained earnings: a lending limit of 1:1 or 100%. AIIB's lending limit can be raised to 250% by super majority decision of the Board of Governors, based on the Bank's financial position and financial standing. Most MDBs had a 1:1 lending limit, a few also permitted

[92] *See* paragraph 6.25 (regional definition) and paragraphs 6.30–6.35 (regional distinctions). Regional may describe the area for the MDB's operations, or regional members may have different rights than non-regional members.

[93] EBRD has amended its Charter three times to expand the scope of its operations from the Central and Eastern European countries specified in its Charter (to Mongolia, to Southern and Eastern Mediterranean, and most recently, to sub-Saharan Africa). *See* paragraph 3.18.

[94] *See* paragraphs 5.26–5.27.

[95] *See* paragraph 5.21.

higher increases.[96] Recently, inspired by the G20 Independent Review of MDB's Capital Adequacy Frameworks, several counterparts—AsDB, IBRD, and EBRD—have taken steps towards a charter amendment to eliminate their lending limits.[97]

One other area of flexibility in AIIB's establishment was the detailed set of Interim Arrangements agreed to keep all Prospective Founding Members involved in AIIB decision-making from the end of negotiations until all had become full members. (See Chapter 10, Section D.)

3.54 In sum, AIIB's governance features both MDB heritage and innovation, as AIIB takes its place in the family of MDBs.

96 EIB Article 16-5 (250%); NIB Section 7 (250%); and BSTDB Article 15-1 (150%).
97 *See* paragraph 7.44, discussing amendments at AsDB, EBRD, EIB, and IBRD.

4
MANDATE

The mandate of a new institution lies at the core of discussions on its establishment. For the Asian Infrastructure Investment Bank (AIIB), that mandate is crystallized in the AIIB Charter. The legal provisions that encapsulate AIIB's mandate address several key questions. What were the overarching objectives that the Prospective Founding Members (PFMs) saw for AIIB? What was to be its purpose, and through what functions would that purpose be achieved? What does the AIIB Charter reveal about the choice of a multilateral development bank (MDB) structure for this purpose and these functions? **4.01**

This chapter describes AIIB's legal purpose and functions, against the backdrop of the Preamble. It concludes by enumerating the clauses in the AIIB Charter where the purpose and functions have particular legal significance. **4.02**

A. Preamble

The Preamble to the AIIB Charter reflects the aims of the parties to the Memorandum of Understanding on Establishing the Asian Infrastructure Investment Bank among Prospective Founding Members (MOU), as refined through their multiple multilateral consultations and the Chief Negotiators' Meetings, and agreed by all fifty-seven PFMs in Singapore. It is perhaps best quoted and read first in full: **4.03**

> The countries on whose behalf the present Agreement is signed agree as follows:
>
> CONSIDERING the importance of regional cooperation to sustain growth and promote economic and social development of the economies in Asia and thereby contribute to regional resilience against potential financial crises and other external shocks in the context of globalization;
>
> ACKNOWLEDGING the significance of infrastructure development in expanding regional connectivity and improving regional integration, thereby promoting economic growth and sustaining social development for the people in Asia, and contributing to global economic dynamism;
>
> REALIZING that the considerable long-term need for financing infrastructure development in Asia will be met more adequately by a partnership among existing multilateral development banks and the Asian Infrastructure Investment Bank (hereinafter referred to as the "Bank");

CONVINCED that the establishment of the Bank as a multilateral financial institution focused on infrastructure development will help to mobilize much needed additional resources from inside and outside Asia and to remove the financing bottlenecks faced by the individual economies in Asia, and will complement the existing multilateral development banks, to promote sustained and stable growth in Asia;

HAVE AGREED to establish the Bank . . .

4.04 The structure of the AIIB Preamble is reminiscent of the preambles to the Charters for the Asian Development Bank (AsDB), African Development Bank (AfDB), Inter-American Development Bank (IADB), and European Bank for Reconstruction and Development (EBRD). Yet each is highly specific to the reasons and timing for establishing the particular MDB.[1] There is an especial resonance with the AsDB Preamble, in its references to cooperation for economic development, economic growth and mobilization of resources from inside and outside the region. Several themes stand out for AIIB: regional economic development; infrastructure; mobilization of resources; and cooperation and partnership. The emphasis on infrastructure is specific to AIIB; the other themes are common to AfDB, AsDB, and EBRD.[2] Unlike some other Charters, the AIIB Charter does not mention trade in its Preamble, as trade was not directly connected to the infrastructure financing gap that inspired its focus.[3]

(1) Regional economic development

4.05 First among the tenets agreed by the parties is sustaining growth and promoting the economic and social development of economies in Asia, reiterated as economic growth and sustained social development for the people of Asia. The anticipated impacts of this growth and development are both regional and global. On the one hand, regional growth and development can "contribute to regional resilience against potential financial crises and other external shocks in the context of globalization." In that regard, AIIB is aimed in part at strengthening the economies of

[1] The IBRD and IADB Charters do not have preambles as such. In the IBRD Charter, the purposes section (Article I) includes the kinds of references later found in the preambles and purposes and functions sections of other MDB charters. The IADB Charter, which followed the IBRD Charter some fifteen years later, separates purpose and functions, in IADB Article I, as do many of the later MDB Charters.

[2] AfDB Preamble; AsDB Preamble; and EBRD Preamble. Much more prominent in EBRD's Preamble, however, are its unique focus on investment in Central and Eastern Europe and its commitment to fundamental principles of multi-party democracy, the rule of law, respect for human rights, and market economics.

[3] The AsDB Charter's preamble and functions link economic growth and external trade, reflecting discussions on regional trade that featured in early proposals for its establishment. AsDB Preamble, third clause, and AsDB Article 2 (iii). For instance, a 1963 ECAFE paper was prepared on "The Case for a Regional Bank for the ECAFE Region—with Special Reference to the Development of Intra-Regional Trade." Wilson (1987) at 5. IBRD Article I also includes among its purposes "to promote the long-range balanced growth of international trade and the maintenance of equilibrium in balance of payments . . ."

the region and promoting sustained and stable growth in Asia. On the other hand, by promoting economic growth and development in Asia, AIIB is also expected to contribute to global economic dynamism.[4]

(2) Infrastructure

4.06 Through the Preamble, the parties acknowledge the significance of infrastructure for achieving regional economic growth and development. In particular, infrastructure development is portrayed as key to expanding regional connectivity and improving regional integration. The considerable long-term need for the financing of infrastructure development in Asia is presented as the driver for AIIB's establishment as a multilateral financial institution focused on infrastructure development.

(3) Mobilization of resources

4.07 The Preamble highlights the belief that the considerable need for financing infrastructure development will be met more adequately by a partnership among existing MDBs and AIIB. The Preamble also states clearly the rationale that AIIB's establishment will help "mobilize much needed additional resources from inside and outside Asia" and help remove financing bottlenecks faced by individual Asian economies.

(4) Cooperation and partnership

4.08 The twin themes of cooperation and partnership are intertwined through the Preamble. It begins with the importance of regional cooperation to sustain growth and promote economic and social development. Alongside regional cooperation, the importance of expanding regional connectivity and improving regional integration is emphasized. At the same time, a cooperative relationship with existing MDBs is also highlighted, both in the realization that the financing needs will be met more adequately by a partnership among existing MDBs and AIIB and in the conviction that AIIB, focused on infrastructure development, will complement existing MDBs.

[4] AIIB's Board of Directors have also recognized that regional development can be enhanced by investments outside Asia. AIIB's Strategy on Financing Operations in Non-Regional Members states as its basic parameter: "[A] project located outside the Region must benefit Asia, i.e., it must foster economic development, create wealth or improve infrastructure connectivity in Asia, and such benefits must be significant." *See* paragraph 5.10.

B. Purpose

4.09 AIIB's purpose under the Charter is twofold, and derives directly from the Preamble's themes laid out in Section A.

(1) Investment

4.10 The first listed purpose is to *foster sustainable economic development, create wealth and improve infrastructure connectivity in Asia by investing in infrastructure and other productive sectors*.[5] This first purpose is most directly tied to the Preamble's themes of regional economic growth and sustainable economic development, and to investment in infrastructure and other productive sectors. Both AsDB and IADB focus specifically on the economic development of regional developing member countries; AfDB also focuses on its regional members and their economic development.[6] AIIB investment is not limited to developing member countries, while its focus is slightly narrowed by its attention to investment in infrastructure and other productive sectors.

4.11 This legal purpose governs AIIB's infrastructure and other operations in many ways. For instance, "sustainable" economic development is used in the description of AIIB's purpose, and was highlighted in the Chief Negotiators' Report.[7] This reference brings in discussions of environmental and social impact that have become a critical aspect of development over the decades since many other MDBs were established.[8]

4.12 AIIB's sectoral focus is laid out broadly in its purpose. The reference to improving infrastructure connectivity can be expected to cover many different kinds of connectivity over time, such as physical and electronic, to name but two. Infrastructure

[5] AIIB Article 1-1 (i).

[6] AsDB Article 1; IADB Article I, Section 1. The limitation to "regional developing" members was added to the IADB Charter in 1976, in the context of the admission of non-regional members. IADB Board of Governors' Resolution No. AG-9/76, *Amendments to the Agreement Establishing the Bank in Respect to the Creation of the Inter-Regional Capital Stock of the Bank and to Related Matters*, approved June 1, 1976. Similarly, AfDB's purpose focuses on sustainable economic development and social progress of its "regional" members, following its admission of non-regional members. AfDB Article 1.

[7] The Chief Negotiators' Report states with regard to the Preamble: "Representatives highlighted that the Bank would be established as a multilateral financial institution to promote sustained and stable growth in Asia."

[8] Negotiated in 1944, the IBRD Charter does not mention the environment, though the World Bank later became one of the first MDBs to have environmental policies. By 1990, the EBRD Charter included the promotion of environmentally sound activities and sustainable development in its functions. EBRD Article 2-1 (vii). The AfDB Charter was amended in 2001 to include the term "sustainable" in its purpose: "to contribute to the sustainable economic development and social progress of its regional members—individually and jointly." AfDB Board of Governors' Resolution No. B/BG/2001/08, *Amendments to the Agreement Establishing the African Development Bank*, adopted May 29, 2001, entered into force July 5, 2002. The IADB Charter was amended in 1976 to add reference to social development. IADB Board of Governors' Resolution No. AG-9/76, *Amendments to the Agreement Establishing the Bank in Respect to the Creation of the Inter-Regional Capital Stock of the Bank and to Related Matters*, approved June 1, 1976.

as a sector is likely to encompass a broad range of investment sectors, as discussed in Chapter 5.[9] The reference to infrastructure and "other productive sectors" adds flexibility to the investment sectors, and echoes the use of the term "productive" in the International Bank for Reconstruction and Development (IBRD) Charter.[10] For AIIB, the reference to other productive sectors (in addition to infrastructure) can be found even in the earliest days of the AIIB discussions.[11]

AIIB's purpose of fostering regional economic development is viewed through the impact of its investments rather than the location of the recipient or the operation itself. AIIB investments in infrastructure, as well as in other productive sectors, should aim at fostering development, creating wealth and improving infrastructure connectivity *in Asia*. Investments located outside the region would need to be balanced with AIIB's mandate to have special regard to the needs of less developed members in the region in the utilization of its resources.[12] **4.13**

(2) Collaboration

The second listed purpose highlights other themes from the Preamble, namely cooperation and partnership: *promote regional cooperation and partnership in addressing development challenges by working in close collaboration with other multilateral and bilateral development institutions.*[13] Regional cooperation and partnership connects to the goal of promoting regional economic growth and development. The imperative for close collaboration with other multilateral and bilateral development institutions connects to the conviction in the Preamble that AIIB's establishment will mobilize additional resources in combination with these other institutions. Cooperation with other institutions features in the Charters of other MDBs, not in purposes but rather among the functions of the institution or separately.[14] The inclusion of this clause (ii) in AIIB's purpose is in sync with the Preamble, and is also seen in a separate AIIB provision on cooperation with members and international organizations.[15] **4.14**

AIIB's collaboration with other MDBs and international financial institutions (IFIs) is visible in many ways. From the beginning, AIIB set up bilateral partnerships with **4.15**

[9] *See* paragraphs 5.06–5.07.

[10] *See* IBRD Article I.

[11] "[Lou Jiwei responds to reporters' questions on AIIB preparations] 楼继伟就筹建 亚洲基础设施投资银行答记者问," Ministry of Finance of the People's Republic of China Press Release, March 7, 2014 (on file with author).

[12] This distinction (and AIIB's Strategy on Financing Operations in Non-Regional Members) is also discussed in paragraphs 5.08–5.10 on investment objectives and in paragraph 6.25 on the definition of Asia.

[13] AIIB Article 1-1 (ii).

[14] *See* AfDB Article 2-2; AsDB Article 2 (v); EBRD Article 2-2; EIB Article 14; and IADB Article 1, Section 2 (b). For IBRD, cooperation with other international organizations is addressed in a separate clause (IBRD Article V, Section 8), and not highlighted in its purposes.

[15] AIIB Article 35.

MDBs and other counterparts. In the first few years, these included Memoranda of Understanding (MOUs) to cement its operational and technical cooperation with AsDB, EBRD, European Investment Bank (EIB), IADB, International Finance Corporation (IFC), New Development Bank (NDB), and the World Bank Group. These non-binding MOUs generally laid out the basis for exchanges of information and staff, coordination in areas of common interest and potential co-financing, and they serve as high-level expressions of collaborative relationships.

4.16 The scope of AIIB's collaboration has grown dramatically. AIIB's first ever Partnership Report in June 2025 highlights four core principles for its partnerships (client focus, value addition, operational adaptability and institutional trust), as well as several dimensions of partnerships (partnering through co-financing, mobilizing resources for clients' support, AIIB Special Funds and AIIB's Digital Partnership Tools).[16] The AIIB 2025 Partnerships Report lists AIIB's partners in several categories: multilateral partners[17] and bilateral partners,[18] as well as multipartner facility and philanthropic partners, technical partners, knowledge partners, and global and regional platforms.[19]

4.17 In the multilateral space, AIIB has taken its place in many international fora related to MDBs and similar international financial institutions. These include: Finance in Common (FiCS), Group of Twenty (G20), Heads of MDBs Meeting, United Nations Climate Change Conference (UNFCCC COP), and United Nations General Assembly (UNGA).[20] For instance, AIIB has been a participant in the

[16] *Scaling Impact Through Collaboration: AIIB's Partnerships in Action*, June 2025 (AIIB 2025 Partnerships Report) at 10–13. https://www.aiib.org/en/publications/partnerships-reports/2025/pdf/partnerships-report-2025.pdf (last visited July 14, 2025).

Digital Partnership Tools include: the Infratech Portal to expand engagement with infrastructure stakeholders, technology providers, and investors, and the Global Collaborative Co-Financing Platform, launched with nine peer MDBs to strengthen collaboration, streamline co-financing processes, and provide a centralized hub for project information. AIIB 2025 Partnerships Report at 13.

[17] Multilateral partners listed in the AIIB 2025 Partnerships Report (at 45) are: African Development Bank (AfDB); African Union Development Agency (AUDA-NEPAD); Asian Development Bank (ADB); Corporación Andina de Fomento (CAF - Development Bank of Latin America and the Caribbean); Eurasian Development Bank (EDB); European Bank for Reconstruction and Development (EBRD); European Investment Bank (EIB); Fonplata Development Bank (FONPLATA); Inter-American Investment Bank (IADB); International Fund for Agricultural Development (IFAD); Islamic Development Bank (IsDB); New Development Bank (NDB); Nordic Investment Bank (NIB); OPEC Fund for International Development (OPEC Fund); The World Bank Group (WB).

[18] Bilateral partners listed in the AIIB 2025 Partnerships Report (at 45) are: Abu Dhabi Fund for Development (ADFD); Agence française de développement (AFD); Banco Nacional de Desenvolvimento Econômico e Social (BNDES); Cassa Depositi e Prestiti (CDP); China International Development Cooperation Agency (CIDCA); Export Finance Australia (EFA); Export-Import Bank of China (CEXIM); Export-Import Bank of Korea / Economic Development Cooperation Fund (KEXIM / EDCF); Foreign, Commonwealth, and Development Office (FCDO); Germany Agency for International Cooperation (GIZ); Japan International Cooperation Agency (JICA); Kreditstanstalt für Wiederaufbau (KfW); National Bank of Financing Infrastructure and Development (NaBFID); National Infrastructure Fund (NIF); Nederlandse Financierings-Maatschappij voor; Ontwikkelingslanden N.V. (FMO Entrepreneurial Development Bank); Neighboring Countries Economic Development Cooperation Agency (NEDA); Public Investment Fund (PIF); Saudi Fund for Development (SFD); and State Secretariat for Economic Affairs for Switzerland; (SECO).

[19] AIIB 2025 Partnerships Report at 45–6.

[20] AIIB Partnerships https://www.aiib.org/en/about-aiib/who-we-are/partnership/index.html (last visited July 14, 2025).

MDB Heads group which meets at least annually; meetings in 2021 were chaired by AIIB's President.[21] AIIB has joined some of the specific MDB groupings, such as the Independent Accountability Mechanisms Network, Global Delivery Initiative, and Ethics Network of Multilateral Organizations, as well as MDB Heads of Procurement and Heads of Integrity.[22]

AIIB collaborates with other multilateral institutions in the financing of its investment operations. AIIB co-finances investment operations with several MDBs, including AfDB, AsDB, EBRD, IBRD, IFC and IsDB, among others; about 43% of AIIB's projects have been co-financed.[23] AIIB's projects funded under the COVID-19 Crisis Recovery Facility were for the most part co-financed, enabling quicker and broader response.[24] Cofinancing also has a role to play in the reforms of the MDB system, as noted in AIIB's 2025 Partnerships Report: "At the October 2023 meeting in Marrakesh, the Heads of MDBs Group agreed on the need for closer, more systematic collaboration to improve collective performance and maximize system-wide impact. Co-financing was identified as one of the five critical areas for partnership."[25] **4.18**

C. Functions

To implement its purpose, the AIIB Charter specifies that AIIB has four functions: investment promotion; development finance; supplementing private investment; and other activities and services. **4.19**

(1) Investment promotion

AIIB is mandated *to promote investment in the region of public and private capital for development purposes, in particular for development of infrastructure and other productive sectors.*[26] Investment promotion features in the purposes of AfDB, AsDB, IADB, and IBRD as well. The phrase "to promote investment in the region of public and private capital for development purposes" in the AIIB Charter is identical to the wording used in the AsDB Charter and IADB Charter, and is reflected in **4.20**

[21] AIIB Annual Report 2021 at 3.

[22] AIIB Annual Report 2017 at 25; AIIB Annual Report 2019 at 16; and AIIB Annual Report 2024 at 82.

[23] The AIIB 2025 Partnerships Report at 16 notes 131 co-financed projects out of 303 projects at December 2024, around 43%. Co-financing with AsDB totaled sixty-seven projects (AIIB contributed US$16.36 billion in financing) and with EBRD, there were fifteen projects (totaling more than US$1.86 billion). With World Bank, there were fifty-six projects totaling US$13.6 billion and with IFC, nine projects with $850 million in approved financing. AIIB 2025 Partnerships Report at 16, 18, and 20.

[24] AIIB (2024) [Final Review of the COVID-19 Crisis Recovery Facility] at 6: 84% of Facility financing (US$15.59 billion) was co-financing led by other MDBs, including 53% with ADB (US$9.79 billion); 31% with World Bank Group (IBRD and IFC) (US$5.72 billion); and 0.4% with EBRD (US$82.60 million).

[25] AIIB 2025 Partnerships Report at 16.

[26] AIIB Article 2 (i).

other phrasing in the IBRD and AfDB Charters.[27] Specific to AIIB in this function is its unique objective, namely, the particular development of infrastructure and other productive sectors.

(2) Development finance

4.21 AIIB is mandated *to utilize the resources at its disposal for financing such development in the region, including those projects and programs which will contribute most effectively to the harmonious economic growth of the region as a whole and having special regard to the needs of less developed members in the region.*[28] Several aspects of the development finance function deserve mention. First, the reference to "such development in the region" refers to the development of infrastructure and other productive sectors in Asia. Second, AIIB's development finance function is not restricted to developing member countries, in contrast to AsDB, AfDB, and IADB.[29] Third, the projects and programs financed by AIIB should include those contributing most effectively to harmonious regional economic growth and having regard to the needs of the less developed regional members. These last two considerations borrow from the AsDB Charter.[30]

(3) Supplementing private investment

4.22 AIIB is mandated *to encourage private investment in projects, enterprises and activities contributing to economic development in the region, in particular in infrastructure and other productive sectors, and to supplement private investment when private capital is not available on reasonable terms and conditions.*[31] This function dates back to the IBRD Charter at Bretton Woods, where the promotion of private

[27] AfDB Article 2-d; AsDB Article 2 (i); IADB Article I, Section 2 (a)(i); and IBRD Article I (ii).

[28] AIIB Article 2 (ii).

[29] AfDB Article 2-1-a; AsDB Article 2 (ii). IADB's purpose is limited to economic and social development of regional member countries (IADB Article I, Section 1). IBRD's purposes (Article I) do not strictly limit development finance to developing members, though there is one specific reference to "the encouragement of the development of productive facilities and resources in less developed countries," among several other purposes.

[30] AsDB Article 2 (ii): "to utilize the resources at its disposal for financing development of the developing member countries in the region, giving priority to those regional, sub-regional as well as national projects and programmes *which will contribute most effectively to the harmonious economic growth of the region as a whole, and having special regard to the needs of the smaller or less developed member countries in the region*" (emphasis added). AsDB founders' emphasis on smaller regional countries was reportedly a reflection of the high proportion of World Bank financing for Asia then being directed to larger Asian developing countries (65% of IBRD and 95% of IDA financing for Asia went to India and Pakistan). Wilson (1987) at 6. The AsDB wording includes "smaller or less developed." The inclusion of "or" was important to the larger developing countries. Huang (1975) at 74 (note 15). In AIIB's text, there is no reference to the size of less developed regional members, putting large and small less developed regional countries on an equal footing in this regard.

[31] AIIB Article 2 (iii).

foreign investment was expected primarily through guarantees of, and participation in, loans by private investors, rather than through direct loans that became the predominant mode for IBRD's development finance.[32] Even at Bretton Woods, the potential borrowers (Europeans and less developed countries) were more interested in direct loans, and the latter countries could have anticipated difficulty in borrowing directly on the private market to the extent that they were still in default at that time.[33] Historically, the preponderance of IBRD finance has been in the form of direct loans rather than guarantee of loans by private investors. The AIIB provision is similar to the others that followed IBRD's actual evolution, without specifying the ways in which it will supplement private capital.[34]

All three Charters (IBRD, IADB, and AIIB) contain a similar element in their functions—providing development finance only when private capital is not available on reasonable terms and conditions.[35] This time-honored phrase is operationalized in all three institutions and in AsDB as a condition for financing. The AIIB Charter expresses that common requirement as follows: "In considering an application for financing, the Bank shall pay due regard to the ability of the recipient to obtain financing or facilities elsewhere on terms and conditions that the Bank considers reasonable for the recipient, taking into account all pertinent factors."[36] The AIIB wording is virtually identical in this respect to the clause in the AsDB Charter.[37] **4.23**

(4) Other activities and services

In addition to the three specified functions related to investment promotion, development finance and supplementing private investment, AIIB is authorized *to undertake such other activities and provide such other services as may further these functions.*[38] This clear authorization for additional functions is closely modeled on the Charters for AfDB, AsDB, and EBRD.[39] **4.24**

[32] *See* Bittermann (1971) at 67. IBRD Article 1 (ii) provides: "To promote private foreign investment by means of guarantees or participations in loans and other investments made by private investors; and when private capital is not available on reasonable terms, to supplement private investment by providing, on suitable conditions, finance for productive purposes out of its own capital, funds raised by it and its other resources."

[33] Bittermann (1971) at 71.

[34] AfDB Article 2-1 (d); AsDB Article 2 (i); and IADB Article I, Section 2 (iii).

[35] The same concept is found in the provisions on operational principles also in AfDB Article 17-1 (c); EBRD Article 13 (vii); and EIB Article 16-1.

[36] AIIB Article 13-5. *See* AsDB Article 14 (v); IADB Article II, Section 7 (a)(ii); and IBRD Article III, Section 4 (ii).

[37] The AIIB wording refers to "recipient" instead of "borrower," to clarify the application to financing other than in the form of loans.

[38] AIIB Article 2 (iv).

[39] AfDB Article 2-1-f; AsDB Article 2 (vi); EBRD Article 2-1 (viii).

4.25 A few other roles that are sometimes listed as functions in some other MDB Charters are not found among AIIB's functions. Technical assistance is listed among the specific functions for AfDB, AsDB, EBRD, and IADB,[40] while the provision of technical assistance by AIIB is specifically provided for as a method of operation and detailed in a separate Article.[41] As noted previously, cooperation with members and institutions is included in the functions for AsDB and IADB,[42] but is part of AIIB's purposes and appears in a separate Article.[43]

D. Significance of Purpose and Functions

4.26 The Preamble provides a backdrop for the Charter, illuminating the intent of the founders and those who join them as members. In addition, the provisions on purpose and functions offer a significant legal litmus test under the AIIB Charter.[44] Serving AIIB's purpose in Article 1 and coming within its functions in Article 2 are legal requirements for many powers and decisions under the AIIB Charter. To illustrate: AIIB's resources and facilities may only be used to implement the purpose and functions as set out in the AIIB Charter;[45] technical assistance must serve the purpose and come within the functions;[46] and the Board of Governors may only approve financial assistance to an entity not in a member's territory if it is designed to serve the purpose and come within the functions of the Bank.[47] Serving the purpose and coming within the functions also forms a prerequisite for the acceptance of trust funds[48] and special funds,[49] for the establishment of subsidiaries[50] and for the exercise of incidental functions.[51] AIIB's purpose and functions are also a consideration in situations as diverse as underwriting of securities,[52] acceptance of loans or assistance,[53] publication of reports,[54] and freedom of assets from restrictions.[55]

[40] AfDB Article 2-e; AsDB Article 2 (iv); EBRD Article 2-1 (iv); and IADB Article I, Section 2 (a) (v).
[41] AIIB Article 11-2 (v) and Article 15.
[42] *See, e.g.*, AsDB Article 2 (v) and IADB Article 1, Section 2 (b).
[43] AIIB Article 35.
[44] AIIB Article 1. The clause follows some regional MDBs in having a singular purpose clause and a multi-pronged functions clause, combined in later references to purpose and functions. However, it might have been easier linguistically to follow the older IBRD practice of referring to "purposes" in the plural.
[45] AIIB Article 9.
[46] AIIB Article 15.
[47] AIIB Article 11-1 (b).
[48] AIIB Article 16-7.
[49] AIIB Article 17-1.
[50] AIIB Article 16-8.
[51] AIIB Article 16-9.
[52] AIIB Article 16-4.
[53] AIIB Article 31-1.
[54] AIIB Article 34-4.
[55] AIIB Article 48.

Under other MDB Charters, furtherance of the MDB's purpose and functions has a similar legal impact.[56] Because MDBs generally enjoy "functional immunity" in national legal systems, national courts may also look to an MDB's purpose and functions in deciding whether there should be immunity from suit.[57] 4.27

[56] For example, conforming to the purpose and functions is required for use of resources, exercise of incidental powers, and scope of privileges and immunities for AfDB, AsDB, EBRD, and IADB, and the constraint on acceptance of loans or assistance that would alter purpose or functions is shared by AfDB, AsDB, and EBRD. AfDB Articles 12, 32 (g), 38-1, 50, and 54; AsDB Articles 8, 21 (vii), 36-1, 48 and 53; EBRD Articles 8-1, 20-1 (vii), 32-1, 44, and 49; and IADB Article III, Section 1; Article VII, Section 1 (v); and Article XI, Sections 1 and 6.

[57] *See* Reinisch and Wurm (2010) at 135, referring to immunities of international financial institutions (IFIs): "a recent strand of US case law particularly emphasizes functional aspects in determining the restricted immunity of IFIs. These cases typically allude to the purpose of the activity of an IFI as stated in its governing instruments . . . "

5
INVESTMENT OPERATIONS

The investment operations of the Asian Infrastructure Investment Bank (AIIB) are its raison d'être. AIIB's members have joined together, subscribed to its capital, and organized its governance for the common purpose of infrastructure investment in Asia. The AIIB Charter provisions described in other chapters are essential for AIIB to reach its goals, but not sufficient to achieve the desired results. AIIB's finance and assistance for Asian infrastructure are delivered through the basic framework for investment operations described in this chapter. **5.01**

The modalities for AIIB investment operations are based on similar principles and the experience of other multilateral development banks (MDBs). Among the advantages of opting for similarity were jumpstarting AIIB's portfolio of investment operations, providing familiarity for recipients, and facilitating partnerships with other MDBs in co-financing operations. Given its origins, one would expect AIIB to implement these principles in ways that address concerns with current practices elsewhere. **5.02**

This chapter presents the Charter-based framework for AIIB's investment operations, including investment objectives, types of operations, recipients, operational principles, and operational policies and procedures. It concludes with an overview of AIIB's first years of investment operations (2016–2025). **5.03**

A. Investment Objectives

(1) Purpose

AIIB's objectives in its investment operations stem from its overarching purpose. Indeed, the first listed purpose in the AIIB Charter is *to foster sustainable economic development, create wealth and improve infrastructure connectivity in Asia by investing in infrastructure and other productive sectors.*[1] This first purpose is most directly tied to the themes of regional economic growth and sustainable economic development, and to investment in infrastructure and other productive sectors, as discussed in Chapter 4.[2] **5.04**

[1] AIIB Article 1-1 (i).
[2] *See* paragraphs 4.10–4.13.

5.05 AIIB's legal purpose sets the parameters for its infrastructure and other operations. Notably, the reference to "sustainable" economic development heightens the importance of environmental and social impact that has become a critical aspect of development. Sustainability was emphasized in the Chief Negotiators' Report, noting as to the Preamble: "Representatives highlighted that the Bank would be established as a multilateral financial institution to promote sustained and stable growth in Asia."

(2) Sectors

5.06 The reference to improving infrastructure connectivity can be expected to cover different kinds of connectivity over time, such as physical and electronic, to name but two. Infrastructure as a sector is likely to encompass a broad range of investment. AIIB's Corporate Strategy for 2020–2030 (Financing Infrastructure for Tomorrow) states that "all investments across infrastructure and other productive sectors should *ordinarily* add value through one or more of the four cross-cutting themes of Infrastructure for Tomorrow [AIIB's thematic priorities of Green Infrastructure, Connectivity and Regional Cooperation, Technology-enabled Infrastructure, and Private Capital Mobilization]."[3]

5.07 AIIB is not limited to infrastructure sectors; it is also authorized to finance investment in other "productive" sectors. That open-ended term has its origins in the focus on productive purposes in some other MDB charters, dating back to Bretton Woods and the concern over such non-productive lending as financing of war and budget deficits and refinancing of old debts.[4] In the case of the International Bank for Reconstruction and Development (IBRD), the term "productive purposes" figures prominently in the purposes of the Bank,[5] and, since its introduction at

[3] AIIB Corporate Strategy, Financing Infrastructure for Tomorrow, revised June 2025, at 13–14.

[4] *See* IBRD Article I and EBRD Article 2-1, and Bittermann (1971) at 67. Harry Dexter White had focused on lending for productive purposes for Latin America as early as a June 1939 draft for a bank and for the Inter-American Bank (IAB) as discussed in Chapter 2. Helleiner (2014) at 57 and 61. The focus on productive purposes in development lending can also be seen in the work of Sun Yat Sen, first President of the Republic of China in 1912, whose 1920 work *The International Development of China* discussed the potential role of foreign capital in supporting China's economic development. Helleiner (2019) at 148–9.

[5] IBRD's purposes under IBRD Article I include:

(i) To assist in the reconstruction and development of territories of members by facilitating the *investment of capital for productive purposes*, including the restoration of economies destroyed or disrupted by war, *the reconversion of productive facilities to peacetime needs* and the encouragement of *the development of productive facilities and resources* in less developed countries.

(ii) To promote private foreign investment by means of guarantees or participations in loans and other investments made by private investors; and when private capital is not available on reasonable terms, to supplement private investment by providing, on suitable conditions, *finance for productive purposes* out of its own capital, funds raised by it and its other resources.

(iii) To promote the long-range balanced growth of international trade and the maintenance of equilibrium in balances of payments by *encouraging international investment for the development of the productive resources of members*, thereby assisting in raising productivity, the standard of living and conditions of labor in their territories. (Emphasis added.)

Bretton Woods to improve the quality of loans,[6] has figured prominently in decades of IBRD legal interpretations.[7]

(3) Location

AIIB investments in infrastructure, as well as in other productive sectors, should aim at fostering development, creating wealth, and improving infrastructure connectivity in Asia. The AIIB Charter does not specify that the investment itself must be located in Asia.[8] Indeed, the Chief Negotiators' Report states: 5.08

> Representatives noted that the Preamble and the functions and purposes of the Bank in Articles 1 and 2 focus on the economic development of the Asia region. To the extent permitted under its operational policies, the Bank could provide financing to recipients located outside the region under Article 11, paragraph 1, consistent with its purpose and functions.

How AIIB's purpose and functions will be met by particular investment operations that provide finance to non-regional recipients is a matter for the Board of Directors to decide in construing the AIIB Charter.

AIIB's first investment operation located in a non-regional member was the Egypt Round II Solar PV Feed-In Tariffs Program in 2017. The program included eleven greenfield solar power plants. AIIB supported this program "because it contributes to Egypt's renewable energy capacity and it will help position the country as a regional energy hub, which will have economic benefits for the entire region."[9] 5.09

In February 2018, the AIIB Board of Directors adopted AIIB's Strategy on Financing Operations in Non-Regional Members.[10] The Strategy notes that under the AIIB Charter, AIIB may invest in any member, and all financing must further its purposes and functions, referencing AIIB Article 11-1(a), and Articles 1 and 2. The Strategy sets out the basic parameter: "[A] project located outside the Region must benefit Asia, i.e., it must foster economic development, create wealth or improve 5.10

[6] Bittermann (1971) at 67 points out the view from Bretton Woods that loan quality would be better if loans were restricted "to productive purposes in contrast to the pre-depression bonds financing wars, budget deficits or refunding old debts."

[7] *See* Shihata (2000) at 160: "The emphasis the Articles place on the productive purposes of the loans made or guaranteed by the Bank is overwhelming; the term 'productive' appears five times in the text of Article I, and the concept was uppermost in the minds of the framers of the Articles who wanted to avoid the negative experience of past international lending."

[8] The definition of Asia used throughout the AIIB Charter is in AIIB Article 1-2: "Wherever used in this Agreement, references to 'Asia' and 'region' shall include the geographical regions and composition classified as Asia and Oceania by the United Nations, except as otherwise decided by the Board of Governors." *See* paragraphs 6.24–6.29 for a more detailed discussion.

[9] "AIIB supports renewable energy development in Egypt," AIIB Press Release, September 5, 2017.

[10] AIIB Strategy on Financing Operations in Non-Regional Members, February 24, 2018, and Financing Operations in Non-Regional Members (Technical Note), February 24, 2018.

infrastructure connectivity in Asia, and such benefits must be significant." Three principles are outlined:

- Cross-Country Connectivity. Under this principle, investments should support trade and connectivity with Asia, including ports, transport links, power generation and transmission, and gas pipelines. When the Strategy was adopted in 2018, the majority of non-regional financing was expected to meet this principle, and projects meeting this principle would be given priority.
- Sustainable Infrastructure. Under this principle, investments should support global public goods, specifically renewable energy generation projects (including transmission and storage), in line with country commitments under the Paris Agreement.[11]
- Proximity and Economic Integration. Under this principle, investments that are geographically proximate and economically integrated with Asia could be considered by the Board of Directors. Egypt is noted as an example.

The Strategy also sets a ceiling on investment in non-regional members as a share of total Bank approved financing. From 2018, the ceiling was set at a 15% share.

5.11 Through 2024, regional projects accounted for 251 investment operations (83%), along with twenty-two non-regional projects (7%), and thirty multi-country projects (10%), out of AIIB's total of 303 projects. Of the eighteen projects approved in the first half of 2025, fifteen are listed for regional members, one for a non-regional member, and two as multi-country. The non-regional recipients for these operations include: Argentina, Brazil, Cote d'Ivoire, Ecuador, Egypt, Hungary, Romania, and Rwanda.[12] Under the COVID-19 Crisis Recovery Facility, all non-regional operations required approval by the Board of Directors.[13]

(4) Functions

5.12 Four functions are listed in the AIIB Charter: promoting investment; development finance; supplementing private investment; and other activities and services, as

[11] The Paris Agreement was adopted by 196 Parties at the UN Climate Change Conference (COP21) in Paris, France, on 12 December 2015. It entered into force on 4 November 2016. https://unfccc.int/process-and-meetings/the-paris-agreement (last visited July 14, 2025).

[12] AIIB Annual Report 2024 at 13. For 2025 projects, *see* AIIB website, Approved Projects, https://www.aiib.org/en/projects/list/index.html (last visited July 14, 2025). In July 2025, AIIB approved a US$10 million equity co-investment in Chile, to support climate-resilient water infrastructure. "AIIB Approves First Investment in Chile to Support Climate-Resilient Water Infrastructure," AIIB Press Release, July 31, 2025. A proposed project for Morocco, co-financed with the World Bank, is also listed.

[13] AIIB, *Paper on the Decisions to Support the AIIB COVID-19 Crisis Recovery Facility*, April 16, 2020, sections D–F and *Decisions to Support the AIIB COVID-19 Crisis Recovery Facility*, adopted April 16, 2020. According to AIIB (2024) [Final Review of the COVID-19 Crisis Recovery Facility] at 7: "Total financing (regular and Facility) in non-regional Members as a share of the Bank's total financing approved between Dec. 31, 2020 and Dec. 31, 2023 was 7.6%, far below the 15% ceiling set out in the Bank's Strategy on Financing Operations in Non-Regional Members."

discussed in Chapter 4, Section C. Development finance and supplementing private investment are most relevant for AIIB's investment objectives.

AIIB's development finance function derives from the mandate "to utilize the resources at its disposal for financing such development in the region, including those projects and programs which will contribute most effectively to the harmonious economic growth of the region as a whole and having special regard to the needs of less developed members in the region."[14] For the scope of AIIB's investment operations, three points merit reiteration. First, development finance refers to capital mobilized for the development of infrastructure and other productive sectors in Asia. Second, development finance in AIIB is not restricted to developing member countries, as it is in the Asian Development Bank (AsDB), African Development Bank (AfDB), and Inter-American Development Bank (IADB).[15] Third, AIIB's investment operations should take note of the impact on regional economic growth and on the needs of the less developed regional members.[16] 5.13

AIIB's goal of supplementing private investment derives from its mandate "to encourage private investment in projects, enterprises and activities contributing to economic development in the region, in particular in infrastructure and other productive sectors, and to supplement private investment when private capital is not available on reasonable terms and conditions."[17] An important tenet here is the concept that AIIB should provide finance when not otherwise available on reasonable terms, as noted in paragraphs 4.22–4.23. 5.14

B. Methods of Operation

The AIIB Charter specifies several ways in which AIIB may carry out its financing operations: loans and guarantees; equity investments; technical assistance; Special Operations; and other types of financing.[18] 5.15

(1) Loans and guarantees

AIIB is authorized to make, co-finance, or participate in direct loans. These are not restricted by type of recipient, so direct loans could be made to both sovereign 5.16

[14] AIIB Article 2 (ii).

[15] AfDB Article 14-1 (restricted to regional members); AsDB Article 2 (ii) (financing restricted to regional developing member countries); IADB Article I, Section 1 (purpose restricted to regional developing member countries).

[16] Both of these considerations are borrowed from the AsDB Charter, although in AIIB the emphasis is on less developed regional members, regardless of size. AsDB Article 2 (ii). *See* note 30 in Chapter 4.

[17] AIIB Article 2 (iii).

[18] AIIB Article 11-2.

and non-sovereign borrowers; AIIB may require a member guarantee where the member is not the borrower. Unlike IBRD, however, AIIB is not required to obtain a member guarantee in these cases.[19] AIIB is authorized to guarantee loans, in whole or in part, without differentiating among the types of borrowers. Direct loans and guarantees are authorized methods of financing in AIIB's predecessor MDBs.[20] Under AIIB's Operational Policy on Financing, three types of financing are listed for sovereign-backed projects: Investment Project Financing, Results-based Financing, and Climate Policy-based Financing.[21]

(2) Equity investments

5.17 AIIB is authorized to invest funds in the equity capital of an institution or enterprise. A recipient of AIIB equity investment would necessarily have an equity capital structure, which could in principle be sovereign or non-sovereign. It is worth noting that the AIIB Charter has followed AfDB, AsDB, and the European Bank for Reconstruction and Development (EBRD) in permitting equity investments from the outset.[22] In the case of IBRD, IADB, and the European Investment Bank (EIB), the original charters made no provision for equity operations.[23] Instead, separate

[19] IBRD Article III, Section 4 (i).

[20] AfDB Article 14-1; AsDB Article 11; EBRD Article 11 (with some particular requirements related to its purposes); IADB Article III, Section 4; and IBRD Article III, Section 4 (requiring sovereign guarantee). An important feature in the EBRD Charter that reflects its focus on private sector development is the requirement that loans, guarantees, and equity investments provided to the state sector not exceed 40% of the total. EBRD Article 11-3.

[21] AIIB Operational Policy on Financing describes these types as follows:

> Investment Project Financing (IPF) is a Sovereign-backed Financing modality designed to support a specific Investment Project in order to promote sustainable development, create wealth, and improve infrastructure connectivity. (Section 4.1 of Annex 1.)
>
> Results-based Financing (RBF) is a Sovereign-backed Financing modality designed to promote sustainable development and improve the efficiency and effectiveness of expenditures, consistent with the Bank's strategies, by: (a) financing the expenditures of a Results-based Project (RBP) through disbursement of the RBF's proceeds on the basis of the achievement of key results under the RBP; (b) using (and, as appropriate, strengthening) the systems used for the RBP to provide assurance that the funds allocated to it are used appropriately and that environmental and social impacts are adequately addressed by the RBP; and (c) strengthening, where appropriate, the institutional capacity necessary for the RBP to achieve its intended results. (Section 5.1 of Annex 1.)
>
> Climate Policy-based Financing (CPBF) is a Sovereign-backed Financing modality designed to support a Member's specific program of policy and institutional reform actions (Climate-based Policy Program or CPBP) aimed at scaling up climate finance and accelerating the Member's transition towards a low carbon and climate resilient future. (Section 6.1 of Annex 1.)

[22] AfDB Article 14-1; AsDB Article 11 (iii); and EBRD Article 11-1. In the case of AsDB, the Charter required that equity investments could only be made after a qualified majority decision by the Board of Governors (a majority of the Governors representing a majority of the total voting power) that "the Bank is in a position to commence such type of operations." The AIIB Charter does not restrict when equity operations can commence.

[23] Investments without government guarantee and equity investments were considered at Bretton Woods, but not adopted. The first public draft document for the IBRD Charter (Preliminary Draft Outline of a Proposal for a Bank for Reconstruction and Development, November 1943) permitted IBRD to invest up to 10% of its paid-in capital in equities. Bittermann (1971) at 65 (equity) and 75 (Netherlands' proposal of loans to private entities without government guarantee but with governmental approval). The same percentage limit on equity participation (10%) was agreed for AsDB (AsDB Article 12-3) and AfDB (AfDB Article 15-4 (a)), with the AfDB Charter later amended to refer only to a percentage fixed by the Board of Governors.

affiliates were set up to provide equity investments: the International Finance Corporation (IFC) in the World Bank Group, the Inter-American Investment Corporation in the Inter-American Development Bank Group, and the European Investment Fund with EIB.[24]

(3) Technical assistance

AIIB is authorized to provide technical advice and assistance and other similar forms of assistance which serve its purpose and come within its functions.[25] The reference to technical assistance is further expanded in the Chief Negotiators' Report: 5.18

> Representatives noted that the inclusion of "other similar forms of assistance" was intended to permit the possibility of investment grants and similar instruments commonly used in infrastructure financing by multilateral development banks and others. Project preparation support could also be provided under this paragraph.

Other MDBs are also authorized to provide technical assistance.[26]

AIIB provides project preparation support, a form of technical assistance, through its Project Preparation Special Fund. This Special Fund provides grants to the Bank's low- and middle-income member countries for preparation activities, including environmental, social, legal, procurement and technical assessments and analyses, and advisory services.[27] Projects that benefit AIIB members classified as recipients of International Development Association (IDA) financing are the target group; however, other projects may be eligible in exceptional circumstances, such as innovative and complex projects and regional or cross-border projects with significant regional impacts.[28] Project preparation support may also be provided through some of AIIB's other Special Funds, such as the Global Infrastructure Facility (GIF) Special Fund and the Multilateral Cooperation Center for Development Finance (MCDF) Special Fund.[29] 5.19

[24] IFC was first founded to provide loans and guarantees without government guarantee, and the IFC Charter was amended in 1961 to permit investment in capital stock. IFC Article III, Section 2. The EIB Charter was amended to allow for equity investments by EIB itself in 2009. EIB Article 18-2.

[25] AIIB Articles 11-2 and 15-1.

[26] AfDB Article 2-1 (e); AsDB Article 2 (iv); EBRD Article 11-1 (v); EIB Article 18-7; and IADB Article VI. There is no specific provision in the IBRD Charter. The AIIB formulation is closest to EBRD.

[27] "AIIB's Board of Directors establish a Project Preparation Special Fund: China provides initial $50 million start-up contribution," AIIB Press Release, June 25, 2016. *See* paragraph 7.57.

[28] AIIB 2016 Financial Statements, note 5.15 in AIIB (2017) at 50.

[29] AIIB website, Special Funds Resources, https://www.aiib.org/en/how-we-work/partnerships/special-funds-resources/index.html (last visited July 14, 2025). *See* paragraphs 7.57–7.58.

(4) Special operations

5.20 Under the AIIB Charter, operations are categorized by the type of resources used to finance them. Ordinary operations are those financed from AIIB's ordinary resources (authorized capital, funds raised, repayments and returns from ordinary operations, and related income); special operations are those financed from Special Funds resources.[30] Special Funds are donor resources that are provided to an MDB for specific purposes, often for financing on concessional terms, such as the Project Preparation Special Fund described in paragraph 5.19. For AIIB, ordinary operations and special operations may separately finance elements of the same project or program.[31] As of June 2025, AIIB had approved 37 Project Preparation Special Fund grants since the Fund's inception.[32]

(5) Other types of financing

5.21 The AIIB Charter also includes an express provision to permit new types of financing to be added to the list of authorized investment operations in the future.[33] The addition of such other types of financing requires a Special Majority vote by the Board of Governors. This provision gives AIIB the room to develop new products in the future that may not be strictly characterized as loans, guarantees, equity investment, or technical assistance. Rather, new products can be designed in an optimal way that best benefits recipients and AIIB, and that can garner substantial support at the Board of Governors. Without such a clause, MDBs should design new products in a way that either fits within decades-old legal provisions, or relies on Charter interpretation or amendment as needed.

C. Recipients

5.22 Under the AIIB Charter, there are several types of recipients for investment operations: members and member-based entities; international and regional entities; and other recipients.[34]

[30] AIIB Article 10-1.

[31] AIIB Article 10. Ordinary resources and Special Funds resources must be held and used separately, and losses on special operations cannot be charged to ordinary resources. *See* paragraphs 7.55–7.56 for a description of the rules applicable to AIIB Special Funds.

[32] AIIB website, Special Funds Resources, https://www.aiib.org/en/what-we-do/special-funds/project-list/index.html (Approved Special Fund Grants) (last visited July 14, 2025).

[33] The list of ways that AIIB may carry out its operations includes: "through other types of financing as may be determined by the Board of Governors, by a Special Majority vote." AIIB Article 11-2 (vi).

[34] AIIB Article 11-1.

(1) Members and member-based entities

AIIB may provide or facilitate financing to any member, or any agency, instrumentality, or political subdivision thereof, or any entity or enterprise operating in the territory of a member. This definition follows similar provisions in other MDB charters.[35] Under this provision, finance can be provided not only to member states and political subdivisions (such as provinces) and to governmental agencies and instrumentalities, but also to non-government entities or enterprises of any kind that operate in the territory of an AIIB member. Where the recipient of a loan or guarantee is not the member itself, AIIB is authorized to require a member guarantee.[36] 5.23

To recall, the AIIB Charter does not limit recipients to those in the territory of regional members, but the purpose of AIIB financing should be focused on development in the Asia region (paragraphs 5.08–5.11). Neither is AIIB financing limited to developing or regional members (paragraph 5.13). 5.24

(2) International and regional entities

AIIB is authorized to provide or facilitate financing to international or regional agencies or entities concerned with economic development of the region. This provision mirrors a similar provision in the AsDB Charter, and would allow AIIB to support other international organizations and agencies.[37] For AIIB, this type of financing is also aligned with its purpose to promote regional cooperation and partnership in addressing development challenges by working in close collaboration with other multilateral and bilateral development institutions.[38] 5.25

(3) Other recipients

The AIIB Charter recognizes that there are occasionally potential recipients that do not fit within the categories of members and member-based entities, or international and regional entities. Where AIIB members reach a consensus that AIIB financing for another type of potential recipient is in line with its objectives, the AIIB Charter provides for a determination that assistance can be provided, including a specific decision on which type of financing would be appropriate. In these special circumstances, a determination must be made by the Board of Governors that such assistance is designed to serve the purpose and come within the functions of the 5.26

[35] AfDB Article 14-1; AsDB Article 11; IADB Article III, Section 4; and IBRD Article III, Section 4.
[36] AIIB Article 14-2.
[37] AIIB Article 11-1 (a) and AsDB Article 11.
[38] AIIB Article 1 (ii).

AIIB, and that it is in the interest of AIIB's membership; the Board of Governors must also specify the types of assistance that may be provided to that recipient.[39] This decision by the Board of Governors requires a Super Majority vote.

5.27 This provision would permit AIIB to provide assistance to other entities, including non-member entities, through any of its types of investment operations found suitable. For example, loans to an entity in a non-member territory could be excluded if the necessary legal and financial protections are not available, while grants or other technical assistance may be easier to provide. Provisions and practice in other MDBs may provide some actual examples for AIIB if this question arises. For the World Bank, grants (often from trust funds) have been made to non-member recipients in limited circumstances; this required some creativity in view of the IBRD Charter's emphasis on use of resources for the benefit of IBRD members and the need for a member's guarantee on IBRD loans.[40]

5.28 Some other MDBs, such as EIB[41] and the New Development Bank (NDB),[42] also have some flexibility built into their charters. For the EBRD, however, Charter amendments were found necessary to expand the scope of operations, first to Mongolia and then to the countries of the Southern and Eastern Mediterranean.[43] Most recently, EBRD members agreed to amend the EBRD Charter to enable the expansion of its operations to selected countries in sub-Saharan Africa and Iraq.[44]

[39] AIIB Article 11-1 (b).

[40] *See* Rigo Sureda (2004) at paragraphs 358–73, describing the cases of the Soviet Union, West Bank and Gaza, Kosovo, and East Timor.

[41] The EIB, whose membership is restricted to members of the European Union, is authorized to grant finance for investment to be carried out outside the territories of Member States, if so decided by the Board of Governors by a qualified majority. EIB Article 16-1. (A qualified majority is eighteen Member States (out of twenty-seven) representing 68% of capital, under EIB Article 8.) Historically, the EIB has provided assistance outside its membership, including to associated countries, Associated African and Madagascan States and Overseas Countries and Territories. EIB (2008), Part II, Chapter 3, "New Activities outside the Community." In June 2025, the EU website noted investments over time in 160 countries, shown on a map: https://www.eib.org/en/projects/map (last visited July 14, 2025).

[42] NDB's Board of Governors can approve a general policy for operations in a non-member emerging economy or developing country, if it involves a material interest of an NDB member. NDB Article 19 (d). NDB's Board of Directors can exceptionally approve a specific project in a non-member emerging economy or developing country. NDB Article 19 (e). Both decisions require a special majority vote. A special majority for NDB means an affirmative vote of four of the founding members concurrent with an affirmative vote of two-thirds of the total voting power of members. NDB Article 6 (b). The NDB's founding members are Brazil, Russia, India, China, and South Africa. NDB Article 1(a).

[43] While Mongolia and later the Southern and Eastern Mediterranean countries could have become EBRD members under the original charter, as non-European members of IMF under EBRD Article 3-1, they would not have been included in the Central and Eastern European countries where EBRD was intended to operate. Accordingly, the scope of operations was amended. EBRD Board of Governors' Resolution No. 90, *Amendment to the Agreement Establishing the Bank in order to Admit Mongolia as a Country of Operations*, adopted January 30, 2004, entered into force October 15, 2006. EBRD Board of Governors' Resolution No. 137, *Amendment of the Agreement Establishing the Bank in order to Enable the Bank to Operate in Countries of the Southern and Eastern Mediterranean*, adopted September 30, 2011, entered into force September 12, 2013.

[44] "EBRD shareholders take further step towards geographical expansion," EBRD Press Office, April 23, 2025, available at https://www.ebrd.com/home/news-and-events/news/2025/ebrd-shareholders-take-further-step-towards-geographical-expansi.html (last visited July 14, 2025). EBRD Board of Governors' Resolution No. 259, *Amendment to Article 1 of the Agreement Establishing the Bank to Enable a Limited and Incremental Expansion of the Geographic Scope of the Bank's Operations to Sub-Saharan Africa and Iraq*, adopted 18 May 2023, entered into force July 22, 2025.

Conversely, recipient access to EBRD resources can be restricted by a qualified majority decision by the Board of Governors.[45]

D. Operational Principles

(1) General principles

The general principles governing investment operations set out in the AIIB Charter address several key dimensions, mostly along the lines of other MDB charters.[46] 5.29

- Sound Banking Principles. AIIB, as a financial institution, should be guided by sound banking principles in its operations.[47]
- Forms. AIIB's operations should principally focus on three forms: financing of specific projects or specific investment programs, equity investment, and technical assistance.[48]
- Operational and Financial Policies. The importance of AIIB's policy framework is cemented by the requirement that "each of its operations complies with the Bank's operational and financial policies, including without limitation, policies addressing environmental and social impacts."[49] While this is a requirement in practice at other MDBs, the AIIB Charter is unique in stating it among its operating principles. The inclusion of this requirement also reflects the expanded influence of operational policies in MDB operations, and the importance of environmental and social considerations.
- Procurement. Procurement of goods and services financed by AIIB is open to members and non-members alike, as AIIB may "place no restriction upon the procurement of goods and services from any country from the proceeds of any financing undertaken in the ordinary or special operations."[50] Universal procurement is also required under the EBRD Charter.[51] In AfDB, AsDB, and IADB, procurement is generally restricted to member countries.[52] It is

[45] The EBRD Board of Governors is authorized to decide on suspension or other modification of access to its resources by a member that might be implementing policies inconsistent with EBRD's purpose, or in exceptional circumstances. EBRD Article 8-3, requiring such decisions by two-thirds of the Governors representing not less than three-fourths of total voting power. EBRD Article 8-4 also provided for a member to limit its access to EBRD resources to the amount of its capital actually paid in, for a period of three years; access beyond that required a decision of the Board of Governors by a higher majority (three-fourths of Governors representing 85% of total voting power). Such requests were to be attached to the EBRD Charter, and a letter from the Soviet Union delegation to the negotiations is the only such attachment on EBRD's website. This provision reportedly reflected the position of the US in the negotiations, seeking to limit Soviet borrowing. Weber (1994) at 21, note 63.

[46] AIIB Article 13. *See* AfDB Articles 16–18; AsDB Articles 13–15; EBRD Articles 13 and 14; IADB Article III; and IBRD Article III.

[47] AIIB Article 13-1.

[48] AIIB Article 13-2.

[49] AIIB Article 13-4.

[50] AIIB Article 13-8.

[51] EBRD Article 13 (xii).

[52] AfDB Article 17-1 (d) and AsDB Article 14 (ix), where procurement is restricted to member countries with provision for the Board of Directors to make exception; for IADB, procurement policy restricts

important to note that AIIB's universal procurement also applies to Special Fund operations.

- Use of Proceeds. Due attention should be paid to economy and efficiency in the use of the proceeds of AIIB financing. This requirement is normally addressed through procurement processes. In parallel, AIIB should take measures to ensure that these proceeds are used for the purposes intended. This is the legal basis for disbursement, accounting, auditing, and anti-corruption rules in investment operations.[53]
- Members. The special position of members is respected by the requirement that AIIB not finance any undertaking in the territory of a member if that member objects to such financing.[54] Fairness among members is recognized by the requirement that AIIB "pay due regard to the desirability of avoiding a disproportionate amount of its resources being used for the benefit of any member."[55]

(2) Financial principles

5.30 The AIIB Charter includes several other requirements in the operating principles for investment operations that are particularly important for AIIB's financial management.

- Financial Alternatives. As noted above, AIIB is mandated generally to supplement private investment by providing finance when not otherwise available on reasonable terms.[56] Here, this is implemented through the requirement for each investment operation that AIIB shall pay due regard to the ability of the recipient to obtain financing or facilities elsewhere on terms and conditions that AIIB considers reasonable for the recipient, taking into account all pertinent factors.[57]
- Financial Capacity of the Recipient. The financial capacity of the recipient and any guarantor is required to be assessed. For each operation, AIIB shall pay

procurement to member countries, and IADB Article III, Section 9 (a) further provides for the Board of Governors to restrict procurement in the future, for members that do not participate in capital increases. IBRD previously restricted procurement to member countries and certain others, but changed to unrestricted procurement, by decision of its Board of Directors (the Executive Directors) in 2004. There is no restriction required by the IBRD Charter.

[53] AIIB Article 13-9. AIIB's general accounting, auditing and disbursement requirements for Sovereign-backed financing can be found in AIIB's General Conditions for Sovereign-backed Loans, dated October 22, 2021. *See* paragraphs 5.36–5.37. For Sovereign-backed Financing, the financial management policy requirements are also set out in AIIB's Operational Policy on Financing, at Annex 1, Section III, paragraph 3.3. AIIB's anti-corruption rules can be found in AIIB's Policy on Prohibited Practices, December 8, 2016. *See* paragraphs 5.51–5.54.

[54] AIIB Article 13-3.

[55] AIIB Article 13-10.

[56] AIIB Article 2 (iii). This principle is also grounded in other MDB charters. AfDB Article 17-1 (c); AsDB Article 14 (v); EBRD Article 13 (vii); IADB Article I, Section 2 (ii) and Article II, Section 7 (a)(ii); and IBRD Article I (ii) and Article III, Section 4 (ii).

[57] AIIB Article 13-5.

due regard to the prospects of the recipient and guarantor, if any, being in a position to meet their obligations under the financing contract.[58] Moreover, the financial terms should be appropriate for the financing concerned and the risk to AIIB, in AIIB's opinion.[59]

- Terms and Conditions. In setting the terms and conditions for loans made, participated in, or guaranteed by AIIB, AIIB is required to "take fully into account the need to safeguard its income and financial position."[60] As previously noted, where the recipient is not a member of AIIB, AIIB may require a guarantee from the member (or an acceptable public agency or instrumentality).[61] For AIIB loans, a sovereign guarantee is not mandatory, in line with provisions for AfDB, AsDB, EBRD, EIB, and IADB; in contrast, where the member is not itself the borrower, a sovereign guarantee is required for IBRD.[62]
- Equity Investment. For equity investment, there is a requirement for reasonable diversification. Moreover, AIIB's involvement in its equity investments is limited: AIIB "shall not assume responsibility for managing any entity or enterprise in which it has an investment and shall not seek a controlling interest in the entity or enterprise concerned, except where necessary to safeguard the investment of [AIIB]."[63] In addition, the Board of Directors is empowered to set a policy on the percentage of the equity capital of the entity or enterprise concerned for AIIB equity investments.[64]
- Currency. AIIB may provide financing in its operations in the currency of the country concerned, in accordance with policies that minimize currency risk.[65]

These financial requirements ensure that AIIB's investment operations will contribute to AIIB's sound financial management and position.

(3) International character of the institution

The AIIB Charter contains an additional statement of principles on the international character of AIIB that applies to investment operations as it does to all of AIIB's activities: 5.31

> The Bank, its President, officers and staff shall not interfere in the political affairs of any member, nor shall they be influenced in their decisions by the

[58] AIIB Article 13-6.
[59] AIIB Article 13-7.
[60] AIIB Article 14-1.
[61] AIIB Article 14-2.
[62] AfDB Article 18-3 (b); AsDB Article 15-2; EBRD Article 14-2; EIB Article 16-3; IADB Article III, Section 8 (a); and IBRD Article III, Section 4 (i).
[63] AIIB Article 13-11.
[64] AIIB Article 14-3. *See* AfDB Article 15-4; AsDB Article 12-4; and EBRD Article 12-2. AIIB's Board of Directors has set a percentage of 30% in the Operational Policy on Financing, Annex 2, paragraph 4.9.2.
[65] AIIB Article 14-4.

> political character of the member concerned. Only economic considerations shall be relevant to their decisions. Such considerations shall be weighed impartially in order to achieve and carry out the purpose and functions of the Bank.[66]

These bedrock principles emphasize the importance of economic considerations, impartiality, and non-interference in political matters as part of the legal underpinnings of the institution. The AIIB Charter closely follows other MDB charters in this provision.[67]

E. Operational Policies and Procedures

5.32 Operational policies are not set out in the AIIB Charter, but rather are approved under the Charter by the Board of Directors, and prepared and proposed by AIIB management. The Operational Principles outlined above are set in the AIIB Charter, and policies must be consistent with them. Nonetheless, the importance of AIIB's operational policies is apparent from the specific inclusion of policy compliance in the AIIB Charter itself. This importance is further seen in the Chief Negotiators' Report, referring to that provision of the Charter:

> *Article 13, paragraph 4.* Representatives emphasized that the operational and financial policies of the Bank, referred to in paragraph 4, would be subject to approval by the Board of Directors in accordance with Article 26 and should be based on international best practices. These policies would include, among others, environmental and social frameworks, disclosure, procurement, and debt sustainability. A policy on operations in disputed areas would provide that, for financing in a disputed area, member consent is obtained in accordance with paragraph 3, and the Bank does not take a position on territorial claims.

In line with these statements, the AIIB Board of Directors approved a package of policies relevant for investment operations, posted on the AIIB Website in February 2016: the Operational Policy on Financing, Procurement Policy, Environmental and Social Policy, Sovereign-backed Loan and Guarantee Pricing Decision, and Public Information Interim Policy.[68] The General Conditions for

[66] AIIB Article 31-2.

[67] AfDB Article 38-2; AsDB Article 36-2; IADB Article VIII, Section 5 (f); and IBRD Article IV, Section 10. EBRD Article 32-2 refers to its purpose and functions, in line with the role of certain political considerations in its objectives, while highlighting impartiality. *See* paragraphs 11.13–11.14.

[68] The Operational Policy on Financing, the Procurement Policy, the Sovereign-backed Loan and Guarantee Pricing Decision, and the Public Information Interim Policy were all approved by the Board of Directors at their first meeting. Minutes of the Meeting of the Board of Directors of the Asian Infrastructure Investment Bank held on January 17, 2016, paragraph 12. The Board's approval of the Environmental and Social Policy was recorded in subsequent minutes. Minutes of the Meeting of the Board of Directors of the Asian Infrastructure Investment Bank held on April 25–26, 2016, paragraph 10.

Sovereign-backed Loans and the Policy on Prohibited Practices were first approved in April 2016, and the Policy on Prohibited Practices was revised in December 2016.[69] An Operational Policy on International Relations was approved in March 2017.[70] Policies on financing in disputed areas and debt sustainability, mentioned in the Chief Negotiators' Report, are both covered in AIIB's Operational Policy on Financing,[71] and operations in disputed areas are specifically addressed in the Operational Policy on International Relations. Key aspects of these policies, as updated, are noted in the following paragraphs.

(1) Operational Policy on Financing

The Operational Policy on Financing (revised through November 26, 2024) sets out the basic requirements for all of AIIB's investment operations, whether approved as Sovereign-backed financing (SBF) or Non-sovereign-backed financing (NSBF). These terms are used to differentiate the form of AIIB's financing instead of the terms "public sector" and "private sector," as some NSBF operations could be undertaken with public sector entities without sovereign guarantee or other backing. The Operational Policy on Financing sets out the common principles and provisions for both SBF and NSBF, including processes, design, assessment, and decision-making. Separate annexes further detail the differentiated rules for SBF and NSBF. Annex 1 lays out the rules for the conditions and financial terms and contractual arrangements for SBF. Annex 2 lays out the types of NSBF, and the rules for NSBF exposure, assessments, financial terms and conditions, contractual arrangements, monitoring, and remedies. 5.33

The Operational Policy on Financing corresponds to similar policies in other MDBs, simplifying multiple policies elsewhere and introducing flexibility. For AIIB, one integrated document combined policy content that was spread across multiple World Bank policies and other IFC policies, and covers all aspects of preparation and oversight of SBF and NSBF. The Policy contains the essential policy requirements approved by the Board of Directors, complemented by directives on how to meet these requirements issued by the President. In the Policy, staff and member countries have a comprehensive picture of the entire operational policy framework applicable to AIIB's investment operations, linking together the 5.34

[69] Minutes of the Meeting of the Board of Directors of the Asian Infrastructure Investment Bank held on April 25–26, 2016, paragraphs 2 and 3. A revised Policy on Prohibited Practices was adopted in December. Minutes of the Meeting of the Board of Directors of the Asian Infrastructure Investment Bank held on December 8–9, 2016, paragraph 5.

[70] Minutes of the Meeting of the Board of Directors of the Asian Infrastructure Investment Bank held on March 20–22, 2017, paragraph 4.

[71] AIIB Operational Policy on Financing (amended through November 26, 2024), at Section 3.6, regarding disputed areas. For debt sustainability, *see* Section 3.3.1 (b) and Annex 1, Section 3.3.1. Under Conditions of Financing, the requirement of Fiscal Sustainability states in note 22: "In its determination as to the acceptability of the Project's impact on the member's fiscal sustainability, the Bank gives particular attention to debt sustainability analyses conducted by the International Monetary Fund and the World Bank."

requirements of the AIIB Charter and all other applicable AIIB policies, including environmental and social, procurement, international relations, pricing, and public information. Recognizing that projects financed by AIIB are often implemented in rapidly changing environments, the Policy also provides a decision framework designed to facilitate quick yet orderly changes to the terms and conditions of the financings, where warranted.[72]

5.35 The Operational Policy on Financing has been periodically revised as AIIB's operations have developed. For instance, following experience with co-financed operations, especially in the context of the COVID-19 Crisis Recovery Facility (see Chapter 12), it was updated in 2022 to allow AIIB to provide Results-based Financing.[73] It was updated again in 2024 to include Climate Policy-based Financing.[74]

(a) General Conditions for Sovereign-backed Loans

5.36 AIIB's General Conditions for Sovereign-backed Loans (October 22, 2021) (General Conditions) set out basic legal requirements that apply equally to all AIIB sovereign-backed loans, thus ensuring equitable treatment among borrowers. The legal agreements for AIIB's sovereign-backed investment operations incorporate these General Conditions by reference, so that the requirements apply legally without being repeated in each of the legal agreements. This structure is the normal practice for this type of operation at other MDBs, and AIIB's General Conditions are comparable to similar documents in use at AsDB, EBRD, and IBRD.[75] This similarity to other MDB documents offers the benefit of legal and operational familiarity for AIIB recipients, and also facilitates co-financing with these MDBs.

5.37 The aspects of investment operations covered by the General Conditions include, among others: withdrawal of loan proceeds and eligibility for financing; standard loan terms; recipient obligations for funding, execution, maintenance, monitoring, and reporting; a negative pledge clause (regarding AIIB's right to seek security for its loan if other lenders do so); AIIB's right to cancel, suspend, or accelerate the loan; and dispute resolution through arbitration. AIIB's General Conditions provide for international law as the governing law, and arbitration to be conducted in accordance with the UNCITRAL Arbitration Rules.[76] In any case, it must be recalled that, to date, disputes have been resolved in MDBs without resort to arbitration under

[72] *See, e.g.*, Section 3.5.3 of the Policy.

[73] Results-based Financing is similar to the World Bank's Program-for-Results (PforR) financing and AsDB's Results-based lending (RBL). *See* Section 5.1 of Annex 1 to the Operational Policy on Financing.

[74] *See* Section 6.1 of Annex 1 to the Operational Policy on Financing for the key features of Climate Policy-based Financing.

[75] Comparable documents are called Loan Regulations at AsDB, Standard Terms and Conditions at EBRD and General Conditions at IBRD.

[76] AfDB, AsDB, EBRD, and IBRD all specify international law as the governing law for their sovereign-backed loans. For arbitration, AfDB and EBRD have also adopted UNCITRAL Arbitration Rules, whereas IBRD and AsDB have retained their special ad hoc arbitration rules developed before UNCITRAL rules were adopted.

any of these clauses. This preference for amicable resolution can be expected to continue for AIIB as well.

(b) Sovereign-backed Loan and Guarantee Pricing

AIIB's Pricing Policy for Sovereign-backed Products (revised November 26, 2024) describes the elements of AIIB pricing for those products. The Sovereign-backed Loan and Guarantee Pricing Decision (revised June 2021) summarizes AIIB's lending terms for SBF loans and guarantees. The pricing is market-based. The terms for SBF loans provide for interest at a spread with maturities up to thirty-five years (a maximum average maturity of twenty years). Fixed Spread Loans (FSL) over LIBOR were phased out in 2021. The lending spread for Variable Spread Loans (VSL) includes instead a Borrowing Cost Margin calculated for each hard currency and reference rate, updated semi-annually.[77] 5.38

(c) Operational Policy on International Relations

AIIB's Operational Policy on International Relations (March 21, 2017) provides the policy framework for four situations that occasionally arise in MDB practice and raise issues of relations between or among different states. These situations arise in investment operations that involve international waterways, disputed areas, a de facto government, or a UN Security Council measure.[78] Recognizing the difficulty of applying a general policy to a myriad of difficult situations, the Operational Policy on International Relations states that the President may request approval from the Board of Directors for a deviation from the Policy's requirements, to avoid an outcome that is manifestly unwarranted or undesirable having regard to AIIB's purpose and functions.[79] 5.39

This Policy reflects similar policies at other MDBs, combining several at the World Bank;[80] the provisions on disputed areas also reflect the requirement for member non-objection in the AIIB Charter.[81] In some other MDBs, these situations are dealt 5.40

[77] Sovereign-backed Loan and Guarantee Pricing Decision (revised June 2021), Table 3, and Pricing Policy for Sovereign-backed Products (Revised November 26, 2024).

[78] The basic rules set out in the Policy on International Relations are as follows: *International Waterways*: AIIB may provide financing for an investment operation involving an international waterway only if: (a) AIIB is satisfied that the operation will not have a material adverse effect on other riparians; or (b) all riparians provide their no objection. *Disputed Areas*: AIIB may provide financing for an investment operation in a territorial area that is claimed by two or more countries only if AIIB is satisfied that each of the governments agrees that the financing may proceed, pending settlement of the dispute. *De Facto Governments*: Where a de facto government comes into power while AIIB is financing or preparing to finance an investment operation involving that government, AIIB assesses the legal framework with regard to approvals and undertakings by the member concerned, implementation of the operation and its objectives and payments to AIIB. AIIB also assesses the impact on the obligations of all parties to the relevant legal agreements. Resulting concerns could trigger AIIB's rights and remedies under the legal agreements (such as suspension of disbursements and/or cancellation of the loan). *UN Security Council Measures*: AIIB financing may not be used for a payment to a person or entity or for any import of goods if the payment or import is prohibited by a Security Council Measure (taken under Chapter VII of the UN Charter).

[79] AIIB Operational Policy on International Relations, Section VII.

[80] *See, e.g.*, World Bank Operational Policies 7.30 (Dealings with de Facto Governments), 7.50 (Projects on International Waterways) and 7.60 (Projects in Disputed Areas).

[81] AIIB Article 13-3.

with in multiple policies, or as a matter of practice; AIIB's combination streamlines its policy framework. While other MDB policies form the foundation for AIIB's Policy on International Relations, AIIB's policy content has been enhanced in light of experience and developments in international good practice since those policies were adopted. For example, AIIB's policy statement on international waterways codifies the principle, now generally accepted in the international water community, that as a practical matter, it is necessary to include transboundary groundwaters (and not merely transboundary surface waters) when considering the effects on riparians. Other MDBs have had to rely on broad interpretation to include such effects. In addition, AIIB's policy codifies policy interpretations by allowing for an exception to the notification requirement for situations involving truly *de minimis* impacts.

(2) Environmental and Social Policy Framework

5.41 AIIB's Environmental and Social Framework (ESF) was first approved by the Board of Directors in February 2016, with an overall introduction and a vision statement. The ESF has since been amended, like AIIB's Operational Policy on Financing, to reflect the evolution of AIIB's practice. Included in the ESF is AIIB's Environmental and Social Policy (ESP), which includes an Environmental and Social Exclusion List (ESEL) and three Environmental and Social Standards (ESSs). These policies set out the mandatory environmental and social requirements for AIIB's investment operations.

5.42 The ESP establishes AIIB's overarching policy in this realm:

> The Bank recognizes that environmental and social sustainability is a fundamental aspect of achieving outcomes consistent with its mandate to support the development of sustainable infrastructure and other productive sectors. The overarching objective of this policy is to facilitate achievement by the Bank's Clients of these development outcomes, through a system that integrates sound environmental and social management into Projects.[82]

For investment operations to be financed by AIIB, the ESP (including the ESEL and ESSs) provides the principles and considerations that govern the management of environmental and social risks and impacts. The ESP lays out general mandatory environmental and social requirements, and the three associated ESSs set out more detailed mandatory environmental and social requirements in three areas: Environmental and Social Assessment and Management (ESS 1); Land Acquisition and Involuntary Resettlement (ESS 2); and Indigenous Peoples (ESS 3).

[82] AIIB Environmental and Social Policy, paragraph 1 (part of the AIIB Environmental and Social Framework document on AIIB's website).

If an investment operation involves the activities or items included in the ESEL, AIIB will not knowingly finance those activities or items. Finally, there is a Glossary containing definitions of certain terms used in the ESP and ESSs.

The ESF, ESP (including the ESEL), and ESSs were built upon evolving policies and practice at other MDBs, primarily AsDB, EBRD, EIB, and the World Bank.[83] AIIB's overall approach can be considered broadly consistent with these MDBs, providing a robust structure for managing operational and reputational risk for AIIB and its members and partners in relation to the environmental and social risks and impacts of AIIB-financed investment operations. Among several innovations at the time of initial adoption in 2016 were: consolidation of SBF and NSBF policy requirements regarding environmental and social aspects; provisions allowing application of the policies and procedures of another MDB or bilateral development organization that is co-financing the investment operation;[84] selective use of country and corporate environmental and social systems when they have been found to be materially consistent with the ESP;[85] and phased approaches to addressing environmental and social aspects, where duly justified.[86] **5.43**

Since its adoption in 2016, the ESF has been updated several times, primarily to reflect strategic developments at AIIB and AIIB's introduction of new financing modalities. In 2022, AIIB's longstanding practice of excluding AIIB financing from coal and projects functionally related to coal was codified by revisions to the ESEL.[87] The 2022 revisions also addressed how the ESF applies to the environmental and social aspects of Results-based Financing (paragraph 5.35).[88] Similarly, revisions were made in 2024 to clarify how the ESF applies for Climate Policy-based Financing.[89] **5.44**

(3) Project-affected People's Mechanism

AIIB's independent accountability mechanism was approved in 2018, and also envisaged under the AIIB Charter and AIIB's Environmental and Social Policy.[90] The Project-affected People's Mechanism (PPM), effective March 31, 2019, enables **5.45**

83 A major revision of the World Bank's environmental and social policies was adopted in August 2016, after several years of discussion and after AIIB's ESF was approved. The World Bank discussions provided a backdrop for the development of the AIIB policy.

84 AIIB Environmental and Social Policy (2024), Section 10. Since the principle of reliance was adopted in AIIB's ESF in 2016, other development partners have espoused the principle of mutual reliance on each other's policies. *See* paragraphs 5.55–5.56.

85 AIIB Environmental and Social Policy (2024), Section 56.

86 AIIB Environmental and Social Policy (2024), Section 50.

87 AIIB Environmental and Social Exclusion List (2024), Section 15.

88 AIIB Environmental and Social Policy (2024), Section 15.

89 AIIB Environmental and Social Policy (2024), Section 16.

90 Sharif (2023) at 4 points out that no member of the AIIB Board contested the need for the PPM, in contrast to acrimonious exchanges between developed and developing country members in other MDBs.

- Project Processing Queries. **A Project Processing Query is designed to enable Project-affected** people to obtain rapid resolution of their concerns about simple matters that arise during AIIB's environmental and social due diligence of a Project and do not require dispute resolution. The due diligence includes screening, categorization and assessment of the environmental or social impacts of the Project.
- Requests for Dispute Resolution. Requests for Dispute Resolution allow the PPM to seek to facilitate and coordinate the resolution of a dispute that has arisen over measures required to **mitigate known and quantifiable, potential or actual material adverse environment and social** impacts that arise during AIIB's due diligence of a Project or during Project implementation. The aim of this process is to reach a time-bound and monitorable dispute resolution agreement between the parties concerned on actions to mitigate these impacts. Under this process, the PPM explores with the concerned parties mutually acceptable dispute resolution methods.
- Requests for Compliance Review. The process under a Request for Compliance Review involves **an investigation by the PPM of allegations by Project-affected people that AIIB has failed to** comply with its obligations under the AIIB Environmental and Social Policy (ESP) in its environmental and social due diligence of a Project during Project preparation or its oversight of the Project during implementation, thereby causing or being likely to cause material adverse **environmental or social impacts on the Project-affected people. If the allegations are substantiated,** the process includes a review of any action plan proposed by Management to address these impacts. Unlike the two other processes, a Request for Compliance Review requires that the PPM assess whether AIIB is in compliance with its ESP.

Figure 5.1 Project-affected People's Mechanism Functions
Source: AIIB website, Project-affected People's Mechanism.

project-affected people to file submissions if they have been or are likely to be adversely affected by AIIB's failure to implement AIIB's Environmental and Social Policy when their concerns cannot be addressed satisfactorily through Project-level grievance redress mechanisms or AIIB Management's processes.[91]

5.46 The PPM's three submission-handling functions are summarized in Figure 5.1.

5.47 The Complaints-resolution, Evaluation and Integrity Unit (CEIU) is responsible for PPM functioning through its Managing Director (MD-CEIU). As head of the PPM, the MD-CEIU reports directly to AIIB's Board of Directors and oversees the handling of submissions to the PPM, the issuance of PPM reports, and PPM's outreach, learning, and training activities.[92] The PPM is assisted by a Secretariat headed by a CEIU staff member. The MD-CEIU supervises and provides guidance and direction to the Head-PPM Secretariat and PPM personnel. The placement of the PPM in AIIB's Oversight Mechanism is discussed further in Chapter 12, Section C.

[91] AIIB website, Project-affected People's Mechanism, https://www.aiib.org/en/about-aiib/who-we-are/project-affected-peoples-mechanism/how-we-assist-you/index.html (last visited July 14, 2025).

[92] Sharif (2023) at 3 points out from the vantage point of AIIB's Inaugural Managing Director, CEIU, that placing the PPM under the CEIU is unique "as it enables the MD-CEIU to directly influence policymaking relating to project-affected people, and directly liaise with the management and the board on matters of policy and practice through regular interaction. Ready access to the board without presence of management through the Directors' Forum is a check on any management non-cooperation or interference with CEIU's independence . . . Regular contact with management and the board also militates against the possibility that the [PPM] or other functions of the CEIU are shelved and forgotten."

(4) Procurement Policy

AIIB's Procurement Policy was drafted in a period of procurement policy reform at several MDBs. Consequently, its principles and rules reflect an updating and evolution in MDB procurement policy, moving towards a principle-based and more flexible approach emphasizing "fit for purpose" and "value for money." The Procurement Policy (revised through June 26, 2024) applies to procurement by both public sector and private sector recipients and implementing entities under AIIB-financed investment operations. A separate Corporate Procurement Policy governing AIIB's procurement of goods and services for AIIB as an international institution was also adopted at the Inaugural Meeting of the Board of Directors and is discussed in Chapter 11 (at paragraph 11.48). **5.48**

Under the Procurement Policy, AIIB's Core Procurement Principles are defined: economy, efficiency, effectiveness, fairness and governance, value for money, fit for purpose, and transparency. Procurement standards are also spelled out. For procurement methods, AIIB's normal method is an international open competitive tender process. Alternative methods may be permitted, providing that AIIB is satisfied that these other methods would both promote the best strategic procurement approach for the successful delivery of the project and ensure compliance with the Core Procurement Principles. AIIB's requirement of universal procurement is implemented through the eligibility provision in paragraph 5.9.1: **5.49**

> The Bank permits firms and individuals from all countries to offer goods, works and services for a Bank-financed contract, regardless of whether the country is a member of the Bank. Any conditions for participation are limited to those that are essential to ensure the eligible firm or individual's capability to fulfill the contract in question.

The Procurement Policy also addresses the procurement arrangements for co-financed operations,[93] permits e-procurement, and, under special circumstances, permits government provisions for the development of the domestic industry. Detailed instructions for recipients implementing AIIB-financed investment operations are found in an operational directive, available on AIIB's website.[94]

Since 2021, AIIB has been publishing an annual Operational Procurement Report on its website. This Report provides statistics and analysis of AIIB-financed procurement contracts under Sovereign-backed Financing, including co-financed operations, as well as under Project Preparation Special Fund grants. Standard **5.50**

[93] For parallel co-financing, each co-financier applies its procurement policy to the contracts it alone finances. Where there is joint co-financing of the same contracts, AIIB normally would apply the AIIB Procurement Policy to those contracts. AIIB Procurement Policy (June 26, 2024) at Section 5.12.

[94] AIIB Directive, Procurement Instructions for Recipients (June 26, 2024), AIIB website.

procurement documents for goods, large works, and consultant services are also available on the website.[95]

(5) Policy on Prohibited Practices

5.51 The Policy on Prohibited Practices seeks to enable AIIB and its clients to do business with trustworthy parties who adhere to the highest standards of integrity, and to endeavor that, with respect to investment operations, its funds are used for the purposes intended.[96] In line with the current practice at other MDBs, AIIB has established a regime for the sanctioning of firms and individuals that are found to have engaged in specified forms of fraud, corruption, and other prohibited practices in connection with AIIB-financed projects and AIIB's corporate procurement. This regime protects AIIB's funds and serves as a deterrent to those who might otherwise engage in fraud, corruption, or misuse.

5.52 AIIB's Policy on Prohibited Practices draws largely from the policies and procedures in use at the MDBs that have joined the 2010 Agreement for the Mutual Enforcement of Debarment Decisions (AMEDD), currently AfDB, AsDB, EBRD, IADB, and World Bank (called Comparator Institutions here). AIIB has targeted the following prohibited practices: (i) coercive practice; (ii) collusive practice; (iii) corrupt practice; (iv) fraudulent practice; (v) misuse of resources; (vi) obstructive practice; and (vii) theft.[97] The general public is invited to report any suspicion of a prohibited practice to AIIB, including through its hotline. Board Officials and Bank Personnel have an obligation to report suspected misconduct, as well as to refrain from retaliation against others who report suspected misconduct in good faith.[98] Reports may be made on an anonymous basis.

5.53 AIIB has established a three-tiered process for enforcement of the Policy on Prohibited Practices, again in line with practice at Comparator Institutions.[99]

[95] AIIB, Project Procurement Opportunities, https://aiib.org/en/opportunities/business/project-procurement/index.html (last visited July 14, 2025).

[96] AIIB Article 13-9.

[97] AIIB Policy on Prohibited Practices (December 8, 2016) defines the Prohibited Practices in Section 3.2. Most of these practices are included in the harmonized definitions used by Comparator Institutions, except for misuse and theft (used in AsDB and EBRD only) and obstructive practice (included in procedures for the Comparator Institutions).

[98] These obligations are found in the AIIB Code of Conduct for Board Officials (paragraph 5 (c)) and the AIIB Code of Conduct for Bank Personnel (paragraphs 38 and 39).

[99] The AIIB enforcement process includes the following:

- An internal *Investigations Officer* (in CEIU) reviews suspicion of Prohibited Practices, and assesses whether there is sufficient evidence to support the allegations.
- An internal *Sanctions Officer* (AIIB Vice-President and Corporate Secretary, to date), independent of the Investigations Officer, reviews allegations referred by the Investigations Officer, and makes determinations on sanctions. If the Sanctions Officer issues a finding of a Prohibited Practice, supported by the preponderance of the evidence, the Respondent Party may appeal to AIIB's Sanctions Panel.
- The AIIB *Sanctions Panel* is a three-person body, with one internal and two external members appointed by the President, and with an external member serving as Chairperson. The AIIB

In December 2016, AIIB unilaterally debarred all entities already debarred by others under the AMEDD, through the AIIB Policy on Prohibited Practices.[100] AIIB's unilateral debarment is in line with the AMEDD, under which the Comparator Institutions undertook to recognize and enforce the principal sanctions decided by the others pursuant to their respective integrity procedures. Until AIIB is accepted by the Comparator Institutions as a party to the AMEDD, the Comparator Institutions are not obliged to cross-debar other entities debarred by AIIB itself. AIIB has also stated its intention to join the AMEDD as soon as reasonably possible.[101] Where AIIB co-finances an investment operation with one of the Comparator Institutions, AIIB may agree to apply the co-financier's sanctions policy and processes, and may agree to give full force and effect to the co-financier's sanctions decisions with respect to a joint co-financing.[102]

A review of AIIB's Annual Reports shows one integrity case handled in 2020.[103] In subsequent years, no cases have been reported as appealed to the Sanctions Panel, nor is there mention of investigations referred to the Sanctions Officer.[104] **5.54**

(6) Co-financing

These operational policies have, from the outset, provided for AIIB to co-finance investment operations with others, whether MDBs or other public and private financial institutions. **5.55**

- The Operational Policy on Financing includes specific arrangements for co-financed investment operations. During AIIB's due diligence assessments of projects proposed for financing, co-financing is part of its financial assessment (paragraph 3.3.1(c)). In the context of these due diligence assessments, AIIB is permitted to rely on assessments conducted for this purpose by third parties, provided it is satisfied with the assessment capacity and process of the third party and with the assessment (paragraph 3.3.2). The Policy also provides for

Sanctions Panel will consider appeals from determinations by the Sanctions Officer, and will decide whether to dismiss the findings, in whole or in part, or to impose a sanction on the Respondent Party.

100 AIIB Policy on Prohibited Practices (December 8, 2016), Sections 12.1 and 12.2.

101 AIIB Policy on Prohibited Practices (December 8, 2016), Section 12.4.

102 AIIB Policy on Prohibited Practices (December 8, 2016), Section 12.3.

103 "The remaining elements of the Policy on Prohibited Practices were put in place in 2020 by mobilizing the Sanctions Panel and inducting its newly appointed members. The importance of having a sanctions process was highlighted when the Complaints-resolution, Evaluation and Integrity Unit completed its first investigation. This led to the Bank's Sanctions Officer imposing sanctions on counterparties under a public-private partnership for the first time. No appeal was filed with the Sanctions Panel." Annual Report 2020 at 21.

104 AIIB Annual Report 2023 at 30 notes that no investigations went to the Sanctions Officer, and no cases were filed for appeal to the Sanctions Panel. *See also* AIIB Annual Report 2022 at 40; AIIB Annual Report 2024 at 83.

additional conditions and remedies in co-financed projects, such as cross-effectiveness and cross-default clauses (Annex 1, Section 8.1.10).

- The Procurement Policy provides for both parallel and joint co-financing, as discussed previously.
- The Environmental and Social Policy permits AIIB to apply the policies and procedures of another MDB or bilateral development organization that is co-financing the project, as noted previously. To do so, AIIB must be satisfied that these are consistent with the AIIB Charter and materially consistent with AIIB's Environmental and Social Policy (including the Environmental and Social Standards and Environmental and Social Exclusion List), and that appropriate environmental and social arrangements and monitoring procedures are in place (Section 10.1).
- The Policy on Prohibited Practices allows AIIB to apply the comparable policies and processes of some MDB co-financiers, if these are consistent with the AIIB Charter and materially consistent with the Policy (Section 12.3).[105]

AIIB has entered into partnerships with many other MDBs, many of which facilitate co-financing.[106] As of end 2024, AIIB projects co-financed with other MDBs included co-financings with AfDB, AsDB, EBRD, EIB, IBRD, IFC, and IsDB.[107]

5.56 In 2025, other MDBs have been establishing bilateral arrangements for a deeper co-financing relationship, known as full mutual reliance. The arrangement between the World Bank and AsDB notes that it is the first of its kind (though it echoes the AIIB co-financing policies outlined in paragraph 5.55):

> Under FMRF [Full Mutual Reliance Framework], borrowers in WB-ADB co-financings can rely on one set of rules – using the policies and procedures of either WB or ADB – on all aspects of project design, preparation, appraisal, supervision, completion and evaluation. FMRF is expected to generate efficiencies, time and cost-savings, better outcomes and a closer alignment of policies – advancing the aims of a more cohesive "Multilateral Development Bank System".
>
> The framework also responds to calls by the international community, including the G20, for multilateral development banks (MDBs) to work more cohesively to

[105] For AIIB to apply another co-financier's policies under this provision, the co-financier would have to be one of the parties to the Agreement for the Mutual Enforcement of Debarment Decisions between some Multilateral Development Banks, known in the Policy as Comparator Institutions.

[106] *See* paragraphs 4.15–4.18.

[107] The AIIB 2025 Partnerships Report notes 131 co-financed projects out of 303 projects at December 2024, around 43%. Co-financing with AsDB totaled 67 projects (AIIB contributed US$16.36 billion in financing); with EBRD, there were 15 projects (totaling more than US$1.86 billion); and with World Bank, 56 projects totaling US$13.6 billion, and IFC 9 projects with US$850 million in approved financing. AIIB 2025 Partnerships Report at 16, 18, and 20. *See also* Standard and Poor's (2025) at 2: "We view AIIB's increased share of stand-alone projects as positive. Taking on a bigger share of stand-alone projects or acting as lead arranger in projects is vital, in our view, given the institution's role as a key provider of infrastructure financing. As of end 2024, 43% of the bank's projects were co-financed with other MLIs such as the World Bank Group and the European Investment Bank. This is down from 75% in 2016. The higher share of stand-alone projects signal AIIB's increasing expertise in sourcing deals, risk assessment, and project management."

maximize impact and address escalating development challenges more efficiently and with better results.[108]

Similarly, EIB and EBRD signed a mutual reliance agreement on environmental and social aspects of operations.[109] These are in line with declarations by the MDB Heads on expanding mutual reliance, and the experience with multiple mutual reliance arrangements in the procurement area.[110]

While co-financing is part of the investment operations of most MDBs, there are several reasons why it is likely to continue to play a significant role in AIIB investment operations for some time to come. First, co-financing allowed AIIB to expand operations more quickly and efficiently as the Bank took the time necessary to complete its staffing and full panoply of internal procedures. It also allowed AIIB to move quickly to support its members during the COVID-19 pandemic (see Chapter 12). At the same time, the general policy compatibility with other MDBs should facilitate AIIB's assurance that each operation meets its own requirements. Second, co-financing can have benefits for the recipient entities and countries, as co-financiers' requirements are likely to be harmonized for the operation.[111] Third, some of these operations will require considerable on-the-ground supervision during the implementation phase, and many of AIIB's partners have a network of country offices. The development of a similar network has not yet been identified as part of AIIB's plans. Thus, considerable reliance on the locally based staff of co-financiers could assist AIIB in confirming compliance with the relevant rules and procedures, such as procurement, disbursement, and environmental and social aspects. Lastly, some of the projects in the infrastructure sector can be quite large, with financing needs beyond the risk appetite of individual MDBs. **5.57**

(7) Procedures

The preparation of investment operations generally falls within the President's mandate to conduct the current business of AIIB under the direction of the **5.58**

[108] "ADB and World Bank Group Partner on Full Mutual Reliance Framework to Increase Development Impact," World Bank Press Release, February 20, 2025.

[109] "EIB signs agreement with EBRD to strengthen impact of projects around the world," European Investment Bank Press Release, May 7, 2025.

[110] *See* Viewpoint Note: MDBs Working as a System for Impact and Scale, endorsed by MDB Heads, April 20, 2024, at 9. https://coebank.org/documents/1495/Heads_of_MDBs_Viewpoint_Note_20_April_2024_lixFobs.pdf (last visited July 14, 2025). *See* also "Heads of Multilateral Development Banks Commit to Strong Joint Action on Development Priorities," AIIB Press Release, June 30, 2025, noting: "In 2025 alone, five mutual reliance agreements have been signed, helping streamline the preparation and implementation of co-financed projects across institutions." Among these are an agreement between IFC and EBRD, signed in April 2025 (noted on social media).

[111] The policy flexibility to accept other MDBs' policies as detailed previously makes it easier for AIIB to accept co-financiers' policies than is the case for some other MDBs, whose operational policies have not permitted that even when there is broad compatibility between them.

Board of Directors.[112] The Board of Directors' role in respect of investment operations is further detailed in its specific powers to establish AIIB's policies and take decisions on investment operations.[113] The Board of Directors is further expressly authorized by the AIIB Charter to delegate authority to the President under AIIB policies, as well as to delegate to the president its authority to take decision on investment operations—in each case, by a 75% majority vote. In 2018, the Board of Directors approved AIIB's Accountability Framework, delegating decision authority on investment operations to the President within specified parameters.[114]

5.59 The Board of Directors' oversight role also encompasses AIIB's role in preparing and supervising investment operations. Here, it is essential to recall that these investment operations are not implemented by AIIB itself, but rather carried out by the recipients with AIIB financing and supervision. The oversight mechanism established by the Board of Directors to supervise the management and operation of AIIB covers some aspects of project supervision, as noted in the Chief Negotiators' Report:

> Representatives agreed that the oversight mechanism to be established by the Board of Directors under Article 26 (iv) would be designed in line with the principles of transparency, openness, independence and accountability, and would address such areas as audit, evaluation, fraud and corruption, project complaints and staff grievances, and reflect the Bank's character as a multilateral financial institution focused on infrastructure development.

As in other MDBs, this mechanism covers integrity, project complaints, and evaluation, functions that are grouped for AIIB under the CEIU.[115] The formalization of the Oversight Mechanism in 2019 is detailed in Chapter 12, Section C.

F. Overview of Investment Operations

5.60 AIIB's first investment operations were approved at the Board of Directors' meeting in June 2016, some five months after AIIB's legal establishment and one year after the signing of the AIIB Charter. Nine years later, AIIB has 322 approved projects totaling US$61.49 billion.

[112] AIIB Article 29-4. The policy parameters for preparation of AIIB financing are laid out in the Operational Policy on Financing, supplemented by the Environmental and Social Policy and Procurement Policy, all approved by the Board of Directors.

[113] AIIB Article 26 (ii) and (iii). For an authoritative overview of AIIB's institutional setup and early experience in financing investment operations, *see* Sanders (2017b).

[114] *See* paragraphs 9.26–9.27 and Chapter 12, Section B.

[115] *See* paragraphs 9.28–9.31 and Chapter 12, Section C.

AIIB Projects by Sector (end 2024)			
SECTORS		2024	Total
Energy		13	68
Transport		18	61
Water		1	16
Multi-sector		11	53
Urban		2	16
Digital Infrastructure and Technology		—	9
Rural Infrastructure and Agricultural Development		—	1
Education Infrastructure		1	2
Health Infrastructure		1	4
Other productive sectors		1	1
Others		3	4
COVID-19 CRISIS RECOVERY FACILITY (CRF)	CRF-Public Health	—	18
	CRF-Finance/Liquidity	—	15
	CRF-Economic Resilience / Policy-based financing	—	35
TOTAL		51	303*

Figure 5.2 AIIB Projects by Sector (end 2024)
*Total does not include projects on hold, terminated or cancelled.
Source: AIIB Annual Report 2024 at 15, Projects by Sector.

AIIB Projects by Type and Location					
AIIB Projects	Sovereign	Non-Sovereign	Regional	Non-Regional	Multicountry
June 2025	56% (181)	44% (141)	83% (266)	7% (23)	10% (32)
2024	53% (27)	47% (24)	84% (43)	6% (3)	10% (5)

Figure 5.3 AIIB Projects by Type and Location
For 2024, AIIB Annual Report 2024 at 24.
Source: For June 2025, AIIB website, Project Summary and Project List (June 30, 2025).

AIIB's Investment Operations[116] are focused on the four thematic priorities under its Corporate Strategy: Green Infrastructure; Connectivity and Regional Cooperation; Technology-enabled Infrastructure; and Private Capital Mobilization.[117] Within these priorities, AIIB invested primarily in infrastructure sectors, as shown in Figure 5.2. **5.61**

Through June 2025, AIIB's reported cumulative operations totaled 322 projects (US$61.49 billion in approved financing). Distribution by sovereign/non-sovereign and location (regional/non-regional/multicountry) is shown in Figure 5.3. **5.62**

[116] With the approval of Results-based Financing and Climate-based Policy Financing (paragraph 5.16), AIIB financing is not limited to investment projects. The term "investment financing" is used here to cover all three types of operations.

[117] AIIB Annual Report 2024 at 14 lists the goals of its fifty-one projects approved in 2024 against these priorities (not mutually exclusive): Green Infrastructure (fifty projects); Connectivity and Regional Cooperation (twenty projects); Technology-enabled Infrastructure (twenty-one projects); and Private Capital Mobilization (eighteen projects). AIIB reported a cumulative total of US$13,057.62 billion in private capital mobilized. AIIB Annual Report 2024 at 21.

AIIB Projects by Sector (end 2024)						
NUMBER OF PROJECTS				APPROVED AIIB FINANCING (USD million)		
TOTAL	SBF	NSBF	MEMBER	SBF	NSBF	TOTAL
1	—	1	AZERBAIJAN	—	170.0	170.0
3	3	—	BANGLADESH	760.0	—	760.0
1	1	—	CAMBODIA	80.0	—	80.0
3	1	2	CHINA	400.0	195.0	595.0
1	1	—	EGYPT	300.0	—	300.0
1	1	—	GEORGIA	140.0	—	140.0
1	—	1	HUNGARY	—	200.0	200.0
9	3	6	INDIA	674.7	505.1	1,179.8
2	1	1	KAZAKHSTAN	650.0	113.9	763.9
2	1	1	LAO PDR	40.0	40.0	80.0
1	1	—	MALDIVES	15.0	—	15.0
5	—	5	MULTICOUNTRY*	—	498.7	498.7
3	3	—	PHILIPPINES	582.2	—	582.2
1	1	—	RWANDA	100.0	—	100.0
1	—	1	SINGAPORE	—	350.0	350.0
2	2	—	TAJIKISTAN	345.5	—	345.5
2	1	1	THAILAND	423.1	200.0	623.1
8	3	5	TÜRKIYE	785.0	339.5	1,124.5
2	1	1	UZBEKISTAN	250.0	30.0	280.0
2	—	2	VIET NAM	—	225.0	225.0
51	24	27	GRAND TOTAL	5,545.5	2,867.2	8,412.7

Figure 5.4 AIIB PROJECTS APPROVED 2024

SBF = Sovereign-backed financing; NSBF = Non-sovereign-backed financing.

* Multicountry covers projects financed through financial intermediaries (e.g., private equity funds, bonds). Projects categorized as "multicountry" may indirectly benefit AIIB Members, even when AIIB does not provide direct financing to these beneficiary Members.

Source: Adapted from AIIB Annual Report 2024 at 17.

5.63 For more detail, AIIB's approved operations in 2024 are shown in Figure 5.4.

5.64 Portfolio performance is measured and reported under AIIB's Corporate Scorecard. Through 2024, this measured implementation readiness in terms of number of months elapsed from approval to first cash disbursement, as an indication of the quality of project preparation. For sovereign projects, this indicator was stable at around fourteen months, and for non-sovereign projects, this indicator was eight to nine months. The overall share of projects without severe or unresolved issues impacting implementation performance results, another indicator, was over 90%, reaching 95% in 2024.[118]

5.65 Special Fund grant approvals through end 2024 covered sixty-six grants (US$171 million). On a cumulative basis, there were thirty-seven grants from

[118] AIIB Annual Report 2024 at 16.

AIIB PROJECTS BY MEMBER				
MEMBER	2024 Projects		Approved Projects through June 2025	
	Number	Percentage	Number	Percentage of Approvals
ARGENTINA	-		1	0.3%
AZERBAIJAN	1	2.0%	3	1.0%
BANGLADESH	3	5.9%	26	8.5%
BRAZIL	-		4	1.3%
CAMBODIA	1	2.0%	8	2.6%
CHINA	3	5.9%	21	6.9%
COOK ISLANDS	-		1	0.3%
COTE D'IVOIRE	-		2	0.7%
ECUADOR	-		1	0.3%
EGYPT	1	2.0%	8	2.6%
FIJI	-		2	0.7%
GEORGIA	1	2.0%	6	2.0%
HONG KONG, CHINA	-		1	0.3%
HUNGARY	1	2.0%	2	0.7%
INDIA	9	17.6%	52	17.0%
INDONESIA	-		14	4.6%
JORDAN	-		2	0.7%
KAZAKHSTAN	2	3.9%	7	2.3%
KYRGYZSTAN	-		2	0.7%
LAO PDR	2	3.9%	5	1.6%
MALDIVES	1	2.0%	4	1.3%
MONGOLIA	-		3	1.0%
MYANMAR	-		1	0.3%
NEPAL	-		2	0.7%
OMAN	-		3	1.0%
PAKISTAN	-		11	3.6%
PHILIPPINES	3	5.9%	11	3.6%
ROMANIA	-		1	0.3%
RUSSIA			--	0.0%
RWANDA	1	2.0%	3	1.0%
SAUDI ARABIA	-		1	0.3%
SINGAPORE	1	2.0%	6	2.0%
SRI LANKA	-		3	1.0%
TAJIKISTAN	2	3.9%	4	1.3%
THAILAND	2	3.9%	2	0.7%
TÜRKIYE	8	15.7%	31	10.1%
UZBEKISTAN	2	3.9%	17	5.6%
VIET NAM	2	3.9%	4	1.3%
MULTI-COUNTRY	5	9.8%	31	10.1%
TOTAL	51		306*	

Figure 5.5 AIIB PROJECTS BY MEMBER

*AIIB's online Project List includes 306 approved projects of the 322 approvals. "Approved projects" does not reflect those subject to deferred disclosure and those listed as terminated, cancelled, or on hold.

Source: AIIB website Project List (visited June 30, 2025).

the Project Preparation Special Fund, fifteen grants from MCDF, one grant from Global Infrastructure Facility, one grant from the Special Fund Window, two grants from the Pandemic Fund, and one grant from the Project Specific Window.[119]

5.66 According to AIIB's Investor Presentation, the largest recipients by Total Investment Operations Exposure as of March 31, 2025 were: India (20%); Indonesia (11%); Türkiye (9%); Philippines (8%); Bangladesh (8%); China (8%); Multi-country (7%); Uzbekistan (7%); Pakistan (5%); and Egypt (3%).[120] The distribution of AIIB financing by member is shown in Figure 5.5 (AIIB Projects by Member), showing the number and percentage of operations (instead of the exposure volume). By number of projects, the largest recipients were: India; Multicountry; Türkiye; Bangladesh; China; Uzbekistan; Indonesia; Philippines; Pakistan; Egypt; Cambodia; and Pakistan.

[119] AIIB Annual Report 2024 at 19. *See* paragraph 5.19 and paragraphs 7.55–7.58 for more information on these Special Funds.

[120] AIIB Investor Presentation, Investing with Impact: AIIB's Sustainable Development Bonds (May 2025) at 27.

6
MEMBERSHIP

Membership is one of the first questions that can arise in setting up a multilateral development bank (MDB) as an intergovernmental organization. At a practical level, who will be represented at the table as the Charter is negotiated? Which parties are going to participate in its establishment, and which ones will be able to join later as future members? For an MDB, membership rules may also affect which countries can benefit from the institution's development finance and which countries will be key to its financial base. 6.01

Countries interested in establishing the Asian Infrastructure Investment Bank (AIIB) had been engaged in consultations for nearly one year when charter negotiations began, as outlined in Chapter 3. Whatever scope of membership was chosen would need to encompass not only those in the room at the start of negotiations (the signatories of the Memorandum of Understanding on Establishing the Asian Infrastructure Investment Bank among Prospective Founding Members) but also those countries still discussing the possibility of joining the negotiations and those countries already anticipating joining after AIIB's establishment. Following the model of many other MDBs, membership could also be open to even more countries that might become interested in joining AIIB in the future. 6.02

In addition to its scope, there were other aspects of membership to be decided. Would there be special provisions for the countries that took the initiative and contributed their efforts and resources to AIIB's founding? Would there be recognition of a difference between regional and non-regional members, in light of AIIB's focus on infrastructure in Asia? In that case, what would define "regional" for AIIB? 6.03

This chapter lays out the framework that was agreed for AIIB membership: scope of membership; Prospective Founding Members and Signatories; Founding Members; regional and non-regional members; future members; and withdrawal and suspension of membership. AIIB had 110 approved members by September 2025, fifty-three regional and fifty-seven non-regional. Of these approved members, 104 members had finalized membership after AIIB approval: fifty-two regional and fifty-two non-regional.[1] Figure 6.1 shows AIIB membership composition as of September 15, 2025. 6.04

[1] AIIB's approved members represent over 80% of global population and over 65% of global GDP. AIIB Annual Report 2024 at 10.

	Regional	Non-Regional	Total
Membership Approved	53	57	110
Current Members	52	52	104

Figure 6.1 AIIB Membership at September 15, 2025

A. Scope of Membership

6.05 Membership in AIIB is open to members of the International Bank for Reconstruction and Development (IBRD) or the Asian Development Bank (AsDB).[2] The scope of AIIB membership therefore relies on the IBRD and AsDB Charters and practice for its definition. Generally, other MDBs also rely on membership in other institutions to define their scope of membership.[3]

(1) IBRD membership

6.06 Membership in IBRD is open only to members of the International Monetary Fund (IMF).[4] Membership in IMF is open to countries that were represented at the United Nations Monetary and Financial Conference (at Bretton Woods in July 1944) and accepted membership by December 21, 1945, and to other countries as decided by IMF Board of Governors.[5] As of June 2025, 189 countries were members of IBRD and 191 countries were members of IMF.[6] Membership has grown considerably over more than seventy years: forty-five countries were listed in each of the IMF and IBRD Charters as eligible to sign in 1945.[7]

(2) AsDB membership

6.07 Membership in AsDB is open to two groups: (1) Members and Associate Members of the United Nations Economic Commission for Asia and the Far East (ECAFE,

[2] AIIB Article 3-1.

[3] Examples of membership requirements in other MDBs:

AfDB membership is open to African countries and non-regional members of the African Development Fund (AfDB Article 3).

EBRD membership is open to IMF members as well as the EU and EIB (EBRD Article 3-1).

EIB membership is open to EU members (EIB Article 3).

IADB membership is open to members of the Organization of American States (OAS), IMF, and named countries (Canada, Bahamas, Guyana, and Switzerland) which were not OAS or IMF members at the time (IADB Article II, Section 1).

IBRD and AsDB membership eligibility is discussed in paragraphs 6.06 and 6.07 of this chapter.

[4] IBRD Article II.

[5] IMF Article II.

[6] For IBRD, *see* http://www.worldbank.org/en/about/leadership/members. For IMF, *see* https://www.imf.org/external/np/sec/memdir/memdate.htm (both last visited July 14, 2025).

[7] IMF Article XXXI, Section 2 (e) and Schedule A, and IBRD Article XI, Section 2 (e) and Schedule A.

now ESCAP);[8] and (2) other regional countries and non-regional developed countries which are members of the UN or of any of its specialized agencies.[9] As of June 2025, AsDB had sixty-nine members: fifty regional and nineteen non-regional. AsDB membership has also grown over the past sixty years: in 1965, thirty-three countries were listed in the AsDB Charter as eligible to sign.[10]

(3) Types of IBRD and AsDB members

Only countries may be IBRD members, as this status is required for IMF membership. AsDB membership, however, includes countries, as well as ESCAP Associate Members that are not necessarily countries. AsDB membership applications from ESCAP Associate Members not responsible for the conduct of their international relations are presented by the relevant AsDB member.[11] Historically, AsDB members admitted under this provision included Hong Kong, China; Cook Islands; Fiji; Kiribati; Papua New Guinea; and Solomon Islands.[12] AsDB classifies its members as regional and non-regional, as does AIIB, as discussed in paragraphs 6.24–6.25. IBRD does not classify members under its Charter, as it is not tied to one region. Neither AsDB nor IBRD are open to membership by other entities, such as international organizations or financial institutions, as is the case in a few other MDBs.[13] **6.08**

(4) AIIB's scope of membership

By including both pillars for membership (IBRD and AsDB), AIIB maintains its regional focus as well as a tie to nearly universal IMF and IBRD membership, recognizing both global and regional support for Asian infrastructure. What **6.09**

[8] The United Nations Commission for East Asia and the Pacific (ESCAP) is the successor to the United Nations Commission for Asia and the Far East (ECAFE). ECAFE played a seminal role in developing the AsDB concept and in the consultations and negotiations. Wilson (1987), especially Chapter 2, "The Birth of the Bank." The name ECAFE was changed in 1974 to ESCAP to reflect both the economic and social aspects of development and the geographic location of its member countries. http://www.unescap.org/about (last visited July 14, 2025).

[9] AsDB Article 3-1. Non-regional developing countries are not mentioned in the AsDB Charter provision on membership.

[10] AsDB Article 63-1 and Annex A.

[11] AsDB Article 3-3. *See* paragraph 6.37 in this chapter.

[12] Wilson (1987) at 278 and Kappagoda (1995) at 117–18. Of these, only Kiribati has not been approved for or become a member of AIIB.

[13] *See, e.g.*, EBRD Article 3-1 (the EU and EIB are members); CDB Article 3-1 (institutions may join though none are listed as members); and CAF Article 5 (shareholders may include governments as well as public, semi-public or private institutions, and, as of 2025, include thirteen private banks). The EBRD Chairman's Report on the Agreement Establishing the European Bank for Reconstruction and Development notes, as to the membership of the EU (originally, the European Economic Community) and EIB: "It was not intended that their membership would be a precedent for other organizations or banks to become members of the Bank, or that their membership would be used as a precedent for them to become members of other organizations or banks."

do these two pillars of membership mean for AIIB? The combination of the two broadens the scope for AIIB membership. To illustrate, limiting AIIB membership to AsDB members only would have excluded some Prospective Founding Members (PFMs).[14] Many of the new members approved since 2016 are not AsDB members and were eligible based on IBRD membership.[15]

6.10 Some of these differences arise from the specifics of the AsDB membership definition (paragraph 6.07). For AsDB regional members, the definition of the Asia region is slightly narrower than under the AIIB Charter,[16] so there are fewer countries that would be considered regional at AsDB than at AIIB. Moreover, only developed countries may join AsDB as non-regional members. These two factors combined mean that more countries are eligible to join AIIB than AsDB, whether as regional members under a broader regional definition or as non-regional developing countries.[17] (See Figure 6.2.)

6.11 Neither would IBRD membership alone have been a sufficiently broad prerequisite for future AIIB members. Using only IBRD membership as a criterion would have ruled out the possibility for AIIB membership for three of AsDB's current regional members that are not IBRD members: Cook Islands; Hong Kong, China; and Taipei, China.[18] AsDB membership also opens the AIIB door to ESCAP Associate Members that may later become AsDB members.[19]

6.12 The actual impact of applying these membership criteria, and the different definitions of "regional" for AsDB and AIIB, are shown in Figures 6.2 and 6.3.

[14] Among AIIB Prospective Founding Members (PFMs), Iran, Israel, Jordan, Oman, Qatar, Russia, Saudi Arabia, and United Arab Emirates (regional PFMs) and Brazil, Egypt, Iceland, Malta, Poland, and South Africa (non-regional PFMs) were IBRD members but not AsDB members in 2015. (Israel joined AsDB in 2024.)

[15] Of the sixteen new AIIB regional members approved through June 2025, Bahrain, Cyprus, Iraq, and Lebanon are IBRD members and not AsDB members. Of the thirty-seven new non-regional members approved through June 2025, all are IBRD members; Canada and Ireland are also AsDB non-regional members. The only AsDB non-regional member that is not a member of AIIB is the United States.

[16] Under AIIB Article 1-2, regional means "the geographical regions and composition classified as Asia and Oceania by the United Nations" and the Chief Negotiators' Report provides a link to the UN listing, http://unstats.un.org/unsd/methods/m49/m49regin.htm (last visited July 14, 2025). Under AsDB Article 1, regional means "the territories of Asia and the Far East included in the Terms of Reference of the United Nations Economic Commission for Asia and the Far East." The main difference is that AIIB's definition includes all of the UN's Western Asia grouping, while the AsDB definition includes only Armenia, Azerbaijan, Georgia, and Türkiye from that group. A detailed listing illustrating the coverage of both definitions is provided in Figure 6.2. Türkiye's status in AsDB was changed to regional in 2025.

[17] For instance, developing countries that are AIIB non-regional members (or have been approved as AIIB non-regional members) would not likely have been eligible for AsDB membership as non-regional developed countries (depending on definitions). Non-regional AIIB members that would likely be considered developing countries (i.e., listed as low-income or middle-income by the World Bank) and therefore not eligible for AsDB membership include: Argentina, Belarus, Benin, Bolivia, Brazil, Cote d'Ivoire, Djibouti, Ecuador, Egypt, El Salvador, Ethiopia, Ghana, Guinea, Kenya, Liberia, Libya, Madagascar, Mauritania, Morocco, Nigeria, Peru, Rwanda, Senegal, Serbia, South Africa, Sudan, Tanzania, Togo, Tunisia, and Venezuela. *See* World Bank list of economies in the 2025 World Bank Development Indicators (available on www.worldbank.org).

[18] These three are eligible for AIIB membership solely on the basis of AsDB membership. Membership for Hong Kong, China was approved and took effect in 2017. Cook Islands was approved for membership in December 2017 and became an AIIB member in June 2020. *See* Figure 6.2.

[19] *See* note 83 in this chapter.

AIIB Regional Membership and Eligibility: Comparison with AsDB and IBRD			
REGIONAL (AIIB Definition)	**AIIB Members**	**AsDB Members**	**IBRD Members**
Afghanistan	✓	✓	✓
Armenia	✓	✓	✓
Australia	✓	✓	✓
Azerbaijan	✓	✓	✓
Bahrain	✓	—	✓
Bangladesh	✓	✓	✓
Bhutan	*potential regional*	✓	✓
Brunei Darussalam	✓	✓	✓
Cambodia	✓	✓	✓
China	✓	✓*	✓
Cook Islands	✓	✓	—
Cyprus	✓	—	✓
Fiji	✓	✓	✓
Georgia	✓	✓	✓
Hong Kong, China	✓	✓	—
India	✓	✓	✓
Indonesia	✓	✓	✓
Iran	✓	—	✓
Iraq	✓	—	✓
Israel	✓	✓ *non-regional*	✓
Japan	*potential regional*	✓	✓
Jordan	✓	—	✓
Kazakhstan	✓	✓	✓
Kiribati	*potential regional*	✓	✓
Korea**	✓	✓	✓
Kuwait	✓	—	✓
Kyrgyz Republic	✓	✓	✓
Lao People's Democratic Republic	✓	✓	✓
Lebanon	***prospective***	—	✓
Malaysia	✓	✓	✓
Maldives	✓	✓	✓
Marshall Islands	*potential regional*	✓	✓
Micronesia	*potential regional*	✓	✓
Mongolia	✓	✓	✓
Myanmar	✓	✓	✓
Nauru	✓	✓	✓
Nepal	✓	✓	✓
New Zealand	✓	✓	✓
Niue	*potential regional*	✓	—
Oman	✓	—	✓

(continued)

AIIB Regional Membership and Eligibility: Comparison with AsDB and IBRD			
REGIONAL (AIIB Definition)	AIIB Members	AsDB Members	IBRD Members
Pakistan	✓	✓	✓
Palau	*potential regional*	✓	✓
Papua New Guinea	✓	✓	✓
Philippines	✓	✓	✓
Qatar	✓	—	✓
Russia***	✓	—	✓
Samoa	✓	✓	✓
Saudi Arabia	✓	—	✓
Singapore	✓	✓	✓
Solomon Islands	✓	✓	✓
Sri Lanka	✓	✓	✓
Syrian Arab Republic	*potential regional*	—	✓
Taiwan Province of China	*potential regional*	✓****	—
Tajikistan	✓	✓	✓
Thailand	✓	✓	✓
Timor-Leste	✓	✓	✓
Tonga	✓	✓	✓
Türkiye	✓	✓	✓
Turkmenistan	*potential regional*	✓	✓
Tuvalu	*potential regional*	✓	✓
United Arab Emirates	✓	—	✓
Uzbekistan	✓	✓	✓
Vanuatu	✓	✓	✓
Viet Nam	✓	✓	✓
Yemen	*potential regional*	—	✓

Figure 6.2 AIIB Regional Membership and Eligibility: Comparison with AsDB and IBRD

* AsDB member is People's Republic of China.

** Republic of Korea and Democratic People's Republic of Korea are listed as regional. Republic of Korea is a member of AsDB, AIIB, and IBRD; the Democratic People's Republic of Korea is not.

*** Russia in not listed in the UN classification of Asia and Oceania but is an AIIB regional member by virtue of AIIB Article 3–1 (a) and AIIB Schedule A.

**** AsDB member is Taipei, China.

Source: UN listing for Asia and Oceania (http://unstats.un.org/unsd/methods/m49/m49regin.htm). Membership tables are found on the websites for AIIB, AsDB, and IBRD.

- Figure 6.2 lists potential and current regional members of AsDB and AIIB, alongside current members of IBRD located in AIIB's regional definition. Under the definition of Asia used under the AIIB Charter, the applicable UN listing for Asia and Oceania includes territories and areas that may not be eligible for membership in international organizations.[20] Only those territories

[20] The UN Listing for Asia and Oceania (note 16 in this chapter) includes: (a) in Western Asia, the State of Palestine; (b) in Oceania, Christmas Island, Cocos (Keeling) Islands, Heard Island and McDonald Islands, and Norfolk Island; (c) in Melanesia, New Caledonia; (d) in Micronesia, Guam and Northern Mariana Islands; and (e) in Polynesia, American Samoa, French Polynesia, Pitcairn, Tokelau, and Wallis and Futuna Islands. UN listing (http://unstats.un.org/unsd/methods/m49/m49regin.htm).

and countries that are already members of AsDB or IBRD are shown as potential regional members for AIIB.[21]

- Figure 6.3 lists current non-regional members of AsDB and AIIB, alongside current IBRD members located outside of AIIB's regional definition, shown separately by World Bank regions: Africa (Figure 6.3A), Europe and Central Asia (Figure 6.3B), Latin America and Caribbean (Figure 6.3C), Middle East and North Africa (Figure 6.3D), and North America (Figure 6.3E).

Compared to AsDB's current members, there are ten that are not AIIB members or approved for AIIB membership.[22] Of IBRD's 189 members, eighty-one are not AIIB members or approved for AIIB membership.[23] **6.13**

B. Prospective Founding Members and Signatories

(1) Prospective Founding Members

In AIIB's formative phase, interested countries participated in five Multilateral Consultation Meetings on AIIB's establishment, organized by China, leading up to the MOU signed in October 2014. The twenty-two countries that signed the MOU were the first wave of PFMs.[24] They were considered "prospective" because countries could legally join AIIB as members only after the AIIB Charter was agreed and AIIB established; participation as a PFM did not represent a country's formal legal commitment to join the future AIIB. "Founding Member" was a concept introduced in this preparatory phase, as discussed in paragraphs 6.19–6.23. **6.14**

In addition to the MOU signatories, others could join the negotiations on the AIIB Charter as PFMs. In all, the initial PFMs were joined by another thirty-five PFMs. Thus, fifty-seven PFMs were represented in the Chief Negotiators' Meeting (CNM) when negotiations on the AIIB Charter were concluded at the fifth CNM in Singapore in May 2015.[25] All PFMs were listed in Schedule A, making them eligible to sign the AIIB Charter and thereafter to become members of AIIB. **6.15**

[21] Other potential AsDB members are ESCAP Associate Members, under AsDB Article 3. Some ESCAP Associate Members are already AsDB members: Cook Islands; Hong Kong, China; and Niue. Other ESCAP Associate Members include: American Samoa; French Polynesia; Guam; Macao, China; New Caledonia; and the Northern Mariana Islands. https://www.unescap.org/about/member-states.

[22] Ten AsDB regional members are not AIIB members: four in Asia (Bhutan; Japan; Taipei, China; and Turkmenistan) and six in Oceania (Kiribati, Marshall Islands, Micronesia, Niue, Palau, and Tuvalu). Only one AsDB non-regional member is not an AIIB member: the United States.

[23] *See* Figure 6.2 and Figure 6.3.

[24] *See* paragraph 3.25.

[25] Figure 3.1 lists the AIIB Prospective Founding Members and when they joined the establishment process.

Non-Regional Member Comparison: AFRICA		
IBRD Members (outside AIIB Regional definition)	AIIB Non-Regional	**AsDB Non-Regional** (only developed countries eligible)
Angola		
Benin	✓	
Botswana		
Burkina Faso		
Burundi		
Cabo Verde		
Cameroon		
Central African Republic		
Chad		
Comoros		
Congo, Democratic Republic of		
Congo, Republic of		
Cote d'Ivoire	✓	
Equatorial Guinea		
Eritrea		
Ethiopia	✓	
Gabon		
Gambia		
Ghana	✓	
Guinea	✓	
Guinea-Bissau		
Kenya	✓	
Lesotho		
Liberia	✓	
Madagascar	✓	
Malawi		
Mali		
Mauritania	✓	
Mauritius		
Mozambique		
Namibia		
Niger		
Nigeria	***prospective***	
Rwanda	✓	
Sao Tome and Principe		
Senegal	***prospective***	
Seychelles		
Sierra Leone		
Somalia		
South Africa	✓	

Non-Regional Member Comparison: AFRICA		
IBRD Members (outside AIIB Regional definition)	**AIIB Non-Regional**	**AsDB Non-Regional** (only developed countries eligible)
South Sudan		
Sudan	✓	
Swaziland		
Tanzania	*prospective*	
Togo	✓	
Uganda		
Zambia		
Zimbabwe		

Figure 6.3A Non-Regional Member Comparison: Africa

(2) Signatories

"Signatories" is the term used in the AIIB Charter for the PFMs listed in Schedule A who signed before the signing deadline of December 31, 2015. The AIIB Charter itself does not refer to PFMs. All fifty-seven PFMs signed and became Signatories under the AIIB Charter.[26] **6.16**

In common with many other MDB charters, the AIIB Charter specifies additional steps after signing for Signatories to complete the membership process. Signatories are required to deposit an instrument of ratification, acceptance or approval (instrument of ratification) with the depository.[27] The AIIB Charter set a deadline for the deposit of instruments of ratification by Signatories at December 31, 2016, offering Signatories a minimum of one year to complete the domestic processes for treaty ratification.[28] The Board of Governors is empowered to extend the deadline by a Special Majority[29] and has extended it multiple times, with a final deadline of June 30, 2025.[30] **6.17**

[26] All fifty-seven of the Signatories have become Founding Members as of June 2025.

[27] AIIB Article 58-1. The Depository for the AIIB Charter is the Government of the People's Republic of China, under AIIB Article 57-1; more specifically that role has been assigned to the Ministry of Foreign Affairs. *See* further discussion in paragraph 11.04.

[28] Whether a Signatory deposits an instrument of ratification, acceptance or approval depends on domestic legal requirements. As explained by the UN Treaty Section: "Most multilateral treaties expressly provide for States to express their consent to be bound by signature subject to ratification, acceptance or approval. Providing for signature subject to ratification allows States time to seek approval for the treaty at the domestic level and to enact any legislation necessary to implement the treaty domestically, prior to undertaking the legal obligations under the treaty at the international level . . . Acceptance or approval of a treaty following signature has the same legal effect as ratification, and the same rules apply, unless the treaty provides otherwise (see article 14 (2) of the Vienna Convention 1969)." Treaty Handbook, UN Treaty Section (2012), Sections 3.3.2 and 3.3.3.

[29] AIIB Article 58-1. A comparable provision for extension is found in EBRD Article 61-2, requiring a decision by a majority of Governors, representing a majority of the total voting power of the members (same as an AIIB Special Majority).

[30] The deadline was last extended to June 30, 2025, for the remaining Signatory (Kuwait); Kuwait became a member on May 26, 2025. AIIB Board of Governors' Resolution No. 132, *Extending the Deadline for the State of Kuwait's Ratification of the Articles of Agreement of the Asian Infrastructure Investment Bank*, adopted

Non-Regional Member Comparison: EUROPE AND CENTRAL ASIA		
IBRD Members (outside AIIB Regional definition)	AIIB Non-Regional (potential members)	AsDB Non-Regional (only developed countries eligible)
Albania		
Austria	✓	✓
Belarus	✓	
Belgium	✓	✓
Bosnia and Herzegovina		
Bulgaria		
Croatia	✓	
Czech Republic		
Denmark	✓	✓
Estonia		
Finland	✓	✓
France	✓	✓
Germany	✓	✓
Greece	✓	
Hungary	✓	
Iceland	✓	
Ireland	✓	✓
Italy	✓	✓
Kosovo		
Latvia		
Lithuania		
Luxembourg	✓	✓
Macedonia, FYR of		
Moldova		
Montenegro		
Netherlands	✓	✓
Norway	✓	✓
Poland	✓	
Portugal	✓	✓
Romania	✓	
San Marino		
Serbia	✓	
Slovak Republic		
Slovenia		
Spain	✓	✓
Sweden	✓	✓
Switzerland	✓	✓
Ukraine		
United Kingdom	✓	✓

Figure 6.3B Non-Regional Member Comparison: Europe and Central Asia

Non-Regional Member Comparison: LATIN AMERICA AND CARIBBEAN		
IBRD Members (outside AIIB Regional definition)	AIIB Non-Regional (potential members)	AsDB Non-Regional (only developed countries eligible)
Antigua and Barbuda		
Argentina	✓	
Bahamas		
Barbados		
Belize		
Bolivia	***prospective***	
Brazil	✓	
Chile	✓	
Colombia		
Costa Rica		
Dominica		
Dominican Republic		
Ecuador	✓	
El Salvador	✓	
Grenada		
Guatemala		
Guyana		
Haiti		
Honduras		
Jamaica		
Mexico		
Nicaragua		
Panama		
Paraguay		
Peru	✓	
St. Kitts and Nevis		
St. Lucia		
St. Vincent and the Grenadines		
Suriname		
Trinidad and Tobago		
Uruguay	✓	
Venezuela	***prospective***	

Figure 6.3C Non-Regional Member Comparison: Latin America and Caribbean

Non-Regional Member Comparison: MIDDLE EAST AND NORTH AFRICA		
IBRD Members (outside AIIB Regional definition)	**AIIB Non-Regional (potential members)**	**AsDB Non-Regional (only developed countries eligible)**
Algeria		
Djibouti	✓	
Egypt	✓	
Libya	✓	
Malta	✓	
Morocco	✓	
Tunisia	✓	

Figure 6.3D Non-Regional Member Comparison: Middle East and North Africa

Other Middle East and North Africa IBRD members are considered Regional for AIIB:

Bahrain, Iran, Iraq, Israel, Jordan, Kuwait, Lebanon, Oman, Qatar, Saudi Arabia, Syrian Arab Republic, United Arab Emirates, Yemen.

See Figure 6.2 for AIIB regional members.

Non-Regional Member Comparison: NORTH AMERICA		
IBRD Members (outside AIIB Regional definition)	**AIIB Non-Regional (potential members)**	**AsDB Non-Regional (only developed countries eligible)**
Bermuda		
Canada	✓	✓
United States		✓

Figure 6.3E Non-Regional Member Comparison: North America

6.18 To complete membership, Signatories are also required to subscribe to AIIB capital stock and pay in the first installment of their subscriptions to the paid-in capital stock of the Bank on or before the date of deposit of their instrument of ratification.[31] Delays in payment of these subscriptions to paid-in capital in AIIB result in the loss of proportionate voting power.[32]

June 28, 2024. In that Resolution extending the deadline, the Board of Governors noted "its Resolutions No. 20 of November 28, 2016, No. 55 of December 17, 2017, No. 67 of December 18, 2018, No. 88 of December 30, 2019, No. 116 of December 28, 2022, and No. 120 of June 29, 2023, on extension of the deadline for Prospective Founding Members to ratify the Articles of Agreement of the Asian Infrastructure Investment Bank (AIIB)."

[31] AIIB Article 6-1 also provided that Signatories who deposited their instruments of ratification on or before the date thirty days after entry into force of the Charter (January 24, 2016) had until that date to make those payments. There are similar provisions in other charters, such as AsDB Article 6-1 (within thirty days of entry into force) and EBRD Article 6-1 (within sixty days of entry into force). Payments before AIIB's establishment were to be paid to a Trustee for the Bank (the Government of the People's Republic of China), and thereafter as directed by the Bank, under AIIB Article 6-4. Trustees were also used in other MDBs for this pre-establishment period. *See* AsDB Article 6-7 (UN Secretary-General); AfDB Article 7-5 (Trustee to be appointed); EBRD Article 6-6 (EIB); IADB Article XV, Section 1 (c) (General Secretariat of OAS); and IBRD Article XI, Section 2 (d) (Government of the United States).

[32] AIIB Articles 6-2 and 28-1, discussed in paragraph 7.14 and paragraph 9.06.

C. Founding Members

The AIIB Charter offers the status of Founding Member to Signatories. Founding Member status requires that a Signatory deposits its instrument of ratification and undertakes its capital subscription by the deadline.[33] The concept of Founding Member is rare among MDBs.[34] It offers a recognition of their special role to those members who participated in and contributed to the Bank's establishment. As of June 2025, all fifty-seven Signatories of the Charter have become Founding Members of the AIIB. **6.19**

Founding Members have two special benefits under the AIIB Charter: Founding Member votes and rotation privileges for Director/Alternate Director on the Board of Directors. **6.20**

(1) Founding Member votes

All AIIB members are assigned basic votes and share votes; in addition, each Founding Member is assigned an additional 600 Founding Member votes.[35] The assignment of Founding Member votes increases the voting power of each Founding Member, above the standard assignment of basic votes and share votes. At the time of negotiations, the weight of all Founding Member votes in total voting power would have been around 3%, based on Schedule A. That would compare with basic votes at 12% and share votes at 85%. As of September 2025, Founding Member votes represented 3% of total votes. In reality, the relative benefit of Founding Member votes will decline over time, because Founding Member votes are fixed in number, while the number of total votes will increase as Signatories actually subscribe to specific amounts of capital and AIIB takes on new members and, eventually, increases its capital stock. Thus, the impact of this benefit for Founding Members will lessen as other members join and contribute to AIIB's finances through their capital subscriptions. **6.21**

(2) Board rotation

Founding Members have a certain priority in the rotations for Director and Alternate Directors in the constituencies of the Board of Directors. In many MDB **6.22**

[33] AIIB Article 3-1 (b). The deadline was December 31, 2016, extended to June 30, 2025. *See* note 30 in this chapter.

[34] In the Black Sea Trade and Development Bank, Founding Members have preferences in share subscription and have a majority shareholding. BSTDB Articles 3-3 and 5. The Islamic Development Bank also has Founder Members. ISDB Article 3. In the New Development Bank, the five NDB founding members have several privileges, including: a minimum combined voting power of 55% (NDB Article 8 (c)(i)); Special Majority (requires four of the five, in NDB Article 6 (b)); appointment of a Director and Alternate (NDB Article 12 (b)); and nationality of the President and Vice Presidents (NDB Article 13 (a) and (c)).

[35] AIIB Article 28-1 prescribes the voting power of members. *See* paragraphs 9.04–9.09 on voting power.

Boards, the members represented by a Director are considered to form a Board constituency (not a legal construct but a practical one). Within each constituency, the members agree among themselves on a pattern of nationalities to hold the positions of Director, Alternate Director, and any advisors.[36] The larger shareholders often have a greater say in designating their nationals for these positions, so that assuring a voice at the Board is an advantage for smaller shareholders.

6.23 For AIIB, the rotation privileges within constituencies that are offered to Founding Members are stated as follows:

> The nomination and voting by Governors for Directors and the appointment of Alternate Directors by Directors shall respect the principle that each Founding Member shall have the privilege to designate the Director or an Alternate Director in its constituency permanently or on a rotating basis.[37]

This clause provides a priority in representation for Founding Members. The Charter itself could not dictate the nationality choice for Directors and Alternate Directors, because constituency rotations differ. Moreover, legally speaking, it is the votes of Governors that elect Directors and the decision of Directors to appoint Alternate Directors.[38] Consequently, this privilege is cast as a principle to be respected by Governors and Directors.

D. Regional and Non-Regional Members

6.24 Under the AIIB Charter, regional members are "those members listed in Part A of Schedule A and other members included in the Asia region in accordance with paragraph 2 of Article 1."[39] All other members are then classified as non-regional members.

(1) What is regional?

6.25 This classification of a member as regional or non-regional has two bases. First, for the Signatories, their listing in AIIB Schedule A as regional means that they will be considered regional members.[40] Second, future members will be included in the Asia region on the basis of the definition of "regional" in the AIIB Charter:

[36] For an illustration of country groupings, *see* Figure 8.3, showing AIIB's Board of Directors in June 2016 and in June 2025.

[37] AIIB Schedule B, paragraph 10.

[38] AIIB Article 25-1 (election of Directors) and Article 25-3 (appointment of Alternate Directors).

[39] AIIB Article 3-1 (a).

[40] For Signatories, the decisive action is listing in Schedule A. The reference to inclusion in the Asia region refers only to "other members." Russia was accepted as a regional member in the negotiations and listed as such in Schedule A, but is not listed as located in Asia and Oceania under the UN classification referenced in the Chief Negotiators' Report.

> Wherever used in this Agreement, references to "Asia" and "region" shall include the geographical regions and composition classified as Asia and Oceania by the United Nations, except as otherwise decided by the Board of Governors.[41]

As discussed earlier, this definition of Asia and region is given further detail through the Chief Negotiators' Report, which records the understandings of the Chief Negotiators for future reference in interpreting the AIIB Charter. The Chief Negotiators' Report provides:

> *Article 1, paragraph 2.* Representatives noted that the current geographical region and composition listing for Asia and Oceania by the United Nations for statistical purposes formed the basis for their consideration of "Asia" and "region". The listing can be found at http://unstats.un.org/unsd/methods/m49/m49regin.htm.[42]
>
> Representatives further noted that future decisions on regional classification, if needed, would be made by the Board of Governors under paragraph 2 of Article 1, and that decisions on new members would be made by the Board of Governors under paragraph 2 of Article 3.

This statement in the Chief Negotiators' Report provides a link to the then current listing of Asia and Oceania as classified by the UN, giving a specific set of potential regional members. In addition, should the listing change or other questions arise, the Board of Governors is empowered to make decisions on future classification. As the Chief Negotiators' Report highlights, any decisions by the Board of Governors related to the regional status of new members would be made in acceptance of membership, which requires a Special Majority vote. A listing of territories currently included in this definition is provided in Figure 6.2.

6.26 This multi-step definition of "regional" recognizes some challenges faced by other regional MDBs with geographic classifications and countries under their Charter definitions. First, there are different approaches to defining "regional." Regional membership could be based solely on geography, as in the case of Africa for AfDB.[43] Regional membership has also been based on membership in the regional international organization that hosted the charter negotiations, such as the UN's ECAFE/ESCAP in the case of AsDB and the Organization of American States (OAS) in the case of the Inter-American Development Bank (IADB).[44] In the case of the European Bank for Reconstruction and Development (EBRD), members are

[41] AIIB Article 1-2.

[42] In 2025, that link leads to https://unstats.un.org/unsd/methodology/m49/, the online version of the United Nations publication "Standard Country or Area Codes for Statistical Use" originally published as Series M, No. 49 and now commonly referred to as the M49 standard. Selecting Geographic Regions yields the 2015 list.

[43] The AfDB Charter defines the geographical areas for regional membership as the continent of Africa and African islands. AfDB Article 3-2.

[44] The IADB Charter (IADB Article II, Section 1) implies that regional countries are members of the OAS, Canada, Bahamas, and Guyana, as other potential members (members of IMF and Switzerland) are referred to as "non-regional countries."

referred to as European and non-European rather than regional, with some but not all European members defined with respect to what was then the European Community.[45] As both AfDB and IADB were entirely regional at the start, the regional distinction was grafted on later, when non-regional membership was introduced.[46]

6.27 For AIIB, Asia is subject to different geographical definitions, probably more so than for Africa. There was no host organization for the negotiations or other appropriate regional organization that would include all the PFMs. The choice of a UN classification offers a degree of international acceptance and neutrality for AIIB's diverse membership.

6.28 Second, there is the question of how detailed the Charter should be in its definition of regional. Taking a long view, a country's classification and even existence can change over time. In the AIIB case, the Charter has a general description, tied to the UN. The Chief Negotiators' Report has a more specific expression of the same concept, linked to a UN website. The UN list and weblink are more likely to change over time than the general statement in the Charter. A general statement in the Charter is less likely to require amendment if there are changes.

6.29 Third, the AIIB Charter recognizes that adjustments in the definition could be needed in the future. To that end, future decisions that touch on regional classification can be made by the Board of Governors, without resort to amendment of the AIIB Charter. Decisions on regional classification that do not involve the admission of new members can be made by the AIIB Board of Governors by a simple majority of the votes cast, whereas admission of members requires a Special Majority decision.[47] As an example of changes in circumstances and geographic scope, the EBRD Charter was amended twice to expand the scope of potential recipient member countries: first for Mongolia, effective 2006;[48] second for countries of the Southern and Eastern Mediterranean, effective 2013.[49] The EBRD

[45] While there is no specific definition of "European" in the EBRD Charter, the distinction is clarified by separate listings in Annex A of the EBRD Charter for: European Communities; Other European countries; Recipient countries; and Non-European countries.

[46] Wilson (1987) at 9, noting that AsDB was the first regional development bank to be constructed as an international partnership from the start. IADB membership was originally restricted to members of the OAS, opened up to Canada in 1972 and Switzerland and other non-regional members of IMF in 1976. Non-regional members were admitted to AfDB only in 1982. Kappagoda (1995) at 45 (notes 3 and 4). *See* notes 55 and 58 in this chapter.

[47] AIIB Article 28-2 (i) on simple majority votes.

[48] While Mongolia and later the countries of the Southern and Eastern Mediterranean were eligible for EBRD membership as non-European IMF members under EBRD Article 3-1, they would not have fallen within the Central and Eastern European scope of operations. The Mongolia amendment is in EBRD Board of Governors' Resolution No. 90, *Amendment to the Agreement Establishing the Bank in order to Admit Mongolia as a Country of Operations*, adopted January 30, 2004, entered into force October 15, 2006.

[49] EBRD Board of Governors' Resolution No. 137, *Amendment of the Agreement Establishing the Bank in order to Enable the Bank to Operate in Countries of the Southern and Eastern Mediterranean*, adopted September 30, 2011, entered into force September 12, 2013. A companion amendment allowed the use of EBRD Special Funds in recipient and potential recipient countries. EBRD Board of Governors' Resolution

definition of Southern and Eastern Mediterranean countries used both geography (countries that have a shoreline on the Mediterranean) and political economy (adding Jordan, "which is closely integrated into this region").[50] A third amendment of the EBRD Charter has enabled its expansion to operations in sub-Saharan Africa, approved in 2025.[51]

(2) Regional and non-regional distinctions

The distinction between regional and non-regional members is relevant under the AIIB Charter in several ways. As in some regional MDBs, these distinctions include combined ownership share, decision-making, representation, and scope of operations. 6.30

(a) Combined ownership share

The minimum percentage for regional shareholding in AIIB is set at 75%, with the Board of Governors authorized to vary that percentage by a Super Majority vote.[52] This percentage is based on the combined shares held by all regional members, and it will be different from the percentage of regional voting power (as total voting power includes basic votes and Founding Member votes in addition to share votes).[53] Considering that this power of the Board of Governors to vary the percentage of regional shareholding could be quite open-ended, the Chief Negotiators provided an indication of their understanding in the Chief Negotiators' Report: 6.31

> *Article 5, paragraphs 2 and 3.* While representatives recognized that the Board of Governors might need to exercise some flexibility in the future that would reduce the regional shareholding percentage in paragraphs 2 and 3 below 75%, representatives agreed that a minimum of 70% regional shareholding would be important in preserving the regional character of the Bank.

No. 138, *Amendment to the Agreement Establishing the Bank in order to Allow the Use of Special Funds in Recipient Countries and Potential Recipient Countries*, adopted September 30, 2011, entered into force August 22, 2012.

[50] EBRD Report of the Board of Directors to the Board of Governors on the Geographic Expansion of the Bank's Region of Operations to the Southern and Eastern Mediterranean, as approved by the Board of Directors at their meeting on July 26–27, 2011, Section 3.2.

[51] "EBRD shareholders take further step towards geographical expansion," EBRD Press Office, April 23, 2025 at https://www.ebrd.com/home/news-and-events/news/2025/ebrd-shareholders-take-further-step-towards-geographical-expansi.html (last visited July 14, 2025).

EBRD Board of Governors' Resolution No. 259, *Amendment to Article 1 of the Agreement Establishing the Bank to Enable a Limited and Incremental Expansion of the Geographic Scope of the Bank's Operations to Sub-Saharan Africa and Iraq*, adopted 18 May 2025, entered into force July 22, 2025.

[52] AIIB Article 5-2 and 5-3.

[53] As of June 2025, for instance, total regional shareholding was 76.1% and total regional voting power was 72.5%, while total non-regional shareholding was 23.9% and total non-regional voting power was 27.5%. *See* Figures 6.5 and 6.6.

By comparison, the minimum regional percentage is 60% in AsDB[54] and AfDB[55] and 50% in EBRD.[56] For AfDB, it is regional voting power that is protected; in AsDB and EBRD, it is regional shareholding that is legally protected. For EBRD, however, shareholding is identical to voting power, as EBRD does not have basic votes.[57] In IADB, regional voting power is protected, in a sub-divided manner: the voting power of regional developing members cannot fall below 50.005%, that of the member having the largest number of shares (the United States) cannot fall below 30%, and that of Canada cannot fall below 4%.[58]

6.32 Note that these percentages, whether by shareholding or voting power, do not necessarily relate directly to the distinction between developed and developing countries. In AsDB and AIIB, regional shareholders include developed countries such as Australia, Korea, New Zealand, and Singapore (and, for AsDB, one of its two largest shareholders, Japan). In EBRD, many "regional" European members are EU developed countries. In IADB, as noted, the total regional percentage of 84.005% is specifically divided between regional developing members (50.005%) and the United States and Canada (34%). In AfDB, however, most regional members would be considered developing countries.

(b) Decision-making

6.33 AIIB voting majorities in decisions of the Board of Governors and Board of Directors do not require separate majorities for regional and non-regional members. AsDB, which also included regional and non-regional members from its inception, does not have separate majorities either. EBRD, which included

[54] AsDB Article 5-3. When the AsDB Charter was being negotiated, both IADB and AfDB had regional membership only. There was some debate on whether AsDB should also be regional only, yet the need for non-Asian financing was an important consideration. "The more enlightened Asian officials preferred a wide spread of membership as long as developing Asia had a majority share of the ownership and a majority on the Board." Wilson (1987) at 8. This led to AsDB's 60% regional shareholding provision, which has remained unchanged.

[55] AfDB Article 5-4 requires that capital allocations result in 60% regional voting power and 40% non-regional voting power. When AfDB first admitted non-regional members, the proportion was two-thirds regional, one-third non-regional. AfDB Board of Governors' Resolution 05-79, *Concerning the Amendments of the Agreement Establishing the African Development Bank to Enable Non-African Countries to Become Members Thereof*, approved May 17, 1979, entered into force May 7, 1982, Annex, paragraph 5 (ii). This was later amended to 60:40 in 1998. AfDB Board of Governors' Resolution No. B/BG/98/04, *Amendments to the Agreement Establishing the African Development Bank, Revised Stock Allocation, Quorum and Voting Structure*, approved May 29, 1998, entered into force September 30, 1999, paragraph 1.

[56] EBRD Article 5. The minimum percentage of 50% in EBRD applies for shareholding by countries which are EU members, together with EU and EIB.

[57] EBRD Article 29-1.

[58] IADB Article VIII, Section 4 (b). At its inception, IADB did not have these limitations. When the IADB Charter was first amended in the opening to non-regional membership, the percentages were added so that the voting power of regional developing members would not fall below 53.5%, that of the member having the largest number of shares (the United States) would not fall below 34.5% and that of Canada would not fall below 4%. IADB Board of Governors' Resolution No. AG-9/76, *Amendments to the Agreement Establishing the Bank with Respect to the Creation of the Inter-Regional Capital Stock of the Bank and to Related Matters*, approved June 1, 1976. The current percentages (50.005%, 30%, and 4%) were established by amendment in 1995. IADB Board of Governors' Resolution No. AG-12/95, *Amendments to the Agreement Establishing the Inter-American Development Bank, the Regulations of the Board of Governors and the General Rules Governing Admission of Nonregional Countries to Membership in the Bank*, adopted July 12, 1995, Section 1, paragraph 8.

both from the start, has only one regional voting requirement.[59] In contrast, AfDB and IADB do differentiate some voting majorities by regional and non-regional status, principally capital increases, changes in composition of the Board of Directors, election of the President, quorum for the Board of Governors and for the Board of Directors, Charter amendment, suspension of membership, and termination and distribution of assets.[60] For IADB and later AfDB, these special majorities differentiated by regional and non-regional members were first introduced when each institution decided to admit non-regional members some years after each was founded, in part to access capital from outside the region.[61]

(c) Representation

The AIIB Charter designates Directors as representing regional and non-regional members, respectively,[62] following practice in some other MDBs.[63] Currently, there are nine Regional Directors and three Non-Regional Directors on the AIIB Board of Directors. In addition, the AIIB President must be a national of a regional member country, following the practice in AsDB and AfDB.[64] There is no prescription in the AIIB Charter on nationality for other management positions. There is a preference for staff selection on as wide a *regional* geographical basis as possible, subject to the paramount importance of securing the highest standards of efficiency and technical competence.[65] 6.34

[59] EBRD requires approval by at least two Central and Eastern European members for Charter amendments under EBRD Article 56-1.

[60] Among the majorities that require separate majorities for regional members in AfDB and IADB are: *capital increases* (not in AfDB; IADB Article II, Section 2 (e)); *changes in composition of the Board of Directors*, with a special regional majority for changes in regional rules (AfDB Article 33-1; IADB Article VIII, Section 3 (b) (ii)); *election of the President* (AfDB Article 36; IADB Article VIII, Section 5 (a)); *quorum for the Board of Governors and for the Board of Directors* (AfDB Articles 31-2 and 34-2, later amended to delete the regional majority and require 70% of total voting power; IADB Article VIII, Sections 2 (e) and 3 (f)); *suspension of membership* (AfDB Article 44, later amended to delete the regional majority and require 70% of total voting power; IADB Article IX, Section 2—depending on whether the member is regional or non-regional); *termination and distribution of assets* (AfDB Article 47-1, later amended to delete the regional majority and require 70% of total voting power; and Article 49-1 (ii), later amended to delete any qualified majority; IADB Article X, Sections 2 and 4 (a)); and *amendment* (AfDB Article 60-1; IADB Article XII(a)). There are also separate majorities required for non-regional members when it comes to changes in the rules for admission of non-regional members (AfDB Article 3-3; IADB Article II, Section 1 (b)) and to changes in composition of the Board of Directors, with a special non-regional majority for changes in non-regional rules (AfDB Article 33-1; IADB Article VIII, Section 3 (b)(ii)).

[61] *See* AfDB Board of Governors' Resolution 05-79, *Concerning the Amendments of the Agreement Establishing the African Development Bank to Enable Non-African Countries to Become Members Thereof*, approved May 17, 1979, entered into force May 7, 1982; and IADB Board of Governors' No. Resolution AG-9/76, *Amendments to the Agreement Establishing the Bank with Respect to the Creation of the Inter-Regional Capital Stock of the Bank and to Related Matters*, approved June 1, 1976.

[62] AIIB Article 25-1 and Schedule B.

[63] AfDB Article 33-1 and Annex B; AsDB Article 30-1 and Annex B; EBRD Article 26-1 and Annex A (groupings are specified European members, Central and Eastern Europe, other European and non-European) and IADB Article VIII, Section 3 (b)(ii). In EBRD, as in AIIB, Directors also represent members who assign their votes to them, as discussed in paragraphs 9.11–9.12. *See* Figure 8.4 for Regional and Non-Regional Directors on other MDB boards.

[64] AIIB Article 29-1. AfDB Article 36-1 and AsDB Article 34-1.

[65] AIIB Article 30-3. The wording is identical to AsDB Article 34-6.

(d) Scope of operations

6.35 The definitions of Asia and region are also relevant for AIIB's scope of operations.[66] AIIB's first purpose is to "foster sustainable economic development, create wealth and improve infrastructure connectivity *in Asia* by investing in infrastructure and other productive sectors" and AIIB's functions refer to development in the region.[67] AIIB is not restricted to financing investment operations in the Asia region, but its mandate under the AIIB Charter dictates that its operations contribute to economic development in Asia. From a membership perspective, this means it is not necessary to be a regional member to benefit from AIIB financing, but the scope for AIIB financing in non-regional members is constrained by these requirements.[68] In 2018, AIIB's Board of Directors adopted the Strategy on Financing Operations in Non-Member Countries, which lays out principles for non-regional investments that benefit Asia.[69] In comparison, the AsDB Charter refers to financing for developing member countries in the region, and the Charters for AfDB and IADB also focus on financing for regional members.[70]

E. Future Members

6.36 AIIB membership is open to members of IBRD or AsDB, as noted above. For those who were not Signatories, membership requires a Special Majority vote in the Board of Governors.[71] The terms and conditions of membership are determined by AIIB,[72] including the initial allocation of shares which must respect the minimum percentage for regional shareholding.[73]

6.37 The process for membership also includes several requirements, including ratification, acceptance or approval of the AIIB Charter by the new member and subscription to its allocated shares of capital stock (and payments on paid-in shares). For an AsDB member applicant that is "not sovereign or not responsible for the

[66] See paragraphs 5.08–5.11.

[67] Emphasis added. AIIB Articles 1-1 and 2.

[68] AIIB Article 11-1 includes all members in its definition of recipients, and the Chief Negotiators' Report reinforces the option for AIIB to provide financing to recipients located outside the region, consistent with its purpose and functions and taking into account its focus on economic development of the Asia region.

[69] *See* paragraph 5.10. Under that Strategy, a "project located outside the Region must benefit Asia, i.e., it must foster economic development, create wealth or improve infrastructure connectivity in Asia, and such benefits must be significant." Three principles apply for types of non-regional projects: cross-country connectivity, sustainable infrastructure, and proximity and regional integration. A ceiling on non-regional investment was also specified (at the time, 15%).

[70] AsDB Article 2 (ii). IADB's purpose is also focused on the development of regional developing member countries. IADB Article I, Section 1. AfDB's purpose is focused on the development of regional members, most of whom are developing. AfDB Article 1.

[71] AIIB Article 3-2. The required majority for admission of new members is also two-thirds of the Governors representing 75% of total voting power in AsDB (AsDB Article 3-2) and in EBRD (EBRD Article 3-2).

[72] AIIB Article 3-2.

[73] AIIB Article 5-2.

conduct of its international relations," its application for full membership in AIIB would be presented or agreed by the AIIB member responsible for its international relations.[74] This provision derives from the AsDB Charter, where it applies specifically to AsDB membership applications from Associate Members of ESCAP that are not responsible for the conduct of their international relations.[75] AIIB members that are ESCAP Associate Members as of June 2025 are Hong Kong, China and Cook Islands.[76] All IBRD members are countries, so this provision would not be relevant for IBRD members applying for AIIB membership.

The decision to admit new members and determine the conditions of their admission is a reserved power of the Board of Governors, and not delegated to the Board of Directors.[77] AIIB and other MDBs have followed a Bretton Woods precedent of retaining admission and suspension of membership among the reserved powers of the Board of Governors.[78] In the case of IMF, it has been noted that "the drafters of the Articles believed that decisions on whether or not to admit applicants . . . might be affected by political considerations, and that for this reason it would be more appropriate for the plenary and not the executive organ to take the decisions."[79] Nonetheless, the AIIB By-Laws provide that the Board of Governors will consider applications for membership that have been submitted by the Board of Directors with a recommendation for admission (along with a proposed capital share and other conditions), so that agreement in the Board of Directors would precede a decision by the Board of Governors.[80] **6.38**

[74] AIIB Article 3-3.

[75] AsDB Article 3-3 states: "In the case of associate members of the United Nations Economic Commission for Asia and the Far East which are not responsible for the conduct of their international relations, application for membership in the Bank shall be presented by the member of the Bank responsible for the international relations of the applicant and accompanied by an undertaking by such member that, until the applicant itself assumes such responsibility, the member shall be responsible for all obligations that may be incurred by the applicant by reason of admission to membership in the Bank and enjoyment of the benefits of such membership. 'Country' as used in this Agreement shall include a territory which is an associate member of the United Nations Economic Commission for Asia and the Far East." This provision is reported to have been designed with Hong Kong (then a British colony) and Brunei in mind. White (1970) at 53. Historically, AsDB members admitted under this provision include Hong Kong, China; Cook Islands; Fiji; Kiribati; Papua New Guinea; and Solomon Islands. Wilson (1987) at 278 and Kappagoda (1995) at 117–18.

[76] The Hong Kong membership resolution does not refer to this procedure. However, unlike the resolutions approving membership for other new members, the Hong Kong resolution does not require the deposit of an instrument of ratification, acceptance or approval. Rather, Hong Kong is obliged to furnish AIIB with a letter of confirmation of its acceptance of its obligations as a member. AIIB Board of Governors' Resolution No. 28, *Admission of Hong Kong, China to Membership in the Asian Infrastructure Investment Bank*, adopted March 21, 2017. Hong Kong gave effect to AIIB's privileges and immunities prior to its membership, under the International Organizations (Privileges and Immunities) (Asian Infrastructure Investment Bank) Order L.N. 52 of 2016, effective July 11, 2016.

[77] AIIB Article 23-2(i).

[78] AfDB Article 29-2; AsDB Article 28-2; EBRD Article 24-2; IADB Article VIII, Section 2 (b); IBRD Article V, Section 2 (b); and IMF Article II, Section 2.

[79] Gold (1974) at 20.

[80] AIIB By-Laws, Section 4 (a) provides: "Applications for membership in the Bank in accordance with Article 3 of the Articles of Agreement shall be considered by the Board of Governors when submitted by the Board of Directors with a recommendation that the applicant be admitted to membership along with the proposed number of shares of capital stock to be subscribed and such other conditions as, in the opinion of the Board of Directors, the Board of Governors may wish to prescribe." Practice is similar in the other MDBs.

6.39 Since 2017, AIIB's Board of Governors has approved fifty-three new membership applications, bringing the total number of approved members to 110. Under the Resolutions of the Board of Governors approving these memberships, a deadline is typically set for each prospective member to confirm its acceptance of the obligations of an AIIB member and complete the legal formalities of membership (legislative approvals may be needed under the country's legal system) and subscription of shares.[81] Those with membership applications approved that have not yet completed these formalities are referred to as prospective members. The new memberships approved since 2017 have resulted in forty-seven members and six prospective members as of September 15, 2025. (See Figure 6.4.)

As of September 15, 2025, the total number of AIIB members that completed the membership process was 104, including fifty-two regional members and fifty-two non-regional members; there are six prospective members. Figures 6.5 and 6.6 list AIIB's members in June 2025 by regional and non-regional, showing dates of membership approval and finalization, shareholding, and voting power.

6.40 Future members of IBRD and AsDB would also be eligible to apply for AIIB membership.

- For IBRD, future members are limited to countries that are IMF members. Currently, there are not many countries outside IMF and IBRD membership. For comparison, there are three states that are UN members but not IMF members;[82] countries that are not UN members may also apply for IMF (and then IBRD) membership.
- For AsDB, future members could include ESCAP Members or Associate Members that are not already AsDB members, or regional countries and non-regional developed countries that are members of the UN or its specialized agencies. There are seven current ESCAP Members and Associate Members that are not AsDB members.[83]

Countries (and for AsDB, ESCAP Associate Members) that are eligible for IBRD or AsDB membership would need to become IBRD or AsDB members first in order to meet AIIB's membership requirements.

6.41 Other MDBs and IMF have also added new members since AIIB's establishment. In AsDB, Niue became a regional member in 2019 and Israel became a non-regional member in 2024; Türkiye changed its status to regional in 2025.[84] In New Development Bank (NDB), the five founding members (Brazil, China,

[81] AIIB Board of Governors Resolutions are listed on the AIIB website under Board of Governors, including the text of the resolution.

[82] Cuba, Democratic People's Republic of Korea, and Monaco are UN members but not IMF members.

[83] The Democratic People's Republic of Korea is an ESCAP Member (and UN Member), but not a member of AsDB. ESCAP Associate Members that are not currently AsDB members are: American Samoa; French Polynesia; Guam; Macao, China; New Caledonia; and Northern Mariana Islands: http://www.unescap.org/about/member-states (last visited July 14, 2025).

[84] https://www.adb.org/who-we-are/about (last visited July 14, 2025).

AIIB APPROVAL OF NEW MEMBERS BY YEAR		
YEAR	REGIONAL	NON-REGIONAL
2017	**Afghanistan** *Armenia* **Bahrain** **Cook Islands** **Cyprus** **Fiji** **Hong Kong, China** **Samoa** **Timor-Leste** **Tonga** **Vanuatu**	**Argentina** **Belarus** **Belgium** *Bolivia* **Canada** **Chile** **Ecuador** **Ethiopia** **Greece** **Hungary** **Ireland** **Madagascar** **Peru** **Romania** **Sudan** *Venezuela*
2018	*Lebanon* **Papua New Guinea**	**Algeria** **Ghana** **Kenya** **Libya** **Morocco** **Serbia** **Togo**
2019		**Benin** **Cote d'Ivoire** **Croatia** **Djibouti** **Guinea** **Rwanda** *Senegal* **Tunisia** **Uruguay**
2020		**Liberia**
2021	**Iraq**	*Nigeria*
2022		**Mauritania**
2023	**Solomon Islands**	**El Salvador** *Tanzania*
2024	**Nauru**	

Figure 6.4 AIIB Approval of New Members by Year
Members as of September 2025 in bold; prospective members shown in italics.
Source: Figure 6.5 and AIIB Website.

India, Russia, and South Africa) were joined by Bangladesh (2021), the United Arab Emirates (2021), Egypt (2023), and Algeria (2025).[85] In IMF, Andorra (2020) and Liechtenstein (2024) became members.[86] IBRD has not added new members since 2016.[87]

[85] NDB website listing: http://www.ndb.int/about-ndb/members (last visited July 14, 2025).

[86] For IMF, *see* https://www.imf.org/external/np/sec/memdir/memdate.htm (last visited July 14, 2025). Now that Andorra and Liechtenstein are IMF members, they would be eligible to join IBRD.

[87] Nauru became an IBRD member in 2016. https://www.worldbank.org/en/about/leadership/members.

Subscriptions and Voting Power of AIIB Regional Member Countries					
	MEMBERSHIP		SUBSCRIPTIONS		VOTING POWER
Regional Member	Membership Year	Approval Year	Amount (million USD)	Percent of Total	Percent of Total
Afghanistan	2017	2017	86.6	0.0887%	0.1625%
Australia	2015	PFM	3,691.2	3.7826%	3.4358%
Azerbaijan	2016	PFM	254.1	0.2604%	0.3945%
Bahrain	2018	2017	103.6	0.1062%	0.2082%
Bangladesh	2016	PFM	660.5	0.6768%	0.7541%
Brunei Darussalam	2015	PFM	52.4	0.0537%	0.2160%
Cambodia	2016	PFM	62.3	0.0638%	0.2248%
China	2015	PFM	29,780.4	30.5175%	26.5211%
Cook Islands	2020	2017	0.5	0.0005%	0.1170%
Cyprus	2018	2017	20.0	0.0205%	0.1342%
Fiji	2017	2017	12.5	0.0128%	0.1276%
Georgia	2015	PFM	53.9	0.0552%	0.2173%
Hong Kong, China	2017	2017	765.1	0.7840%	0.7935%
India	2016	PFM	8,367.3	8.5744%	7.5735%
Indonesia	2016	PFM	3,360.7	3.4439%	3.1434%
Iran	2017	PFM	1,580.8	1.6199%	1.0089%
Iraq	2022	2021	25.0	0.0256%	0.1387%
Israel	2016	PFM	749.9	0.7685%	0.8332%
Jordan	2015	PFM	119.2	0.1222%	0.2751%
Kazakhstan	2016	PFM	729.3	0.7473%	0.8150%
Korea	2015	PFM	3,738.7	3.8312%	3.4779%
Kuwait	2025	PFM	536.0	0.5493%	0.1696%
Kyrgyz Republic	2016	PFM	26.8	0.0275%	0.1933%
Lao PDR	2016	PFM	43.0	0.0441%	0.2077%
Malaysia	2017	PFM	109.5	0.1122%	0.2665%
Maldives	2016	PFM	7.2	0.0074%	0.1760%
Mongolia	2015	PFM	41.1	0.0421%	0.2060%
Myanmar	2015	PFM	264.5	0.2710%	0.3101%
Nauru	2025	2024	0.5	0.0005%	0.1170%
Nepal	2016	PFM	80.9	0.0829%	0.2412%
New Zealand	2015	PFM	461.5	0.4729%	0.5780%
Oman	2016	PFM	259.2	0.2656%	0.3990%
Pakistan	2015	PFM	1,034.1	1.0597%	1.0847%
Papua New Guinea	2024	2018	5.0	0.0051%	0.1210%
Philippines	2016	PFM	979.1	1.0033%	1.0360%
Qatar	2016	PFM	604.4	0.6194%	0.7044%

Subscriptions and Voting Power of AIIB Regional Member Countries					
	MEMBERSHIP		SUBSCRIPTIONS		VOTING POWER
Regional Member	Membership Year	Approval Year	Amount (million USD)	Percent of Total	Percent of Total
Russia	2015	PFM	6,536.2	6.6980%	5.9533%
Samoa	2018	2017	2.1	0.0022%	0.1184%
Saudi Arabia	2016	PFM	2,544.6	2.6076%	2.4212%
Singapore	2015	PFM	250.0	0.2562%	0.3908%
Solomon Islands	2025	2023	0.5	0.0005%	0.1170%
Sri Lanka	2016	PFM	269.0	0.2757%	0.4077%
Tajikistan	2016	PFM	30.9	0.0317%	0.1970%
Thailand	2016	PFM	1,427.5	1.4628%	1.4328%
Timor-Leste	2017	2017	16.0	0.0164%	0.1307%
Tonga	2021	2017	1.2	0.0012%	0.1176%
Türkiye	2016	PFM	2,609.9	2.6745%	2.4790%
UAE	2016	PFM	1,185.7	1.2150%	1.2188%
Uzbekistan	2016	PFM	219.8	0.2252%	0.3641%
Vanuatu	2018	2017	0.5	0.0005%	0.1170%
Viet Nam	2016	PFM	663.3	0.6797%	0.7566%
TOTAL Regional			74,424.0	76.2660%	72.6046%

Figure 6.5 Subscriptions and Voting Power of AIIB Regional Member Countries

PFM = Prospective Founding Member.

The listing does not include Prospective Members as of June 2025: Armenia (2017) and Lebanon (2018). Armenia became a member on September 4, 2025.

Source: AIIB website List of Members (July 7, 2025) and Figure 7.2. Armenia became a member on September 4, 2025.

EBRD has not only added members but also increased its scope of operations, launching investments in sub-Saharan Africa. China joined EBRD in 2016, about the same time as AIIB opened its doors. Since then, new EBRD members include: Lebanon in 2017; India in 2018; Libya and San Marino in 2019; Algeria and United Arab Emirates in 2021; Benin, Cote d'Ivoire and Iraq in 2024; and Nigeria in 2025. As of June 2025, memberships for Ghana, Kenya, and Senegal were in progress; in July 2025, Kenya and Senegal became EBRD members, bringing the total number of shareholders to seventy-nine.[88] 6.42

For European Investment Bank (EIB), one member withdrew in this period. Because EIB membership is tied to membership in the European Union (EU), the 6.43

[88] "EBRD to launch investments in sub-Saharan Africa," EBRD Press Release, May 15, 2025. This press release also states that Iraq is becoming a country of operation, and that Benin, Cote d'Ivoire, and Nigeria are expected to do so also.

"Kenya and Senegal become EBRD shareholders," EBRD Press Release, July 23, 2025.

Subscriptions and Voting Power of AIIB Non-Regional Member Countries

	MEMBERSHIP		SUBSCRIPTIONS		VOTING POWER
Non-Regional Member	Membership Year	Approval Year	Amount (million USD)	Percent of Total	Percent of Total
Algeria	2019	2018	5.0	0.0051%	0.1210%
Argentina	2021	2017	5.0	0.0051%	0.1210%
Austria	2015	PFM	500.8	0.5132%	0.6128%
Belarus	2019	2017	64.1	0.0657%	0.1733%
Belgium	2019	2017	284.6	0.2916%	0.3684%
Benin	2020	2019	5.0	0.0051%	0.1210%
Brazil	2020	PFM	5.0	0.0051%	0.1741%
Canada	2018	2017	995.4	1.0200%	0.8212%
Chile	2021	2017	10.0	0.0102%	0.1236%
Côte d'Ivoire	2020	2019	5.0	0.0051%	0.1202%
Croatia	2021	2019	5.0	0.0051%	0.1210%
Denmark	2016	PFM	369.5	0.3786%	0.4966%
Djibouti	2024	2019	0.5	0.0005%	0.1170%
Ecuador	2019	2017	5.0	0.0051%	0.1210%
Egypt	2016	PFM	650.5	0.6666%	0.7452%
El Salvador	2025	2023	5.0	0.0051%	0.1210%
Ethiopia	2017	2017	45.8	0.0469%	0.1571%
Finland	2016	PFM	310.3	0.3180%	0.4442%
France	2016	PFM	3,375.6	3.4591%	3.1566%
Germany	2015	PFM	4,484.2	4.5952%	4.1375%
Ghana	2020	2018	5.0	0.0051%	0.1210%
Greece	2019	2017	10.0	0.0102%	0.1254%
Guinea	2019	2019	5.0	0.0051%	0.1183%
Hungary	2017	2017	100.0	0.1025%	0.2050%
Iceland	2016	PFM	17.6	0.0180%	0.1852%
Ireland	2017	2017	131.3	0.1345%	0.2327%
Italy	2016	PFM	2,571.8	2.6355%	2.4453%
Kenya	2024	2018	5.0	0.0051%	0.1210%
Liberia	2021	2020	5.0	0.0051%	0.1192%
Libya	2023	2018	52.6	0.0539%	0.1631%
Luxembourg	2015	PFM	69.7	0.0714%	0.2313%
Madagascar	2018	2017	5.0	0.0051%	0.1210%
Malta	2016	PFM	13.6	0.0139%	0.1817%
Mauritania	2025	2022	5.0	0.0051%	0.1210%
Morocco	2022	2018	5.0	0.0051%	0.1210%
Netherlands	2015	PFM	1,031.3	1.0568%	1.0822%

Subscriptions and Voting Power of AIIB Non-Regional Member Countries					
	MEMBERSHIP		SUBSCRIPTIONS		VOTING POWER
Non-Regional Member	Membership Year	Approval Year	Amount (million USD)	Percent of Total	Percent of Total
Norway	2015	PFM	550.6	0.5642%	0.6568%
Peru	2022	2017	154.6	0.1584%	0.2533%
Poland	2016	PFM	831.8	0.8524%	0.9057%
Portugal	2017	PFM	65.0	0.0666%	0.2271%
Romania	2018	2017	153.0	0.1568%	0.2519%
Rwanda	2020	2019	5.0	0.0051%	0.1210%
Serbia	2019	2018	5.0	0.0051%	0.1210%
South Africa	2023	PFM	5.0	0.0051%	0.1741%
Spain	2017	PFM	1,761.5	1.8051%	1.7283%
Sudan	2018	2017	59.0	0.0605%	0.1315%
Sweden	2016	PFM	630.0	0.6456%	0.7271%
Switzerland	2016	PFM	706.4	0.7239%	0.7947%
Togo	2023	2018	5.0	0.0051%	0.1210%
Tunisia	2022	2019	5.0	0.0051%	0.1210%
United Kingdom	2015	PFM	3,054.7	3.1303%	2.8726%
Uruguay	2020	2019	5.0	0.0051%	0.1210%
TOTAL Non-Regional			23,160.8	23.7340%	27.3954%

Figure 6.6 Subscriptions and Voting Power of AIIB Non-Regional Member Countries

PFM = Prospective Founding Member.

The listing does not include Prospective Members as of June 2025: Bolivia (2017), Nigeria (2021), Senegal (2019), Tanzania (2023), Venezuela (2017).

Source: AIIB website List of Members (July 7, 2025) and Figure 7.2.

withdrawal of the United Kingdom from the EU led to its withdrawal from EIB in 2020.[89]

89 "EIB President regrets Brexit and welcomes EU 27 united support for EIB Group," EIB Press Release, January 31, 2020. https://www.eib.org/en/press/news/eib-president-regrets-brexit-welcomes-eu27-united-support-for-eib-group. According to this Press Release, the UK's withdrawal from the European Union automatically ended its membership of the EIB and its 16.11% subscribed capital in the bank. Specific arrangements were as follows:

> "The UK's share of the EIB's paid-in capital prior to Brexit represents EUR 3.5 billion, alongside EUR 35.7 billion of callable capital. The UK's callable capital disappears on Brexit day and is replaced by the UK's liability on callable capital.
>
> On 1 March 2020 two member states, Romania and Poland, will contribute additional capital, providing the EIB with a higher capital base than before Brexit.
>
> The UK will remain liable for the EIB's pre-Brexit operations. This liability will be reduced as the EIB's pre-Brexit exposure declines.
>
> The EIB will reimburse the UK's EUR 3.5 billion paid-in share over 12 annual instalments following Brexit."

F. Withdrawal and Suspension of Membership

6.44 The AIIB Charter includes a chapter on withdrawal and suspension of membership. Based closely on similar provisions in other MDBs, this chapter provides for withdrawal by a member and settlement of accounts on its departure, and for the suspension of a member that fails to fulfill any of its obligations to AIIB. Withdrawal requires notice from the member, and can take effect after six months.[90] Suspension requires a Super Majority vote by the Board of Governors, and takes effect after one year, unless the Board of Governors decides to restore membership, also by Super Majority vote.[91]

[90] AIIB Articles 37 and 39.
[91] AIIB Article 38.

7
CAPITAL AND FINANCE

Capital is the foundation for the financial resources that allow the Asian Infrastructure Investment Bank (AIIB) to carry out its activities and fund its investment operations. Capital is also a key driver in AIIB's governance and financial management. 7.01

This chapter describes AIIB's capital structure, including authorized capital (paid-in and callable capital shares), capital increases, and allocation of capital, followed by discussion of AIIB's financial resources and management and other vehicles. We begin with a short introduction to multilateral development bank (MDB) capital structure. 7.02

Capital structure is one of the defining aspects of MDBs that distinguishes them from many other membership-based international organizations. To simplify, MDBs since Bretton Woods have been built on a corporate structure where members subscribe to shares of capital. Each member's shareholding is divided into paid-in and callable capital, so that members actually pay in a small percentage of the cost of their capital subscriptions (paid-in capital), with a binding commitment by each member to pay in the remainder if and when called upon by the MDB (callable capital).[1] Calls would be made by the MDB if funds were needed to meet the MDB's financial obligations. To date, there has never been a call on callable capital for the MDBs surveyed in this book.[2] 7.03

To raise the funds needed for its investment operations,[3] however, the MDB would then borrow in capital markets, backed by these callable capital commitments of its members. This reliance on callable capital has a number of implications: 7.04

- While the MDB has access to funds to meet its purposes, the upfront cost for members to join and subscribe is reduced.[4]

[1] Most but not all MDBs have been based on this structure. IFC capital, for example, is all paid-in. IFC Article II, Sections 2 and 3. Most concessional arms of the MDBs are not based on this model, but rather on paid-in subscriptions and periodic contributions.

[2] Humphrey (2024) at 6: "No major MDB has ever come remotely close to triggering a capital call."

[3] In this book, the term "investment operations" has been used to refer to AIIB's development financing of projects through its financing products, such as loans, guarantees, and equity investment. In MDB financial work, "investment operations" often means the investment of MDB funds pending use for development financing or administrative expenses.

[4] The efforts of war-torn European countries (including the UK) to reduce the percentage and timing of paid-in capital in the IBRD Charter discussions is an early case in point. Oliver (1996) at 169 and 176. Subscribing members in other MDBs since have had the same incentives to reduce the actual payment

- This upfront cost is leveraged by the MDB to generate substantial amounts of financing for investment operations.[5]
- The MDB is somewhat less dependent on member government approvals for its ongoing financing,[6] relying instead on worldwide markets; the MDB will need member support when it needs to expand its capital base.
- The strength of the callable capital commitments of various member governments influences the MDB's market rating; in turn, better ratings for the MDB would be reflected in better financing terms for recipients of the MDB's financing.
- The reliance on market perceptions, coupled with members' desires to avoid calls on capital and future capital increases, heightens the importance of sound financial management for the MDB.

This overall pattern has been considered a hallmark of the success of the MDB structure.[7] This combination was innovative in its time, as summarized in Figure 7.1 on the origins of MDB callable capital.

7.05 Capital plays another important role, in the governance of many MDBs. Voting power is not equal among members[8] but rather weighted, principally tied to size of shareholding. (Weighted voting of this sort is common to the corporate structures on which MDBs are based.) As a result, larger shareholders tend to have more say in the institutions, and qualified majority voting requirements for important decisions amplify the impact of capital-based voting power. Which members subscribe to how many shares is a function of capital allocation rules, and often capital

amounts required to subscribe, usually funds that must be approved by national legislatures with budget implications.

[5] Humphrey (2020) notes at 12 that with IBRD's share capital of US$18 billion paid in through 2020, "IBRD extended over $750 billion in loans . . . income of IBRD loan repayments generated nearly $30 billion in retained earnings, $23 billion in donated grants to the poorest countries, and covered the costs of creating the most comprehensive body of global development data and expertise in the existence. And the original share capital has not been used up—it is still on the books of the World Bank and will support operations for years to come."

[6] For those legacy MDBs requiring consent for borrowing in a member's market or currency, access to borrowing can still be restricted by a member, as noted in paragraph 7.41 in this chapter.

[7] Humphrey (2016) at 92 summarizes the view: "Perhaps the one trait that goes farthest in explaining the success of this organizational model [family of MDBs] is that they are mainly self-financing: MDBs borrow most of their money on international capital markets, and then on-lend these resources to recipient countries for development projects. Thus, regular operations imply no direct budgetary cost to shareholder governments, apart from relatively minimal capitalization costs, and MDBs (arguably) generate the public good of development promotion, as well as potential geo-political benefits to powerful shareholders . . . In light of the limited generosity of shareholder governments, accessing private financial markets to raise resources is the only realistic option if an MDB is to fulfill its development mission. Relying on international capital markets rather than fiscal allocations gave MDBs a degree of financial security and independence from the fickle generosity of shareholder countries."

[8] Equal shareholding at NDB by its five founding members (Brazil, China, India, Russia, and South Africa) is a notable exception. NDB Charter, Attachment 1. As NDB has admitted additional members in recent years, the shares of the five founders remain equal (18.98% each) while the shareholding of new members varies (Bangladesh, 1.79%; Egypt, 2.27%; United Arab Emirates, 1.06%). https://www.ndb.int/about-ndb/shareholding/ (last visited July 14, 2025). Algeria became an NDB member in May 2025.

When callable capital was introduced as a backstop for development financing by IBRD, it was untested as a mechanism. The initial expectation for IBRD was that callable capital would function as surety for IBRD guarantees of private investors' loans to borrowing countries. As explained by the US Treasury Department on the eve of IBRD Charter negotiations:

> Because the Bank's principal function is to encourage international investment by private investors, the surety aspect of the Bank's capital will be of particular importance. The Bank will encourage international investment primarily by acting as guarantor on approved loans made by private investors. The effectiveness of the Bank's guarantee must depend on the confidence of the investing public in the capacity of the Bank to meet its liabilities.[1]

In fact, direct loans funded by IBRD borrowing in capital markets became the mainstay of IBRD operations, rather than IBRD guarantees. Issuance of securities for sale to private investors also brought in private capital needed for international investment.

> The Bank must also be in a position to borrow some private funds for the loans it makes or in which it participates with the public. In order to perform these functions satisfactorily, the institution must have large resources relative to its liabilities and it must be able at all times to meet its obligations as a guarantor and issuer of securities. Although a part of the subscribed capital of the Bank will be needed for current operations, a substantial portion will be required exclusively as a reserve that provides additional protection to private investors.[2]

Since IBRD's establishment, callable capital has indeed served as a protection for IBRD bondholders.

How did this untested mechanism find its way into the IBRD Charter? Two similar corporate-style structures in international financial institutions are described in Chapter 2.

- In 1930, the Bank for International Settlements (BIS) was established to handle German reparation payments after World War I and as a forum for central bank cooperation. BIS can be seen as the first international financial organization. BIS has a corporate structure, based on the form of a joint-stock company inspired by its central bank founders. For BIS, paid-up capital was set at 25% and the remainder subject to call from shareholders at the discretion of the Board, with three months' notice. BIS, however, does not include loans for reconstruction or development among its functions, or public issuance of securities among its powers.[3] BIS had private shareholders at its inception.
- In 1940, the Inter-American Bank was proposed as a regional financial institution, under a convention signed by the United States and eight Latin American countries. US participation was never authorized by the US Congress, and the institution never came into existence. The Inter-American Bank would also have had a corporate structure, with paid-up capital at 50% and the remainder subject to call with three months' notice. This Bank would have been authorized to make loans, take deposits, and issue bonds, among its other purposes and powers.[4] This aborted Inter-American Bank proposal influenced the US Treasury team leading preparations for the IBRD.

[1] US Department of Treasury (1944), Question 2 at 6.

[2] Id., Question 8 at 13.

[3] BIS Articles 7 and 21. *See* Chapter 2, Section B in this volume.

[4] Signatories were Bolivia, Brazil, Colombia, Dominican Republic, Ecuador, Mexico, Nicaragua and Paraguay, and the United States. US Department of State Bulletin (1940) at 516 (Inter-American Bank By-Laws, Section 2A and 5A). *See* Chapter 2, Section C in this volume.

Figure 7.1 Origins of MDB Callable Capital

is allocated on the strength of each member's economy among the economies of members as a whole. This focus on economic strength is derived, in part, from the reliance on members' callable capital commitments, and market assessment of the value of these commitments from major shareholders. Since the allocation of the capital to members determines their relative control through voting power, the standard for allocation is important—and so are the rules for capital increases and new members and the protections for current shareholders. At the same time, a member's willingness and ability to pay for its capital subscription, and geopolitical concerns about its standing vis-à-vis other members, all become critical considerations in capital allocation.

A. Capital Structure

(1) Authorized capital

7.06 The original authorized capital stock of AIIB was one hundred billion US dollars (US$100,000,000,000).[9] The amount had been mentioned in the public statements about AIIB before and during the negotiations on AIIB's Charter, and definitively agreed in the final text at Singapore.[10] Schedule A of the AIIB Charter lists the allocation of the initial number of shares available for subscription by the Signatories,[11] with a small number of unallocated shares.[12] The Chief Negotiators' Report indicates the intention for these unallocated shares to be taken up by new regional and non-regional members.[13] Shares have been allocated to fifty-three new members since 2017.[14] By May 2025, AIIB's capital was 99% subscribed, representing the subscriptions of 100 members.[15]

7.07 The unit of account for AIIB is the US dollar, defined as the official currency of payment of the United States of America.[16] It is noteworthy that the US dollar was chosen to denominate AIIB's capital, as the United States was not a participant in the preparatory stage or the Chief Negotiators' Meetings. The New Development Bank (NDB) also uses the US dollar as its unit of account, without US participation or membership.[17]

7.08 Several other MDBs also have a US dollar-based unit of account, often originally defined by reference to the gold value of the US dollar at the time the Charter was agreed. Thus, the International Bank for Reconstruction and Development (IBRD) Charter refers to the 1944 gold dollar. The 1959 gold dollar in the Inter-American Development Bank (IADB) Charter and the 1966 gold dollar in the Asian Development Bank (AsDB) Charter had the same gold value as the 1944 gold dollar;

[9] AIIB Article 4-1. The NDB also has an initial authorized capital of US$100 billion, with an initial subscribed capital of US$50 billion. NDB Article 7 (a).

[10] China's Finance Minister mentioned US$50 billion registered capital as a preliminary consideration, noting that the final amount would depend on discussions and PFM views. "[Lou Jiwei responds to reporters' questions on AIIB preparations] 楼继伟就筹建 亚洲基础设施投资银行答记者问," Ministry of Finance of the People's Republic of China Press Release, March 7, 2014 (on file with author).

[11] AIIB Article 5-1.

[12] Of the total 1,000,000 shares of AIIB authorized capital stock, Schedule A lists some 16,150 shares as unallocated for regional members and 2,336 shares as unallocated for non-regional members.

[13] The Chief Negotiators' Report states: "Representatives noted that, in Schedule A, unallocated shares had been shown for regional members (Part A) and non-regional members (Part B), respectively, in anticipation of additional members joining in each category."

[14] Additional allocations have been made for the new members approved since 2017. The total allocations of shares for these new members, listed in Table 7.2, is 36,222 shares (US$3.6222 billion). Paragraph 7.36 discusses the share allocations for new members.

[15] AIIB Investor Presentation, "Investing with Impact, AIIB's Sustainable Development Bonds," May 2025, https://www.aiib.org/en/treasury/_common/_download/AIIB-Investor-Presentation.pdf (last visited July 14, 2025), at 7. By September 2025, 104 members had subscribed to AIIB's capital. As of December 31, 2024, paid-in capital was US$19.4 billion.

[16] AIIB Article 4-1 and 4-4.

[17] The NDB Charter also defines the dollar as the official currency of payment of the United States of America. NDB Article 7 (a). For reference, NDB members at the time were Brazil, China, India, Russia, and South Africa.

this same gold value was the unit of account in the 1963 African Development Bank (AfDB) Charter and the 1957 European Investment Bank (EIB) Charter.[18] In these examples, the US dollar was essentially the unit of account, even where the United States was not a participant in the negotiations (AfDB and EIB). After the introduction of the Special Drawing Right (SDR) by the International Monetary Fund (IMF) and the demise of the gold standard and fixed exchange rates, each of these institutions had to take steps to interpret or amend its charter to reflect this changed circumstance.[19] Another example of change in the unit of account over time in an MDB charter is the European Bank for Reconstruction and Development (EBRD), where capital was originally denominated in terms of European Currency Units (ECUs), now replaced by euros.[20]

(2) Share structure

In addition to the overall amount of the AIIB's capital, the AIIB Charter specifies the value of the shares. The value of each share is US$100,000, so that AIIB has one million (1,000,000) shares of authorized capital stock.[21] Both IBRD and NDB set the value of each share of capital stock as US$100,000,[22] while AfDB, AsDB, EBRD, and IADB used 10,000 units.[23] Using 10,000 units for share value would have given AIIB ten million shares, which could have been somewhat unwieldy in administration. **7.09**

[18] IBRD Article II, Section 2 (a) and IADB Article II, Section 2 (a); AsDB Article 4-1; and AfDB Article 5-1 (now amended to refer to the SDR as the unit of account instead of 0.88867088 grammes of fine gold). The EIB's original unit of account was set at the same value in fine gold. Treaty Establishing the European Economic Community, Protocol on the Statute of the European Investment Bank (Rome, March 25, 1957) at Article 4-1.

[19] *See* Shihata (2000) at 11–12 and note 37. In AfDB, this change was reflected in an amendment to AfDB Article 5-1 (b) in 2001. AfDB Board of Governors' Resolution B/BG/2001/08, *Amendments to the Agreement Establishing the African Development Bank*, adopted May 29, 2001, entered into force July 5, 2002, paragraph 2. For IBRD, the 2024 Information Statement describes the situation: "*Valuation of Capital Stock*: In the Articles of Agreement, the capital stock of IBRD is expressed in terms of 'U.S. dollars of the weight and fineness in effect on July 1, 1944' ('1944 dollars'). Following the abolition of gold as a common denominator of the monetary system and the repeal of the provision of the U.S. law defining the par value of the U.S. dollar in terms of gold, the pre-existing basis for translating 1944 dollars into current dollars or into any other currency was eliminated. The Executive Directors of IBRD have decided, until such time as the relevant provisions of the Articles of Agreement are amended, that the words 'U.S. dollars of the weight and fineness in effect on July 1, 1944' in Article II, Section 2 (a) of the Articles of Agreement of IBRD are interpreted to mean the Special Drawing Right (SDR) introduced by the International Monetary Fund, as valued in terms of U.S. dollars immediately before the introduction of the basket method of valuing the SDR on July 1, 1974, such value being $1.20635 for one SDR ('1974 SDR')." IBRD (2024) at 107–8.

[20] EBRD Article 4-1. The European Currency Unit (ECU) was replaced with the Euro (€) from January 1, 1999.

[21] AIIB Article 4-1.

[22] IBRD Article II, Section 2 (a) (initial capital of 100,000 shares with par value of US$100,000 each); NDB Article 7 (b) (initial capital of 1,000,000 shares with par value of US$100,000 each).

[23] AfDB Article 5-1 (initial capital of 25,000 shares with par value of 10,000 units of account, now specified as SDR); AsDB Article 4 (original capital of 100,000 shares with par value of US$10,000 each); EBRD Article 4-1 (initial capital of 1,000,000 shares with par value of 10,000 ECU each) and IADB Article II, Section 2 (a) (initial capital of 85,000 shares with par value of US$10,000 each).

7.10 AIIB's original authorized capital of US$100 billion is composed of US$20 billion in paid-in shares (20%, equal to 200,000 shares) and US$80 billion in callable shares (80%, equal to 800,000 shares).[24] Members are obliged to subscribe to shares in this same proportion of 2:8.[25] The initial capital structure of other MDBs also provided for a significant percentage of paid-in capital, though the current proportion of paid-in capital is significantly less. At IBRD, initial capital was 20% paid-in; currently the percentage is slightly above 6%.[26] For IADB, the percentage was 47% originally and is currently 3.5%; AfDB and AsDB capital was 50% paid-in initially and is now around 7% for AfDB and 5% for AsDB.[27] EBRD capital was 30% paid-in at the start and is currently around 26%; EIB capital was initially 25% paid-in and is currently around 9%.[28] For NDB, the percentage of initial paid-in capital is also set at 20%.[29]

7.11 AIIB's two-class share structure (paid-in and callable) is in line with the share structure at AfDB, AsDB, EBRD, and IADB. The paid-in to callable ratio must be reflected in a member's subscription to a whole number of paid-in shares and callable shares; thus, rounding is needed to avoid fractional shares. In these MDBs, the percentage of paid-in shares has been reduced over time, as noted in paragraph 7.10; the mechanism to reduce this percentage has been decisions by the Board of Governors specifying a higher proportion of callable shares in later capital increases. For AIIB, the Board of Governors could similarly change the ratio of paid-in and callable capital in future increases, as it is explicitly authorized to decide on the proportion of paid-in shares in each capital increase.[30]

7.12 IBRD is slightly different legally, because IBRD has only one type of share, and the IBRD Charter provides for a portion of each share to be paid-in and the remainder to be callable.[31] This leads to two differences from the MDBs previously described. First, there is no need for rounding to avoid fractional shares. Second, the ratio of paid-in to callable has been adjusted over time through decisions by the IBRD Board of Governors to reduce the percentage to be paid-in on each share, effectively increasing the percentage that is subject to call.[32] Though the legal and financial

[24] AIIB Article 4-2.

[25] AIIB Article 5-1.

[26] IBRD Article II, Section 7 and IBRD (2024), at 3 states: "As of June 30, 2024, IBRD's shareholders have subscribed to $323.1 billion of capital, $22.5 billion of which has been paid in [6.9%] and the remainder of which is callable."

[27] AfDB Article 6-1; AsDB Article 4-2; and IADB Article II, Section 2 (b). *See* AfDB Information Statement, July 12, 2024, at 2; AsDB Information Statement, April 24, 2025, at 3; and IADB Information Statement, February 26, 2025, at 131.

[28] EBRD Article 5-1 and EBRD's Investor Presentation June 2025 (Investment of Choice) at 15; EIB Article 5-1 ("The subscribed capital shall be paid in by Member States to the extent of 8.919255272% on average of the amounts laid down in Article 4(1)"); and EIB 2016 Financial Report at Note H.

[29] NDB Article 7 (c).

[30] AIIB Article 4-3.

[31] For IBRD, the 20% portion that corresponds to paid-in shares was divided into a 2% portion payable in gold or US dollars, and an 18% portion payable on call in the currency of the member. IBRD Article II, Section 7.

[32] The IBRD Charter specifies 20% to be paid in for each share, and the IBRD Board of Governors has provided in subsequent capital increases for a smaller percentage of each share to be paid in, with the remaining

mechanisms for IBRD are somewhat more intricate than the straightforward authorization of paid-in and callable shares in a transparent ratio, the same result has effectively been achieved over time.

(3) Paid-in shares

The AIIB Charter regulates payment by Signatories on the paid-in shares of their initial subscriptions, providing generally for payment in five installments of 20% each, in US dollars or other convertible currency.[33] The first installment is due no later than the date the Signatory deposits its instrument of ratification, acceptance or approval required for membership.[34] The remaining installments became due on the second, third, fourth, and fifth anniversaries of the entry into force of the AIIB Charter on December 25, 2015—namely, December 25 in 2016, 2017, 2018, and 2019.[35] This payment schedule mirrors the schedules for payment of initial capital in the AsDB and EBRD Charters.[36] 7.13

There is no bar on payment of installments before the due date. Late payments would result in suspension of voting and other rights in respect of the paid-in and associated callable shares until full payment is received by AIIB.[37] This incentive for timely payment is modeled on a similar provision in the EBRD Charter, and also reflects practice in some other MDB capital increases.[38] For a start-up institution 7.14

paid-in percentage (up to the 20% stipulated in the IBRD Charter) to be treated in the same manner as callable. IBRD has also issued fully callable shares (0% paid-in at the time of subscription). IBRD's Information Statement describes these additional callable portions as follows: "As of June 30, 2024, the total uncalled portion of subscriptions was $300,620 million. The amount may be called only when required to meet IBRD's obligations for funds borrowed or loans guaranteed and is, thus, not available for use by IBRD in making loans. Of this amount, $42,162 million was restricted pursuant to resolutions of the Governors (though such conditions are not required by IBRD's Articles). While these resolutions are not legally binding on future Governors, they do record an understanding among members that this amount will not be called for use by IBRD in its lending activities or for administrative purposes." IBRD (2024) at 42. Although the legal rules for this additional callable capital created by resolutions of the IBRD Board of Governors are not identical to the obligations under IBRD Article II, Section 5, IBRD and its members have treated them as substantially the same.

[33] AIIB Article 6-1 and 6-2.

[34] Under AIIB Article 6-1, Signatories that deposited their instruments of ratification, accession or approval more than thirty days before the Charter entered into force had until thirty days after entry into force to pay the first installment due on paid-in shares. The AIIB Charter entered into force on December 25, 2015, so that deadline was January 24, 2016. Since that date, each remaining Signatory's payment of the first installment on its paid-in shares has been due on or before the date of deposit of the instrument of ratification, accession or approval.

[35] For the memberships approved since 2017 (utilizing shares of the original authorized capital), payment on paid-in shares has also been divided into five installments, and payable over four years. *See, e.g.*, the most recent Resolution, AIIB Board of Governors' Resolution No. 134, *Admission of the Republic of Nauru to Membership in the Asian Infrastructure Investment Bank*, adopted September 26, 2024.

[36] AsDB Article 6-1 and EBRD Article 6-1 (five installments of 20% each). Others also provided for payment over time, as in AfDB Article 7-1 (six installments of 5%, 35%, 15%, 15%, 15%, and 15%) and IADB Article II, Section 4 (a) (three installments of 20%, 40%, and 40%).

[37] AIIB Articles 6-2 and 28-1.

[38] EBRD Article 29-1; BSTDB Article 28-1. Suspension of rights in the 2010 IBRD General Capital Increase applies when timely payments are not made for the encashment of notes. IBRD Board of Governors' Resolution No. 613, *2010 General Capital Increase*, adopted March 16, 2011, paragraph 4. Another example

such as AIIB, timely payment of paid-in capital is of particular value, considering that the flow of loan repayments to AIIB from its investment operations will not add to its resources for some time to come.

(4) National currency subscription payments

7.15 The general rule, noted previously, is that payments on paid-in shares of AIIB's initial capital are required to be made entirely in US dollars or other convertible currency. In many of AIIB's predecessors, a portion of paid-in capital is paid in the currency of a member (national currency), dating back to the very different currency situation when the IBRD Charter was negotiated in 1944, where many countries anticipated a shortage of foreign exchange.[39] Payment in national currency is likely to be more advantageous for the members, especially developing countries, as it does not drain foreign currency resources.

7.16 National currency payments of non-convertible currencies may be less advantageous for an MDB in its financial operations. Other MDBs whose subscription payments are made in part in national currencies, often non-convertible, have needed to maintain complicated arrangements to use and manage these non-convertible national currencies.[40] Additional payments may be required in the future from the member or the MDB to maintain the value of such subscriptions against the MDB's unit of account as the national currency fluctuates. Payments may be required from the member in the event of currency depreciation, to protect the MDB against a reduction in the value of its capital; payments may be required from the MDB in the event of currency appreciation, to maintain fairness to the member. Recent capital increases at some MDBs have reflected a trend away from national currency payments, for these and other reasons.[41]

7.17 Balancing these concerns for AIIB members and for AIIB, only less developed countries among the AIIB Signatories were offered an option for national currency

of proportionate reduction in voting rights for delays in payment can be found in AfDB. AfDB Board of Governors' Resolution B/BG/2010/08, *Authorizing the Sixth General Capital Increase*, adopted May 27, 2010, sub-paragraph 6-4. In EIB, the granting of loans and guarantees to a Member State or its nationals may be suspended by the Board of Governors if the Member State fails to meet its obligations of membership, including the obligation to pay its share of subscribed capital. That decision requires a qualified majority (eighteen of twenty-seven members, with 68% of capital). EIB Article 24.

[39] IBRD Article II, Section 7. For initial capital provisions in other MDBs, *see* AsDB Article 6-2 (50% in gold or convertible currency, 50% in the member's currency), and IADB Article II, Section 4 (a)(i) (50% in gold or dollars, 50% in the member's currency). For AfDB, initial subscriptions were entirely payable in convertible currency (AfDB Article 7-2) and for EBRD, initial subscriptions were payable in ECU, US dollars or Japanese yen (EBRD Article 6-3).

[40] *See* IBRD (2024) at 108 (Note A—Summary of Significant Accounting and Related Policies).

[41] *See* IBRD Board of Governors' Resolution No. 613, *2010 General Capital Increase*, adopted March 16, 2011, paragraph 3(c). IADB's Ninth General Capital Increase was payable entirely in US dollars. IADB Board of Governors' Resolution No. AG-1/12, *Increase of US$70 billion in the Authorized Ordinary Capital Stock and Subscriptions Thereto*, adopted January 18, 2012, paragraph 2 (c)(iii).

subscription payments. There were two alternatives to the general rules for paid-in capital installments included in the AIIB Charter:[42]

- Alternative A allowed a less developed country to pay in ten annual installments (instead of five installments) of 10% each (instead of 20% each), entirely in US dollars or other convertible currency. Alternative A offered eligible members twice as long to pay in, with each installment half the amount paid by other members. There would be no national currency subscription payments under Alternative A.
- Alternative B required a less developed country to pay on the same schedule as other members (five annual installments of 20% each), but allowed payment of up to 50% of each installment in the member's currency and the remainder in US dollars or other convertible currency.[43] Alternative B offered eligible members a smaller convertible currency requirement for each installment, without any extension of time or reduction in installment amounts.[44]

Both alternatives were only available to those members considered as less developed countries, based on the Chief Negotiators' Report:

> *Article 6, paragraph 5.* Representatives agreed that a member that is eligible to borrow from the International Development Association (but not from the International Bank for Reconstruction and Development) would be considered a less developed country for purposes of this paragraph.[45]

However, none of the eligible members elected to make payments in national currency.[46] Payment in convertible currency in ten smaller installments over ten years may have proved more beneficial for these members than payment in national currency. Their choice was also beneficial for AIIB, as all of its subscription payments will be in US dollars or other convertible currency and no special arrangements for other subscription currencies will be required.

[42] AIIB Article 6-5. Coincidentally, a similar choice of partial payment in national currency on the same schedule as others, or full payment in convertible currency over a longer time was offered to regional members in AfDB, in connection with the capital increase to allow for non-regional members in 1979. AfDB Board of Governors' Resolution 06-79, *Concerning the General Increase in the Capital Stock of the African Development Bank in Connection with the Admission of Nonregional Member Countries*, May 17, 1979, paragraph 6.

[43] Members were required to advise AIIB at the time of subscription of the proportion to be paid in the member's currency. AIIB Article 6-5 (b)(i).

[44] Alternative B also included provisions for maintenance of value, and payment in the form of promissory notes. AIIB Article 6-5 (iii)–(v) and 6-6. Neither the maintenance of value provisions nor the use of promissory notes apply to subscriptions under Alternative A or to the regular installment payments of other members. The provisions regarding maintenance of value are nearly identical to those in AfDB Article 28; AsDB Article 25; IADB Article V, Section 3; and IBRD Article II, Section 9.

[45] Eight PFMs were eligible as "IDA-only" borrowers from the World Bank Group: Bangladesh, Cambodia, Kyrgyz Republic, Lao PDR, Maldives, Myanmar, Nepal, and Tajikistan. World Bank Operational Manual, Operational Policies, OP 3.10, Annex C (July 2015) lists member eligibility for IBRD and IDA lending.

[46] AIIB's 2016 financial statements state that less developed countries may pay in 10 installments (Note 5.7) and show all paid-in capital as a US$ financial asset (Note 5.13(d) Currency Risk). AIIB (2017) at 39 and 48. Since all eligible countries became members in 2016, this confirms that they opted for the ten-year, all-US$ option (Alternative A).

(5) Callable shares

7.18 Payments on the callable shares of AIIB stock are not required either at the time of subscription or on a schedule of installments as provided for paid-in shares. Rather, payment by members on their callable shares is subject to call by AIIB (demand for payment) "only as and when required by the Bank to meet its liabilities."[47] Such calls by AIIB are further required to be in the same percentage on all callable shares, so that the obligation is equitable among members.

7.19 Here, several aspects merit mention. First, to reiterate, none of the MDBs discussed in this book has ever needed to make a call on its callable capital. Callable capital has nonetheless been considered an important foundation for the financial position of the MDBs, both for the financial support it represents and for the prudent financial management it requires. Indeed, the decreasing percentages of paid-in capital at some MDBs, as noted in paragraph 7.10, meant that they correspondingly increased the percentage of callable capital as they built their financial foundations and track record—without negatively affecting their financial reputations.[48]

7.20 Second, the standard that must be met by AIIB in order to make a call on callable capital reflects an evolution. AIIB's standard is that the funds are required to meet its liabilities in general. IBRD and other MDBs founded in the 1940s–1970s tie calls on capital specifically to the MDB's liabilities on funds borrowed for its investment operations.[49] At heart, callable capital can be seen as a protection for MDB bondholders, regardless of the purpose of the bonds issued. As a result, the standard for calling capital in AIIB is more closely aligned to EBRD (and EIB), referring generally to calls when required by the Bank to meet its liabilities.[50]

7.21 Third, a member's obligation to respond to a call on callable capital continues in certain circumstances even after the member has withdrawn.[51] This provision

[47] AIIB Article 6-3.

[48] In connection with the Group of Twenty (G20) Independent Review of Multilateral Development Banks' Capital Adequacy Frameworks, several MDBs undertook reviews of their Callable Capital. *See, e.g.*, African Development Bank Group, *Analysis of the Call on Callable Capital Process of the African Development Bank*, 2024; Asian Development Bank, *Callable Capital of the Asian Development Bank*, April 2024; Inter-American Development Bank, *Callable Capital of the Inter-American Development Bank*, 2024; European Bank for Reconstruction and Development, *MDB Callable Capital Review, European Bank for Reconstruction and Development*, 2024; and World Bank, *IBRD Callable Capital*, 2024.

[49] IBRD Article II, Section 5 (ii): "the remaining eighty percent shall be subject to call by the Bank only when required to meet obligations of the Bank created under Article IV, Sections 1 (a) (ii) and (iii)." These Sections of Article IV refer to IBRD's direct loans out of borrowed funds and guaranteeing loans made by private financiers through the usual investment channels. Similar provisions can be found in AfDB Article 7-4; AsDB Article 6-5; CDB Article 7-6; and IADB Article II, Section 4 (a)(ii).

[50] EBRD Article 6-4. The EIB Charter provides that the unpaid balance of subscriptions may be called by the Board of Directors to meet the Bank's obligations (Article 5-3).

[51] AIIB Article 39-3 (iv) provides that a former member "shall remain liable on any call for unpaid subscriptions in accordance with paragraph 3 of Article 6, to the same extent that it would have been required to respond if the impairment of capital had occurred and the call had been made at the time the repurchase price of its shares was determined."

corresponds directly to provisions related to settlement of accounts with former members in most other MDBs.[52]

Before a call against callable capital could be made, losses arising from AIIB's investment operations would be charged, in order, to provisions, net income, reserves and retained earnings, and unimpaired paid-in capital.[53] Even in the institutionally catastrophic event that AIIB were to terminate its operations, members would remain liable on uncalled subscriptions until the claims of all creditors have been discharged.[54] 7.22

Another factor here is that MDBs generally benefit from preferred creditor status, under which borrowers continue to repay MDBs even if they default or delay payment to other creditors.[55] Preferred creditor status is informal, meaning that it is not based on legal requirements. Rather, it can be seen as a reflection of each member's regard for the other countries that are the MDB's shareholders, as well as potentially negative market perceptions of a default to an MDB. Preferred creditor status benefits AIIB as well, as noted in its first issuer ratings.[56] 7.23

(6) Terms of shares

Certain key terms for AIIB shares are also stipulated in the AIIB Charter, as they are for other MDBs. Shares are available only for subscription by members,[57] and only transferable to AIIB; shares may not be pledged or encumbered.[58] A member's liability is limited to the unpaid portion of its subscription,[59] and members are not liable for obligations of AIIB merely by reason of membership.[60] Shares are 7.24

[52] AfDB Article 45-3 (d); AsDB Article 43-3 (iv); CDB Article 42-3 (d); EBRD Article 39-3 (iv); IADB Article IX, Section 3 (d)(iii); and IBRD Article VI, Section 4 (c)(iv).

[53] AIIB Article 20. There are similar provisions in other charters, with EBRD wording being closest to AIIB. AfDB Article 21-1; AsDB Article 18; EBRD Article 17; IADB Article VII, Section 3; and IBRD Article IV, Section 7.

[54] AIIB Article 42. In line with the structure of other MDB charters, the AIIB Charter includes provisions for AIIB to suspend and ultimately to terminate its operations. *See* AIIB Chapter VIII, Suspension and Termination of Operations of the Bank, and AfDB Articles 46–49; AsDB Articles 44–47; EBRD Articles 40–43; IADB Article X; and IBRD Article VI, Section 5.

[55] Humphrey (2015b) at 11–15 has a fuller description of how preferred creditor treatment (PCT) is reflected in MDB credit ratings.

[56] *See* "Moody's assigns first-time Aaa issuer rating to Asian Infrastructure Investment Bank; outlook stable," Moody's Investors Service, June 29, 2017: "We expect that AIIB will, like other MDBs, enjoy preferred creditor status." Moody's view is maintained in its most recent rating of April 2, 2025. *See also* "Fitch assigns Asian Infrastructure Investment Bank 'AAA': outlook stable," Fitch Ratings, June 17, 2024 and "Asian Infrastructure Investment Bank 'AAA' Rating Affirmed; Outlook Stable," Standard and Poor's Research Update, March 13, 2025.

[57] AIIB Article 4-1. AfDB Article 5-1 (a); AsDB Article 4-1; EBRD Article 4-1; IADB Article II, Section 2 (a); and IBRD Article II, Section 2 (a).

[58] AIIB Article 7-2. AfDB Article 6-6; AsDB Article 5-5; EBRD Article 5-6; IADB Article II, Section 3 (e); and IBRD Article II, Section 10.

[59] AIIB Article 7-3. AfDB Article 6-5; AsDB Article 5-6; EBRD Article 5-7; IADB Article II, Section 3 (d); and IBRD Article II, Section 6.

[60] AIIB Article 7-4. AsDB Article 5-7; EBRD Article 5-7. This further limitation of member liability does not appear in the AfDB, IADB, or IBRD Charters.

issued at par, although future AIIB shares could be issued on other terms in special circumstances decided by the Board of Governors by a Special Majority.[61]

B. Capital Increases

7.25 AIIB's capital can be increased by its Board of Governors, "under such terms and conditions as it may deem advisable, including the proportion between paid-in and callable shares."[62] Capital increases must be approved by a Super Majority vote of the Board of Governors. Similar qualified majorities are required in other MDBs.[63] Final decisions on capital increases are specifically reserved for the Board of Governors, and cannot be delegated to the Board of Directors—for AIIB as well as for its counterparts.[64]

7.26 An indirect constraint on increases in capital is the regional/non-regional shareholding proportion. The AIIB Charter applies the minimum 75% regional shareholding requirement to the allocation of shares to members for subscription, not directly to the power to increase authorized capital.[65] This constraint is similar for AfDB, AsDB, EBRD, and IADB, although the legal structure varies.[66]

7.27 In addition, each AIIB member retains the right to subscribe to enough shares in each capital increase to maintain its percentage of total shareholding.[67] This so-called "pre-emptive right" to subscribe is common in MDBs.[68] Pre-emptive rights mean that a reduction in any member's shareholding percentage can only come about if that member agrees not to exercise its right to subscribe to additional shares. Moreover, an increase in any member's shareholding percentage (and the

[61] AIIB Article 7-1. AfDB Article 6-4; AsDB Article 5-4; EBRD Article 5-5; IADB Article II, Section 3 (c); and IBRD Article II, Section 4.

[62] AIIB Article 4-3.

[63] AfDB Article 5-3 (two-thirds of Governors representing three quarters of total voting power, unless solely to provide for initial subscription of a member); AsDB Article 4-3 (two-thirds of Governors representing three-quarters of total voting power); EBRD Article 4-3 (two-thirds of Governors representing three-quarters of total voting power); IADB Article II, Section 2 (e) (three-quarters of Governors including two-thirds of Regional Governors, representing three-quarters of total voting power); and IBRD Article II, Section 2 (b) (three-quarters of total voting power). In EIB, however, unanimous approval is required. EIB Article 4-3.

[64] AIIB Article 23-2 (ii) reserves to the Board of Governors the power to increase or decrease the authorized capital stock, as in other MDBs, though decrease in capital is not mentioned elsewhere in the Charter. *See* AfDB Article 29-2 (a) (only the power to decrease is reserved); AsDB Article 28-2 (ii); EBRD Article 24-2 (ii); IADB Article VIII, Section 2 (b)(ii); and IBRD Article V, Section 2 (ii).

[65] *See* discussion of AIIB Article 5-2 and 5-4 in Regional and Non-Regional Shareholding at paragraphs 7.29–7.30.

[66] AsDB Article 5-1 and 5-3 (regional shareholding minimum of 60%) and EBRD Article 5-2 and 5-4 (EEC members, EEC and EIB combined shareholding majority) are similar to AIIB Article 5-2 and 5-4. AfDB Article 5-3 conditions the power to increase capital with requirement of 60/40 regional/non-regional shareholding in AfDB Article 5-4. In IADB, the power to increase capital in IADB Article II, Section 2 (e) is subject to the voting power limitations in IADB Article VIII, Section 4 (b) (regional developing members hold at least 50.005%, the largest member not below 30% and Canada not below 4%, all of total voting power).

[67] AIIB Article 5-4.

[68] AfDB Article 6-2; AsDB Article 5-2 (exception for increases in new or existing member subscriptions); EBRD Article 5-3; IADB Article II, Section 3 (b); and IBRD Article II, Section 3 (c).

addition of new members' shareholding) can only come about if there is forbearance by some other members. Recognition of the fundamental nature of this preemptive right is evidenced in AIIB, as elsewhere, by its inclusion as one of the three Charter provisions that require unanimous agreement for amendment.[69] In parallel, the AIIB Charter provides that no member is obligated to subscribe to any part of a capital increase.[70]

C. Allocation of Capital

For an MDB with a shareholding structure, agreement on allocation of shares is critical. Where each member's voting power depends in largest part on the size of its capital subscription,[71] allocation of capital establishes the respective roles of members in institutional governance. For a financial institution whose soundness rests in large part on the availability of its paid-in capital and the backing of its callable capital, an allocation mechanism ideally takes into account the financial strength of its shareholders. The history of other MDBs also highlights the challenges for an allocation mechanism to adjust to the changes in member countries' relative positions over decades, as noted in paragraphs 7.31–7.32. **7.28**

(1) Regional and non-regional shareholding

The AIIB Charter follows the practice of other regional MDBs in specifying a floor for the shareholding of its regional members. As noted in paragraph 7.26, AIIB shares cannot be allocated to new members and additional shares cannot be allocated to existing members if the effect would reduce the percentage of capital stock held by regional members below 75% of total subscribed capital stock.[72] For AsDB, the regional shareholding minimum is 60%, and for EBRD, there is provision for the European Economic Community (now the EU), members of the European Economic Community (the EU), and the European Investment Bank, taken together, to maintain a shareholding majority.[73] For AfDB, the proportion of regional/non-regional shareholding is set at 60/40.[74] In IADB, the power to increase capital is subject to the specific percentages of total voting power: regional **7.29**

[69] AIIB Article 53-2. AfDB Article 60-3 (a); AsDB Article 59-2 (iii); EBRD Article 56-2 (i)(b); IADB Article XII (b)(ii); and IBRD Article VIII (b)(ii).

[70] AIIB Article 5-4. AfDB Article 6-2; AsDB Article 5-2; EBRD Article 5-3; IADB Article II, Section 3 (b); and IBRD Article II, Section 3 (c).

[71] Voting power in AIIB has three components: basic votes, share votes, and founding member votes. *See* discussion in paragraphs 9.04–9.09.

[72] AIIB Article 5-2 (new members) and 5-3 (existing members, requiring a Super Majority vote in the Board of Governors). *See* the discussion in paragraphs 6.25–6.26 and 6.31–6.32 for the definitions of regional and non-regional members and discussion of combined regional ownership share.

[73] AsDB Article 5-1 and 5-3 and EBRD Article 5-2 and 5-4.

[74] AfDB Article 5-4.

developing members must hold at least 50.005%, the largest member (the United States) not below 30% and Canada not below 4%.[75]

7.30 These limitations in MDB Charters set a floor for regional shareholding but not a ceiling. In the case of the AIIB Charter, however, there is an additional element of flexibility to the restriction on reducing regional shareholding below 75%, as the Board of Governors can 'otherwise agree' by a Super Majority vote.[76] This flexibility is circumscribed to an extent by the related statement in the Chief Negotiators' Report:

> While representatives recognized that the Board of Governors might need to exercise some flexibility in the future that would reduce the regional shareholding percentage in paragraphs 2 and 3 below 75%, representatives agreed that a minimum of 70% regional shareholding would be important in preserving the regional character of the Bank.

The initial allocations in Schedule A of the AIIB Charter would, if all fully subscribed within each group, result in a regional shareholding of 75%. As of June 2025, AIIB regional shareholding stood at 76.2%.

(2) Standard for allocation

7.31 Beyond the overall prescriptions on the shareholding of regional members and non-regional members, the AIIB Charter has no specific mention of a standard for allocation. Neither do the other MDBs mentioned above.[77] At IBRD, which is global in membership and reach and without regional or other voting restrictions, updating the shareholding standard has been the topic of extensive debate in the World Bank Group for more than a decade; a new Dynamic Formula was agreed in 2016.[78]

[75] IADB Article II, Section 2 (e) and Article VIII, Section 4 (b).

[76] AIIB Article 5-2 (new members) and 5-3 (existing members).

[77] Rigo Sureda (2004) at paragraphs 56–61 surveys the initial allocation criteria in some of the other MDBs. For IADB, the starting point was the US capital contribution, with capital allocated so that the US could be the majority shareholder without controlling the institution. For AfDB, allocation was based on the economic capacity of each member (at a time when AfDB members were all regional). For AsDB, several formulae were used for regional members, reflecting economic capacity as in AfDB. For AsDB non-regionals, who were part of AsDB from the start, the minimum capital contribution was US$5 million.

[78] Since 2003, the World Bank's governing bodies, in particular the Development Committee (formally, the Joint Ministerial Committee of the Boards of Governors of the Bank and the Fund on the Transfer of Real Resources to Developing Countries), have had repeated discussions on IBRD shareholding principles. Historically, IBRD has applied as a fundamental principle that members' subscriptions should reflect their relative position in the world economy, subject to each member's pre-emptive rights, implemented primarily, though not exclusively, through the use of IMF quotas until 2010. Development Committee (2007) at paragraphs 12–13. In 2010, the IBRD Governors agreed to adopt unique IBRD Shareholding Principles and establish a dynamic formula which primarily reflects countries' evolving economic weight and the World Bank's development mission. For the application of those principles and further discussion of the challenges of setting and maintaining a standard for allocation of capital shares, *see* Development Committee (2010); Development Committee (2016); and Development Committee Communique, October 8, 2016, paragraph 13. *See also*

Perhaps mindful of these World Bank Group discussions, the AIIB Chief Negotiators did record the standard of allocation that was applied in reaching agreement on the initial subscriptions in Schedule A. Instead of enshrining that standard in the AIIB Charter, where it might someday become outdated, the Chief Negotiators included a statement in the Chief Negotiators' Report: 7.32

> Representatives noted that the basic parameter for allocation of capital stock to members would be the relative share of the global economy of members within the regional and non-regional groupings, respectively. Members' shares of the global economy would be measured by reference to Gross Domestic Product (GDP), with the understanding that GDP share would be indicative only for non-regional members.[79]

It has also been noted that the GDP measurement used in the Chief Negotiators' Meetings was a blend of GDP measured at market exchange rates (60%) and GDP on a purchasing power parity (PPP) basis (40%).[80] The same 60/40 GDP blend was one of the factors in the IMF quota formula adopted in 2008 and was used for the measurement of economic weight in the IBRD 2010 Shareholding Realignment.[81]

When new members join, the decision on the initial allocation of shares is made by the Board of Governors as part of the membership terms and conditions.[82] Their decision would be expected to reflect the regional shareholding percentage, as well as the standard of allocation set out in the Chief Negotiators' Report, particularly the reference to relative GDP shares. If existing members request additional shares, this standard of allocation would also be relevant, and a Super Majority vote by the Board of Governors would in any event be required.[83] In either case, if available authorized and unallocated shares are insufficient, the Board of Governors would also have to decide on a capital increase to increase the available number of shares, in conformity with the rules on capital increases, including pre-emptive rights as described in paragraph 7.27. 7.33

Development Committee Communique, April 22, 2017, at paragraph 9, recalling the commitment "to the principles we endorsed in Lima [October 2016] toward a WBG that reflects the evolution of the global economy and contributions to the WBG's mission."

In 2025, preparations are underway for the next shareholding review. *See* Development Committee (2024) on technical preparations for the 2025 review.

[79] The Chief Negotiators' Report does not specify a source for GDP calculations. A common source is the IMF World Economic Outlook data set, updated in April and September/October in each year.

[80] "Vice Minister Shi Yaobin answers reporters' questions about AIIB Articles of Agreement," [史耀斌副部长就《亚投行协定》相关问题答记者问], Ministry of Finance of the People's Republic of China Press Release, June 29, 2015 (on file with author).

[81] Development Committee (2010) at paragraph 11.

[82] AIIB Articles 3-2 and 5-2.

[83] AIIB Article 5-3.

(3) Capital reviews

7.34 The percentage for regional shareholding and the continuing applicability of GDP weights for members will also be relevant in future shareholding reviews. The AIIB Charter provides for the Board of Governors to review AIIB's capital stock at least at five-year intervals, but the Board of Governors is not obliged to consider a capital increase in each review—nor does this section preclude earlier reviews if appropriate.[84] While the AsDB and EBRD Charters have provisions for regular reviews, others do not.[85] In IBRD, regular shareholding reviews were not required under the IBRD Charter, and were introduced through a decision of the Board of Governors as part of the World Bank Group reforms in 2010.[86] The AIIB provision on regular reviews offers a mechanism to continue alignment with economic developments into the future, aided by the explicit agreement on GDP as the basic parameter. Two reviews have been undertaken, in 2020 and 2025; no changes were made.[87]

(4) Allocations

7.35 The initial allocation of AIIB capital was made in Schedule A of the AIIB Charter. Capital allocations for the fifty-seven Prospective Founding Members (PFMs) were listed separately for regional and non-regional groups, at a 75:25 ratio. In Schedule A, the regional group was allocated 73.4% and the non-regional group was allocated 24.7%. A small amount of total authorized capital was left unallocated under the regional group (16,150 shares) and under the non-regional group (2,336 shares). The Chief Negotiators' Report addressed the future allocation of these unallocated shares, noting:

> Representatives noted that, in Schedule A, unallocated shares had been shown for regional members (Part A) and non-regional members (Part B), respectively, in anticipation of additional members joining in each category.

As the PFMs became Signatories and later members, these allocations set a maximum subscription for each one; there is no minimum subscription under the AIIB Charter.[88] Actual subscriptions for each member could be for a smaller total

84 AIIB Article 5-4. With respect to this paragraph, the Chief Negotiators' Report confirms: "Representatives further noted that reviews of capital stock by the Board of Governors need not result in a capital increase, and any such increase would require Board of Governors' approval in accordance with paragraph 3 of Article 4."

85 AsDB Article 5-2 and EBRD Article 5-3.

86 IBRD Board of Governors Resolution No. 612, *2010 Selective Increase in Authorized Capital Stock to Enhance Voice and Participation of Developing and Transition Countries*, adopted March 16, 2011. Regular quota reviews at least every five years are featured in the IMF structure (IMF Article III, Section 2), and it should be noted that until the 1980s, IMF quotas were the primary basis for IBRD shareholding.

87 AIIB Board of Governors Resolution No. 101, *Review of the Capital Stock of the Asian Infrastructure Investment Bank*, adopted December 17, 2020, and AIIB Board of Governors Resolution No. 140, *Review of the Capital Stock of the Asian Infrastructure Investment Bank*, adopted April 18, 2025.

88 The EBRD Charter provides that the minimum initial subscription is 100 shares. EBRD Article 5-1.

number of shares, in the same 20:80 proportion of paid-in and callable shares. As of June 2025, subscriptions by the Signatories that have become AIIB members have been for the amounts in Schedule A, except for Brazil which subscribed initially for a significantly smaller number of shares.[89]

The shares identified as unallocated in Schedule A and any shares not subscribed by Signatories can be allocated by the AIIB Board of Governors to new members, through decisions on the membership.[90] AIIB has approved membership applications since 2017 for fifty-three new prospective members, with allocations of 12,162 shares to new regional members and 24,060 shares to new non-regional members (a total of 36,222 shares, equal to US$3.6222 billion).[91] Figure 7.2 lists the share allocations by member. **7.36**

Note that shareholding in AIIB is not identical to voting power. Share votes (equal to shareholding) are one component of each member's AIIB voting power, albeit the largest component; each member also has basic votes, and Founding Members also hold 600 Founding Member votes each.[92] As a result, there is a difference between a member's percentage of AIIB shareholding and a member's percentage of AIIB voting power. In general, voting power will be less than shareholding for large members and greater than shareholding for smaller shareholders. As of June 2025, total regional shareholding was 76.3% and total regional voting power was 72.6%, while total non-regional shareholding was 23.7% and total non-regional voting power was 27.4%.[93] This difference between voting power and shareholding is also seen in AfDB, AsDB, IADB, and IBRD.[94] **7.37**

D. Financial Resources

AIIB's financial resources are separated into ordinary resources, principally derived from AIIB capital, and Special Funds resources.[95] This distinction is made because **7.38**

[89] Members' shareholding on the AIIB Website under Members can be compared with the shares allocated in Schedule A of the AIIB Charter. Brazil subscribed to fifty shares, instead of the 31,810 shares allocated in Schedule A. That action would have added 31,760 shares to the unallocated pool for allocation to new members. Without those unallocated shares, it is unlikely AIIB could have allocated the 42,677 shares for members since 2017 (without a capital increase).

An additional subscription of 6,455 shares for Brazil was approved by the Board of Governors in 2024. AIIB Board of Governors Resolution No. 130, *Brazil's Increase in its Subscription of Shares in the Asian Infrastructure Investment Bank*, adopted April 9, 2024.

[90] *See* paragraphs 6.36–6.38.

[91] *See* paragraph 6.39. The allocations to each new member are shown in the relevant AIIB Board of Governors' Resolutions approving each membership, and summarized in Figure 7.2.

[92] AIIB Article 28-1. *See* paragraphs 9.04–9.09 for a discussion of voting power.

[93] *See* Members on AIIB website at https://www.aiib.org/en/about-aiib/governance/members-of-bank/index.html (last visited July 14, 2025). Figures 6.5 and 6.6 show the status of subscriptions and voting power as of June 30, 2025.

[94] AfDB Article 35-1; AsDB Article 33-1; IADB Article VIII, Section 4 (a); and IBRD Article V, Section 3. EBRD has only share votes, without basic votes, so voting power and shareholding percentages are the same (if subscriptions are fully paid up). EBRD Article 29-1.

[95] *Ordinary resources* include: (i) paid-in and callable shares; (ii) funds raised; (iii) repayments and income on loans or guarantees and returns on equity investments and other financing, where the loan,

New Membership Approvals and Share Allocations (September 15, 2025)		
Member	*Shares*	***Date of Approval (membership effective date)***
REGIONAL MEMBERS		
Afghanistan	**866**	March 2017 (effective October 13, 2017)
Armenia	374	March 2017 (effective September 4, 2025)
Bahrain	**1036**	May 2017 (effective August 27, 2018)
Cook Islands	**5**	December 2017 (effective June 1, 2020)
Cyprus	**200**	May 2017 (effective June 25, 2018)
Fiji	**125**	March 2017 (effective December 11, 2017)
Hong Kong, China	**7651**	March 2017 (effective June 7, 2017)
Iraq	**250**	December 2021 (effective August 4, 2022)
Lebanon	1397	June 2018
Nauru	**5**	September 2024 (effective February 28, 2025)
Papua New Guinea	**50**	May 2018 (effective May 13, 2024)
Samoa	**21**	May 2017 (effective April 3, 2018)
Solomon Islands	**5**	September 2023 (effective June 9, 2025)
Timor-Leste	**160**	March 2017 (effective November 22, 2017)
Tonga	**12**	June 2017 (effective January 5, 2021)
Vanuatu	**5**	December 2017 (effective March 6, 2018)
Regional allocated	12162	
NON-REGIONAL MEMBERS		
Algeria	**50**	December 2018 (effective December 27, 2019)
Argentina	**50**	June 2017 (effective March 30, 2021)
Belarus	**641**	December 2017 (effective January 17, 2019)
Belgium	**2846**	March 2017 (effective July 12, 2019)
Benin	**50**	July 2019 (effective May 27, 2020)
Bolivia	261	May 2017
Canada	**9954**	March 2017 (effective March 19, 2018)
Chile	**100**	May 2017 (effective July 2, 2021)
Cote d'Ivoire	**50**	April 2019 (effective February 26, 2020)
Croatia	**50**	December 2019 (effective December 17, 2021)
Djibouti	**5**	July 2019 (effective September 5, 2024)
Ecuador	**50**	December 2017 (effective November 1, 2019)
El Salvador	**50**	September 2023 (effective February 10, 2025)
Ethiopia	**458**	March 2017 (effective May 13, 2017)
Ghana	**50**	December 2018 (effective February 21, 2020)
Greece	**100**	May 2017 (effective August 20, 2019)
Guinea	**50**	April 2019 (effective July 12, 2019)
Hungary	**1000**	March 2017 (effective June 16, 2017)
Ireland	**1313**	March 2017 (effective October 23, 2017)
Kenya	**50**	May 2018 (effective September 4, 2024)
Liberia	**50**	July 2020 (effective January 4, 2021)
Libya	**526**	December 2018 (effective September 12, 2023)

New Membership Approvals and Share Allocations (September 15, 2025)		
Member	*Shares*	***Date of Approval (membership effective date)***
Madagascar	**50**	**June 2017 (effective June 25, 2018)**
Mauritania	**50**	**December 2022 (effective June 24, 2025)**
Morocco	**50**	**December 2018 (effective May 4, 2022)**
Nigeria	50	October 2021
Peru	**1546**	**March 2017 (effective January 14, 2022)**
Romania	1530	**May 2017 (effective December 28, 2018)**
Rwanda	50	**July 2019 (effective April 16, 2020)**
Senegal	50	December 2019
Serbia	**50**	**December 2018 (effective August 15, 2019)**
Sudan	**590**	**March 2017 (effective Sept 18, 2018)**
Tanzania	50	September 2023
Togo	**50**	**December 2018 (effective December 19, 2023)**
Tunisia	**50**	**April 2019 (effective April 29, 2022)**
Uruguay	**50**	**April 2019 (effective April 28, 2020)**
Venezuela	2090	March 2017
Non-regional Allocated	24060	
TOTAL Allocated	36222	Regional (12,162) + Non-regional (24,060)

Figure 7.2 New Membership Approvals and Share Allocations (September 15, 2025)
Source: AIIB Board of Governors' Resolutions on membership and allocation and AIIB website on membership.

AIIB is empowered to set up Special Funds, with donor contributions, for purposes that meet the purpose and functions of AIIB; once contributed, these resources become resources of AIIB. The separation ensures that the ordinary resources and related finances are not affected by the Special Funds and related operations, which may be for specific purposes and influenced by donor priorities. These distinctions are found in other MDB Charters where the MDB is authorized to establish Special Funds with resources, often concessional, contributed from outside parties (including members). (Special Funds are discussed further in Section F of this chapter.)

To implement this separation, the investment operations of AIIB are divided into ordinary operations (financed from ordinary resources) and special operations (financed from Special Funds resources). Furthermore, the AIIB Charter requires that ordinary resources and Special Funds resources be managed separately, shown separately in AIIB's financial statements, and charged separately for expenses. The ordinary resources cannot be used to discharge losses arising out of special operations. **7.39**

guarantee, investment, or financing was made with funds under (i) or (ii); and (iv) any other funds or income received that are not Special Funds resources. AIIB Article 8. *Special Funds* resources means the resources of any Special Fund, including: (i) funds accepted for any Special Fund; (ii) funds received in respect of loans or guarantees, and the proceeds of any equity investments financed from the resources of any Special Fund; (iii) income from investment of Special Funds resources; and (iv) any other resources placed at the disposal of any Special Fund. AIIB Article 17-4.

(1) Raising additional resources

7.40 AIIB is authorized to undertake several types of transactions as part of its financial operations. Specifically, the AIIB Charter empowers AIIB to:

- raise funds, through borrowing or other means, in member countries or elsewhere, in accordance with the relevant legal provisions;
- buy and sell securities the Bank has issued or guaranteed or in which it has invested;
- guarantee securities in which it has invested in order to facilitate their sale;
- underwrite, or participate in the underwriting of, securities issued by any entity or enterprise for purposes consistent with the purpose of the Bank; and
- invest or deposit funds not needed in its operations.[96]

In addition, the AIIB Charter authorizes AIIB to exercise such other powers as may be necessary or appropriate to further its purpose and function, consistent with the other provisions of the AIIB Charter.[97]

7.41 These powers are comparable to the powers in other MDBs, with a number of streamlined features:

- Consents. For borrowings and similar financial market transactions, many of the other MDBs are required by their Charters to obtain consent from the member in whose market funds are raised and the member in whose currency the transaction is denominated.[98] AIIB is not. These consents are no longer specifically required under domestic financial regulations, and thus keeping an outdated requirement would not be useful.[99] Where governmental approvals

[96] AIIB Article 16.

[97] AIIB Article 16-9. These incidental powers are common at other MDBs. AfDB Article 23 (g); AsDB Article 21 (vii); EBRD Article 20-1 (vii); and IADB Article V, Section 1 (v). While the IBRD Charter is silent on this point, such powers have long been considered implied powers at IBRD. *See* Shihata (2000) at 852–4.

[98] Several of these provisions also require agreement of members to exchange the proceeds for currencies of other members, such as IBRD Article IV, Section 1 (b). *See* AfDB Article 23 (a); AsDB Article 21-1; IADB Article VII, Section 1 (i). The EBRD provision does not have this currency requirement. EBRD Article 20-1 (i).

[99] The member consent provision in the IBRD Charter was viewed as an important power for countries to protect their financial markets in the financial world of 1944. As explained in the US Treasury's Questions and Answers on the Bank for Reconstruction and Development just prior to the Bretton Woods conference: "The provisions of the proposed Bank are designed to prevent disturbances in the security markets of member countries as a result of its operations. Each member country has a safeguard against undesirable action in requirement that securities may be sold in its markets only with the consent of its representatives on the Bank board." US Department of the Treasury (1944) at 22 (Question 16). The final text agreed at Bretton Woods referred to the consent of the member in whose market IBRD would borrow (not to its Board representative), as well as the consent of the country in whose currency the loan was denominated, if different. Bittermann explains that this latter requirement would guard against the contingency that the currency of denomination might become scarce under the IMF Charter, and thus subject to exchange restrictions. Bittermann (1971) at 76–7. By the 1990s, however, markets had changed. Mistry (1995) at 55 observed that the requirement for IBRD and others to obtain permission from members to borrow in their markets and in their currencies no longer served any useful purpose. He also noted the prospect that members could use this requirement as a tool to restrain MDB borrowing for political and other reasons. For example, the US restricted IBRD borrowings in the 1960s. *See* Mason and Asher (1973) at 136–7.

are necessary, AIIB would be obliged in any event to obtain them under the AIIB Charter requirement to raise funds "in accordance with the relevant legal provisions."[100]

- Purposes. AIIB's borrowings and other transactions are not legally categorized by specific uses of the proceeds, such as for loans and guarantees. In some older MDB Charters, by comparison, requirements may differ for borrowing for different purposes.[101] In practice, this flexibility means that AIIB can borrow for its general purposes without earmarking particular borrowings for particular purposes. This could, in turn, foster efficiency in its financial management.
- Power to Raise Funds. The basic power to raise funds is cast in broader terms than just borrowing. The AIIB is empowered to "raise funds, through borrowing or other means, in member countries or elsewhere." While many transactions will fall easily into a legal definition of borrowing, there may be other transactions, now or in the future, where the term "borrowing" alone could be too narrow a term. AIIB's incidental powers could make it possible to undertake such a transaction in any case, but having the flexibility built into the basic power to raise funds could simplify the mechanics.

Like other MDBs, AIIB's financial management can be expected to adapt over time to changes in market and financial industry practices, within the confines of these legal provisions.

E. Financial Management

The AIIB Charter follows MDB precedents in mandating expressly that AIIB's resources (and facilities) be used exclusively to implement its purpose and functions,[102] adding for AIIB a general requirement to follow sound banking practices.[103] 7.42

[100] AIIB Article 16-1. The AIIB provision is similar to the provision enabling EIB to borrow in the capital markets of Member States "in accordance with the legal provisions applying to those markets." EIB Article 20-2. AIIB, like many other MDBs, may also be raising funds in the capital markets of countries that are not members. In IBRD's early years, for instance, funds were raised in Switzerland, which was not then a member. As AIIB's capital base is in US dollars, borrowing funds in US dollars could be expected even if the United States is not a member of the AIIB.

[101] *See* AfDB Article 15-3; AsDB Article 12-2; IADB Article III, Section 5 (b); and IBRD Article IV, Section 1 (b). In the AsDB Charter, the authorization for the Bank's operations refers separately to direct loans out of funds raised in capital markets. AsDB Article 11 (i) and (ii).

[102] AfDB Article 12; AsDB Article 8; EBRD Article 8; and IADB Article III, Section 1. IBRD Article II, Section 1 (a) requires that resources be used for the benefit of members.

[103] AIIB Article 9.

(1) Financial ratios

7.43 There are two financial ratios stipulated in the AIIB Charter. The first is its lending limit (limitation on ordinary operations). This ratio requires that total AIIB investment financing not exceed its unimpaired capital, reserves, and retained earnings. The design of this 1:1 ratio is similar to other MDBs, although the precise wordings and calculations differ.[104] In the AIIB Charter, the ratio is stated as follows:

> The total amount outstanding of loans, equity investments, guarantees and other types of financing provided by the Bank in its ordinary operations under subparagraphs 2 (i), (ii), (iii) and (vi) of Article 11 [meaning direct loans, equity, guarantees, and other types of financing] shall not at any time be increased, if by such increase the total amount of its unimpaired subscribed capital, reserves and retained earnings included in its ordinary resources would be exceeded.[105]

There is an additional provision in the AIIB Charter, however, which empowers the Board of Governors to increase that limit from 100% of unimpaired subscribed capital, reserves, and retained earnings up to 250%, "based on the Bank's financial position and financial standing." A Super Majority vote in the Board of Governors is required for such an increase.[106] Among the MDBs, most have had a 1:1 ratio, while at the time the AIIB Charter was negotiated, EIB and the Nordic Investment Bank (NIB) had a lending limit set at 250% and the Black Sea Trade and Development Bank (BSTDB) had a lending limit set at 150%.[107]

7.44 In recent years, discussions among the MDBs and their shareholders on a reform agenda for the MDBs have included specific attention to their capital adequacy frameworks, notably the G20 Independent Review of MDB's Capital Adequacy Frameworks (CAF Review).[108] The CAF Review recommended that MDBs should relocate specific numeric leverage targets (such as those discussed in paragraph 7.43) from MDB statutes to MDB capital adequacy frameworks. That change would enhance flexibility by enabling the MDB to make necessary future adjustments to the targets without the need to amend its charter.[109] Some of the actions taken by other MDBs in this area include:

[104] AfDB Article 15-1; AsDB Article 12-1; EBRD Article 12-1; IADB Article III, Section 5 (a); and IBRD Article III, Section 3.

[105] AIIB Article 12-1.

[106] AIIB Article 12-1.

[107] EIB Article 16-5; NIB Section 7; and BSTDB Article 15-1. In the Bretton Woods discussions, the US had suggested a limit of 200% or 300%, as for banks; other proposals ranged from 75% to 500%. In the end, it was agreed that financial markets at the time would only be likely to rely on the US subscription in any case. Bittermann (1971) at 75.

[108] Boosting MDBs' investing capacity: An Independent Review of Multilateral Development Banks' Capital Adequacy Frameworks (2022), https://www.dt.mef.gov.it/export/sites/sitodt/modules/documenti_it/news/news/CAF-Review-Report.pdf (last visited July 14, 2025).

[109] Id. at 29 (Recommendation 1C): "Statutory changes would need to be accompanied by very clear communication that they imply no loosening of financial prudence. Instead, they represent an updating of MDB statutes in light of modern financial practices and a streamlining of the framework around MDB capital adequacy."

- As of June 2025, the EBRD Charter has been amended to move from its 1:1 ratio to a more flexible provision (Article 12.1): "The Board of Directors shall establish and maintain appropriate limits with respect to capital adequacy metrics, in order to protect the financial soundness and sustainability of the Bank."[110]
- EIB has also removed its former 250% limit and replaced it with a more flexible structure.

In March 2025, the EIB Statute was amended to remove the numerical determination of the Bank's Gearing Ratio (the Gearing Ratio) (currently 250%) from the EIB Statute itself, granting the EIB Board of Governors the power to determine the Gearing Ratio by unanimous decision . . . The amendment to the EIB Statute implemented one of the recommendations of the CAF Review to remove statutory lending limits from the statutes of MDBs. In June 2024, the EIB Board of Governors unanimously decided to increase the Gearing Ratio of the Bank from 250% to 290%, subject to the approval of the EIB Statute amendment, to allow the Bank to deliver on the priorities and goals set out in the Strategic Roadmap.[111]

- NIB took a similar action in 2020, replacing its statutory gearing limit with a risk-based comprehensive framework for capital and liquidity management.[112]
- IBRD has an amendment in process that would remove the statutory lending limit.[113]
- AsDB has an amendment in process that would remove the statutory lending limit.[114] The proposed amendment has been approved by the AsDB Board of Directors and transmitted to the Board of Governors for a vote without a meeting:

On 20 October 2023, the Board of Directors approved the proposal to recommend to the Board of Governors to vote (once the Governors had taken appropriate legal and legislative actions to subsequently vote on a resolution) and approve the removal of the Charter lending limitation [AsDB Article 12.1]. This initiative is in line with the Group of Twenty Expert Panel recommendations to maximize the financing capacity of multilateral development banks. It will support ADB's future

[110] EBRD Board of Governors' Resolution, No. 260, *Amendment to Article 12.1 of the Agreement Establishing the European Bank for Reconstruction and Development to Remove the Statutory Capital Limitation on Ordinary Operations*, May 18, 2023, entered into force June 26, 2025.

[111] EIB Financial Report 2024 at 9. The EIB amendment was approved, and the current EIB Charter (Article 16-5) reads: "The aggregate amount outstanding at any time of loans and guarantees granted by the Bank shall not exceed a maximum ratio in respect of its subscribed capital, reserves, non-allocated provisions and profit and loss account surplus to be established by the Board of Governors acting unanimously."

[112] "NIB's updated Statutes enter into force on 29 July," NIB Press release, July 9, 2020, https://www.nib.int/news/nibs-updated-statutes-enter-into-force-on-29-july.

[113] IBRD Board of Governors Resolution; No. 696, *Amendment of the Articles of Agreement - Removal of Lending Limitation*, adopted July 10, 2023. IBRD Article III, Section 3 would be deleted.

[114] AsDB Management's Report to the 58th Annual Meeting of the AsDB Board of Governors (May 5, 2025) confirms that "We are amending our Charter for the first time to remove the lending limitation."

lending operations as expanded by ADB's new capital adequacy framework. In parallel with the ADB Charter amendment process, ADB will assess the potential integration of a nominal lending limitation into the CAF [Capital Adequacy Framework]."[115]

7.45 The other financial ratio in the AIIB Charter governs the extent of AIIB's equity investments. That ratio requires that the amount AIIB has disbursed for equity investments not exceed the total of unimpaired paid-in subscribed capital and general reserves. There are limitations on equity investments in other MDB Charters, though formulations vary.[116]

(2) Other financial management considerations

7.46 The AIIB Charter also includes financial considerations among its operating principles for investment operations.[117] In addition, AIIB adopted a Risk Management Framework early on, revised in 2022, that provides an overview.[118] AIIB's 2024 Annual Report gives more detail:

> Our Risk Management Framework has been pivotal in developing a diverse and resilient portfolio, ensuring the stability of our operations. The Risk Management Department operates under the well-established "three lines of defense" model, with our Risk Appetite Statement (RAS) serving as a cornerstone, approved by our Board of Directors . . . This statement actively engages the Board and its Audit and Risk Committee in strategic risk deliberations. The RAS not only defines the Bank's appetite for core and noncore risks but also underscores our low tolerance for risks that could jeopardize the institution or compromise the Bank's mandate, such as reputational or compliance-related risks. It establishes thresholds for key risk indicators across multiple tiers, which are regularly reported to management and the Board. Any breaches or deviations trigger action plans to steer both Investment and Treasury operations.[119]

(3) Income and reserves

7.47 The AIIB Charter establishes the powers of the Board of Governors to allocate and distribute AIIB's net income and to determine reserves; these are reserved powers of the Board of Governors.[120] In particular, the Board of Governors is empowered

[115] *Status of the Financial Resources of the Asian Development Bank, Report of the Board of Directors*, AsDB Document No. BG57-6 (9 April 2024), paragraph 4.
[116] AfDB Article 15-4 (a); AsDB Article 12-3; EBRD Article 12-3; and EIB Article 16-5.
[117] *See* paragraph 5.30.
[118] AIIB's Risk Management Framework (December 2022) provides an overview of the different aspects of risk covered under AIIB policies and processes.
[119] AIIB Annual Report 2024 at 86.
[120] AIIB Article 23-2 (viii).

to determine, at least annually, any provision for reserves, allocation of net income to retained earnings or for other purposes, and any distribution of net income to the members.[121] Comparable powers are given to the Board of Governors in other MDBs.[122] Moreover, a decision by the AIIB Board of Governors to allocate net income to purposes other than retained earnings requires a Super Majority vote, similar to the EBRD Charter provisions.[123] Distribution of net income is specifically authorized but rare among the MDBs, as net income is more likely to be allocated for the MDB's ongoing needs and purposes.[124] For AIIB, a distribution of income would be in proportion to the number of shares held by each member, as in other MDBs.[125]

(4) Currencies

The AIIB Charter requirements for the use of currencies have been substantially simplified, in comparison with the Charters of many older MDBs.[126] This simplification has been made possible by the changes in the use and convertibility of currencies and in currency markets over the intervening decades. With simpler restrictions and obligations, AIIB and its members may find it easier to address new types of currencies in the future, such as electronic currencies. **7.48**

There are two general provisions governing AIIB's use of currencies. First, the AIIB Charter mandates that members shall not impose any restrictions on currencies, including the receipt, holding, use, or transfer by AIIB or by any recipient from AIIB, for payments in any country.[127] Second, the valuation of currencies and the determination of convertibility under the AIIB Charter is made by AIIB.[128] **7.49**

The AIIB Charter does specify the currency of payment for capital subscriptions, as discussed in Section A of this chapter. For installment payments of paid-in capital, members are required to pay in US dollars or other convertible currency, except as noted above, and AIIB may convert other currencies to US dollars.[129] Payments by **7.50**

[121] AIIB Article 18-1.
[122] AfDB Article 42; AsDB Article 40; EBRD Article 36; and IBRD Article V, Section 14. IADB Article VII, Section 4 addresses the issue with reference to distribution of net profits, including to the Fund for Special Operations.
[123] AIIB Article 18-1. EBRD Article 36-1 requires that allocations for other purposes be approved by the Board of Governors—by two-thirds of the Governors representing not less than two-thirds of total voting power.
[124] Often, net income is transferred to the institution's own concessional lending arm, whether a separate entity or separate funding mechanism. As yet, AIIB does not have a concessional lending function, though the Special Fund mechanism could eventually be used for that purpose, as it is in AsDB.
[125] AIIB Article 18-2.
[126] *See* AfDB Articles 16, 26, 27; AsDB Chapter V; EBRD Chapter V; IADB Article V; and IBRD Article IV, Section 2.
[127] AIIB Article 19-1.
[128] AIIB Article 19-2.
[129] AIIB Article 6-2. *See* the discussion of Alternatives A and B for national currency subscription payments, in paragraphs 7.16–7.17.

members on callable capital subscriptions in response to calls by AIIB may be made at the option of the member in dollars or in the currency required to discharge the obligations of AIIB for the purpose of which the call is made.[130]

7.51 In its investment operations, AIIB may provide financing in the currency of the country concerned, in accordance with policies that minimize currency risk.[131]

(5) Accounts and audits

7.52 The AIIB Charter continues an MDB tradition in setting the basic parameters for AIIB's financial accounts and audits. The Board of Directors is specifically required to submit the audited accounts for each financial year for the approval of the Board of Governors.[132] The reserved powers of the Board of Governors include the approval, after reviewing the auditors' report, of the general balance sheet and the statement of profit and loss of AIIB.[133] With respect to accounts, the AIIB By-Laws further detail the basic requirements:

> The accounts of the Bank shall be prepared in accordance with generally accepted accounting principles and, at least once a year, audited in accordance with generally accepted auditing standards by independent external auditors of international reputation chosen by the Board of Directors on the basis of a proposal by the President. On the basis of this audit, the Board of Directors shall submit promptly to the Board of Governors for approval a statement of accounts, including a general balance sheet and a statement of profit and loss.[134]

The AIIB By-Laws also mandate that AIIB's financial year shall begin on January 1 and end on December 31 of each year.[135] AIIB is obliged by the AIIB Charter to transmit to members and publish an annual report containing an audited statement of its accounts; members also receive quarterly summaries.[136]

7.53 The AIIB Board of Directors established an Audit and Risk Committee in January 2017, which is composed of four Directors and two external committee members. As seen in Figure 8.5, the functions of the Audit and Risk Committee include: review of AIIB's financial statements and accounting, auditing, and financial reporting practices, procedures, and issues; review of the selection procedures for and the qualification and performance of the external auditors as well as reports from the external auditors; review of the internal audit function; and review of risk-related

130 AIIB Article 6-3.
131 AIIB Article 14-4.
132 AIIB Article 26 (vii).
133 AIIB Article 23-2 (vii).
134 AIIB By-Laws, Section 5 (b).
135 AIIB By-Laws, Section 5 (a).
136 AIIB Article 34-3.

policies and the risk appetite statement. AIIB's external auditor was appointed in 2016.[137]

Overall, one measure of the anticipated soundness of AIIB's financial management and practices can be seen in its first issuer ratings, in July 2017, by the main financial ratings agencies: all were at AAA or equivalent.[138] AIIB's current ratings have remained at that high level.[139] In October 2017, the Basel Committee on Banking Supervision, a standard setter for financial regulators worldwide, agreed that supervisors may allow banks to apply a zero risk weight to AIIB liabilities. This action puts AIIB's future issuance of securities on a par with other MDBs, which is expected to facilitate AIIB's fundraising in international markets.[140] 7.54

F. Other Vehicles

(1) Special Funds

AIIB is positioned to add to its resources by establishing Special Funds with resources contributed by other parties, including its members, as noted previously. Any Special Fund must be designed to serve the purpose and come within the functions of AIIB, and be used on terms and conditions consistent with the purpose and functions of AIIB.[141] Special Funds are resources of AIIB, with administration costs charged to the Special Fund.[142] The rules and regulations adopted by AIIB for the establishment, administration, and use of each Special Fund must also conform to the AIIB Charter.[143] 7.55

[137] A new external auditor is expected in 2026. AIIB Audit and Risk Committee, Annual Report to the Board of Directors 2024–2025, at 4.

[138] *See* "Moody's assigns first-time Aaa issuer rating to Asian Infrastructure Investment Bank; outlook stable," Moody's Investors Service, June 29, 2017; "Fitch assigns Asian Infrastructure Investment Bank 'AAA': outlook stable," Fitch Ratings, July 13, 2017; and "Asian Infrastructure Investment Bank assigned 'AAA/A-1+' rating: outlook stable," Standard and Poor's Research Update, July 18, 2017.

[139] "Moody's Ratings affirms AIIB's Aaa rating, outlook remains stable," Moody's Investors Service, April 2, 2025; "Fitch assigns Asian Infrastructure Investment Bank 'AAA': outlook stable," Fitch Ratings, June 17, 2024; and "Asian Infrastructure Investment Bank 'AAA' Rating Affirmed; Outlook Stable," Standard and Poor's Research Update, March 13, 2025. Standard and Poor's notes at 3: "The early months of the Russia-Ukraine conflict, combined with overall complicated market dynamics, saw AIIB's spreads widen relative to peers. This led the bank then to rely more on private placements to reduce its overall funding cost. In line with our expectations, the impact was transitory and did not limit AIIB's ability to tap hard currency markets. From the start of 2024, bond spreads of the bank narrowed meaningfully and are now on par with much older 'AAA' rated institutions such as the International Bank for Reconstruction and Development and the Asian Development Bank."

[140] "The Basel Committee on Banking Supervision assigns eligible AIIB liabilities a 0% risk weighting," AIIB Press Release, October 11, 2017.

[141] AIIB Article 17-1 and 17-2.

[142] AIIB Article 17-1. AIIB charges an administration fee equal to 1% of any contribution, and the Special Fund bears all expenses appertaining directly to operations financed from the resources of the Special Fund. AIIB 2016 Financial Statements, Note 5.15 in AIIB (2017) at 50.

[143] AIIB Article 17-3.

7.56 In other MDBs, similar Special Funds have been established, often to provide concessional resources, either for operations similar to the MDB's non-concessional financing (such as the Asian Development Fund at AsDB) or for specific objectives.[144] In AIIB, it is worth noting that the requirement of unrestricted procurement in AIIB-financed operations expressly applies to ordinary and special operations alike.[145]

7.57 AIIB has established several Special Funds, with various purposes and funding sources.[146] Internal Special Funds are established by AIIB to receive and manage direct contributions from donors and are governed by the Bank's policies and decision-making bodies.

- Project Preparation Special Fund. Established in June 2016, AIIB's Project Preparation Special Fund (PPSF) is a multi-donor facility created to provide technical assistance grants to support the preparation of high-quality bankable projects for AIIB Members, especially less developed Members.
- Special Fund Window for Less Developed Members (SFW). The Special Fund Window for Less Developed Members (SFW) provides interest rate buydown for eligible sovereign-backed financing projects to make AIIB financing more affordable for its less developed Members. As mentioned in paragraph 12.53, this Special Fund was inspired by AIIB's experience with the COVID-19 Crisis Recovery Facility.
- Project Specific Window (PSW). The Project Specific Window (PSW) is a special fund that allows AIIB to accept, manage, and disburse grant co-financings on behalf of contributors into eligible AIIB projects in AIIB Members classified as either low- or middle-income or small island economies.[147]

7.58 External Special Funds are created within AIIB to receive and manage resources from facilities established by external parties for whom the Bank acts as an implementing entity. Each external Special Fund is subject to its specific governance arrangements. Three external Special Funds were established to channel resources from the Multilateral Cooperation Center for Development Finance

[144] AfDB Articles 8, 9, 10, 11, 13; AsDB Articles 9, 10, 19, 20; EBRD Articles 9, 10, 18, 19; and IADB Article III, Sections 2 and 3 (Fund for Special Operations). The IBRD Charter does not contain similar provisions. In AsDB, for instance, eight funds are listed as Special Funds: ADB Institute Special Fund, Asia Pacific Disaster Response Fund, Asian Development Fund, Climate Change Fund, Financial Sector Development Partnership Special Fund, Japan Special Fund, Regional Cooperation and Integration Fund, and Technical Assistance Special Fund, https://www.adb.org/site/funds/funds#special (last accessed July 14, 2025). As of December 31, 2024, EBRD was administering sixteen Special Funds, with aggregate pledged contributions and associated fees of €4.3 billion. EBRD Financial Report 2024 at 91.

[145] AIIB Article 13-8, derived from EBRD Article 13 (xii).

[146] Information here comes from the AIIB website, Special Funds Resources, https://www.aiib.org/en/how-we-work/partnerships/special-funds-resources/index.html (last visited July 14, 2025), supplemented by AIIB Annual Report 2023 at 74.

[147] AIIB website, Project Specific Window, at https://www.aiib.org/en/what-we-do/special-funds/project-specific-window-fund/index.html (last visited July 14, 2025).

(MCDF), the Global Infrastructure Facility (GIF), and the Pandemic Prevention, Preparedness and Response Intermediary Fund (Pandemic Fund).[148]

- Global Infrastructure Facility (GIF) Special Fund. The Global Infrastructure Facility Special Fund was established to administer grants received by AIIB as a Technical Partner of the Global Infrastructure Facility (GIF). The GIF is a global collaboration platform that supports the preparation, structuring, and de-risking of high-quality, bankable, sustainable infrastructure programs and projects in emerging markets that are attractive to private capital.
- Pandemic Fund Special Fund. The Pandemic Fund Special Fund was established to administer grants received by AIIB as Implementing Entity of the Pandemic Fund. The Fund, hosted by the World Bank, is the first multilateral financing mechanism dedicated to providing multiyear grants to help low- and middle-income countries become better prepared for future pandemics.
- Multilateral Cooperation Center for Development Finance (MCDF) Special Fund. The Multilateral Cooperation Center for Development Finance (MCDF) Special Fund was established to administer grants received by AIIB as Implementing Partner of the Finance Facility of the MCDF. The MCDF is a multilateral financial mechanism designed to promote high-quality infrastructure and connectivity investments in developing countries in compliance with IFI standards, including by encouraging other investors and financial institutions to adopt such standards.

The MCDF platform extends beyond AIIB's Special Fund, and includes a Finance Facility and separate governance structure. AIIB also serves as MCDF Administrator, and the MCDF Secretariat is housed at AIIB. The MCDF is further discussed in Chapter 12, Section E.

(2) Trust funds

Many MDBs also establish trust funds, managed by the MDB to utilize outside funds for its purposes. The AIIB Charter is unusual in its explicit recognition of this practice.[149] AIIB may only establish trust funds that are designed to serve the purpose and come within the functions of AIIB, under a trust fund framework approved by the Board of Governors.[150] Trust fund resources are managed by AIIB, but do not become assets of AIIB (unless otherwise provided in their setup). **7.59**

[148] AIIB Annual Report 2023, at 74.
[149] The ISDB has specific provisions for trust fund resources in its Charter. ISDB Articles 11, 13, and 14.
[150] AIIB Article 16-7.

(3) Subsidiaries

7.60 The AIIB Charter is also unusual in its express reference to AIIB's power to establish subsidiary entities.[151] Subsidiaries, like Special Funds and trust funds, must be designed to serve the purpose and come within the functions of AIIB. The establishment of subsidiaries requires the approval of the Board of Governors by a Special Majority vote.[152] Subsidiaries and similar vehicles have been considered and sometimes established in a number of ways at other MDBs, without express authorization or approval processes set out in their Charters.[153]

[151] For IBRD, for instance, the power to establish subsidiaries would be read into its implied powers. *See* Shihata (2000) at 851–4.

[152] AIIB Article 16-8. Article 24-4 further provides that the Board of Governors, and the Board of Directors to the extent authorized, may establish such subsidiary entities as may be necessary or appropriate to conduct the business of AIIB. The Chief Negotiators' Report further clarified that Article 16-8 and Article 24-4 should be read together as providing the framework for the establishment of subsidiary entities with the approval of the Board of Governors.

[153] *See* Rigo Sureda (2004) at paragraphs 374–445, discussing several such exercises at the World Bank (Consultative Group on International Agricultural Research (CGIAR), Onchocerciasis [River Blindness] Control Program, Global Environment Facility (GEF), Prototype Carbon Fund, and proposals that did not come to fruition for an energy affiliate and the "Bank's Bank"); at AfDB (African Development Fund, Africa Capacity Building Foundation); and among the World Bank, IMF and others (Joint Vienna Institute). The IFC has established a wholly owned subsidiary, IFC Asset Management Company, Limited.

8
GOVERNANCE: FRAMEWORK

Governance arrangements are central to the creation of a new multilateral development bank (MDB) in several ways. The governance arrangements establish how the institution will function—what organs will make which decisions and how these organs will be constituted. These elements contribute to the confidence of prospective members that the organization will be well-run and responsive to its shareholders. At the same time, the governance arrangements also regulate the power structure within the institution—determining how voting power will be determined and what majorities will be required for different decisions. In these respects, each prospective member is looking to see how its rights and influence will be cemented, whether as a large or a small shareholder. For the Asian Infrastructure Investment Bank (AIIB), the design of the governance arrangements took place at a time when the need for governance reforms had been debated for some time in MDB circles. The final AIIB arrangements take up some of these reforms, within an overall structure that is broadly comparable to other MDBs. **8.01**

The AIIB Charter provides for a hierarchy of three governance levels. The Board of Governors is the Bank's highest authority, composed of one Governor appointed by each member, meeting annually. The Board of Directors is responsible for the direction of the general operations of the Bank, and is composed of Directors elected by one or more Governors representing particular members, meeting at least quarterly. The President, elected by the Board of Governors, conducts the current business of the Bank, under the direction of the Board of Directors. **8.02**

This chapter describes the organization and powers of each of these governance levels. Chapter 9 (Governance: Decision-Making) presents the rules for these bodies to make decisions: Voting Power, Voting Majorities, and Delegation and Oversight. Chapter 10 (Transitions) then provides an inside look at how these bodies and rules were set up and maintained in AIIB's transition from negotiations to establishment and operation. **8.03**

A. Board of Governors

(1) Composition

Each member appoints a Governor and Alternate Governor, and is represented on the Board of Governors by its Governor or, in the Governor's absence, the Alternate **8.04**

Governor.[1] The size of the Board of Governors is determined by the number of members of the Bank. If all members approved through June 2025 complete the membership process, there will be 110 Governors on the Board of Governors.[2] The Board of Governors elects its Chairman and Vice Chairman at each annual meeting and can establish committees.[3] Overall, the provisions in the AIIB Charter regarding the composition of the Board of Governors are similar to the Charters of its counterparts.[4]

(2) Meetings

8.05 The Board of Governors meets annually, and at other times as called by the Board of Governors or Board of Directors, including at the request of five members.[5] In practice, non-annual meetings of MDB Boards of Governors are held rarely. Between meetings, the Board of Directors can seek a vote by the Board of Governors without a meeting,[6] and this is the most common way for Board of Governors decisions to be taken. The AIIB Charter also authorizes electronic meetings of the Board of Governors in special circumstances, a somewhat novel provision among MDBs.[7] For any meeting of the Board of Governors, the quorum requirement is a majority of Governors representing no less than two-thirds of the total voting power.[8] The meetings of the AIIB Board of Governors through June 2025 are listed in Figure 8.1.

8.06 Other MDBs regularly hold annual meetings in various member countries outside their headquarters.[9] The World Bank and International Monetary Fund (IMF)

[1] AIIB Article 22-1.

[2] At the time of AIIB's 10th Annual Meeting in June 2025, one hundred and three Governors were eligible to attend, representing members that had completed the membership process. There were seven prospective members. *See* Figures 6.5 and 6.6.

[3] AIIB Article 22-2 and AIIB Rules of Procedure of the Board of Governors, Sections 6 (b) and 9. AIIB's Board of Governors added an Advisory Group under its Rules of Procedure (Section 7), composed of the current and prior Chairs and current Vice Chairs. The Advisory Group can advise the Chair on urgent procedural issues related to meetings.

[4] *See generally* AfDB Articles 30 and 31; AsDB Articles 27 and 29; EBRD Articles 23 and 25; IADB Article VIII, Section 2; and IBRD Article V, Section 2.

[5] AIIB Article 24-1. Governors and Alternate Governors may be paid reasonable expenses in attending meetings, but are not entitled to remuneration from the Bank. AIIB Article 22-3.

[6] AIIB Article 24-3.

[7] AIIB Article 24-3, and AIIB Rules of Procedure of the Board of Governors, Section 2 (c). Another example, for the Board of Directors, can be found in the By-Laws of the European Stability Mechanism, Section 3-8 (December 8, 2014). *See also* BIS Article 31-2: "decisions of the Board may be taken by means of teleconferencing, or video conferencing, or by correspondence, unless at least five Directors request that the decisions be referred to a meeting of the Board."

[8] AIIB Article 24-2. The quorum requirement is the same in AsDB, EBRD, and IBRD, and requires a majority of Governors with 70% of total voting power in AfDB. AfDB Article 31-2; AsDB Article 29-2; EBRD Article 25-2; and IBRD Article V, Section 2 (d). In IADB, the quorum requires a majority of Governors, including a majority of regional Governors, representing not less than three-fourths of total voting power. IADB Article VIII, Section 2 (e). Since the United States' voting power in IADB cannot be lower than 30% under IADB Article VIII, Section 4 (b), the United States must participate for any Board of Governors' vote to be effective.

[9] AfDB Article 31-1 provides that the Annual Meetings of the AfDB Board of Governors be held in member countries, regional and non-regional.

o Inaugural Meeting (January 2016), Beijing, China o First Annual Meeting (June 2016), Beijing, China o Second Annual Meeting (June 2017), Jeju, Korea o Third Annual Meeting (June 2018), Mumbai, India o Fourth Annual Meeting (July 2019), Luxembourg o **Fifth Annual Meeting (October 2020), virtual** o Sixth Annual Meeting (October 2021), virtual o Seventh Annual Meeting (July 2022), virtual o Eighth Annual Meeting (September 2023), Sharm El Sheikh, Egypt o Ninth Annual Meeting (September 2024), Samarkand, Uzbekistan o Tenth Annual Meeting (June 2025), Beijing, China

Figure 8.1 Meetings of the AIIB Board of Governors (through June 2025)
Source: AIIB website (Board of Governors, Meetings) https://www.aiib.org/en/about-aiib/governance/board-governors/index.html (last visited July 14, 2025).

annual meetings, for instance, have had a rotation pattern of two years at headquarters in Washington, DC, and the third year in another country. Meeting in different countries provides different members with an opportunity to showcase their country's progress and developments, and shares the cost and administrative burden of hosting across the membership. Many, including AIIB, held virtual meetings during the global pandemic.[10]

(3) Powers

Under the AIIB Charter, all powers of the Bank are vested in the Board of Governors, as is the case in other MDBs.[11] The Board of Governors is authorized to delegate any or all of its powers to the Board of Directors, with the exception of those powers that the AIIB Charter specifically provides cannot be delegated.[12] **8.07**

These non-delegable powers are often known as reserved powers, representing core decisions for the institution that are reserved for its highest organ. The specific reserved powers for AIIB are consistent with, and in some cases nearly identical to, those specified for the Boards of Governors of other MDBs.[13] The AIIB Charter also includes in its list of reserved powers "such other powers as are expressly assigned to the Board of Governors in other provisions of the AIIB Charter," a formulation found in the AsDB and EBRD Charters as well. Other decisions specified throughout the AIIB Charter to be made by the Board of Governors are thus also "reserved powers" and cannot be delegated. Figure 8.2 lists the reserved powers and **8.08**

10 For example, the World Bank Annual Meetings were virtual in 2020 and 2021 as were the EBRD meetings.
11 AIIB Article 23-1. AfDB Article 29-1; AsDB Article 28-1; EBRD Article 24-1; IADB Article VIII, Section 2 (a); and IBRD Article V, Section 2 (a).
12 AIIB Article 23-2.
13 AIIB Article 23-2. AfDB Article 29-2; AsDB Article 28-2; EBRD Article 24-2; IADB Article VIII, Section 2 (b); and IBRD Article V, Section 2 (b).

Powers Reserved Under AIIB Article 23-2	Powers Assigned Under Other Articles
GOVERNANCE AND INSTITUTIONAL	
Admission of members and increases in subscription of a member*	Definition of Asia and region *(AIIB Article 1-2)*
Suspension of members**	Changes in the size or composition of the Board of Directors *(AIIB Article 25-2)*
Election of Directors and determination of expenses to be paid for Directors and Alternate Directors and remuneration, if any	Number of constituency members for Second Alternate Director *(AIIB Article 25-3)*
Election of the President, and suspension or removal from office;** remuneration and other conditions of service	Extension of deadline for Signatories to join *(AIIB Article 58-1)*
Amendment of the AIIB Charter**	
FINANCIAL	
Increase or decrease authorized capital**	Exceptions to 75% regional shareholding** *(AIIB Articles 5-2 and 5-3)*
Determination of reserves and allocation and distribution of the net profits of AIIB	Allocation of net income to other purposes** *(AIIB Article 18-1)*
Approval, after reviewing the auditors' report, the general balance sheet, and the statement of profit and loss of AIIB	Increase in the limitation on lending (up to 250%)** *(AIIB Article 12-1)*
	Establishment of subsidiaries* *(Article 16-8)*
	Approval of the trust fund framework *(AIIB Article 16-7)*
	Issuance of non-par value shares *(AIIB Article 7-1)*
OPERATIONAL	
	Financing for a non-member recipient** *(AIIB Article 11-1 (b))*
	New types of financing* *(AIIB Article 11-2 (vi))*

Figure 8.2 AIIB Board of Governors Reserved Powers

* = a Special Majority decision, requiring a majority of the total number of Governors, representing not less than a majority of the total voting power of the members.

** = a Super Majority decision requiring two-thirds of the total number of Governors, representing not less than three-fourths of the total voting power of the members.

assigned powers of the Board of Governors that cannot be delegated to the Board of Directors.

8.09 At its Inaugural Meeting in January 2016, the AIIB Board of Governors delegated its non-reserved powers to the Board of Directors, through a provision in the AIIB By-Laws. The AIIB By-Laws provide that the Board of Directors shall not take actions pursuant to delegated powers that are inconsistent with the actions of the Board of Governors.[14] Moreover, the AIIB Charter provides that the Board of Governors retains full power to exercise authority over any matter that has been delegated.[15]

One power commonly reserved to the Board of Governors in other MDBs has been assigned directly to the Board of Directors in AIIB: the power to approve arrangements for cooperation with other international organizations.[16] This clause originated in the IMF and IBRD Charters, at a time when other international organizations were also in a formative stage.[17] Discussions on the UN started immediately after the Bretton Woods negotiations, and the Food and Agriculture Organization (FAO) and International Labor Office (ILO) were in discussions about their postwar status. FAO and ILO had delegates at the IBRD negotiations, proposing clauses that recognized their role.[18] Relations with other international organizations could have had political dimensions, which would have been more appropriate for the Board of Governors to decide. 8.10

For AIIB, the AIIB Charter generally directs AIIB to work in close cooperation with other international financial institutions and international organizations concerned with economic development of the region or AIIB's operational areas. AIIB is authorized to enter into arrangements with such organizations, with the approval of the Board of Directors.[19] Moving this authority from the Board of 8.11

[14] Section 6 of the AIIB By-Laws provides: "The Board of Directors is authorized by the Board of Governors to exercise all the powers of the Bank, with the exception of those expressly reserved to the Board of Governors by paragraph 2 of Article 23 and other provisions of the Articles of Agreement, and subject to these By-Laws . . . The Board of Directors shall not take any action pursuant to powers delegated by the Board of Governors which is inconsistent with any action taken by the Board of Governors." This delegation of non-reserved powers to the Board of Directors is also found in AfDB General Regulations Article 4-1; AsDB By-Laws Section 8; EBRD By-Laws Section 8 (a); IADB By-Laws Section 4; and IBRD By-Laws Section 14.

[15] AIIB Article 23-3. *See* AfDB Article 29-3; AsDB Article 28-3; EBRD Article 24-3; and IADB Article VIII, Section 2 (c).

[16] The power to approve general agreements with other international organizations is a reserved power of the Board of Governors in the AfDB, AsDB, EBRD, IADB, and IBRD, in varying terms. *See* AfDB Article 29-2; AsDB Article 28-2; EBRD Article 24-2; IADB Article VIII, Section 2 (b); and IBRD Article V, Section 2 (b).

[17] The reserved power in the IBRD Charter (IBRD Article V, Section 2 (v) was identical to the reserved power in the IMF Charter at the time (Article XII, Section 2 (iv)). In addition, in the IMF and IBRD Charters, there was a specific provision on the relationship with other international organizations (IMF Article X; IBRD Article V, Section 8). The IBRD text stated:

> (a) The Bank, within the terms of this Agreement, shall cooperate with any general international organization and with public international organizations having specialized responsibilities in related fields. Any arrangements for such cooperation which would involve a modification of any provision of this Agreement may be effected only after amendment to this Agreement under Article VIII.
>
> (b) In making decisions on applications for loans or guarantees relating to matters directly within the competence of any international organization of the types specified in the preceding paragraph and participated in primarily by members of the Bank, the Bank shall give consideration to the views and recommendations of such organization.

The IMF Charter does not include subparagraph (b).

[18] *See* paragraph 2.32. A factor at Bretton Woods was a concern that arrangements with other international organizations could impose restrictions on the Bank's activities, particularly in light of arguments made by FAO representatives, who had proposed a role in approving Bank operations relevant to their fields. Bittermann (1967) at 98.

[19] AIIB Article 35.

Governors to the Board of Directors reflects experience in some other MDBs. Nowadays, there are fewer significant and lasting institutional commitments meriting the highest level of attention than was the case when IBRD was designed. Rather, there are now a multiplicity of dealings between MDBs and other international organizations with a more routine scope and level of technical and administrative detail, where decision at the level of the Board of Directors would fit better with the overall allocation of powers. In some cases, approval of an arrangement to cooperate with other international organizations by MDB management within Board-approved parameters might well be considered more appropriate.[20]

B. Board of Directors

(1) Composition

8.12 The AIIB Charter provides that Directors shall be "persons of high competence in economic and financial matters," elected to two-year terms, with the possibility of re-election.[21] AIIB's Board of Directors is composed of twelve Directors: nine elected by the Governors representing regional members (Regional Directors) and three elected by the Governors representing non-regional members (Non-Regional Directors).[22] Each Director represents one or more members, so that there are twelve constituencies of members represented on the Board of Directors. These basic provisions for the composition of the AIIB Board of Directors are comparable to other MDBs in most respects, with some differences highlighted below.[23]

8.13 The 9:3 ratio of Regional Directors to Non-Regional Directors provided in the AIIB Charter corresponds to the 75% regional shareholding.[24] The evolution of the AIIB Board constituencies since 2016 can be seen in Figure 8.3, as Signatories became members along with the fifty-three new members approved since 2017.

The size and composition of the AIIB Board of Directors may be changed by a decision of the Board of Governors by a Super Majority vote.[25] Other MDBs also provide for the Board of Governors to revise the size and composition of the Board of

[20] AIIB has entered into partnership arrangements of various types with many MDBs and others, in its cooperation with other international organizations. *See* paragraphs 4.15–4.18.

[21] AIIB Article 25-1 and 25-5. The general provisions for the biannual election of Directors are set out in Schedule B of the AIIB Charter. Schedule B further provides for the Board of Governors to prescribe rules for the conduct of each election of Directors, in accordance with those provisions.

[22] AIIB Article 25-1. Directors may not be members of the Board of Governors.

[23] AfDB Articles 33 and 34; AsDB Articles 30 and 32; EBRD Articles 26 and 28; IADB Article VIII, Section 3; and IBRD Article V, Section 4.

[24] AIIB Article 5-2 and 5-3.

[25] AIIB Article 25-2.

REGIONAL CONSTITUENCIES
o Bahrain; Djibouti; Iraq; **Jordan; Oman;** Qatar (AD); **Saudi Arabia (D); United Arab Emirates (AD)**
o **Bangladesh (AD);** Malaysia ; **Maldives; Nepal;** Philippines (AD); **Thailand (D)**
o **China (D/AD);** Hong Kong, China
o **Cambodia (AD); Indonesia (D); Lao People's Democratic Republic; Sri Lanka (AD);** Timor-Leste
o Fiji (AD); **Israel (AD); Korea (D); Mongolia;** Samoa; Tonga; Uzbekistan
o **Australia (AD);** Cook Islands; Nauru; **New Zealand (D);** Papua New Guinea; **Singapore (AD); Viet Nam**
o Belarus; Iran (AD); **Kazakhstan (AD); Russia (D); Tajikistan**
o **India (D/AD)**
o Azerbaijan (AD); **Brunei Darussalam; Georgia; Kyrgyzstan; Pakistan (D); Türkiye**
NON-REGIONAL CONSTITUENCIES
o **Austria;** Belgium; Croatia; Cyprus; **Finland; France; Germany (D);** Greece; Ireland; Italy (AD); **Luxembourg; Malta; Netherlands;** Portugal; Spain
o **Denmark;** Hungary; **Iceland; Norway; Poland;** Romania; Serbia; **Sweden (AD); Switzerland (AD); United Kingdom (D)**
o Algeria; Argentina; Benin; Brazil (AD); Chile; Egypt (D); Ethiopia; Liberia; Libya; Madagascar; Morocco; Peru; Rwanda; South Africa; Sudan; Togo; Tunisia; Uruguay
D = Director nationality AD = Alternate Director nationality

Figure 8.3 AIIB Board of Directors Constituencies June 2025

D = Director nationality AD = Alternate Director nationality

Source: June 2016 Election in Summary of Proceedings of the Annual Meeting of the AIIB Board of Governors, June 2016, at 71–2.

June 2025 Listing, from AIIB website listing of Board of Directors, https://www.aiib.org/en/about-aiib/governance/board-directors/board-members/index.html (last visited July 14, 2025).

Directors.[26] Over time, some have expanded the size of the Board of Directors as membership has expanded. For example, there are now twenty-five IBRD Executive Directors for a membership of 189; there were twelve Executive Directors at the beginning, when 45 countries were listed in Schedule A to the IBRD Charter. AsDB began with a Board of Directors of ten members, expanded to twelve with effect from its Fourth Annual Meeting (1971);[27] currently, AsDB has sixty-nine members (thirty-three countries were listed in Annex A to the AsDB Charter).

The size of the Boards differs among the MDBs as does the balance between re- **8.14**
gional and non-regional Directors for the regional MDBs.[28] The length of terms

[26] IBRD Article V, Section 4 (b) authorized the Board of Governors to make the intervening changes by an 80% majority vote. In the AsDB, the Charter provided for a ten-member Board, which could be expanded under AsDB Article 30-1 (ii) at the Second Annual Meeting to increase the representation of smaller less developed countries, by vote of a majority of Governors holding two-thirds of the total voting power. *See* comparable provisions in EBRD Article 26-3; AfDB Article 33-1; and IADB Article VIII, Section 3 (b) (ii).

[27] IBRD Article V, Section 4 (b) authorized the Board of Governors to make the intervening changes by an 80% majority vote. In the AsDB, the Charter provided for a ten-member board, which could be expanded under AsDB Article 30-1 (ii) at the Second Annual Meeting to increase the representation of smaller less developed countries, by vote of a majority of Governors holding two-thirds of the total voting power. *See* comparable provisions in EBRD Article 26-3; AfDB Article 33-1; and IADB Article VIII, Section 3 (b) (ii).

[28] AfDB: AfDB Article 33-1.

AsDB: The printed AsDB Charter cover cites AsDB Board of Governors' Resolution No. 27 as amended by Resolution No. 37, noting: "with effect from the Fourth Annual Meeting of the

	AIIB	AfDB	AsDB	IADB	IBRD	EBRD
MDB members	104	81	69	48	189	79
Directors	12	20	12	14	25	23
Regional Directors (members)	9 (49)	13 (54)	8 (50)	9 (26)	N/A	4 Recipient 4 Non-European
Non-Regional Directors (members)	3 (51)	7 (27)	4 (19)	5 (22)	N/A	
Single member constituencies	India	US	China Japan US	Canada US	US* Japan* China* Germany* France* UK* Saudi Arabia	EIB EU France Germany Italy Japan US UK
Term	2 years	3 years	2 years	3 years	2 years	3 years

Figure 8.4 Comparison of MDB Board Composition

* In IBRD, the five largest shareholders each appoint their own Director under the IBRD Charter (Article V, Section 4 (b)(i)). In 2025, there were seven single-member constituencies on the twenty-five-member Board: one each appointed by the United States, Japan, China, and Germany, as well as one each appointed by the United Kingdom and France, as these two members are tied for fifth-largest shareholder, and one elected by Saudi Arabia. *See* World Bank website, https://www.worldbank.org/en/about/leadership/directors (last visited July 14, 2025).

See IADB website https://www.iadb.org/en/who-we-are/how-we-are-organized/board-executive-directors/executive-directors-and-alternates (last visited July 14, 2025).

also varies, with AIIB following AsDB and IBRD in having two-year terms, while AfDB, EBRD, and IADB have three-year terms.[29] Figure 8.4 summarizes some elements of Board composition.[30]

8.15 Each AIIB Director appoints an Alternate Director, with full power to act when the Director is not present.[31] Directors and Alternate Directors are required to be nationals of member countries, but are not required to be nationals of members

Board of Governors, the size of the Board of Directors was increased to twelve (12) members, eight (8) members elected by the Governors representing regional member countries and four (4) members elected by the Governors representing non-regional member countries."

EBRD: Under EBRD Article 26-1, the twenty-three Directors are grouped in several ways: eleven Directors are elected by Governors representing Belgium, Denmark, France, the Federal Republic of Germany, Greece, Ireland, Italy, Luxembourg, the Netherlands, Portugal, Spain, the United Kingdom, the European Economic Community (now EU), and the EIB, while twelve represent other members, of whom four represent Central and Eastern European countries eligible for assistance from the Bank; four represent other European countries; and four represent non-European countries.

IADB: IADB Article VIII, Section 3 (b)(ii) (one Director is appointed by the largest shareholder (United States), not fewer than three are elected by non-regional members, and not fewer than ten others are elected by the remaining regional members).

[29] AsDB Article 30-3 and IBRD Article V, Section 4 (b) provide for two-year terms. AfDB Article 33-3, EBRD Article 26-5 and IADB Article VIII, Section 3 (iii) provide for three-year terms.

[30] *See* Delikanli (2018) at 102–3 for an expanded table that includes different elements.

[31] AIIB Article 25-3.

they represent.[32] Typically, each Director will represent several member countries in a Board constituency, although a larger shareholder may constitute a single shareholder constituency on its own.[33] Constituency members agree on which members' nationals will serve as Director and Alternate Director in succeeding terms, sometimes in rotation; the relative voting powers can mean that larger shareholders within the constituency end up with more prominent positions.

In AIIB, Directors representing more than a specified number of members may appoint an additional Alternate Director (currently, those Directors representing five or more members).[34] This additional Alternate Director position for larger constituencies could enhance member representation and voice, as more members will have an opportunity to participate more often in the rotation. Moreover, increasing the number of Board positions will facilitate the designation by Founding Members of a Director or Alternate Director on a permanent or rotating basis, a privilege enshrined in the AIIB Charter.[35] Seven of AIIB's Board constituencies have a second Alternate Director.[36] **8.16**

A second Alternate Executive Director position was first introduced in IMF as part of its governance reforms in 2008, and further expanded in the 2010 package of reforms. In IMF, an Executive Director elected by seven or more members is entitled to appoint two Alternate Executive Directors.[37] For comparison, there are twenty-five Executive Directors on the IMF Executive Board, representing 191 IMF members, and nine constituencies with two Alternate Executive Directors.[38] **8.17**

(2) Terms of Service

Directors and Alternates are required to "devote to the activities of the Bank such time and attention as the interests of the Bank may require," and attend physical **8.18**

[32] AIIB Article 25-4.

[33] *See* Figure 8.4 showing single member constituencies as of June 2025.

[34] AIIB Article 25-3. Board of Governors' Resolution No. 8, *Appointment of Additional Alternate Director*, adopted January 16, 2015, provided that Directors who cast the votes of five or more members, whether through election or assignment of votes, shall be entitled to appoint an additional Alternate Director. This decision has now been enshrined in the AIIB By-Laws, Section 10 (b).

[35] AIIB Schedule B, paragraph 10, discussed in paragraphs 6.22–6.23 in this volume.

[36] *See* Figure 8.3. Three other constituencies have more than five members and could have a second Alternate Director.

[37] IMF Article XII, Section 3 (e). The 2008 IMF Board of Governors' Resolution No. 63-2, *Reform of Quota and Voice in the International Monetary Fund*, effective April 28, 2008, provided that an Executive Director elected by at least nineteen members would be entitled to appoint two Alternate Executive Directors. That threshold was adjusted from nineteen to seven by the 2010 IMF Board of Governors' Resolution No. 66-2, *Fourteenth General Review of Quotas and Reform of the Executive Board*, effective December 15, 2010. Once the amendments in Resolution 63-2 went into effect, that adjustment was effective following the first regular Executive Board election in 2016.

[38] The IMF Board of Governors issued a Resolution on July 16, 2024, approving a twenty-fifth chair "to improve Sub-Saharan Africa's voice and representation and the overall balance of regional representation at the Board." *See* "IMF Board of Governors Issues a Resolution to Create a 25th Chair at the IMF's Executive Board," IMF Press Release No. 24/299, August 2, 2024.

and electronic meetings.[39] Directors and Alternate Directors serve without remuneration (in line with the part-time, non-residential position), while the Bank may pay them reasonable expenses incurred in attending meetings.[40] Directors and Alternate Directors are bound by the Code of Conduct for Board Officials, adopted by the Board of Governors at its Inaugural Meeting in January 2016.[41] In addition to one or more Alternate Directors, each Director may designate up to three Advisors as observers for physical meetings of the Board, without any voting or speaking rights.[42]

(3) Non-resident Board

8.19 The AIIB Board of Directors is set up as a part-time board, on a non-residential basis, meeting periodically throughout the year as the business of the Bank requires.[43] The Board of Governors can take a decision to alter the non-residential basis, by a Super Majority vote.[44] Regular in-person meetings are held on a quarterly basis, usually at AIIB headquarters.[45] The Board of Directors can also hold electronic meetings or vote without a meeting, and frequently does so.[46] For any meeting of the Board of Directors, the quorum requirement is a majority of Directors representing not less than two-thirds of the total voting power.[47]

[39] AIIB By-Laws, Section 10 (a).

[40] AIIB Article 25-6. Decisions on remuneration and expenses for Directors and Alternate Directors are among the reserved powers of the Board of Governors. AIIB Article 23-2 (v). Directors and Alternates on resident boards of other MDBs generally receive salary and benefits, which are reflected in the budget of the MDB.

[41] AIIB By-Laws, Sections 8 and 10 (k). The Code of Conduct for Board Officials was approved under Board of Governors' Resolution No. 9, *Codes of Conduct*, adopted January 16, 2016. The Code (Section 14) includes a sanction of mandatory resignation (normally within a specified period) at the decision of the Board Ethics Committee; Directors and Alternates are bound to follow Code-based sanctions by Section 10 (k) of the AIIB By-Laws. These provisions, taken together, address the problem that sometimes occurs in other MDBs, when elected Board officials found to have violated ethical or contractual rules cannot legally be required to resign.

[42] AIIB Rules of Procedure of the Board of Directors, Section 3 (i). The Rules were amended October 9, 2017, to allow a Director representing seven or more members to designate more than three Advisors, provided that the total number of the Director, Alternate(s), and Advisors does not exceed the number of members in the constituency. These Advisor positions offer an opportunity for additional support for the Director and additional involvement by members in the work of the Board, particularly when there are constituency members without a national serving as Director or Alternate. The Board's Rules of Procedure further stipulate that Advisors are not provided travel expenses by AIIB (unlike Directors and Alternate Directors); Advisors are, however, bound by the AIIB Charter, By-Laws, and Board Rules of Procedure, and the Code of Conduct for Board Officials shall apply to them, *mutatis mutandis*.

[43] AIIB Article 27-1.

[44] AIIB Article 27-1. This provision is similar to NDB Article 12 (g). For AIIB, the Super Majority required is approval by two-thirds of Governors representing not less than three-fourths of total voting power.

[45] AIIB By-Laws, Section 10 (a) (quarterly meetings). Under AIIB Article 27-1, meetings are called by the Chairman (AIIB President) or if requested by three Directors.

[46] AIIB Article 27-4. AIIB's Board of Directors meets virtually as needed; it met virtually in particular during the COVID-19 pandemic. *See* paragraph 12.19.

[47] AIIB Article 27-2. The AIIB quorum is the same as AsDB (AsDB Article 32-2) and EBRD (EBRD Article 28-2). Others differ slightly: *see* AfDB Article 34-2 (majority representing not less than 70% of total voting power); IADB Article VIII, Section 3 (f) (majority including majority of regional Directors, representing not less than two-thirds total voting power); and IBRD Article V, Section 4 (f) (majority representing not less than one-half total voting power).

The non-resident Board model for AIIB drew much attention during AIIB's establishment process, as many commentators made comparisons to the resident Board structures at AfDB, AsDB, EBRD, IADB, and IBRD.[48] Yet non-resident boards have long had a place in the governance of international financial institutions, and are the general practice in private companies.[49] As discussed in greater detail in Chapter 12 (Section A), the non-resident Board at IMF and IBRD was itself a departure from practice at that time. During the discussions on the IBRD and IMF Charters at Bretton Woods in 1944, the issue of residency was debated, and not fully settled in favor of resident boards until the inaugural meeting of the Boards of Governors in 1946. The debate included different views of Board functions, as well as cost. The United States prevailed, and the World Bank and IMF were established with full-time, resident boards.[50] Decades later, the issue of Board residency featured again in the negotiations on the AfDB Charter (1963), AsDB Charter (1965), and EBRD Charter (1990), before the resident board option was agreed.[51] **8.20**

Other international financial institutions that have functioned for decades with non-resident Board mechanisms include EIB, the Council of Europe Development Bank, CAF, CDB, Nordic Investment Bank (NIB), ISDB, BSTDB and the International Fund for Agricultural Development, and most recently the European Stability Mechanism and the New Development Bank (NDB). Governance reform discussions at the World Bank have also included proposals for a non-resident Board, though no reforms in this area were adopted.[52] **8.21**

[48] The AIIB Charter not only provides explicitly for the Board of Directors to function "on a non-residential basis" in Article 27-1, but also omits the references found in some other MDB charters to the Board functioning at the principal office of the Bank. *See* AfDB Article 34-1; AsDB Article 32-1; EBRD Article 28-1; IADB Article VIII, Section 3 (e); and IBRD Article V, Section 4 (e). The Chairman's Report on the Report on the Agreement Establishing the EBRD further notes: "Delegates agreed that Directors and their Alternates should be resident at the headquarters of the Bank."

[49] For a discussion of the different roles of boards at intergovernmental organizations including residency, *see* Martinez-Diaz (2009), in particular Table 3 at 106–7 (comparing selected indicators for IMF, IBRD, AsDB, AfDB, IADB, and EBRD Boards) and Table 4 at 109 (comparing EIB, the Organization for Economic Co-operation and Development (OECD) and BIS).

[50] *See* Callaghan and Hubbard (2016) at 131, noting the debate at the origin of the Bretton Woods Institutions between Harry Dexter White and John Maynard Keynes. "Keynes wanted high-level, part-time non-executive boards to focus on the strategic direction of the institution. But White (and the United States) prevailed and the World Bank and IMF were established with full-time, resident executive boards to act as a political check on every decision."

[51] For AfDB, the issue of Board residency had also been debated in the preparation of AfDB, where some felt non-resident Directors "would facilitate the release by governments of people with requisite skills and also result in considerable savings." The Directors did not actually become resident until 1970. Gardiner and Pickett (1984) at 23.

For AsDB, during the negotiations on the Charter, cost-consciousness led to at least one proposal for a part-time Board. Wilson (1987) at 27.

For EBRD, a majority of the European Community countries originally favored a non-resident Board in order to economize on cost, as in the EIB. Menkveld (1991) at 78. Apparently, the United States argued in favor of a resident board at EBRD to have a powerful voice in day-to-day functions, so as to assure that the vague compromises in negotiations would be implemented. Weber (1994) at 19.

[52] One proposal to transform the World Bank Board from its resident, full-time status can be seen in the Report of the High-Level Commission on Modernization of World Bank Group Governance, Zedillo (2009) at Recommendation #2. Dollar (2015) at 3 notes the Zedillo criticisms of the current World Bank arrangement of a resident Board that approves all loans, and the point that the World Bank Group resident Board "represents both a large financial cost to the bank (US$70 million per year) and an extra layer of management that slows down project preparation and makes the bank less efficient." He also comments that slowness of project preparation is among the main client criticisms of MDBs.

(4) Powers

8.22 The powers of the AIIB Board of Directors can be categorized in three ways, for purposes of analysis: general power, delegated powers, and specific powers.

- The "general power" of the Board of Directors is to be responsible for the direction of the general operations of the Bank.[53]
- The "delegated powers" of the Board of Directors are all the non-reserved powers of the Board of Governors that the Board of Governors has delegated to the Board of Directors, as discussed in paragraph 8.09. This delegation of powers includes the authorization from the Board of Governors to the Board of Directors to adopt rules and regulations as may be necessary or appropriate to conduct the business of the Bank.[54]
- The "specific powers" of the Board of Directors are those decisions assigned to the Board of Directors throughout the AIIB Charter, as well as the seven powers enumerated in Article 26 of the AIIB Charter.

These categories are similar to those set out in the AfDB, AsDB, and EBRD Charters, although the enumerated powers differ somewhat in AIIB.[55] The assigned powers include the appointment of Vice-Presidents; arrangements with international organizations (discussed in paragraph 8.10); and the power to interpret the AIIB Charter, subject to appeal to the Board of Governors.[56] Key enumerated powers are described in what follows.

(a) Supporting the Board of Governors

8.23 The Board of Directors is obliged to prepare the work of the Board of Governors.[57] This function can be seen in the preparation of decisions for approval by the Board of Governors, as these decisions are first reviewed and approved by the Board of Directors.[58] This function is routinely carried out by the Board of Directors in other MDBs, although only AfDB, AsDB, and EBRD have provisions to that effect in their Charters.

[53] AIIB Article 26. Reference to "operations of the Bank" in the AIIB Charter means all activities of the Bank, not just its investment operations. This terminology is common in other Charters.

[54] AIIB By-Laws, Section 6, referring to the power to adopt rules and regulations under AIIB Article 24-4.

[55] IADB and IBRD do not have enumerated powers in the same way. The references in this section to the provisions of other MDB Charters on the powers of the Board of Directors refer to AfDB Article 32; AsDB Article 31; EBRD Article 27; IADB Article VIII, Section 3 (a); and IBRD Article V, Section 4 (a).

[56] Decisions of the Board of Directors specifically mentioned in the AIIB Charter include: setting policies on percentage of an entity's equity investment (AIIB Article 14-3); the appointment of Vice-Presidents (AIIB Article 30); arrangements with international organizations (AIIB Article 35); and, perhaps most importantly, the power to issue interpretations of the AIIB Charter, with a final appeal to the Board of Governors (AIIB Article 54-1). On interpretation, *see also* paragraphs 11.10–11.12.

[57] AIIB Article 26 (i).

[58] The Board of Directors decides when a vote of the Board of Governors on a specific question should be taken without a meeting, and the underlying proposal for that vote would first be discussed and decided upon by the Board of Directors. AIIB Article 24-3 and AIIB Rules of Procedure of the Board of Governors, Section 11.

(b) Policy

The Board of Directors has the authority to establish the policies of the Bank.[59] Major operational and financial policies require approval by the Board of Directors by a majority representing not less than three-fourths of total voting power. The Chief Negotiators' Report amplifies the meaning of "major operational and financial policies" by noting that "major policies established by the Board of Directors under Article 26 (ii) would include such policies as environmental and social impact and procurement (Article 13) and disclosure (Article 34)." The Board may, under Bank policies, delegate authority to the President, and decisions on such delegation also require approval of the Board of Directors by a majority representing not less than three-fourths of total voting power. This higher majority for certain decisions by the Board of Directors on policy matters recalls a provision in the EBRD Charter that general policy decisions shall be taken by a majority of not less than two-thirds of the total voting power of the members voting.[60] **8.24**

(c) Decisions on operations

The Board of Directors has the authority to take decisions on the financing operations of AIIB.[61] These operations include: making, co-financing, or participating in direct loans; equity investment; guarantees; use of Special Fund resources; technical assistance; and other types of financing determined by the Board of Governors.[62] The Board of Directors is expressly authorized under the AIIB Charter to delegate decisions on these operations to the President. A decision to make a delegation requires approval by a majority representing not less than three-fourths of total voting power (the same majority as for delegation under policies approved by the Board). Some of the other MDBs, such as AfDB, AsDB, and EBRD, include similar authority in their Charters for the Board to decide on investment operations.[63] **8.25**

Under these provisions, the AIIB Board of Directors has delegated decision authority for financing operations to the President, within specified parameters. That delegation is included in AIIB's Accountability Framework, first adopted in 2018, discussed at greater length at paragraphs 9.24–9.31 and in Chapter 12, Section B. **8.26**

[59] AIIB Article 26 (ii).

[60] EBRD Article 29-3; *see also* BSTDB Article 28-3. The meaning of this provision at the time negotiations on the EBRD Charter were concluded is set out in the Chairman's Report on the Agreement Establishing the European Bank for Reconstruction and Development: "Delegates intended that, in the case of differing views on whether or not issues involved 'general policy', decisions would be made by the Board on the basis of advice from the Legal Counsel. In general, decisions on individual operations would not involve such issues, but 'general policy issues' would include, inter alia, the budget; the annual programme of operations; borrowing policy, including borrowing limits; interest rate policy; exchange risk management policy; the drawing down of notes; underwriting policy and the organizational structure of the Bank."

[61] AIIB Article 26 (iii).

[62] AIIB Article 11-2.

[63] The AIIB Charter does not include provisions found in the AsDB Charter (AsDB Article 14 (iv)) and EBRD Charter (EBRD Article 13 (vi)) that, for each operation, the President presents the Board of Directors with a written report regarding the applicant's proposal with recommendations. Such written reports are included in other charters, without reference to the President, such as in IADB Article III, Section 7 (a)(i) and IBRD Article III, Section 4 (iii).

(d) Supervision and oversight

8.27 The AIIB Board of Directors is expressly required to supervise the management and operation of AIIB on a regular basis.[64] While this function is carried out by other MDB Boards of Directors, the AIIB Charter is unusual in making this responsibility explicit.[65] This provision can be seen as adding more definition to the Board's role in the non-residential context, where physical presence is not an element of oversight. Indeed, the AIIB Charter further requires the Board of Directors to establish an oversight mechanism for this purpose, "in line with principles of transparency, openness, independence and accountability." The Chief Negotiators' Report records more detail that illustrates what the negotiators expected in respect of the oversight mechanism:

> Representatives agreed that the oversight mechanism to be established by the Board of Directors under Article 26 (iv) would be designed in line with the principles of transparency, openness, independence and accountability, and would address such areas as audit, evaluation, fraud and corruption, project complaints and staff grievances, and reflect the Bank's character as a multilateral financial institution focused on infrastructure development.

With principles in the AIIB Charter and some details in the Chief Negotiators' Report, this arrangement has given AIIB the scope to innovate in fulfilling this mandate, so that functions comparable to those at other MDBs can be designed to reflect AIIB's unique characteristics. The oversight bodies at other MDBs—such as evaluation, accountability, integrity, and internal dispute resolution—have been added and refined over time, necessarily in a piecemeal fashion. AIIB has the opportunity and the challenge to draw up these functions in a coordinated way from the start. In 2019, the Board of Directors approved AIIB's Oversight Mechanism, formally grouping these functions, as discussed in paragraphs 9.28–9.29 and Chapter 12, Section C.

(e) Strategy, annual plan, and budget

8.28 The Board of Directors has the authority to approve AIIB's strategy, annual plan, and budget.[66] How the content of the strategy and annual plan evolves over time is likely to be worked out between the Board and management. Other MDBs have similar planning documents without Charter-based requirements. The annual budgets are also approved by the Board of Directors and generally reported to the Board of Governors in AfDB, AsDB, EBRD, IADB, and IBRD.[67] The summaries of AIIB's annual Business Plan and Budget documents, approved by the Board of Directors, are posted on the AIIB website.[68]

64 AIIB Article 26 (iv).

65 The EIB Rules of Procedure, Article 18-2, provide that the Board of Directors, also non-resident, shall ensure that EIB is properly run in accordance with its Charter and other texts.

66 AIIB Article 26 (v).

67 AsDB Article 31 (iv); EBRD Article 27 (iv); and IADB Article VIII, Section 3 (i). The requirement to submit the annual budget approved by the Board of Directors to the Board of Governors for information is found in the AIIB By-Laws, Section 5 (c). The approval and reporting requirements are found in the By-Laws for IBRD (Section 18 (b)) and the General Regulations for AfDB (Section 8-1).

68 AIIB Website, https://www.aiib.org/en/policies-strategies/strategies/business-plan-summaries.html (last visited July 14, 2025).

(f) Committees

The Board of Directors is also empowered to appoint committees,[69] as in some other MDBs.[70] There is no requirement that Committee members be members of the Board. There are four Committees under the Board of Directors: the Audit and Risk Committee (ARC); the Budget and Human Resources Committee (BHRC); the Policy and Strategy Committee (PSC); and the Ethics Committee. The Directors are appointed for a term of two years. The external members of the ARC are appointed for a term of three years. These Committees are described in Figures 8.5 and 8.6. **8.29**

Audit and Risk Committee (ARC): Four Directors and two external members.

- Review AIIB's financial statements and accounting, auditing, and financial reporting practices, procedures, and issues.
- Review the selection procedures for and the qualification and performance of the external auditors; review the reports from the external auditors and ensure appropriate action be taken in respect of major improvement areas identified.
- Review the scope of work and internal audit plan and the effectiveness of the internal audit function.
- Review the effectiveness of the internal control system.
- Review AIIB's financial and risk-related policies; annually review the Bank's risk management framework and its risk appetite statement.
- Receive reports on violations of the Prohibited Practices Policy (PPP) from the Managing Director of the Complaints-resolution, Evaluation and Integrity Unit (CEIU).

Budget and Human Resources Committee (BHRC): Six Directors.

- Review the proposed annual administrative budget, taking into account the annual business plan, review the quarterly budget execution update, and report thereon to the Board.
- Review and assess the implementation of the staffing strategies, the compensation and benefits policies and related issues periodically and make recommendations to the Board as appropriate.
- Review the human resources update report semi-annually.
- Undertake the functions of the Committee provided for under the Code of Conduct for Board Officials.
- Receive the summary of an Administrative Review Decision generated as part of Staff Rule 8.01.
- Consider any other aspects of the annual administrative budget and the Bank's human resources as the Board may request and report thereon to the Board.
- Receive briefings on significant actions proposed by the President under the terms of the Policy on Compensation and Benefits, prior to their implementation.

Policy and Strategy Committee (PSC): Six Directors.

- Review AIIB's operational policies (other than financial and risk-related policies), including but not limited to the environment and social and procurement policies, and report thereon to the Board.
- Advise on the development of AIIB's strategies and report thereon to the Board.
- Review the proposed annual business plan, taking into account the annual administrative budget, and report thereon to the Board.
- Undertake any other activities consistent with these Terms of Reference as the Board may request and report thereon to the Board.
- Receive updates on the findings of project evaluations, and requests filed by Project-affected People under the Project-affected People's Mechanism, as part of the Oversight Mechanism.

Figure 8.5 AIIB Board of Directors: Committee Responsibilities (Audit and Risk, Budget and Human Resources, Policy and Strategy)

Source: AIIB website (Board of Directors, Committees) https://www.aiib.org/en/about-aiib/governance/board-directors/board-committees/index.html (last visited July 14, 2025).

[69] AIIB Article 26 (vi).

[70] The Board's power to appoint committees is found in the Charters for IADB (Article VIII, Section 3 (i)) and IBRD (Article V, Section 4 (i)). It is not found in the Charters for AfDB, AsDB, and EBRD; rather, AsDB By-Laws Section 12 and EBRD Rules of Procedure of the Board of Directors Section 11 contain a similar power. The AfDB Board of Directors also has a committee structure similar to these others.

Ethics Committee: Membership is co-extensive with that of the BHRC.

- Receive any notice to it from a Board Official that such Board Official has been arrested, charged, or convicted of any criminal offense; the Ethics Committee may consider such notice as equivalent to an allegation of misconduct constituted by a violation of the Code.
- Receive information from the Chief Ethics Officer as to the resolution of any concerns related to disclosure of financial and business interests of Board Officials or those of their immediate family members, together with any outstanding concerns; the Ethics Committee shall consider and resolve such outstanding concerns.
- Receive information from a Board Official of a matter unresolved with the Chief Ethics Officer; the Ethics Committee shall consider and resolve such a matter.
- Receive reports and regularly obtain advice from the Chief Ethics Officer on any matter concerning Board Officials brought to the attention of the Chief Ethics Officer, and on the resolution of such matter.
- Receive requests for, and issue as needed, guidance concerning conflicts of interest, annual financial disclosures, and other ethical aspects of conduct in respect of Board Officials.
- Receive and consider allegations of misconduct constituted by a violation of the Code of Conduct for Board Officials.
- Consider and otherwise resolve all ethical aspects of conduct in respect of Board Officials and make recommendations to the Board of Directors accordingly.

Figure 8.6 AIIB Board of Directors: Committee Responsibilities (Ethics)
Source: AIIB website (Board of Directors, Committees) https://www.aiib.org/en/about-aiib/governance/board-directors/board-committees/index.html (last visited July 14, 2025).

(g) Accounts

8.30 Approving AIIB's balance sheet and statement of profit and loss is a reserved power of the Board of Governors. Submitting the audited accounts for each financial year for approval by the Board of Governors is the responsibility of the Board of Directors. This allocation of responsibilities is found in other MDBs as well, whether in the Charters, as in AfDB, AsDB, and EBRD, or in the By-Laws, as in IBRD and IADB.[71]

C. President

(1) Election

8.31 The AIIB President is elected by the Board of Governors.[72] The election of the President requires a Super Majority vote in the Board of Governors; some other MDBs also require a qualified majority vote for President, though a lower one.[73]

71 AfDB Articles 29-2 (g) and 32-4; AsDB Articles 28-2 (viii) and 31 (iii); EBRD Articles 24-2 (viii) and 27 (iii); IADB By-Laws, Section 10; and IBRD By-Laws, Section 18.

72 AIIB Article 29-1. The Board of Governors adopted Rules for the Election of the President in December 2019. AIIB Board of Governors Resolution No. 87, *Rules for the Election of the President*, adopted December 30, 2019, https://www.aiib.org/en/news-events/news/2020/_download/Rules-for-the-Election-of-the-President-adopted-Dec-2019.pdf.

73 AIIB Article 29-1. A Super Majority vote requires two-thirds of Governors with three-fourths of total voting power. This is higher than the majority votes required for election of the President among AfDB, AsDB, EBRD, IADB, and IBRD. AfDB Article 36-1 and IADB Article VIII, Section 5 (a) (a majority of total voting power including a majority of total regional voting power); AsDB Article 34-1 and EBRD Article 30-1 (a majority of Governors with a majority of total voting power). In IBRD, the selection of the President is decided by the Executive Directors (the Board of Directors), not the Board of Governors, and by a simple majority. IBRD Article V, Section 5 (a).

The Super Majority requirement, including 75% of the total voting power, ensures that the President elected has very substantial support from the shareholders, while it also could allow one or a handful of shareholders to exercise a veto. That said, there have been longstanding nationality traditions for the heads of IBRD (United States), IMF (European), and AsDB (Japanese) with only a simple majority required and without any veto power that would affect the decision.[74]

AIIB's first President, Mr. Jin Liqun, was elected to his first term at the Inaugural Meeting of the Board of Governors, in January 2016.[75] He had previously been chosen as AIIB's President-designate in August 2015, with the stated expectation of the Chief Negotiators that he would be elected as the first President.[76] In 2020, he was re-elected to a second term beginning in January 2021, which will conclude on January 15, 2026.[77] AIIB's Board of Governors elected Madame Zou Jiayi as AIIB's second President at their 10th Annual Meeting in June 2025, for a term to commence in January 2026.[78] **8.32**

The AIIB Charter formally includes an open, transparent and merit-based selection process, a requirement that has been mentioned in other MDBs but not included in their Charters.[79] Election of the President by the Board of Governors in AIIB follows the practice at AfDB, AsDB, EBRD, and IADB;[80] in comparison, a model based on the World Bank and IMF would empower the Board of Directors to select the President.[81] **8.33**

[74] *See* Cogan (2009) at 227–9 and 241–4, detailing practice and suggesting that the IBRD-IMF deal has ended. In fact, the results since 2009 have not changed (US national at IBRD; European national at IMF), but there have been candidates of other nationalities publicized as serious contenders in each case (e.g., former Mexican Finance Minister Agustin Carstens at IMF and former Nigerian Finance Minister Ngozi Okonjo-Iweala at IBRD, among others).

[75] AIIB Board of Governors' Resolution No. 5, *Election of the President*, approved January 16, 2016.

[76] *See* paragraph 10.19.

[77] *See* "AIIB Launches 2025 President Election," AIIB Press Release, March 31, 2025. The Board of Governors approved Rules for the Election of the President in December 2019. AIIB Board of Governors' Resolution No. 87, *Rules for the Election of the President*, adopted December 30, 2019. The election of the President is found in AIIB Board of Governors' Resolution No. 97, *Election of the President*, adopted July 28, 2020.

[78] AIIB Board of Governors' Resolution No. 141, *Election of the President*, adopted June 24, 2025.

[79] AIIB Article 29-1. *See* the Report on the Selection Process of the President, adopted by the IBRD Executive Directors, in response to Development Committee communiques calling for an open, merit-based and transparent selection process, at Development Committee (2011). The Development Committee, in its Communique of April 16, 2011, welcomed this Report addressing an open, merit-based and transparent selection process, and the IBRD Executive Directors announced that a new process was followed in 2012. "World Bank's Executive Directors select Dr. Jim Yong Kim 12th President of the World Bank Group," World Bank Press Release, April 16, 2012. The selection of Ajay Banga as World Bank Group President in 2023 also refers to an open, merit-based and transparent nomination process. "Ajay Banga Selected 14th President of the World Bank," World Bank Press Release, May 3, 2023.

Similarly, the IMF process for the selection of Managing Director has referred to an open, merit-based and transparent selection process following evolving reforms dating back to 2007. *See, e.g.*, Communiqué of the International Monetary and Financial Committee of the Board of Governors of the International Monetary Fund, October 4, 2009, paragraph 5.

[80] AfDB Article 36-1; AsDB Article 34-1; EBRD Article 30-1; IADB Article VIII, Section 5 (a); and IBRD Article V, Section 5 (a). Originally, the AfDB President was elected by the Board of Directors; this was changed to election by the Board of Governors by amendment of the AfDB Charter in 1979. AfDB Board of Governors' Resolution 05-79, *Concerning the Amendments of the Agreement Establishing the African Development Bank to Enable Non-African Countries to Become Members Thereof*, approved May 17, 1979, entered into force May 7, 1982, Annex, paragraphs 12 and 16.

[81] IBRD Article V, Section 5 (a) (selection of the President by the Executive Directors) and IMF Article XII, Section 4 (a) (selection of the Managing Director by the Executive Board).

(2) Qualifications and terms of service

8.34 The AIIB President is required to be a national of a regional member country, as in the AfDB and AsDB, and following precedent, may not serve concurrently as a Governor, Alternate Governor, Director, or Alternate Director.[82] The term of office is five years, with the possibility of being re-elected once.[83] AIIB's two-term limit is also found in AfDB and has been discussed at IADB.[84] The AIIB President may be suspended or removed from office by a Super Majority decision of the Board of Governors,[85] reflecting comparable practice elsewhere.[86] The AIIB Board of Governors determines the terms of service and remuneration of the President, among its reserved powers.[87]

(3) Powers

8.35 The powers of the President under the AIIB Charter flow from the dual role as the chief executive of AIIB and as Chairman of the Board of Directors. As the Bank's chief executive, the President is "chief of the staff of the Bank" and conducts, under the direction of the Board of Directors, the current business of AIIB.[88] That broad role is not further limited by the provisions of the AIIB Charter. Additional specific powers of the President include the responsibility for the organization, appointment, and dismissal of officers and staff, in accordance with regulations adopted by the Board of Directors,[89] and the preparation of the administrative budget to be presented to the Board of Directors for approval.[90] The Board of Directors may

[82] AIIB Article 29-1. AfDB Article 36-1 and AsDB Article 34-1.

[83] AIIB Article 29-2. The President's term is five years in the AfDB (AfDB Article 36-1), AsDB (AsDB Article 34-2), and IADB (IADB Article VIII, Section 5 (a)) and four years at the EBRD (EBRD Article 30-1). The President's initial term in IBRD is also five years, and successive terms may be up to five years. IBRD By-Laws, Section 13 (c).

[84] AfDB Article 36-1. For IADB, *see* Section 2 (c) of the Regulations for the Election of the President at IDB: "The Governors state their firm will that no President shall hold office for more than two consecutive terms of five years." The terms of the NDB President and Vice-Presidents are non-renewable. NDB Article 13 (d).

[85] AIIB Article 29-2. This Article also provides that if the office of the President for any reason becomes vacant during his term, the Board of Governors shall appoint an Acting President for a temporary period or elect a new President. This possibility of having an Acting President for a temporary period is included in the AfDB Charter in case the President is suspended by the Board of Governors. AfDB Article 36. In the IADB, the Executive Vice President would act in the President's absence or incapacity to act. IADB Article VIII, Section 5 (b). The Charters for the AsDB, EBRD, and IBRD do not refer to the appointment of an Acting President.

[86] AfDB Article 36-1 (majority of total voting power including majority of regional total voting power); AsDB Article 34-2 (two-thirds of Governors exercising two-thirds majority of total voting power); EBRD Article 30-2 (two-thirds of Governors exercising two-thirds majority of total voting power); and IADB Article VIII, Section 5 (a) (majority of total voting power including majority of regional total voting power). In IBRD, there is no special majority required for the Executive Directors to decide that the President shall cease to hold office, or to select the President. IBRD Article V, Section 5 (a).

[87] AIIB Article 23-2 (vi). There are similar provisions in AfDB Article 29-2 (d); AsDB 28-2 (vii); EBRD Article 24-2 (vii); IADB Article VIII, Section 2 (b)(iii); and IBRD Article V, Section 2 (h).

[88] AIIB Article 29-4. By virtue of this clause, the President is also the legal representative of AIIB.

[89] AIIB Article 30-2.

[90] AIIB By-Laws, Section 5 (c).

also delegate authority to the President, under Bank policies and for decisions on operations.[91]

As the Chairman of the Board of Directors, the President calls meetings on his initiative or at the written request of at least three Directors, including regular meetings at least quarterly.[92] The agenda is prepared and circulated by or on the instructions of the President, with the possibility for any Director to add any matter on which the Board has power to act before the meeting; matters may be added during the meeting unless any Director or the Chairman objects.[93] When the decision on a specific question should not, in the view of the President, be postponed until the next regular meeting of the Board, he may request a vote by the Board of Directors between meetings; if the decision is suitable to be made on a no-objection basis, he may instead request an absence of objection approval.[94] The President as Chairman of the Board has no vote, except a deciding vote in case of an equal division.[95] **8.36**

The President plays a similar role with respect to meetings of the Board of Governors, but does not act as Chairman or vote.[96] The President is responsible for preparation and circulation of the agenda for meetings of the Board of Governors, under direction of the Board of Directors, and has charge of all the arrangements for these meetings, together with the Chairman of the Board of Governors.[97] **8.37**

(4) Vice-Presidents

The AIIB Charter provides for one or more Vice-Presidents, to be appointed by the Board of Directors on the recommendation of the President, on the basis of an open, transparent and merit-based process.[98] While this process requirement is novel, the other AIIB provisions on the appointment of Vice-Presidents are **8.38**

[91] AIIB Article 26. For the delegation of decision authority for financing operations to the President, *see* 9.24–9.27 and Chapter 12, Section B.

[92] AIIB Article 29-3 (Chairman of the Board) and 27-1 (calling of meetings). Under the Board's Rules of Procedure, the President may designate a Vice-President to chair in his absence; if both are absent, the Board selects a Director as Chairman. However, the President, Vice-Presidents, and Directors shall not chair a meeting in the event of a conflict of interest related to an item on the agenda at that meeting. AIIB Rules of Procedure of the Board of Directors, Section 3.

[93] AIIB Rules of Procedure of the Board of Directors, Section 4.

[94] AIIB Rules of Procedure of the Board of Directors, Section 5 (d) (voting without meeting) and Section 5 (e) (approval in absence of objection).

[95] AIIB Article 29-3. This provision for a deciding vote dates back to BIS and IAB (*see* paragraph 2.40). Because voting in the Board of Directors is by voting power and not by number of Directors (*see* paragraph 9.11), it is mathematically unlikely for there to be an equal division.

[96] AIIB Article 29-3.

[97] AIIB Rules of Procedure of the Board of Governors, Section 2 (g) and 4.

[98] AIIB Article 30-1. As of June 2025, AIIB has four Vice-President positions listed on its website (Corporate Secretary, Investment Solutions, Policy & Strategy, and Chief Administration Officer); previously, there have been five. AIIB senior management also includes the General Counsel, two Chief Investment Officers, the Chief Economist, Chief Financial Officer, and Chief Risk Officer, appointed by the President. *See* AIIB website,
https://www.aiib.org/en/about-aiib/governance/_common/_download/AIIB_organizational_structure.pdf (last visited July 14, 2025).

familiar. The appointment of Vice-Presidents by the Board of Directors on the President's recommendation in AIIB follows AsDB, EBRD, and IADB, while in the World Bank and AfDB these appointments are made by the President.[99] Nationality considerations are found at the Vice-President level in most of these MDBs.[100]

8.39 In recommending candidates for Vice-President, the AIIB President is obliged, in his recommendations, to give paramount importance to the highest standards of efficiency and technical competence and to pay due regard to recruitment on as wide a regional geographical basis as possible.[101] Remuneration and terms of service for Vice-Presidents are determined by the Board of Directors.[102] The President and Vice-Presidents are bound by the Code of Conduct for Bank Personnel adopted by the Board of Governors.[103]

[99] AsDB 35-1 and EBRD Article 31-1. For the IADB, the Executive Vice President and other Vice Presidents are also appointed by the Board of Directors on the recommendation of the President. IADB Article VIII, Section 5 (b) and (c). IBRD Article V, Section 5 does not refer to Vice-Presidents but only to officers and staff, all appointed by the President. AfDB Article 37-2 empowers the President to appoint Vice-Presidents, "provided that he shall act in consultation with the Board of Directors in the exercise of his powers of appointment and release of Vice-Presidents." Originally, AfDB Vice-Presidents were also appointed by the Board of Directors on the recommendation of the President; the AfDB Charter was amended to the language quoted above by AfDB Board of Governors' Resolution B/BG/97/05, *Concerning Measures to Enhance Governance of the African Development Bank and Amending the Agreement Establishing the Bank*, adopted May 29, 1997, entered into force May 2, 1998, paragraph 5.

[100] *See* Cogan (2009) at 227–9.

[101] AIIB Article 30-3.

[102] AIIB Article 30-1. Section 12 of the AIIB By-Laws further provides: "The salary and any other terms of remuneration and any allowances, and the term of office, authority and functions, of the Vice-President(s) shall be determined by the Board of Directors and included in the relevant contracts. The Vice-Presidents may participate in such medical, pension, retirement and other plans as may be established for the staff of the Bank."

[103] AIIB By-Laws, Section 8. The Code of Conduct for Bank Personnel was adopted under Board of Governors' Resolution No. 9, *Codes of Conduct*, adopted January 16, 2016.

9

GOVERNANCE: DECISION-MAKING

AIIB's governance framework is set out in detail in Chapter 8. The Board of Governors is AIIB's highest authority, made up of Governors appointed by each of AIIB's members. The Board of Governors is solely responsible for certain important decisions.[1] The Board of Governors can delegate its other powers to the Board of Directors, and has done so.[2] The Board of Directors, a body of twelve Directors elected by and representing groups of Governors, is generally responsible for the direction of AIIB's general operations, and takes many of AIIB's most important decisions.[3] The President conducts AIIB's current business under the direction of the Board of Directors, as both Chairman of the Board and AIIB's chief executive officer.[4] **9.01**

Decision-making in AIIB under this framework can be described from different perspectives. Voting power is the starting point. Decisions in AIIB reflect its weighted voting model, derived from other MDBs, with special features, such as Founding Member votes. Required majorities are another dimension of decision-making. Simple majority decisions are the rule at AIIB and its comparators. However, key decisions require a higher majority, and these are prescribed by the AIIB Charter and its counterparts. Moreover, one of AIIB's unique features is the potential for the Board of Directors to delegate decision authority to the President as it deems appropriate. In 2018, the Board of Directors established AIIB's Accountability Framework to cover these decisions, underpinned by the Board's Oversight Mechanism. **9.02**

This chapter lays out AIIB's voting structure and voting majorities in comparison to other MDBs. Comparison charts highlight the similarities and differences across the comparator MDBs. Following that, AIIB's innovative Accountability Framework for delegation of decisions on investment operations from the Board to the President is summarized, along with the Oversight Mechanism. **9.03**

1 *See* Figure 8.2, AIIB Board of Governors Reserved Powers.
2 *See* paragraphs 8.07–8.09.
3 *See* paragraphs 8.22–8.30.
4 *See* paragraph 8.35.

A. Voting Power

9.04 Voting power in AIIB has three components: share votes, basic votes, and Founding Member votes. The total voting power of each member consists of the sum of its share votes, basic votes, and, in the case of a Founding Member, its Founding Member votes.[5]

(1) Share votes

9.05 Share votes are equal to one vote for each share of stock held by a member. Larger shareholders consequently hold more share votes. When capital is increased, a member's share votes will increase by the number of shares actually subscribed. Share votes are common in the MDBs, and lead to the weighted voting system that differentiates them from many other international organizations. In AIIB, the initial allocations of stock in Schedule A of the AIIB Charter would have given share votes a weight of about 85% of total voting power; with new members and actual subscriptions, that percentage will be different in reality.

9.06 AIIB members subscribe to both callable and paid-in shares, and all subscribed shares are counted for share votes. Payment of initial subscriptions of paid-in shares is permitted to be paid in installments over time. Delays, if any, in installment payments result in a temporary reduction in the number of share votes for the member.[6] Accordingly, where there are installment payment delays on AIIB shares, the number of share votes exercised by the member is reduced proportionately during the period of delay.[7] This reduction serves to encourage timely payment of installments and to ensure that those members making timely payments are not disadvantaged.

(2) Basic votes

9.07 Each member is assigned the same number of basic votes, with the exact number recalculated each time voting power is determined. This is because the AIIB

[5] AIIB Article 28-1.

[6] AIIB Article 6-2 provides for suspension of all rights, including voting rights, in respect of paid-in and associated callable shares for which payments are due but have not been received—until full payment is received by the Bank. The reduction in voting power is specified in AIIB Article 28-1. As discussed in paragraph 7.14, similar provisions can be found in the EBRD and BSTDB Charters, and in capital increases for IBRD and AfDB.

[7] AIIB Article 28-1 provides: "In the event a member fails to pay any part of the amount due in respect of its obligations in relation to paid-in shares under Article 6, the number of share votes to be exercised by the member shall, as long as such failure continues, be reduced proportionately, by the percentage which the amount due and unpaid represents of the total par value of paid-in shares subscribed to by that member." This reduction in share votes for the member also reduces the number of total share votes of all members, and thus affects the calculation of basic votes and voting power for all members.

Charter does not specify the number of basic votes allocated to each member; instead, it specifies a proportion. The total number of basic votes allocated to all members must always equal 12% of total votes. Total votes are equal to the sum of total basic votes, total share votes, and total Founding Member votes. Thus, the number of basic votes assigned to each member changes with changes in the number of share votes and Founding Member votes, and changes in the number of members. Basic votes have the effect of increasing the relative voting power of smaller shareholders (above their shareholding percentage) while reducing the relative voting power of larger shareholders (below their shareholding percentage).

Why use a percentage instead of a fixed number of votes? When the concept of **9.08** basic votes was introduced in IBRD in 1945, each member had 250 votes (basic votes) plus one vote for each share of stock held (share votes).[8] At that time, IBRD basic votes represented about 11% of total voting power (basic votes plus share votes).[9] Over time, each member's basic votes remained at the fixed number, while the overall number of share votes increased with each increase in IBRD capital and shares held by members. As a result, IBRD basic votes represented only 2.86% of total voting power when voice reform discussions were underway in the mid-2000s. As part of those reforms, the IBRD Charter was amended to set basic votes as a percentage of total votes, equal to 5.55% of total votes, so that the proportion of basic votes would be maintained when share votes increase.[10] The IMF Charter was amended as part of its reforms in that period, to set its basic votes at 5.502% of total votes instead of its original 250 basic votes per member.[11] In AsDB, basic votes have been set at a percentage of total votes (20%) since the beginning, while a fixed number of basic votes was set in the original Charters for AfDB (625) and IADB (135), now less than 1% in each.[12]

[8] IBRD Article V, Section 3 (a), prior to its amendment in 2012, provided that each member had 250 votes plus one additional vote for each share of stock held. The concept of basic votes seems to stem from the proposed Inter-American Bank in 1940. There, each member government would have had twenty votes for its minimum shares, and one vote for each share of stock subscribed above its minimum. IAB By-Laws, Section 2H.

[9] Development Committee (2008) at paragraph 17.

[10] IBRD Article V, Section 3, as amended effective June 27, 2012. This percentage (5.55%) represented roughly a doubling of the weight of basic votes.

[11] IMF Board of Governors' Resolution No. 63-2, effective April 28, 2008, set out amendments to Article XII, Section 5 (a) of the IMF Charter; the amendments required acceptance by members and became effective on March 3, 2011. Originally, the basic vote provision in the IBRD Charter was based on the IMF Charter; the amended provision in the IBRD Charter also reflects the wording of the IMF provision.

[12] AsDB Article 33-1. IADB Article VIII, Section 4 (a) provides for 135 votes per member, in addition to share votes. AfDB Article 35-1 provides for 625 votes per member, in addition to share votes. The EBRD has only share votes, no basic votes. EBRD Article 29-1. At the time that the AsDB Charter was being negotiated, AfDB basic votes were considered equivalent to 50%, and IADB basic votes at 5%. The World Bank was at about 10%. The decision on 20% was part of an informal bargain with the donors for 30% of the Board for non-regionals. Wilson (1987) at 26. As the numbers of AfDB and IADB basic votes per member have not changed while share votes have increased with capital increases, basic votes now represent a smaller fraction of total votes (less than 1%).

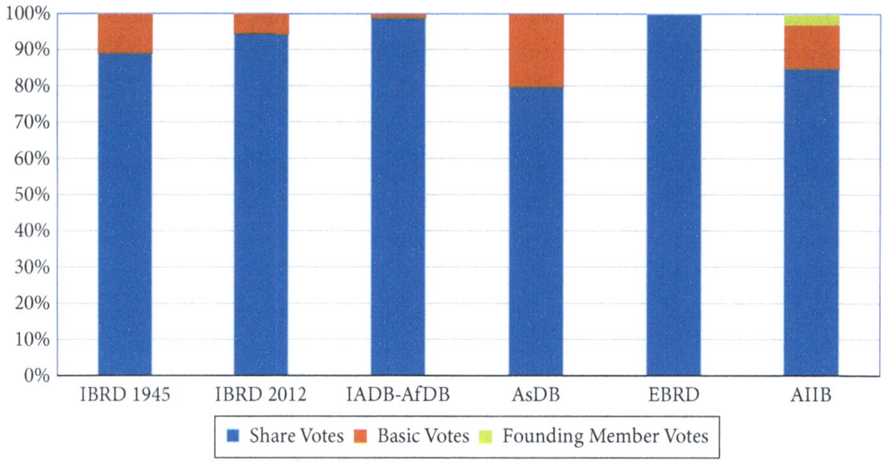

Figure 9.1 MDB Voting Power Comparison

(3) Founding Member votes

9.09 Founding Member votes are fixed at 600 votes per member. Founding Member votes are assigned to those Signatories who become Founding Members by completing membership requirements before the deadline set in the AIIB Charter.[13] The weight of all Founding Member votes in total voting power would have been around 3%, if all Signatories subscribed to the number of shares allocated to them in AIIB Schedule A. Combined with the weight of total basic votes (12%), that would mean that votes not tied to shareholding would account for about 15%, and share votes would weigh about 85%, as noted above. This compares with an 80% weight for share votes in AsDB and a 94.5% weight for share votes in IBRD. This estimate of the weight of Founding Member Votes is hypothetical, however, as the number of members and shares votes has changed.[14] This only illustrates the mathematical impact at the time the AIIB Charter was negotiated; as of September 2025, Founding Member Votes actually represented about 3% of total votes. Figure 9.1 provides a graphic comparison of MDB Voting Power Composition.

B. Voting Majorities

(1) Voting

9.10 In general, decisions by the Board of Governors and the Board of Directors require a majority of votes cast.[15] Abstentions are counted in determining participation for

[13] AIIB Article 3-1 (b). All fifty-seven Signatories became Founding Members before the deadline for completion of membership requirements under Article 58-1, which had been extended to June 30, 2025.
[14] Figure 7.2 shows the allocations of shares to AIIB's new members.
[15] AIIB Article 28-2 (i) and 28-3 (ii).

the purposes of the quorum for the meeting,[16] but only yes and no votes count in determining the number of votes cast. In the Board of Governors, each Governor casts the votes of the member he represents.[17]

In the Board of Directors, each Director casts the votes of all the members whose Governors voted for him in the election, as well as members whose Governors did not participate in the election but have assigned their votes to the Director.[18] A Director may cast each member's votes separately. This ability to split votes in a constituency is found in AsDB and EBRD, while Directors in AfDB, IADB, and IBRD are required to cast all of their votes as a unit.[19] 9.11

Assignment of votes, based on EBRD provisions,[20] offers a mechanism for a member to be represented by a Director even when the Governor does not participate in the election. This can be particularly useful for a new member joining the Bank in the two-year period between elections as well as for a member whose Governor is unable to participate in the biannual election for other reasons. Without assignment of votes, these members would not be formally represented on the Board until the next election, and their votes would not be counted in the Board's decisions in the interim. 9.12

(2) Qualified majorities

For the Board of Governors, the AIIB Charter provides for exceptions to this rule of simple majority decisions by requiring two types of higher majority votes by the Board of Governors. A *Super Majority vote* of the Board of Governors requires an affirmative vote of two-thirds of the total number of Governors, representing not less than three-fourths of the total voting power of the members.[21] A *Special Majority vote* of the Board of Governors requires an affirmative vote of a majority of the total number of Governors, representing not less than a majority of the total voting power.[22] Figure 9.2 lists these qualified majority decisions of the Board of Governors. 9.13

Amendments of the AIIB Charter require a Super Majority vote, with an exception for three core amendments that require unanimity.[23] Unanimous agreement of 9.14

[16] The quorum requirement for a Board of Governors decision is a majority of Governors representing not less than two-thirds of the total voting power of members (AIIB Article 24-2). A quorum for a meeting of the Board of Directors shall be a majority of the Directors representing not less than two-thirds of the total voting power of the members (AIIB Article 27-2).

[17] AIIB Article 28-2.

[18] AIIB Article 28-3, Article 25-1 and Schedule B, paragraph 9.

[19] AIIB Article 28-3 (i). AfDB Article 35-3; AsDB Article 33-3; EBRD Article 29-3; IADB Article VIII, Section 4 (d); and IBRD Article V, Section 4 (g).

[20] EBRD Article 26-1 and Annex B, Section D.

[21] AIIB Article 28-2 (ii).

[22] AIIB Article 28-2 (iii).

[23] Other MDBs have similar unanimity requirements. *See* paragraph 11.09.

SUPER MAJORITY DECISIONS: 2/3 of Governors, representing not less than 75% TVP*	
Increase in capital	*Article 4-3*
Increase of a subscription of a member	*Article 5-3*
Modifying the percentage of capital stock held by regional members	*Article 5-2, 5-3*
Provision of assistance to non-members	*Article 11-1 (b)*
Increase in the lending limit	*Article 12-1*
Allocation of net income to other purposes	*Article 18-1*
Changes in the size or composition of the Board of Directors	*Article 25-2*
Modifying the non-resident basis for the Board of Directors	*Article 27-1*
Election of the President; removal or suspension from office	*Article 29-1; 29-2*
Suspension or restoration of membership	*Article 38*
Termination of operations	*Article 41*
Distribution of assets	*Article 43-1 (ii)*
Amendment of the Charter	*Article 53-1*
SPECIAL MAJORITY DECISIONS: >50% of Governors, representing not less than 50% TVP	
Admission of members	*Article 3-2*
Issuance of non-par stock	*Article 7-1*
Approval of other types of financing	*Article 11-2 (vi)*
Establishment of subsidiaries	*Article 16-8*
Extension of the deadline for deposit of instruments of ratification	*Article 58-1*

Figure 9.2 AIIB Board of Governors: Qualified Majority Decisions
*Percentage of total voting power (TVP) required.

the Board of Governors is required to amend: (i) each member's right to withdraw from the Bank; (ii) the limitations on liability of members; and (iii) the pre-emptive rights pertaining to purchase of capital stock.[24]

9.15 For the Board of Directors, there are three qualified majority provisions, as discussed in paragraphs 8.24–8.25 under the powers of the Board of Directors. A three-quarters majority of total voting power is required for decisions by the Board of Directors to: (i) approve major operational and financial policies; (ii) delegate authority to the President under Bank policies; and (iii) delegate authority to take decisions on operations.[25] The higher majority refers only to a majority of *votes*. A majority of the *number* of Directors voting at the Board of Directors could be difficult to determine, as a Director can cast each constituency member's votes separately, possibly some members' votes for and other members' votes against a particular proposal. In comparison, for voting at the Board of Governors, each Governor casts the votes of only one member, so that double majorities by number and voting power are straightforward to calculate.[26] Thus, double majority

[24] AIIB Article 53-2.
[25] AIIB Article 26 (ii) and (iii).
[26] AIIB Article 28-2.

provisions in the AIIB Charter provisions are limited to the Board of Governors (Super Majority and Special Majority decisions).

It is important to note that the Boards of Directors in MDBs generally operate without formal votes, although voting power plays a role in reaching agreement.[27] In AIIB, this mechanism can be seen in the Board's Rules of Procedure, which follows other precedents in providing: 9.16

> The Chairman shall ordinarily ascertain and announce to the meeting the sense of the meeting with regard to any matter and the Board shall be deemed to have acted in accordance with the announcement by the Chairman without the necessity of taking a formal vote. A Director may require that his views be recorded in accordance with Section 8 (c) [of the Rules of Procedure]. Any Director may request a formal vote to be taken in accordance with the provisions of paragraph 3 of Article 28 of the Articles of Agreement. The Chairman shall not exercise any voting power but shall have a deciding vote in the event of an equal division.[28]

While actual voting is rare, the voting power represented by each Director would be taken into account in ascertaining the sense of the meeting and whether a majority of voting power would be in favor of the decision taken. In addition, the AIIB Board of Directors Rules of Procedure now formally provide for the practice of decision-making on an absence of objection basis, in which the proposal is circulated to the Directors for decision without a meeting.[29] The practice is common elsewhere but not always recognized in the formal rules.

Overall, AIIB's decision majorities and structure fit within the design of other MDBs. This is illustrated in Figure 9.3 (MDB Selected Qualified Majority Decisions), Figure 9.4 (Board of Governors: AIIB Super Majority Decisions Compared), Figure 9.5 (Board of Governors: AIIB Special Majority Decisions Compared), and Figure 9.6 (Board of Directors: Qualified Majority Decisions). In particular, it is worth noting that the highest qualified majority in the other MDBs surveyed is generally 75% of total voting power. There are two exceptions: at IBRD, there are higher majorities for changes in the number of Executive Directors (80%) and Charter amendments (85%);[30] at EBRD, amendments require an 80% 9.17

[27] Rigo Sureda (2004) at paragraph 64.

[28] AIIB Rules of Procedure of the Board of Directors, Section 5 (a). *See* AFDB Rules of Procedure of the Board of Directors, Section 8-1; AsDB Rules of Procedure of the Board of Directors, Section 5 (a); EBRD Rules of Procedure of the Board of Directors, Section 5 (a); IADB Regulations of the Board of Executive Directors, Part III, Section 3 (a); and IBRD Rules of Procedure for Meeting of the Executive Directors, Section 4.

[29] AIIB Board of Directors Rules of Procedure, as amended October 9, 2017, Section 5 (e). If any Director objects to the use of the procedure or the content of the proposal, the item would be discussed at a meeting or decided by a formal vote without a meeting.

[30] IBRD Article V, Section 4 (b) (Governors representing four-fifths majority of total voting power to increase the number of Executive Directors) and Article VIII (a) (three-fifths of members having 85% of total voting power to amend the Charter). The original IBRD threshold was 80% for both; the IBRD Charter was amended in 1989 to change to 85%, in connection with an agreement for US voting power to drop below 20% (and, among others, Japan to increase its voting power, becoming the second largest shareholder). The majority for important decisions at the proposed Inter-American Bank was also 80%. IAB By-Laws, Section 3J.

	Amendment	Capital increase	Change in Board seats	President election	Membership Admission
AIIB	75% with 2/3	75% with 2/3	75% with 2/3	75% with 2/3	50% with 1/2
EBRD	80% with 3/4	75% with 2/3	75% with 2/3	50% with 1/2	75% with 2/3
AsDB	75% with 2/3	75% with 2/3	67% with 1/2	50% with 1/2	75% with 2/3
IADB*	75% with 1/2	75% with 3/4	75% with 2/3	50% with 1/2	50%
AfDB*	75% with 2/3	75% with 2/3	75% with 2/3	50%	50%
IBRD	85% with 3/5	75%	80%	50%	50%

*Some IADB and AfDB decisions have regional/non-regional requirements. See Figure 9.4.
Grey shows decisions requiring 50% voting power.
Orange shows decisions requiring 75% voting power.
Blue shows decisions requiring 80% or 85% voting power.

Figure 9.3 MDB SELECTED QUALIFIED MAJORITY DECISIONS

*Some IADB and AfDB decisions have regional/non-regional requirements. See Figure 9.4.
Grey shows decisions requiring 50% voting power.
Orange shows decisions requiring 75% voting power.
Blue shows decisions requiring 80% or 85% voting power.

majority and certain decisions on country access to its resources require an 85% majority.[31]

The citations for the decisions in Figure 9.4 can be found in note 32.[32]

[31] *See* EBRD Article 56-1 for Charter amendments (three-fourths of members, including at least two Central and Eastern European countries, holding four-fifths of total voting power). The EBRD majority for access decisions is three-fourths of the Governors representing 85% of the total voting power. EBRD Article 8-4 (iii). Accounts of the negotiations identify this as a US proposal seeking to restrict access by the Soviet Union; the United States was expected to have a 10% voting share, so it would presumably have anticipated that Japan (9%) or another ally would join in these decisions. Weber (1994) at 22.

[32] **Super Majority Decisions in Figure 9.4:**

1. Increase in Capital: AIIB Article 4-3; AsDB Article 4-3; EBRD Article 4-3; AfDB Article 4-3; IADB Article II, Section 2 (e); IBRD Article II, Section 2 (b).
2. Increase of a Member's Subscription: AIIB Article 5-3; AsDB Article 5-3; EBRD Article 5-4; AfDB Article 5-3.
3. Change in Regional Shareholding Percentage: AIIB Article 5-3.
4. Assistance to Non-Members: AIIB Article 11-1 (b).
5. Increase in Limitation on Operations [Lending Limit]: AIIB Article 12-1.
6. Allocation of Net Income to Other Purposes: AIIB Article 18-1; EBRD Article 36-1.
7. Changes in Size or Composition of Board of Directors: AIIB Article 25-2; AsDB Article 30-1 (ii); EBRD Article 26-3; AfDB Article 33-1; IADB Article VIII, Section 3 (b)(ii); IBRD Article V, Section 4 (b).
8. Modifying Non-Resident Board: AIIB Article 27-1.
9. Election of President: AIIB Article 29-1; AsDB Article 34-1; EBRD Article 30-1; AfDB Article 36-1; IADB Article VIII, Section 5 (a); IBRD Article V, Section 5 (a) [Executive Directors decide].
10. Suspension/Restoration of Membership: AIIB Article 38; AsDB Article 42; EBRD Article 38-1; AfDB Article 44-1; IADB Article IX, Section 2; IBRD Article VI, Section 2.
11. Termination of Operations: AIIB Article 41-1; AsDB Article 45-1; EBRD Article 41; AfDB Article 47-1; IADB Article X, Section 2; IBRD Article VI, Section 5 (b).
12. Distribution of Assets: AIIB Article 43-1 (ii); AsDB Article 47-1; EBRD Article 43-1 (ii); AfDB Article 49-1 (b); IADB Article X, Section 4 (a); IBRD Article VI, Section 5 (e)(ii).
13. Amendment of Charter: AIIB Article 53-1; AsDB Article 59-1; EBRD Article 56-1; AfDB Article 60-1; IADB Article XII (a); IBRD Article VIII (a).

General Rule: AIIB Article 28-2 (i); AsDB Article 33-2; EBRD Article 29-2; AfDB Article 35-2; IADB Article VIII, Section 4 (c); IBRD Article V, Section 3 (b).

AIIB	AsDB	EBRD	AfDB	IADB	IBRD
1. INCREASE IN CAPITAL					
2/3 *and* 75%	2/3 *and* 75%	2/3 *and* 75%	2/3 *and* 75%	3/4 (2/3 Reg) *and* 75%	- *and* 75%
2. INCREASE OF A MEMBER'S SUBSCRIPTION					
2/3 *and* 75%	General Rule	General Rule	General Rule	No similar provision	No similar provision
3. CHANGE IN REGIONAL SHAREHOLDING PERCENTAGE					
2/3 *and* 75%	No similar provision	No similar provision	No similar provision	No similar provision	No similar provision
4. ASSISTANCE TO NON-MEMBERS					
2/3 *and* 75%	No similar provision	No similar provision	No similar provision	No similar provision	No similar provision
5. INCREASE IN LIMITATION ON OPERATIONS [LENDING LIMIT]					
2/3 *and* 75%	Amendment to remove limit pending	Removed by amendment 2025	No similar provision	No similar provision	Amendment to remove limit pending
6. ALLOCATION OF NET INCOME TO OTHER PURPOSES					
2/3 *and* 75%	No similar provision	2/3 *and* 67%	No similar provision	No similar provision	No similar provision
7. CHANGES IN SIZE OR COMPOSITION OF BOARD OF DIRECTORS					
2/3 *and* 75%	Majority *and* 67%	2/3 *and* 75%	2/3 Regional OR 2/3 Non-Regional *and* 75%	2/3 Regional OR 2/3 Non-Regional *and* 75%	- *and* 80%
8. MODIFYING NON-RESIDENT BOARD					
2/3 *and* 75%	Not applicable	Not applicable	Not applicable	Not applicable	Not applicable
9. ELECTION OF PRESIDENT					
2/3 *and* 75%	Majority *and* >50%	Majority *and* >50%	- *and* >50% including >50% Regional	Majority *and* >50%	Directors' decision (general rule)
10. SUSPENSION/RESTORATION OF MEMBERSHIP					
2/3 *and* 75%	2/3 *and* 75%	2/3 *and* 67%	- *and* 70%	2/3 Regional OR 2/3 Non-Regional and 75%	Majority *and* >50%
11. TERMINATION OF OPERATIONS					
2/3 *and* 75%	2/3 *and* 75%	2/3 *and* 75%	- *and* 75%	2/3 *and* 75%	Majority *and* >50%
12. DISTRIBUTION OF ASSETS					
2/3 *and* 75%	2/3 *and* 75%	2/3 *and* 75%	Majority and 50% Regional	2/3 *and* 75%	Majority and >50%

AIIB	AsDB	EBRD	AfDB	IADB	IBRD
		13. AMENDMENT OF CHARTER			
2/3 *and* 75%	2/3 *and* 75%	Governors: General Rule Members: 3/4 (including 2 Central/ Eastern Europe) 80% Votes	Governors: General Rule Members: 2/3 and 75% Votes, including Regional 2/3 *and* 75%	Majority including 2/3 regional and 75%	Governors: General Rule Members: 3/5 *and* 85% Votes
		GENERAL RULE			
Majority of votes cast	Majority of voting power represented	Majority of voting power of members voting	66 2/3% of voting power represented (if important matter for a member, 70%)	Majority of total voting power	Majority of votes cast

Figure 9.4 Board of Governors: AIIB SUPER MAJORITY Decisions Compared

The citations for the decisions in Figure 9.5 are found in note 33.[33]

AIIB	AsDB	EBRD	AfDB	IADB	IBRD
		1. ADMISSION OF NEW MEMBERS			
Majority *and* >50%	2/3 *and* 75%	2/3 *and* 75%	General Rule and Non-Regional rules	General Rule and Non-Regional rules	General Rule
		2. ISSUANCE OF NON-PAR STOCK			
Majority *and* >50%	Majority *and* 50%	2/3 *and* 67%	General rule	General rule	- *and* >50%
		3. APPROVAL OF OTHER TYPES OF FINANCING			
Majority *and* >50%	No similar provision	No similar provision	No similar provision	No similar provision	No similar provision
		4. ESTABLISHMENT OF SUBSIDIARIES			
Majority *and* >50%	No similar provision	No similar provision	No similar provision	No similar provision	No similar provision
		5. EXTENSION OF DEADLINE FOR RATIFICATION			
Majority *and* >50%	No similar provision	Majority *and* >50%	No similar provision	No similar provision	No similar provision

Figure 9.5 Board of Governors: AIIB SPECIAL MAJORITY Decisions Compared

[33] **Special Majority Decisions in Figure 9.5.**

1. Admission of New Members: AIIB Article 3-2; AsDB Article 3-2; EBRD Article 3-2; AfDB Articles 3-3 and 64-2; IADB Article II, Section 1 (b); IBRD Article II, Section 1 (b).
2. Issuance of Non-Par Stock: AIIB Article 7-1; AsDB Article 5-4; EBRD Article 5-5; AfDB Article 6-4; IADB Article II, Section 3 (c); IBRD Article II, Section 4.
3. Approval of Other Types of Financing: AIIB Article 11-2 (vi).
4. Establishment of Subsidiaries: AIIB Article 16-8.
5. Extension of Deadline for Ratification: AIIB Article 58-1; EBRD, Article 61-2.

(3) Veto power

Discussions of MDB governance often zero in on veto power. In the MDBs, veto power is derived from the percentages of total voting power required for qualified majorities, not from a specific Charter reference to one or more members. MDB voting power fluctuates with capital subscriptions, and in principle, different shareholders or groups of shareholders can use their voting power to block decisions at different times. In the UN, by contrast, the five named permanent members of the Security Council must concur in any non-procedural decision, resulting in an automatic veto.[34] 9.18

In IBRD, for example, there were originally two decisions that required 80% of total voting power (Charter amendments and increases in the number of Executive Directors) and one key decision requiring 75% of total voting power (capital increases); the percentage for amendments was increased to 85% in 1989.[35] In the IBRD Charter as negotiated, the United States would have had more than 30% of total voting power, giving it a veto on all three decisions; since 1989, the United States has maintained its shareholding to keep its voting power above 15% and continues to maintain a veto on amendments but not on other decisions. Other IBRD members could combine to veto Charter amendments; for instance, the BRICS countries together hold almost 14% of voting power, and France, Germany, and the United Kingdom hold nearly 12%.[36] 9.19

For AIIB, the highest percentage required for major decisions in Figure 9.4 is 75% of total voting power. Had AIIB's initial subscriptions matched Schedule A exactly, China's voting power would have been just over 26%—a clear veto power. In June 2025, China's actual voting power was around 26.5%. As a result, China alone can block all of these Super Majority decisions at the Board of Governors and decisions on delegations and major policies at the Board of Directors, requiring a 75% majority. The next five largest AIIB regional shareholders (India, Russia, Korea, Indonesia, Saudi Arabia) could combine to comprise almost 23%. Among non-regionals, France, Germany, and the United Kingdom combine for over 10%.[37] 9.20

Maintaining veto power in the MDBs reflects a significant financial cost, because the members with high percentages of voting power have typically subscribed to 9.21

[34] UN Charter, Article 23-1 lists China, France, Russia, the United Kingdom, and the United States as permanent members of the Security Council, and Article 27-3 requires the concurrence of the permanent members for decisions on other than procedural matters.

[35] IBRD Article VIII (a) (amendments); Article V, Section 4 (b) (increase in the number of Executive Directors); and Article II, Section 2 (b) (capital increases).

[36] Similarly, the US voting share in IADB cannot be lower than 30%, previously 34.5% (IADB Article VIII, Section 4 (b)), yielding veto power over many of the IADB decisions listed in Figure 9.4 that require 75% of total voting power. In AsDB, the United States and Japan combined hold just over 25% of total voting power, sufficient to block AsDB's highest majority decisions that require 75% of voting power.

[37] *See* Figures 6.5 and 6.6. Figure 13.1 also compares the voting power of the twelve largest shareholders at IBRD and AIIB.

AIIB	**Major operational and financial policies (75% Votes)**	*Article 26-(ii)*
	Delegation to President under policies (75% Votes)	*Article 26-(ii)*
	Delegation to President of decisions on operations (75% Votes)	*Article 26 (iii)*
AsDB	Procurement in non-member countries (67% Votes)	*Article 14 (ix)*
AfDB	None	
EBRD	General policy decisions (67% Votes)	*Article 29-3*
	Decisions pursuant to country strategy review (2/3 Directors and 75% Votes)	*Article 11-2 (i)*
IADB	**Loan proposal without staff report (>50% Votes)**	*Article III Sec 7 (a)(i)*
	Reduce special commission (75% Votes)	*Article III Sec 12*
	Decisions on Fund for Special Operations (75% Votes)	*Article IV Sec 9 (b)*
	Invest funds (75% Votes)	*Article VII Sec 1 (iii)*
	Currency purchase (75% Votes)	*Article V Sec 1 (e)*
IBRD	Investment of special reserve (75% Votes)	*Article IV Sec 8 (iv)*
	Specifying currency on loans out of equity (75% Votes)	*Article IV Sec 4 (b)(i)*

Figure 9.6 Board of Directors: Qualified Majority Decisions Compared

a commensurately high proportion of capital. They have strong financial reasons to ensure that the MDB makes sound financial decisions, to protect their callable capital commitments. For the institution, the high percentages required for major decisions ensure a commanding level of support from the membership as a whole for significant changes to proceed, while the potential control by veto can lead to governance concerns. Note that having sufficient voting power to block certain decisions, alone or in combination, does not translate into the ability to ensure that alternative proposals are adopted. The necessary majority of voting power, and where relevant, number of members, must still be on board for adoption.

C. Delegation and Oversight

(1) Delegation of authority

9.22 The AIIB Charter specifically provides for the Board of Directors to delegate decision authority to the President in the case of policy and decisions on investment operations.

(a) Policy delegation

9.23 The Board of Directors has the authority to establish AIIB policies, and major operational and financial policies require approval by the Board of Directors by a majority representing not less than three-fourths of total voting power.[38] Under

[38] AIIB Article 26 (ii).

the same provision, the Board may, under Bank policies, delegate authority to the President, and decisions on such delegation also require approval of the Board of Directors by a majority representing not less than three-fourths of total voting power.

(b) Delegation of decisions on financing operations

Deciding on AIIB's financing operations is a specific function of the Board of Directors.[39] Board decision-making on operations has been the practice in most of the comparator MDBs although it is not always spelled out in the charter.[40] The AIIB Charter is rare among MDB Charters in specifying that the Board of Directors may delegate this function to the President.[41] **9.24**

AIIB's Board of Directors delegated certain decision authority on financing operations to the President in 2018 under an overall Accountability Framework, with three main components:[42] **9.25**

- Strategy Setting comes first, describing how the Board of Directors establishes the directions, contours, and priorities for AIIB's operations.
- Delegation of Financing Decisions to the President can then take place within these Board-established directions, contours, and priorities (as well as all Board-approved operational policies and processes).[43]
- Presidential Accountability is how the Board assesses the decisions that have been made.

Another foundation for the Accountability Framework is the Board's multi-faceted oversight, crystallized in the Oversight Mechanism. Paragraphs 9.28–9.31 summarize the Oversight Mechanism and Chapter 12 discusses the Accountability Framework and the Oversight Mechanism in greater depth.

Decisions on AIIB financing operations are currently delegated to the President unless the operations fall within Board-determined exceptions that require Board approval. Figure 9.7 outlines where the Board has reserved its decision authority for four types of operations. By 2024, just over half of AIIB projects (by number) were approved by the Board rather than the President (paragraph 12.31 and Figure 12.3). **9.26**

[39] AIIB Article 26 (iii).

[40] *See* paragraph 8.25.

[41] EIB and NIB have general provisions for delegation that would include decisions on financing. EIB Article 9-1; NIB Section 14. In EIB, the Board of Directors approves all projects, some through written procedure. EIB (2015) at 6-7. The Board of Directors in some MDBs approves many operations without Board discussion, on a streamlined or absence of objection basis; in principle, these are still approvals by the Board, not delegated to the management. A few MDBs have delegated decision authority for specific operations to management in the context of programs or similar umbrella initiatives approved by the Board. *See* discussion in Chapter 12, noting delegations at EBRD, IFC, and AsDB (paragraph 12.22).

[42] AIIB (2018a) [Decision on Accountability Framework], AIIB (2018b) [Paper on Accountability Framework] and AIIB (2023a) [Regulation on Accountability Framework, as revised].

[43] The Regulation on the Accountability Framework (2023) specifies that the President's authority to make these decisions should be exercised in conformity with the Sector Strategies, Policies, Frameworks, and Annual Business Plan and Budget adopted by the Board of Directors. AIIB (2023a).

Decisions on AIIB financing operations are currently delegated to the President with exceptions that require Board approval. Board decisions are required as described below:

CO-FINANCING: Generally, the Board decides on projects supported by financings of more than US$500 million "that are cofinanced with a lead partner multilateral development bank."*

CATEGORIES: The Board has retained its decision authority for three categories of projects:

Precedent Setting (Category I). This includes the first project in a Member country; the first three projects within a Sector Strategy; and the first project involving a co-financier for which AIIB proposes to apply policies of the co-financier.

Significant Strategic and Policy Issues (Category II). This includes a project in a non-regional Member country; a project where a Sector Strategy has not yet been approved; and a project requiring derogation from a Sector Strategy, Policy, or Framework approved by the Board; a project which directly implicates the Operational Policy on International Relations.

Risk Tolerances (Category III). This includes a project where the amount of AIIB's economic capital (as defined in the Regulation) is in excess of US$37.5 million; and a project where the amount of AIIB financing exceeds US$300 million for sovereign-backed financing or guarantees, US$150 million for non-sovereign-backed financing or guarantees, or US$35 million for equity investments.

Figure 9.7 Decisions on Financing Operations
*Co-financed projects are those that apply the partner MDB's policies in lieu of AIIB's Environmental and Social Framework and for which the partner MDB acknowledges the AIIB co-financing in its documentation.
Source: AIIB Regulation on the Accountability Framework 2023.

9.27 Even for projects that do not fall within the Board's retained authority, Board consideration can be requested ("called-in") by any Director, and the President can request Board consideration in lieu of his approval.[44] For projects approved by the President, changes proposed during implementation that would result in the project falling within the exceptions to delegation should be referred to the Board for consideration. In 2023, the Risk Tolerance limits were adjusted to the amounts specified in Figure 9.7[45] when the co-financing exemption was also added.[46]

(2) Oversight

9.28 The AIIB Charter and Chief Negotiators' Report emphasize the Board's regular supervision of management and operations of AIIB, and require that the Board

[44] AIIB (2023a). In 2024, AIIB's CEIU undertook an independent evaluation of the Accountability Framework, noting that eight projects had been called in, and the President had referred two projects back to the Board for approval. AIIB CEIU (2024) at 18–20.

[45] The limits were adjusted in the 2023 revision: economic capital was increased from US$25 million to US$37.5 million; Sovereign-backed financing was increased from US$200 million to US$300 million; and Non-sovereign-backed financing was increased from US$100 million to US$150 million. The limit for equity investment was unchanged at US$35 million.

[46] AIIB (2023a). The Board delegated to the President the authority to decide on such co-financed projects supported by financings of US$500 million or less. The Regulation specifies: "These are cofinanced projects that apply the partner MDB's policies in lieu of the AIIB's Environmental and Social Framework and for which the partner MDB acknowledges the AIIB cofinancing in its documentation."

of Directors establish an oversight mechanism for this purpose.[47] In 2019, AIIB's Board of Directors' Decision on the Oversight Mechanism set out the contours of the Oversight Mechanism, not as an integrated mechanism but rather as a collection of five components that support the Board's oversight of management.[48] The first three components are housed under AIIB's independent Complaints-resolution, Evaluation and Integrity Unit (CEIU): Project-Related Complaints; Evaluation; and Integrity. The fourth component is the External Audit function. The fifth component is AIIB's rules and process to address Staff Grievances. Separating out these functions for particular attention and periodic review reflects the importance of Board oversight for AIIB, as it was for its founders.

(a) Complaints-resolution, Evaluation and Integrity Unit (CEIU)

The CEIU was established by the President, reports directly to the Board, and **9.29**
engages with management, exercising an unusual dual role. Under its terms of reference,[49] the CEIU's mandate includes project-related complaints, evaluation, and integrity (anti-corruption). The CEIU may also provide independent input to the Board of Directors and the President in relevant policy formulation and review. The CEIU is managed by a Managing Director, appointed by the President after consultation with the Board of Directors, for a single non-renewable five-year term, meeting with the Board of Directors (without management) at least once a year.[50]

- The Project-affected People's Mechanism (PPM), effective March 31, 2019, enables project-affected people to file submissions if they have been or are likely to be adversely affected by AIIB's failure to implement its Environmental and Social Policy when their concerns cannot be addressed satisfactorily through Project-level grievance redress mechanisms or AIIB Management's processes.[51] The PPM is described in more detail in Chapter 5 and Chapter 12.[52]
- Under AIIB's Learning and Evaluation Policy, "CEIU evaluates AIIB's ordinary and special operations and determines whether these projects and processes

[47] AIIB Article 26 (iv) requires that the Oversight Mechanism be in line with principles of transparency, openness, independence, and accountability. The Chief Negotiators' Report further provided that the Oversight Mechanism should address areas such as audit, evaluation, fraud and corruption, project complaints, and staff grievances.

[48] Paper on the Oversight Mechanism, July 10, 2019 and Decision on the Oversight Mechanism, adopted on July 10, 2019, on AIIB website.

[49] Terms of Reference for the Complaints-resolution, Evaluation and Integrity Unit, revised January 27, 2024.

[50] The Terms of Reference for the Complaints-resolution, Evaluation and Integrity Unit, revised January 27, 2024, address some internal aspects of independence. For instance, they provide that "notwithstanding the approved annual budget of CEIU, additional resources for dealing with submissions to PPM, investigating complaints regarding Prohibited Practices, and for evaluation of investment projects will be provided as needed." Furthermore, CEIU staff are not to be subject to management instructions that would be inconsistent with independence and Board reporting.

[51] AIIB website, Project-Affected People's Mechanism, https://www.aiib.org/en/about-aiib/who-we-are/project-affected-peoples-mechanism/how-we-assist-you/index.html (last visited July 14, 2025).

[52] *See* paragraphs 5.45–5.47 and 12.36–12.39.

are producing the expected results and delivering the value expected."[53] The CEIU also shares its findings and lessons with AIIB staff.

- The Integrity function is responsible for investigation of project-related fraud and corruption cases under the Policy on Prohibited Practices. The Sanctions Panel includes two external members and one internal member. The Integrity function is described in more detail in Chapter 5.[54]

(b) Audit

9.30 The AIIB Board of Directors established an Audit and Risk Committee in January 2017, which is now composed of four Directors and two external members. As shown in Figure 8.5, the functions of the Audit and Risk Committee cover: review of financial statements and practices; review of external auditor selection, performance, and reports; review of internal audit plans and effectiveness; review effectiveness of internal control system; review AIIB's financial and risk-related policies, risk management framework, and risk appetite statement; and receive reports on violations of the Policy on Prohibited Practices. There are two external members of the Audit and Risk Committee, with extensive backgrounds in accounting and auditing.[55] In addition, AIIB's external auditor was appointed in 2016 for a ten-year term, so a new external auditor is expected in 2026.[56] The Internal Audit Office (IAO) is responsible for providing independent, risk-based, and objective assurance, advice, insight, and foresight. In 2024, IAO was assessed by the Institute of Internal Auditors as being in conformance with the International Standards on the Professional Practice of Internal Auditing and the Institute of Internal Auditors' Code of Ethics.[57]

(c) Staff dispute resolution

9.31 AIIB's Staff Regulations, approved by the Board of Directors in November 2016, include an article on resolution of employment disputes.[58] AIIB's Staff Regulations provide for the establishment of an internal procedure for staff to challenge employment actions that adversely affect them directly and personally, and for appeals from that internal procedure to an independent administrative tribunal.[59] The Staff Regulations also mandate that there shall be no retaliation for the use

[53] AIIB Learning and Evaluation Policy, approved May 19, 2021, https://aiib.org/en/about-aiib/who-we-are/complaints-resolution-evaluation-integrity-unit/introduction/index.html (last visited July 14, 2025).

[54] *See* paragraphs 5.51–5.54.

[55] "Mr. Jan Engstrom and Mr. Chaly Mah have been appointed as external members of AIIB's Audit Committee," AIIB Press Release, April 28, 2017; "AIIB Appoints Members of its Audit and Risk Committee," AIIB Press Release, May 13, 2020; and "AIIB Appoints New External Member of its Audit and Risk Committee," AIIB Press Release, May 19, 2023.

[56] In 2016, the Board of Directors approved the appointment of PwC as the AIIB's external auditors for a term of ten years, with a mid-term (five-year) review. That appointment was coming to a close in 2025–2026. AIIB Audit and Risk Committee, Annual Report to the Board of Directors 2024–2025, paragraph 4.8.

[57] *See* AIIB Annual Report 2024 at 88.

[58] Staff Regulations of the Asian Infrastructure Investment Bank, approved November 2016, Article 13.

[59] *See* discussion on Officers and Employees in paragraphs 11.35–11.37.

of the Bank's dispute resolution process, a protection enshrined in the Codes of Conduct.[60]

(d) International Advisory Panel

AIIB's International Advisory Panel was established by the President to support the President and senior management on the Bank's strategies and policies, as well as on general operational issues.[61] After the Panel's first meeting in October 2016, AIIB further explained the Panel's role: "The Panel provides impartial, objective and independent advice to the President, allowing the Bank to benefit from the international experience and expertise of Panel members."[62] The dozen or so Panel members meet annually or as requested by the President, and are generally well-recognized senior experts from diverse backgrounds, including from non-member countries, appointed to two-year terms.[63] **9.32**

[60] AIIB Code of Conduct for Board Officials, paragraph 5 (c), and AIIB Code of Conduct for Bank Personnel, paragraph 39.

[61] AIIB website. Interestingly, the IBRD Charter provides for an Advisory Council to advise on general policy matters, meeting annually; the Council was convened twice in its early years, and not since. Bitterman (1971) at 66 and 79, noting that it "proved to be a nuisance" and was dropped. IBRD Article V, Section 6 provided for a Council of at least seven people, selected by the Board of Governors including representatives of banking, commercial, industrial, labor and agricultural interests, and with as wide a national representation as possible.

[62] "International Advisory Panel holds inaugural meeting," AIIB Press Release, October 19, 2016.

[63] The AIIB website lists the members of the Panel. As of June 2025, there were ten Panel members:

> Iwan Azis, Adjunct Professor, Cornell University; Rachel Biderman, Senior Vice President, South America Field Division, Conservation International; Ha-Joon Chang, Professor of SOAS University of London; Ahmed Galal, former Minister of Finance, Egypt; Yukon Huang, Senior Fellow, Asia Program, the Carnegie Endowment for International Peace; Naoko Ishii, Special Presidential Envoy for Global Commons, University of Tokyo, Professor and Director of the Center for Global Commons; Omobola Johnson, Senior Partner, TLcom Capital LLP, former Minister of Communication Technology of Nigeria; Mari Kiviniemi, former Prime Minister of Finland, Chair of the Board of the University of Vaasa; Rachel Kyte, Special Representative on Climate, UK Government; and Nargiz Nasrullayeva, former President of the American Chamber of Commerce and former Principal Advisor to CEO of Sovereign Wealth Fund.

https://www.aiib.org/en/about-aiib/governance/international-advisory-panel/index.html (last visited July 14, 2025).

10

TRANSITIONS

The governance arrangements for the Asian Infrastructure Investment Bank (AIIB) described in Chapters 8 and 9 could operate only after the AIIB Charter took effect and AIIB had been legally established. Before then, a full range of the more detailed basic documents and policies envisaged under the AIIB Charter had to be readied for launch at the Inaugural Meetings of the Board of Governors and Board of Directors. Since these formal governing bodies, as well as management and staff, could not be put in place until after AIIB's establishment, transitional mechanisms for preparation by staff and reviews by Prospective Founding Member (PFM) representatives were crucial. **10.01**

In that interim period, the timing of the different steps to establishment was a key factor. For PFMs, formal AIIB membership depended on the pace and complexity of their domestic approval processes. The timing of PFM membership, in turn, determined the entry into force of the AIIB Charter; entry into force would then trigger AIIB's formal establishment at the Inaugural Meeting. The uncertainty of the timing of each PFM's membership meant uncertainty for Board representation at the Inaugural Meetings—which PFMs would be formally represented as AIIB members and which would not. **10.02**

To address the interplay of these factors, the Chief Negotiators agreed on a set of transitional governance arrangements for the period from conclusion of Charter negotiations to AIIB's commencement of operations and full membership. **10.03**

This chapter describes the context and considerations for the transitional arrangements, including establishment requirements, development of basic documents and policies, transitional arrangements for AIIB's governing bodies (President-designate and the Boards) and the Inaugural Meetings of the Board of Governors and Board of Directors. **10.04**

A. Pre-Establishment Phase

(1) Overview

The timeline was short. The final text of the AIIB Charter was agreed on May 22, 2015, and it was opened for signature on June 29, 2015. AIIB's formal establishment **10.05** was anticipated six months later, at the Inaugural Meetings. In any event, to become Founding Members, PFMs had to sign the AIIB Charter by December 31, 2015.

10.06 For PFMs, the short timeframe contrasted with the longer period of time normally expected in order to obtain domestic approvals. In many countries, two procedures would be involved—one to sign an international treaty and another for its subsequent ratification and AIIB membership (including capital subscriptions and payments). In May 2015, many a PFM could anticipate that its domestic procedures for multilateral development bank (MDB) membership would delay its actual AIIB membership until sometime in 2016. This expectation created a strong interest among PFMs in preserving their role in AIIB's early policy development and activities, prior to membership. Even those PFMs expecting to be among the first group of members could see benefits from ensuring that others could also stay engaged in this formative time, maintaining AIIB as a cooperative among all PFMs.

10.07 AIIB as an institution also faced a transition. AIIB could only hire regular staff and begin to function as an organization after its formal establishment. The Multilateral Interim Secretariat for Establishing the Asian Infrastructure Investment Bank (the Secretariat) continued to operate in this period, as its role extended beyond Charter negotiations. The Secretariat had been charged more generally with technical preparations for establishing the AIIB (including Charter negotiations) and providing technical support and services for the Chief Negotiators' Meeting (CNM). As the precursor to the management and staff of the Bank, the Secretariat was thus also an essential element of the transitional governance arrangements.

(2) Establishment requirements

10.08 The AIIB Charter set out the next legal steps to establishment—signing, membership, entry into force, Inaugural Meeting, and commencement of operations. With the timing for each step dependent on many different actors, there was uncertainty all along the way. These steps and timing considerations are summarized in what follows.

(a) Signing

10.09 The AIIB Charter was opened for signing at a ceremony in Beijing in late June. PFMs had barely five weeks from final agreement in Singapore to complete all the legal and procedural steps required to sign at the ceremony. In actuality, some fifty PFMs sent representatives to sign the AIIB Charter at the Signing Ceremony on June 29, 2015—an unexpected turnout in light of the anticipated hurdles. The remaining seven PFMs completed the signing of the AIIB Charter before expiration of the year-end deadline.[1]

[1] AIIB Article 57-1 set the deadline for signing, which was only open to PFMs. PFMs signing after June 29, 2015 were Denmark, Kuwait, Malaysia, Philippines, Poland, South Africa, and Thailand. For AIIB, all

(b) Membership for Signatories

Signatories were also required to deposit instruments of ratification, acceptance or approval (instruments of ratification)[2] and to subscribe to AIIB's capital, including making their first installment payments on paid-in shares.[3] In many countries, the relevant national legal process for treaty ratification included parliamentary consideration and budgetary appropriations. Completion of these membership requirements by the ratification deadline was a condition of becoming a Founding Member.[4] 10.10

(c) Entry into force

AIIB's establishment did not require that all PFMs sign or become members. For the entry into force of the AIIB Charter, however, an agreed threshold of PFM membership had to be met: the deposit of instruments of ratification by at least ten Signatories whose initial subscriptions totaled not less than 50% of the total subscriptions in Schedule A of the AIIB Charter.[5] This threshold was a moving target in the second half of 2015, as the number of instruments of ratification deposited by PFMs and shares subscribed were counted. The target was met—and the AIIB Charter entered into force—on December 25, 2015, when instruments of ratification had been deposited by seventeen Signatories with 50.1% of the subscriptions in Schedule A of the AIIB Charter.[6] 10.11

(d) Inaugural Meetings and commencement of operations

The Inaugural Meeting of the Board of Governors is specified under the AIIB Charter as the moment for the Board of Governors to determine the date for AIIB to begin to operate as an organization.[7] The Inaugural Meeting is also specified as the time for the Board of Governors to elect the President of the Bank, elect the Board of Directors, and make such other arrangements as necessary to prepare for 10.12

negotiation participants signed the Charter. For some MDBs, on occasion, a country that participated in MDB Charter negotiations and was allocated shares in the Charter did not follow up by becoming a member (e.g., the Union of Soviet Socialist Republics as listed in IBRD Schedule A and Iran as listed in AsDB Annex A).

2 AIIB Article 58-1. Instruments of ratification, acceptance or approval are commonly required for the signatories of MDB charters to become members, as well as for many other types of treaty. Whether the instrument will be one of ratification, acceptance or approval depends on the legal requirements under the country's national legal system. *See* note 28 in Chapter 6.

3 AIIB Article 6-1 and 6-2.

4 December 31, 2016 was the ratification deadline for Founding Members, under AIIB Article 3-1 (b). The deadline was last extended to June 30, 2025, for the remaining Signatory (Kuwait); Kuwait became an AIIB member on May 26, 2025. AIIB Board of Governors' Resolution No. 132, *Extending the Deadline for the State of Kuwait's Ratification of the Articles of Agreement of the Asian Infrastructure Investment Bank*, adopted June 28, 2024. In that Resolution extending the deadline, the Board of Governors noted its Resolutions No. 20 of November 28, 2016, No. 55 of December 17, 2017, No. 67 of December 18, 2018, No. 88 of December 30, 2019, No. 116 of December 28, 2022, and No. 120 of June 29, 2023, on extension of the deadline for Prospective Founding Members to ratify the Articles of Agreement of the Asian Infrastructure Investment Bank (AIIB).

5 AIIB Article 59.

6 "AIIB's Charter enters into force on 25 December 2015," AIIB Press Release, December 25, 2015. *See* note 4 in Chapter 11 for a list of the first seventeen Signatories to ratify.

7 AIIB Article 60-2 (iii).

the commencement of the Bank's operations.[8] As the Inaugural Meeting could only be formally called once the AIIB Charter had entered into force (on December 25)[9] the Inaugural Meeting of the Board of Governors was called for January 16–17, 2016. The Inaugural Meeting of the Board of Directors was scheduled to take place immediately thereafter, after Governors had completed their election of Directors.

10.13 With these considerations as a backdrop, in May 2015 the Chief Negotiators set in motion a transparent process for AIIB's establishment and for the PFMs to continue their close involvement in AIIB governance as these countries went through their national requirements. This transitional process facilitated PFM participation in three main endeavors: (i) the preparation of basic documents and policies for AIIB's initial establishment; (ii) selection of a President-designate to lead and manage pre-establishment start-up; and (iii) the establishment and work of the first Board of Governors and Board of Directors. This process culminated in the Inaugural Meetings of the Board of Governors and the Board of Directors.

B. Basic Documents and Policies

10.14 Many documents and policies needed to be ready in time for AIIB's Inaugural Meeting, to enable AIIB to start its activities as soon as possible thereafter. Basic institutional documents included the By-Laws, the Rules of Procedure for the Board of Governors and for the Board of Directors, and the Codes of Conduct for Board Officials and for Bank Personnel. Institutional policies for AIIB to employ staff and manage its finances and administration included the business plan and budget, compensation and benefits policy, financial policies, corporate procurement policy, and public information policy. Arrangements for temporary and permanent office facilities also had to be in place for AIIB's formal establishment.[10] To prepare its investment operations, AIIB would also need an operational policy on financing, an environmental and social policy, a procurement policy, and a pricing policy.

10.15 The CNM had begun to discuss some of these documents and policies even while the Charter negotiations were ongoing. With the draft Charter agreed, the CNM process continued to discuss and consider drafts through its subsequent meetings: the sixth CNM in Tbilisi, Georgia, in August 2015; the seventh CNM in Frankfurt, Germany, in September 2015; and the eighth CNM in Jakarta, Indonesia, in November 2016, with a virtual review of final documents for the Inaugural Meeting in December 2015–early January 2016.

[8] AIIB Article 60-2.
[9] AIIB Article 60-1.
[10] The location of AIIB's headquarters in Beijing, China was stipulated in AIIB Article 32-1.

This subsequent role of the CNM maintained the inclusive, participatory process that characterized the AIIB Charter negotiations. Indeed, this role had been confirmed in May, at the close of negotiations, in the Chief Negotiators' Report: 10.16

> Representatives agreed that, until the Articles of Agreement had entered into force, the Prospective Founding Members would continue to convene Chief Negotiators' Meetings to provide a broader consultation mechanism for the establishment of the AIIB.

Through the CNM, all PFMs were involved in the discussions leading up to the adoption of the documents and policies at the Inaugural Meeting, regardless of when each PFM signed the AIIB Charter or whether it had fulfilled the requirements for membership. This function of the CNM was akin to the post-signing conferences of the parties that are not uncommon for other treaties.[11]

C. President-Designate

The timetable for AIIB establishment called for intense work in the second half of 2015, preparing the institution and its initial operations and establishing its relationships with other organizations, governments, financiers, and the public. The success of the work in this early period would depend in large part on AIIB's leadership, and on the confidence that it would continue once AIIB was formally established. Temporary leadership had been installed earlier, at the October 2014 Special Ministerial Meeting that launched the negotiations on the AIIB Charter. There, a Secretary-General had been chosen to head the Secretariat.[12] At their next Special Ministerial Meeting, after the AIIB Charter signing ceremony in June 2015, the PFM Ministers agreed on a process to select a President-designate for AIIB. This practice echoed the designation of a President-designate for the European Bank for Reconstruction and Development (EBRD) in its establishment process.[13] 10.17

The decision at the Special Ministerial Meeting of the PFMs on June 29, 2015 emphasized that selecting a President-designate as early as possible was necessary "to provide for continuity of leadership through the Bank's establishment process and its early years and to enable the Bank to be set up and start operations soon after its establishment." The Special Ministerial Meeting endorsed a process for selection 10.18

[11] In the case of EBRD, there were four follow-up conferences to review the basic documents and prepare for establishment in the 11-month period between signing of the Charter and the inaugural meetings. Menkveld (1991) at 82–4.

[12] Mr Jin Liqun was selected as Secretary-General in October 2014. The overall preparation process is described in Jin (2015) at 54.

[13] For EBRD, the negotiators, at their final meeting, selected Jacques Attali as President-designate; Mr Attali had led the meetings, and was the chief personal advisor of French President Mitterrand. It was reported that the vote was thirty-two for Mr Attali and eight for the Dutch Finance Minister Otto Ruding, with two abstentions. At the same meeting, London was selected for the EBRD headquarters. "Frenchman head of new aid bank," *New York Times*, May 21, 1990.

of the President-designate, thereafter posted on the AIIB Secretariat's website.[14] This Special Ministerial Meeting was comprised of minister-level representatives from the PFMs, including those who had not yet signed the AIIB Charter—another example of the continued involvement of all PFMs in the process.

(1) Selection process

10.19 The Process for Selection of the President-designate of the Asian Infrastructure Investment Bank (the Selection Process)[15] provided for a nomination period concluding thirty days later (July 31, 2015), with a decision anticipated at the sixth CNM in August 2015. Qualifications, nomination procedures, and publication of the names of candidates were all specified. The Chief Negotiators were to meet with the candidates at the CNM, and were authorized by their appointing Ministers to reach agreement on the selection at that meeting. The Selection Process also stated clearly that it would apply only to the selection of the President-designate, and that the President-designate was expected to be elected as President by the Board of Governors at the Inaugural Meeting, as provided in the AIIB Charter.[16]

10.20 While the steps in the Selection Process resembled elements of other MDB practice for selecting a President,[17] the Selection Process had to be adapted to the absence of AIIB's formal governance organs and staff. The Special Ministerial Meeting took on the role of the Board of Governors, and the Chair of the Special Ministerial Meeting had a position similar to the Chairman of the Board of Governors. The Chief Negotiators played a role similar to the Board of Directors. The procedural role often played by an MDB's corporate secretary and general counsel was assigned to the AIIB Secretariat's Chief Counsel, inasmuch as the Secretary-General of the AIIB Secretariat himself was promptly nominated as a candidate. To reflect AIIB's decision-making rules, the Chief Negotiators were authorized to reach agreement by consensus, if possible; if not, the agreement of two-thirds of the PFMs was required. This paralleled the number of Governors needed for the Super Majority for election of the AIIB President, where two-thirds of the Governors representing three-fourths of total voting power must agree.[18] In this pre-establishment phase, no comparable percentage of total voting power could be required, as PFMs had not subscribed and become members, and therefore had no actual votes.

[14] Asian Infrastructure Investment Bank, Selection of the President-designate, July 1, 2015.

[15] Process for Selection of the President-designate for the Asian Infrastructure Investment Bank, July 1, 2015.

[16] AIIB Article 60-2 (i).

[17] For AfDB, *see* Rules of Procedure Governing the Election of the President of the African Development Bank, published December 3, 2015. For IADB, *see* Regulations for the Election of the President of the Bank. For IBRD, *see* the Report on the Selection Process of the President, adopted by the IBRD Executive Directors, in Development Committee (2011).

[18] AIIB Article 29-1. The Selection Process also respected this section by requiring that each candidate must be a national of a regional PFM.

(2) Selection decision

In July 2015 two candidates were nominated, and their names were published on the AIIB Secretariat website: Mr Andrei Bugrov, nominated by Russia, and Mr Jin Liqun, nominated by China. At the sixth CNM in Tbilisi, Georgia, the representatives of the PFMs selected Mr Jin Liqun as the President-designate by consensus.[19] The August 24, 2015 CNM decision on the selection of the President-designate further stated: **10.21**

> The President-designate will take over the continuing responsibilities of the Secretary-General of the Multilateral Interim Secretariat for Establishing the Bank. In addition, the President-designate will be responsible for taking the actions needed for the Bank to start operating effectively upon its establishment, including advance temporary recruitment and preparation of the Bank's offices.

Mr Jin served as President-designate from September 1, 2015 until taking up the position of President of AIIB following his election at the Inaugural Meeting of the Board of Governors on January 16, 2016. (He was re-elected in 2020, for a second term ending in January 2026.) **10.22**

D. Interim Arrangements

The formal processes for members to appoint Governors and elect Directors were laid out in the AIIB Charter. PFMs that had signed the AIIB Charter but not yet completed AIIB membership requirements could not be formally represented on the Boards. To maintain the consultative process, all PFMs were enabled to participate in the work of both Boards under the Interim Arrangements recorded in the Chief Negotiators' Report: **10.23**

> Once the Articles of Agreement had entered into force, and until the final date under Article 58, paragraph 1, Interim Arrangements would provide an opportunity for Prospective Founding Members to continue to participate in AIIB governance, pending their completion of the steps for membership. In that period, the Boards would accommodate non-voting representatives as follows,[20] in order to ensure that major decisions will be supported by adequate consultation of all Signatories and reached by consensus to the maximum extent possible.
>
> ...
>
> Once the deadline has passed for Signatories to complete the steps for membership and become members under Article 58, the period to become Founding

[19] "Jin Liqun selected President-designate of the Asian Infrastructure Investment Bank," AIIB Secretariat Press Release, August 24, 2015.

[20] The provisions of the Interim Arrangements for the two Boards are described in the following text.

> Members would end. At that point, all Founding Members would participate in AIIB governance under normal AIIB governance arrangements, and these Interim Arrangements would terminate.[21]

These Interim Arrangements were necessary to fit informal participation within the AIIB's legal requirements, which otherwise required membership as a prerequisite for any form of representation.

(1) Board of Governors

10.24 Each AIIB member appoints one Governor and one Alternate Governor to represent the member on the Board of Governors.[22] Thus, the Board of Governors at its Inaugural Meeting would be composed only of the Governors appointed by AIIB members. As soon as each PFM had signed the Charter and completed its membership requirements, the new member could appoint its Governor and Alternate Governor, and be represented on the Board of Governors.

10.25 For the Board of Governors, the Interim Arrangements were relatively straightforward. Each Signatory that had not yet become a member could send a representative to attend meetings of the Board of Governors as an observer. Observers are normally permitted at meetings of the Board of Governors in other MDBs, especially for prospective members. To formalize and recognize Signatory Observers as part of the Interim Arrangements, the Rules of Procedure of the AIIB Board of Governors, adopted at the Inaugural Meeting, included a specific provision in addition to the usual rules permitting observers:

> Until the final date for deposit of instruments of ratification, acceptance or approval under paragraph 1 of Article 58 of the Articles of Agreement, each Signatory of the Articles of Agreement that has not yet become a Member shall be invited to send a non-voting representative as an observer for each meeting of the Board.[23]

10.26 The Inaugural Meeting was attended by Governors representing thirty members (with about 74% of expected shareholding), along with Signatory Observers from twenty-seven PFMs. By the time of the first Annual Meeting of the Board of Governors in June 2016, forty-six members were represented by Governors, along with ten Signatory Observers.[24] Starting from the Second Annual Meeting in June 2017, there were also observers from newly approved prospective members

[21] Ten years after the Chief Negotiators' Report was agreed, the last Founding Member (Kuwait) joined on May 26, 2025, ending any required vestiges of the Interim Arrangements.

[22] AIIB Article 22-1.

[23] AIIB Rules of Procedure of the Board of Governors, January 16, 2016, Section 3 (c). Generally, Section 3 (b) permits observers at meetings, at the invitation of the Chairman of the Board of Governors, in consultation with the Board of Directors.

[24] Uzbekistan is not listed as having sent a Signatory Observer, as it was entitled to do. In addition, representatives of twenty-four potential members attended the first Annual Meeting.

INAUGURAL MEETING OF THE AIIB BOARD OF GOVERNORS (January 16-17, 2016)[1]
REPRESENTATION AT MEETINGS OF AIIB BOARD OF GOVERNORS (2016)
Members (represented by Governors)
Australia, Austria, Brunei Darussalam, China, Denmark, Finland, Georgia, Germany, India, Indonesia, Israel, Jordan, Republic of Korea, Lao PDR, Luxembourg, Maldives, Malta, Mongolia, Myanmar, Nepal, Netherlands, New Zealand, Norway, Pakistan, Russia, Singapore, Tajikistan, Türkiye, United Arab Emirates, United Kingdom
Prospective Founding Members (Signatories) (represented by Signatory Observers)
Azerbaijan, Bangladesh, Cambodia, Egypt, France, Iceland, Iran, Italy, Kazakhstan, Kuwait, Kyrgyz Republic, Malaysia, Oman, Philippines, Poland, Portugal, Qatar, Saudi Arabia, South Africa, Spain, Sri Lanka, Sweden, Switzerland, Thailand, Uzbekistan, Vietnam
FIRST ANNUAL MEETING (June 24-25, 2016)[2]
Members (represented by Governors)
Australia, Austria, Azerbaijan, Bangladesh, Brunei Darussalam, Cambodia, China, Denmark, Finland, France, Georgia, Germany, Iceland, India, Indonesia, Israel, Jordan, Kazakhstan, Republic of Korea, Kyrgyz Republic, Lao PDR, Luxembourg, Maldives, Malta, Mongolia, Myanmar, Nepal, Netherlands, New Zealand, Norway, Oman, Pakistan, Poland, Qatar, Russia, Saudi Arabia, Singapore, Sri Lanka, Sweden, Switzerland, Tajikistan, Thailand, Türkiye, United Arab Emirates, United Kingdom, Vietnam
Prospective Founding Members (Signatories) (represented by Signatory Observers)
Brazil, Egypt, Iran, Italy, Kuwait, Malaysia, Portugal, South Africa, Spain, Philippines

Figure 10.1 Representation at Meetings of AIIB Board of Governors (2016)

Source:

[1] Summary Proceedings of the Inaugural Meeting of the AIIB Board of Governors, January 16–17, 2016.

[2] Summary Proceedings of the Annual Meeting of the AIIB Board of Governors, June 24–25, 2016.

listed with the Prospective Founding Members.[25] Figure 10.1 lists AIIB members attending the Board of Governors' Inaugural Meeting and First Annual Meeting, along with Signatory Observers from PFMs.

(2) Board of Directors

Under the regular governance provisions, twelve Directors are elected in a process where votes can be cast only by AIIB Governors, and Directors serve a term of two years.[26] Further, each Director appoints an Alternate Director (in some cases, two Alternate Directors); Directors and Alternate Directors must be nationals of member countries.[27] As a result, a PFM would have to complete all membership requirements in order to appoint a Governor to vote for a Director as well as for a national of a PFM to serve as Director or Alternate Director. Here, too, the uneven pace of PFM membership over several months, before and after the Inaugural Meetings, necessitated alternative arrangements. **10.27**

[25] Summary Proceedings of the Annual Meeting of the AIIB Board of Governors, June 16–18, 2017.

[26] AIIB Article 25-1 and 25-5, and Schedule B.

[27] AIIB Article 25-3 and 25-4, and AIIB Board of Governors' Resolution No. 8, *Appointment of Additional Director*, adopted January 16, 2016, deciding that Directors representing five or more members could appoint a second Alternate Director.

10.28 The Board of Governors was authorized under the AIIB Charter to shorten the initial term and to reduce the initial number of Directors to be elected, as needed.[28] This authorization was specifically aimed at the situation in which the timing of both PFM membership and the Inaugural Meeting was in flux, as that decision was to be taken "in consideration of the number of members and Signatories which have not yet become members." In light of the timing of PFM membership and Board constituency arrangements, the Governors made use of this flexibility in establishing the term of the first Board and the timing of elections.

(a) Board constituency arrangements

10.29 PFMs expected to group together in compatible Board constituencies, with each constituency represented by a Director, as is the normal practice in many MDBs. Constituencies usually work out arrangements for the nationalities of Directors and Alternates, often with a rotation pattern tied to the regular elections of Directors.[29] For the first AIIB Board, however, internal constituency rotation arrangements might not prove feasible, because a national from a not-yet-member PFM could not legally be elected as Director even if the PFMs in the constituency agreed. Instead, a national from another PFM in the constituency that was already an AIIB member at the Inaugural Meetings would have to be elected. If no one was elected in a constituency or no PFMs in the constituency were members, that constituency would have no Director—and no representation—on the first Board. (To illustrate, the twelve anticipated constituencies can be seen in Figure 10.2.)

(b) Number of Directors elected

10.30 The number of Directors to be elected was set only on the eve of the Inaugural Meeting, when the final number of PFMs having met the membership requirements in time was known. As it happened, eleven constituencies had at least one member by then and could elect Directors: nine regional and two non-regional.[30] As other PFMs in those eleven constituencies became members after the Inaugural Meeting, they could join their expected constituency by assigning votes to the already elected Director.[31] For the twelfth constituency, those PFMs had a voice in the work of the

[28] AIIB Article 60-2 (ii). Other MDB Charters have had provisions to handle the timing of membership and the first Board of Directors. *See* AfDB Article 66-2 (a) (smaller number); EBRD Article 26-3 (special recognition for size of second board); IADB Article XV, Section 3 (b) (shorter term); and IBRD Article XI, Sections 3 (b) and (c) (selection and appointment of provisional directors to remain in office until first regular election).

[29] There is no legal requirement that a Director or Alternate must represent his own country, though that is often the case. A Director or Alternate may be a national of any member. However, no two or more Directors may be of the same nationality nor may any two or more Alternate Directors be of the same nationality. AIIB Article 25-4.

[30] AIIB Board of Governors' Resolution No. 4, *Rules for the Election of Directors at the Inaugural Meeting*, adopted January 16, 2016.

[31] Not-yet-member Signatories could nonetheless have nationals serve as one of the non-speaking, non-voting Advisors that each Director is entitled to designate under the AIIB Rules of Procedure of the Board of Directors, January 17, 2016, Section 3 (h). The Advisor position is established under the Rules of Procedure of the Board of Directors rather than the AIIB Charter, and there is no nationality requirement. *See* note 42 in Chapter 8 for more details about the Advisor position.

AIIB INAUGURAL BOARD OF DIRECTORS (January 17, 2016)			
Director	**Alternate Director**	**Members (formal representation)**	***Signatories (informal representation)***
Baikuntha ARYAL (Nepal)	Mohamed SAEED (Maldives)	**Maldives** **Nepal**	*Bangladesh* *Malaysia* *Philippines* *Thailand*
Luis BALDUINO* (Brazil)	Sahar NASR (Egypt)**		*Brazil* *Egypt* *South Africa*
Andin HADIYANTO (Indonesia)	Bounthom LOMANY (Lao People's Democratic Republic)	**Indonesia** **Lao People's Democratic Republic** **Myanmar**	*Sri Lanka*
Adel AL HOSANI (United Arab Emirates)	Emad SHANA'AH (Jordan)	**Jordan** **United Arab Emirates**	*Kuwait* *Oman* *Qatar* *Saudi Arabia*
Christopher LEGG (Australia)	Lee Pak SING (Singapore)	**Australia** **New Zealand** **Singapore**	*Cambodia* *Vietnam*
Vanessa MACDOUGALL (United Kingdom)	Henrik HARBOE (Norway)	**Denmark** **Norway** **United Kingdom**	*Iceland* *Poland* *Sweden* *Switzerland*
Timur MAKSIMOV (Russia)		**Russian Federation** **Tajikistan**	*Iran* *Kazakhstan*
Nikolai PUTSCHER (Germany)	Irene JANSEN (Netherlands) Edith FRAUWALLNER (Austria)	**Austria** **Finland** **Germany** **Luxembourg** **Malta** **Netherlands**	*France* *Italy* *Portugal* *Spain*
Dinesh SHARMA (India)		**India**	
In-chang SONG (Korea, Republic of)	Yoel NAVEH (Israel)	**Israel** **Korea, Republic of** **Mongolia**	*Uzbekistan*
Hakan TOKAÇ (Turkey)	Omar Hamid KHAN (Pakistan)	**Brunei Darussalam** **Georgia** **Pakistan** **Turkey**	*Azerbaijan* *Kyrgyz Republic*
YANG Shaolin (China)		**China**	

Figure 10.2 AIIB Inaugural Board of Directors (January 17, 2016)

*Constituency Representative

**Alternate Constituency Representative

Source: Summary of Proceedings, Inaugural Meeting of the AIIB Board of Governors, January 16–17, 2016 at 84–5 and Minutes of the Meeting of the AIIB Board of Directors, January 17, 2016 (attendees).

Board of Directors through their non-voting Constituency Representative, a newly created position described at paragraphs 10.35–10.36.[32]

10.31 Figure 10.2 shows the composition of the AIIB Board of Directors at the time of its Inaugural Meeting, including PFMs in each constituency that had already become members (in bold) and that had yet to become members (in italics). (Figure 8.3 in Chapter 8 shows the Board of Directors in June 2025, for comparison.)

(c) Timing of elections

10.32 MDB elections for the Board of Directors have traditionally taken place at annual meetings, although there has been a move to non-physical virtual elections in some cases.[33] While the AIIB Charter does not tie the election of Directors to the annual meetings of the Board of Governors, coordinating the timing of elections and annual meetings has the advantage of familiarity and convenience, if Governors' presence is needed. With a likely June timing for AIIB's Annual Meeting, the first Board's term could have ended around the time of either the First Annual Meeting in June 2016 (a Directors' term of about six months) or the Second Annual Meeting in June 2017 (a Directors' term of about eighteen months).

10.33 The timing of the election of the second Board thus depended on the term of the first Board. The timing of the second election would then determine the timing for subsequent biennial elections (for regular two-year terms). Electing the first Board for a shorter term would minimize any disconnect with Board constituency arrangements, and would encourage PFMs to join before the second election, at the latest. A second election in a short time would also provide a transparent way to revert to agreed constituency patterns, if needed, once all or most of the PFMs in a constituency had formally joined.

10.34 In view of these considerations, the Board of Governors took two complementary decisions at its Inaugural Meeting. The Board decided that the first Annual Meeting would be held in June 2016, and that the term of the Directors elected at the Inaugural Meeting would end on June 30, 2016.[34] These two decisions taken together meant that the Inaugural Board of Directors would serve less than six months, and that the second Board of Directors would be elected at the first Annual Meeting and serve a term of two years from July 2016. That arrangement also coordinated the future timing of Directors' elections and annual meetings.

[32] As shown in Figure 10.2, the twelfth constituency was composed of Brazil, Egypt, and South Africa. It was not until Fall 2016 that the twelfth Director was elected for that constituency, following Egypt's completion of its membership requirements. AIIB Board of Governors' Resolution No. 21, *First Election of the 3rd Non-Regional Director*, adopted November 28, 2016.

[33] This is the case for the World Bank Group, for example. One factor in this evolution has been the development of suitable technologies; another has been the unpredictability in recent decades in terms of external events that can cause the delay or cancellation of an Annual Meeting.

[34] AIIB Board of Governors' Resolution, No. 4, *Rules for the Election of Directors at the Inaugural Meeting*, adopted January 16, 2016 and AIIB Board of Governors' Resolution No. 11, *Date and Place of the First Annual Meeting*, adopted January 17, 2016.

(d) Constituency Representative

The Constituency Representative position was created under the Interim Arrangements to address the constituency issues outlined above. Where no PFMs in a particular constituency group had yet completed AIIB membership requirements, there could be no Director elected to represent them, even informally. The Constituency Representative would be an informal representative for those PFMs, participating in the work of the Board of Directors in substantially the same manner as a Director but without any formal vote. The Chief Negotiators' Report set out the agreement on the Constituency Representative position as follows: **10.35**

> *Board of Directors.* Signatories could agree on notional constituency groupings, recognizing that actual constituencies would be formed when members' Governors cast their votes for or assign their votes to a Director. Based on these notional constituency groupings, each constituency would either be represented by a Director if one has been elected by a member or members in the constituency, or, if there is no Director yet for the constituency, by a special Constituency Representative selected by the constituency members through consultations. Constituency Representatives could participate in Board of Directors' meetings without voting. A Director would informally represent the Signatories in the constituency that had not yet become members, as well as formally representing the Governors who had cast their votes for or assigned their votes to the Director. Each constituency group would be represented by a Director or by a Constituency Representative, but not both.

The first Board of Directors also provided a solid legal basis for the innovative positions of Constituency Representative and Alternate Constituency Representative. Section 12 of the Rules of Procedure for the Board of Directors, adopted at its Inaugural Meeting, contained the rules applicable to these positions, with the proviso that this Section falls away when the Interim Arrangements have ended.[35] This Section confirmed that constituency groupings for purposes of determining whether there should be a Constituency Representative in lieu of a Director are notional groupings, "recognizing that actual constituencies would be formed when members' Governors cast their votes for or assign their votes to a Director." Moreover, this Section confirmed the informal representation by Directors of Signatories that had not yet become members. In addition, this Section introduced the position of Alternate Constituency Representative, also designated by the constituency, with a role akin to that of an Alternate Director. Constituency Representatives and Alternate Constituency Representatives were entitled to **10.36**

[35] AIIB Rules of Procedure of the Board of Directors, as amended, Section 13, provides: "Once the deadline has passed for Signatories to complete the steps for membership and become Members under Article 58, these Interim Arrangements shall terminate. These Rules shall then be restated without this Section . . . "

reasonable expenses for traveling officially to meetings, and were subject to ethical requirements and confidentiality obligations provided for Directors.

E. Inaugural Meetings

10.37 Through the CNM preparatory process, with the technical support of the Secretariat and under the leadership of the President-designate, the two Boards were presented with decisions at their Inaugural Meetings that were necessary for AIIB to be established and start operations. The presentation of these decisions reflected the division of powers outlined in Chapter 8, including the reserved powers of the Board of Governors and delegated and specific powers of the Board of Directors.

(1) Board of Governors

10.38 The Board of Governors adopted a package of resolutions that approved, inter alia, the Rules of Procedure of the Board of Governors, the elections of officers of the Board of Governors, the AIIB By-Laws, the Rules for the Election of Directors at the Inaugural Meeting, the election of the President, the Headquarters Agreement with China, the threshold for appointment of an additional Alternate Director, the Codes of Conduct for Board Officials and Bank Personnel, and the date and place of the First Annual Meeting.[36] Importantly, the Board of Governors adopted a resolution that determined January 16, 2016 as the date for commencement of operations of the Bank—in essence, a declaration that AIIB was formally established that day.[37]

10.39 Following their adoption of the Rules for the Election of Directors, the Governors proceeded to cast ballots on January 16, electing eleven Directors, who took up office on January 17, 2016. The Directors then appointed Alternate Directors and Advisors to participate in the Inaugural Meeting of the Board of Directors. The Signatories in the twelfth constituency designated a Constituency Representative,[38] who was also authorized to appoint an Alternate Constituency Representative and Advisors.

[36] For AIIB, the Resolutions of the Board of Governors adopted at the Inaugural Meeting can be found in the Summary Proceedings, Inaugural Meeting of the AIIB Board of Governors, January 16–17, 2016 (and on the AIIB website). Resolutions No. 1-9 were adopted on January 16, 2016 and Resolutions No. 10–13 were adopted on January 17, 2016.

[37] EBRD's Board of Governors also declared the first day of the Inaugural Meeting as the date for commencement of operations (April 15, 1991).

[38] *See* the list of attendees in the Minutes of the Meeting of the Board of Directors of the Asian Infrastructure Investment Bank held on January 17, 2016.

(2) Board of Directors

At the Inaugural Meeting of the Board of Directors on the afternoon of January 17, the Board of Directors approved, inter alia, the Rules of Procedure of the Board of Directors; the 2016 Business Plan and Budget, Compensation and Benefits Policies; Financial Policies; the Sovereign-backed Loan and Guarantee Pricing Decision; the General Investment, Borrowing, and Asset Liability Management Authorities; the Operational Policy on Financing; the Public Information Interim Policy; the Procurement Policy; and the Corporate Procurement Policy. They also considered, and subsequently approved, the Environmental and Social Framework.[39] **10.40**

With the Inaugural Meetings, AIIB's governing organs were all formally and legally established: Board of Governors, Board of Directors, and President. The Board of Governors subsequently held its first Annual Meeting in June 2016. At that time the Governors elected a new Board of Directors, to serve a two-year term (July 1, 2016 to June 30, 2018).[40] In accordance with the Interim Arrangements, not-yet-member Signatories could send observers to the 2016 Annual Meeting, and the Board of Directors elected there also had eleven Directors and one Constituency Representative. By December 2016, a twelfth Director had been elected, and the position of Constituency Representative was no longer shown on the Board of Directors' roster.[41] Overall, the Interim Arrangements would terminate when the deadline for Signatories to complete membership requirements passed, which was June 30, 2025.[42] **10.41**

[39] These policies were all approved by the Board of Directors at the meeting, with the exception of the Environmental and Social Policy, which was approved shortly thereafter: "the Board of Directors accepted the President's proposal to circulate by mid-February a revised version of the proposed environmental and social policy for approval on an absence of objection basis." Minutes of the Meeting of the Board of Directors of the Asian Infrastructure Investment Bank held on January 17, 2016, paragraph 12. The Board's approval of the Environmental and Social Policy was recorded in subsequent minutes. Minutes of the Meeting of the Board of Directors of the Asian Infrastructure Investment Bank held on April 25–26, paragraph 10. Chapter 5, Section E, includes summaries of the policies relevant for operations (Operational Policy on Financing, Environmental and Social Policy, Procurement Policy, and Sovereign-backed Loan and Guarantee Pricing Decision) and Chapter 11 includes summaries of the Corporate Procurement Policy (paragraph 11.48) and the Public Information Interim Policy (paragraphs 11.45–11.47).

[40] AIIB Board of Governors' Resolution No. 15, *2016 Election of Directors*, adopted June 13, 2016 and Results of Election, in Summary of Proceedings, Annual Meeting of the Board of Governors, June 24–25, 2016, at 71–2.

[41] Minutes of the Meeting of the Board of Directors of the Asian Infrastructure Investment Bank held on December 8–9, 2016.

[42] Chief Negotiators' Report: "Once the deadline has passed for Signatories to complete the steps for membership and become members under Article 58, the period to become Founding Members would end. At that point, all Founding Members would participate in AIIB governance under normal AIIB governance arrangements, and these Interim Arrangements would terminate." The AIIB Rules of Procedure of the Board of Directors also provide for termination of the Interim Arrangements in Section 12. Once the Interim Arrangements have terminated, the provision for not-yet-member Signatories to send observers to meetings of the Board of Governors would end as well (though observers can always be invited by the Chairman of the Board of Governors). *See* AIIB Rules of Procedure of the Board of Governors, Section 3 (b) and (c).

The deadline was extended until June 30, 2025 and has since passed. *See* note 4 in this chapter.

11
INSTITUTIONAL MATTERS

Like other multilateral development banks (MDBs), the Asian Infrastructure Investment Bank (AIIB) is at once a development institution, a financial institution, and an international organization created by multilateral treaty. Earlier chapters have described how the AIIB Charter regulates AIIB as a development institution (Chapter 5, Investment Operations) and as a financial institution (Chapter 7, Capital and Finance). Some elements related to AIIB as an international organization have been covered as well (Chapter 4, Mandate; Chapter 6, Membership; and Chapters 8 and 9, Governance: Framework and Governance: Decision-Making, respectively). 11.01

Still other elements derive from AIIB's creation by multilateral treaty and its consequent status as an intergovernmental entity. This chapter outlines the provisions of the AIIB Charter most relevant for its status as a treaty, its international character, AIIB's Charter-based privileges and immunities as an international organization, and the framework for the administration of the Bank. 11.02

A. Charter as Treaty

(1) Signature and ratification

To recall, the AIIB Charter was open for signature between June 29, 2015 and December 31, 2015.[1] To become members, each Signatory had to deposit an instrument of ratification, acceptance or approval of the treaty,[2] and complete the membership and subscription process.[3] It was the deposit of these instruments from seventeen Signatories with 50.1% of total subscriptions that brought the AIIB Charter into force as a treaty on December 25, 2015.[4] 11.03

[1] AIIB Article 57-1.

[2] Whether a Signatory deposits an instrument of ratification, acceptance or approval depends on domestic legal requirements. *See* note 28 in Chapter 6.

[3] AIIB Article 58-1.

[4] AIIB Article 59 required a minimum of ten instruments with subscriptions totaling not less than 50% of total subscriptions. "AIIB's Charter enters into force on 25 December 2015," AIIB Press Release, January 16, 2016. The seventeen Signatories whose instruments of ratification counted towards meeting the threshold for entry into force were: Australia, Austria, Brunei Darussalam, China, Georgia, Germany, Jordan, Korea, Luxembourg, Mongolia, Myanmar, Netherlands, New Zealand, Norway, Pakistan, Singapore, and the United Kingdom. (These members are shown with a membership date of December 25, 2015 on AIIB's website, and their allocated shares are shown in Schedule A of the AIIB Charter.)

11.04 This process of signature and deposit of instruments for an international treaty of this nature is normally conducted by a depository, which handles the procedures for signature and subsequent types of accession, as well as treaty events during the life of the treaty.[5] The depository could be another international organization or a member state, for example. For AIIB, the depository was specified as the Government of the People's Republic of China,[6] and, as is common, China's Ministry of Foreign Affairs played this role. By comparison, Charters of other MDBs organized under the auspices of existing international organizations have specified the host organization as the depository, such as the Organization of American States for the Inter-American Development Bank (IADB) and the United Nations Secretary-General for the African Development Bank (AfDB) and Asian Development Bank (AsDB).[7] Where there is no host organization, as was the case for AIIB, the organizing government could serve as depository, as the United States did for the International Bank for Reconstruction and Development (IBRD) and France did for the European Bank for Reconstruction and Development (EBRD).[8]

(2) Amendment

11.05 As an international treaty, the AIIB Charter stipulates a formal process for its amendment. Amendment of the AIIB Charter is a reserved power of the Board of Governors, requiring a Super Majority vote.[9] Any proposal for amendment, whether emanating from a member or from the Board of Directors, must be communicated to the Chairman of the Board of Governors, who has the responsibility to bring the proposal before the Board of Governors.[10]

11.06 The AIIB Charter thus follows the procedure in the Charters for the AsDB and IADB, where the Board of Governors' decision is the final act in amendment.[11]

[5] *See* the 1969 Vienna Convention on the Law of Treaties, Articles 77–80, for a legal description of the functions of depositaries (also referred to as depositories).

[6] AIIB Article 57-1.

[7] IADB Article XV, Section 1; AfDB Article 63 and AsDB Article 63. The UN Secretary-General serves as depositary (depository) for more than 500 multilateral treaties. The Secretary-General's policy has been in principle to restrict the assumption of depositary functions to open multilateral treaties of worldwide interest, usually adopted by the General Assembly or concluded by plenipotentiary conferences convened by the appropriate organs of the United Nations, and to regional treaties that are drawn up within the framework of the United Nations regional commissions and are open for participation to their entire membership. Summary of Practice of the Secretary-General as Depositary of Multilateral Treaties, UN 1999, at paragraph 28. Thus, the UN Secretary-General would not have been a likely depository for the AIIB Charter.

[8] IBRD Article XI, Section 2 and EBRD Article 60. In the case of the IBRD Charter, the US Department of State has continued to play this role since 1945. In parallel, for the IMF Charter, the United States is the depository, "in accordance with the usual practice at the time of the Bretton Woods Conference of depositing multilateral treaties with the state in which the treaty was signed." Gold (1974) at 38. Gold further notes that the UN Charter had not yet been signed at that time, so the UN was not an option for depository.

[9] AIIB Articles 23-2 (ix) and 53-1.

[10] AIIB Article 53-3.

[11] AsDB Article 59 (Board of Governors' decision only, requiring two-thirds of Governors representing not less than three-fourths of the total voting power); and IADB Article XII (a) (Board of Governors' decision only, requiring a majority of Governors including two-thirds of regional Governors, representing

Some other MDBs, notably IBRD, AfDB, and EBRD, require a second-phase acceptance of Charter amendments by a specified majority of members holding a qualified majority of voting power, after approval by the Board of Governors.[12] MDB Charters are amended infrequently, and the qualified majorities for this important act are usually among the highest. Some organizations have experienced very little change. For instance, the AsDB Charter has never been amended, and the IBRD Charter has had three very specific amendments in seventy years.[13] In June 2025, however, both AsDB and IBRD had amendments in process to remove the statutory lending limit.[14]

The EBRD Charter had three limited amendments in its first twenty-five years, first to bring in Mongolia as a country of operations in 2006, and similarly to bring in countries of the Southern and Eastern Mediterranean in 2013.[15] In 2025, however, two additional amendments came into force, one to enable EBRD operations in Sub-Saharan Africa and Iraq[16] and another to revise the statutory capital limitation on ordinary operations.[17] **11.07**

In other organizations, amendments are more common, especially when the nature of the change is significant.[18] The IADB Charter was amended seven times between **11.08**

three-fourths of total voting power). *See* also IFC Article VII (a) (Board of Governors' decision only, requiring three-fifths of the Governors exercising 85% of the total voting power).

[12] *See, e.g.*, AfDB Article 60-1 (requiring acceptance of amendments by two-thirds of members including two-thirds of regional members having three-quarters of total voting power of regional members); EBRD 56-1 (requiring acceptance of amendments by three-fourths of members, including at least two Central and Eastern European members, having not less than four-fifths of the total voting power of members); and IBRD Article VIII (a) (requiring acceptance by three-fifths of the members holding an 85% majority of total voting power).

[13] The IBRD Charter was amended in 1965 to permit loans to IFC (Article II, Section 6), in 1989 to require an 85% majority for amendments instead of four-fifths (80%) (Article VIII (a)), and in 2012 to increase and set basic votes as a percentage (5.55%) of total votes (Article V, Section 3 (a)).

[14] *See* paragraph 7.44.

[15] While Mongolia and later the countries of the Southern and Eastern Mediterranean were eligible for EBRD membership as non-European IMF members under EBRD Article 3-1, they would not have fallen within the Central and Eastern European scope of operations. The Mongolia amendment is in EBRD Board of Governors' Resolution No. 90, *Amendment to the Agreement Establishing the Bank in order to Admit Mongolia as a Country of Operations*, adopted January 30, 2004, entered into force October 15, 2006. EBRD Board of Governors' Resolution No. 137, *Amendment of the Agreement Establishing the Bank in order to Enable the Bank to Operate in Countries of the Southern and Eastern Mediterranean*, adopted September 30, 2011, entered into force September 12, 2013. A companion amendment allowed the use of EBRD Special Funds in recipient and potential recipient countries. EBRD Board of Governors' Resolution No. 138, *Amendment to the Agreement Establishing the Bank in order to Allow the Use of Special Funds in Recipient Countries and Potential Recipient Countries*, adopted September 30, 2011, entered into force August 22, 2012.

[16] EBRD Board of Governors' Resolution No. 259, *Amendment to Article 1 of the Agreement Establishing the Bank to Enable a Limited and Incremental Expansion of the Geographic Scope of the Bank's Operations to Sub-Saharan Africa and Iraq*, adopted May 18, 2023, entered into force July 22, 2025.

[17] EBRD Board of Governors' Resolution, No. 260, *Amendment to Article 12.1 of the Agreement Establishing the European Bank for Reconstruction and Development to Remove the Statutory Capital Limitation On Ordinary Operations*, adopted May 18, 2023, entered into force June 26, 2025. *See* paragraph 7.44.

[18] The IMF Charter has been amended seven times, in some major ways (e.g., introduction of Special Drawing Rights, demise of the par value system). The 2016 publication of the IMF Charter lists the details: amended effective July 28, 1969, by the modifications approved by the Board of Governors in Resolution No. 23-5, adopted May 31, 1968; amended effective April 1, 1978, by the modifications approved by the Board of Governors in Resolution No. 31-4, adopted April 30, 1976; amended effective November 11, 1992, by the modifications approved by the Board of Governors in Resolution No. 45-3, adopted June 28,

1959 and 1995, with substantial changes to bring in non-regional members and their capital approved in 1976; other changes were more limited in scope.[19] The AfDB Charter has been amended five times from 1964 to 2002, with the most extensive changes to introduce non-regional membership in 1982 and to remove obsolete provisions and harmonize with other Charters in 2002.[20]

11.09 The AIIB Charter carries forward the same requirement of unanimity for three core amendments that is found in other MDBs.[21] Unanimous agreement of the Board of Governors is required to amend: (i) each member's right to withdraw from the Bank; (ii) the limitations on liability of members; and (iii) the pre-emptive rights pertaining to purchase of capital stock.[22] The limitations on liability mean that members' liability is limited to the unpaid portion of the issue price of shares and that no member is liable for the obligations of AIIB merely by virtue of its membership.[23] Pre-emptive rights allow each member to subscribe to enough shares of each capital increase to maintain its percentage share of AIIB's capital.[24] Each of these provisions requiring unanimity for amendment offers a core protection for members, and unanimity ensures that these protections cannot be altered without every member's consent.

(3) Interpretation

11.10 Interpretation of MDB Charters is a normal practice to enable the institutions to adapt to particular situations or new circumstances that are not specifically addressed in the Charter. Generally, amendment would be a course of last resort when interpretation would go beyond stretching the Charter. Informal

1990; amended effective August 10, 2009, by the modifications approved by the Board of Governors in Resolution No. 52-4, adopted September 23, 1997; amended effective February 18, 2011, by the modifications approved by the Board of Governors in Resolution No. 63-3, adopted May 5, 2008; amended effective March 3, 2011, by the modifications approved by the Board of Governors in Resolution No. 63-2, adopted April 28, 2008; amended effective January 26, 2016 by the modifications approved by the Board of Governors in Resolution No. 66-2, adopted December 15, 2010.

[19] The IADB Charter was last amended in 1995, according to the published text; six previous amendments are recorded in 1964, 1968, 1971, 1972, 1976, and 1987. The introduction of non-regional membership came through IADB Board of Governors' Resolution No. AG-9/76, *Amendments to the Agreement Establishing the Bank with Respect to the Creation of the Inter-Regional Capital Stock of the Bank and to Related Matters*, approved June 1, 1976.

[20] The 2016 publication of the AfDB Charter lists five amendments, in 1982, 1994, 1998, 1999, and 2002. For non-regional membership, *see* AfDB Board of Governors' Resolution 05-79, *Concerning the Amendments of the Agreement Establishing the African Development Bank to Enable Non-African Countries to Become Members Thereof*, approved May 17, 1979, entered into force May 7, 1982, Annex, paragraph 5 (ii). For the most recent changes, *see* AfDB Board of Governors' Resolution B/BG/2001/08, *Amendments to the Agreement Establishing the African Development Bank*, adopted May 29, 2001, entered into force June 5, 2002.

[21] The provisions requiring unanimity are similar in the other MDBs as well. AfDB Article 60-3; AsDB Article 59-2; EBRD Article 56-2 (adds to the list amendments to its purpose and functions); IADB Article XII (b) (slightly different); and IBRD Article VIII (b).

[22] AIIB Article 53-2.

[23] AIIB Article 7-3 and 7-4.

[24] AIIB Article 5-4.

interpretation of MDB Charters is more frequent than formal interpretation. The AIIB Charter follows a familiar structure in providing for formal interpretation, in the first instance, by the Board of Directors.[25] As elsewhere, the Board of Governors retains a reserved power to take a final decision on interpretation, if a member appeals the initial decision by the Board of Directors.[26] In practice, there have been relatively few formal interpretations of the Charters in the IBRD and other MDBs, but informal interpretations take place frequently through decisions of the Board of Directors in approving proposals as consistent with the Charters.[27] Normally, such decisions of the Board would rely on formal legal opinions from the MDB's General Counsel.[28]

There is a unique provision in the AIIB Charter that mandates that the English text of the AIIB Charter should be relied on for interpretations (and for all other decisions), and also specifies that English is the working language of the Bank.[29] Another novel provision relevant for future interpretations requires that all references in the AIIB Charter to "he" and "his" include any gender, introducing full gender neutrality to the text.[30] **11.11**

AIIB is authorized to exercise such powers as may be necessary or appropriate to further its purpose and function, consistent with the other provisions of the AIIB Charter.[31] The existence of such incidental powers can often alleviate the need to **11.12**

[25] AIIB Article 54-1.

[26] AIIB Articles 23-2 (iv) and 54-2.

[27] *See* Rigo Sureda (2004) at paragraphs 78–80. He notes that there had been fifteen formal interpretations of the IBRD Charter at that time (thirteen occurring in its first five years). There have been two subsequent formal interpretations, one in 2010 (Appointed Executive Directors) and another in 2015 (Waiver of Privileges and Immunities). In the absence of a listing of IBRD Charter interpretations on the World Bank Group website, the two most recent interpretations can be found in the minutes of the meetings of the Executive Directors.For the 2010 interpretation, *see* IBRD Executive Directors' Resolution No. IBRD 2010-0003, *IBRD Articles of Agreement, Interpretation of Article V, Section 4 (b)(i)*, approved July 6, 2010, recorded in paragraph 7 of the Minutes of Joint Meeting of the Executive Directors of the Bank and IDA, and the Board of Directors of IFC (July 15, 2010), M2010-0047, August 9, 2010. That interpretation was extended by the Executive Directors through Resolution No. IBRD 2015-0004, approved on an absence of objection basis on August 27, 2015, recorded (without text) in an annex to the Minutes of Meeting of the Board of Directors of IFC, August 27, 2015.For the 2015 interpretation, the adoption of Resolution Nos. IBRD 2015-0002 and IDA 2015-0001 is recorded in the Minutes of Meeting of the Executive Directors of the Bank and IDA, July 30, 2015. (Both the IBRD and IDA Charters were the subject of that interpretation.)

[28] *See, e.g.*, Shihata (1999) at 1048–9.

[29] AIIB Article 34-1 provides: "The working language of the Bank shall be English, and the Bank shall rely on the English text of this Agreement for all decisions and for interpretations under Article 54." While the signature clause of the AIIB Charter specifies that the English, Chinese, and French texts of the charter are equally authentic, Article 34-1 makes clear that the English text only is used for all of the Bank's decisions and interpretations. The AfDB Charter also refers to different texts in its clause on interpretation, providing that its English and French texts are equally authentic. AfDB Article 61-1.

[30] AIIB Article 36-2 provides: "References in this Agreement to a specific gender shall be equally applicable to any gender." The AfDB Charter has a note (Nota Bene) on the first page of its publication, stating that references to a particular gender shall be applicable to the other gender; there is a similar statement in the AfDB General Regulations.

[31] AIIB Article 16-9. These incidental powers are common at other MDBs. AfDB Article 23 (g); AsDB Article 21 (vii); EBRD Article 20-1 (vii); and IADB Article V, Section 1 (v). While the IBRD Charter is

consider either interpretation or amendment as a means to authorize a particular decision or action.

B. International Character

11.13 For all of AIIB's governance bodies and decisions, the AIIB Charter confirms the international character of the Bank. The foundation for the AIIB's international character is found in three provisions, which are similar to those found in the other MDBs:[32]

- First, AIIB may not accept Special Funds, loans or assistance that may in any way prejudice, limit, deflect, or otherwise alter its purpose or functions.
- Second, AIIB, its President, officers, and staff "shall not interfere in the political affairs of any member, nor shall they be influenced in their decisions by the political character of the member concerned. Only economic considerations shall be relevant to their decisions. Such considerations shall be weighed impartially in order to achieve and carry out the purpose and functions of the Bank."[33]
- Third, the AIIB President, officers, and staff of the Bank, "in the discharge of their offices, owe their duty entirely to the Bank and to no other authority." Each AIIB member is obliged to respect the international character of this duty and refrain from all attempts to influence any of the above in the discharge of their duties.

The second provision, on avoidance of political interference and reliance on economic considerations, and the third provision, on the international character of the duty of the President and staff, are virtually identical in all of these Charters, with the exception of EBRD's explicit political mandate.[34] The first provision addresses

silent on this point, such powers have long been considered implied powers at the IBRD. *See* Shihata (2000) at 852–5.

[32] AIIB Article 31. AfDB Article 38; AsDB Article 36; EBRD Article 32; IADB Article VIII, Section 5 (d) and (f); and IBRD Article IV, Section 10 and Article V, Section 5 (c).

[33] The AIIB text is virtually identical to the IBRD text, with grammatical changes introduced in the AfDB and AsDB Charters. The first sentence on non-interference and political character from the AIIB text is included in the AIIB Staff Regulations (Article 3-2). For the original IBRD text, Bittermann (1971) at 79 suggests that the references to the political character and economic considerations were principally for the USSR—which, in the end, did not become a member. (The Russian Federation became a member of the World Bank in 1992.)

[34] In EBRD Article 32, the first sentence on avoiding political interference and disregarding the political character of the member is replaced with: "The Bank, its President, Vice-President(s), officers and staff shall in their decisions take into account only considerations relevant to the Bank's purpose, functions and operations, as set out in this Agreement." The change is essential in light of EBRD's purpose, as laid out in EBRD Article 1: "In contributing to economic progress and reconstruction, the purpose of the Bank shall be to foster the transition towards open market-oriented economies and to promote private and entrepreneurial initiative in the Central and Eastern European countries committed to and applying the principles of multiparty democracy, pluralism and market economics." Indeed, the EBRD has since its inception implemented its political mandate through procedures approved by the Board of Directors, in its document, "Political Aspects of the Mandate of the European Bank for Reconstruction and Development."

the possibility that donor funds may be offered with certain conditions, and ensures that only conditions consistent with AIIB's purpose and functions can be accepted. This provision is not found in the IBRD or IADB Charters, where there is no similar Charter provision for setting up Special Funds or the like.

These clauses are perhaps best known for the prohibition of political activity in the second clause and the focus on economic considerations. Observance of these principles is sometimes questioned in various MDBs; sometimes they are perceived as constraints.[35] Nonetheless, their inclusion in the AIIB Charter demonstrates a recognition by AIIB's founders that AIIB should function within the MDB framework, as a non-political, international organization, guided by economic decision-making. 11.14

C. AIIB's Privileges and Immunities

International organizations are typically endowed with certain privileges and immunities that exempt them from the operation of the national legal systems of their respective members. The basis for these privileges and immunities relates to the functioning of the international organization: 11.15

> The rationale for the broad immunity usually enjoyed by international organizations is the "functional necessity" of protecting the independent functioning of international organizations. This requirement is usually seen as necessitating an exemption from the jurisdiction and possible interference of national courts in the affairs of international organizations.[36]

The term "functional immunity" is therefore often used to refer to an immunity limited to what is necessary for an organization to meet its objectives. The functional immunity of MDBs is not considered "full" since it does not apply to the exercise of borrowing powers.[37] For the MDBs, each member agrees, as a requirement of membership, to provide the specific privileges and immunities under the MDB's Charter.

For AIIB, the AIIB Charter provides in Chapter IX the particular status, immunities, privileges, and exemptions (referred to here as privileges and immunities) accorded to AIIB in the territory of each member, to enable AIIB to fulfill its purpose and carry out the functions entrusted to it.[38] Moreover, each member is required to promptly take such action as is necessary to make these privileges and immunities 11.16

[35] *See generally* Cisse (2012) for a thorough discussion of World Bank practice under its political prohibition clauses.

[36] Reinisch and Wurm (2010) at 106.

[37] For a comprehensive survey of the interaction of MDB immunities and activities in national courts, *see generally* Reinisch and Wurm (2010).

[38] AIIB Article 44-1.

effective in its own territory.[39] The Board of Governors gave particular emphasis to this requirement at its Inaugural Meeting,[40] and it has been reiterated in the Board of Governors' Resolutions approving new members since 2017.[41]

11.17 The specific privileges and immunities granted to AIIB by virtue of the AIIB Charter and member actions under it are comparable to the privileges and immunities of other MDBs. AIIB's Charter-based privileges and immunities are summarized in the subsections that follow, noting any significant differences from other MDBs.

(1) Status of the Bank

11.18 AIIB possesses full juridical personality and, in particular, the full legal capacity: (i) to contract; (ii) to acquire, and dispose of, immovable and movable property; (iii) to institute and respond to legal proceedings; and (iv) to take such other action as may be necessary or useful for its purpose and activities.[42] The text of this provision includes several additions to other MDB Charter text that are similar to provisions in the Agreement Establishing the Joint Vienna Institute.[43] For instance, the clause stipulates that AIIB is empowered both to institute and respond to legal proceedings; comparable documents for the other MDBs do not expressly refer to responding to legal proceedings. The capacity to take other necessary or useful actions (sub-paragraph (iv)) is not spelled out in the other MDB Charters. In other respects, this provision is nearly identical to the clauses in the Charters for AfDB, AsDB, EBRD, IADB, and IBRD.[44]

(2) Immunity from judicial proceedings

11.19 AIIB enjoys immunity from every form of legal process, except in cases arising out of or in connection with the exercise of its powers to raise funds, through borrowings or other means, to guarantee obligations or to buy and sell or underwrite the sale of securities. This broad statement of immunity with an exception for cases arising from AIIB's issuance or guarantee of securities is similar in structure to the AfDB and AsDB Charters.[45] The text of the exception in the AIIB Charter

[39] AIIB Article 44-2.

[40] AIIB Board of Governors' Resolution No. 10, *Implementation of Chapter IX of the Articles of Agreement of the Bank*, adopted January 17, 2016.

[41] *See, e.g.*, AIIB Board of Governors' Resolution No. 25, *Admission of Canada to Membership in the Asian Infrastructure Investment Bank*, adopted March 21, 2017; and AIIB Board of Governors' Resolution No. 134, *Admission of Republic of Nauru to Membership in the Asian Infrastructure Investment Bank*, adopted September 26, 2024.

[42] AIIB Article 45.

[43] Agreement Establishing the Joint Vienna Institute, Article III (as amended effective 2003).

[44] AfDB Article 51; AsDB Article 49; EBRD Article 45; IADB Article XI, Section 2; and IBRD Article VII, Section 2.

[45] AfDB Article 52-1. AsDB Article 50-1.

is slightly broader than the term "borrowing" in other texts, consistent with the wording of AIIB's borrowing power as the power to "raise funds, through borrowing or other means."[46]

This exception to immunity in the case of MDB fundraising stems from the need for counterparties in these financial transactions to be confident that they can assert their legal rights against the MDBs. Considering that the funds for MDB investment operations come primarily from the financial markets, investor confidence is an important and necessary asset for the MDBs. This consideration was present in the negotiations on the IBRD Charter, at a time when the kind of borrowing envisaged for IBRD was itself unprecedented and market reaction unknown.[47] Bank issuance of securities became even more crucial for its operation through the pre-negotiation discussions in Atlantic City, as it was agreed that capital market borrowings (likely in the US initially) would fund operations without expectation of further calls on callable capital.[48] **11.20**

The AIIB text derives from the AfDB and AsDB texts and reflects an evolution in MDB Charters, where the language has been made more specific although the intent remains comparable.[49] As the AfDB Charter was being drafted in the 1960s, comments from IBRD suggested that the IBRD language could be improved and clarified.[50] The final AfDB Charter first states that the Bank is immune from every form of legal process, and then provides an exception for cases arising out of the Bank's borrowings. That formulation was slightly expanded two years later in the negotiations on the AsDB Charter, with the addition of "cases arising out of or in connection with the exercise of its powers to borrow money, to guarantee obligations, or to buy and sell or underwrite the sale of securities."[51] Subsequently, **11.21**

[46] AIIB Article 16-1. *See* paragraph 7.40. AfDB Article 52-1 refers to "cases arising out of the exercise of its borrowing powers." AsDB Article 50-1 refers to "cases arising out of or in connection with the exercise of its powers to borrow money, to guarantee obligations, or to buy and sell or underwrite the sale of securities."

[47] Bittermann (1967) at 116–18. He notes: "The Fund's operations were primarily with the member governments or their agencies which would not normally give rise to private rights which might appropriately be the subject of suits in the courts of member countries. It was proposed that the Fund be given a general immunity from suits unless it waived its immunity in a particular case or in particular contracts. The Bank on the other hand would be issuing securities in financial markets and would be giving its guarantee to the obligation of members or their nationals, so that suits could properly arise under these transactions."

[48] Bittermann (1971) at 68–9: "The net effect of acceptance of the U.K. proposal was that the Bank initially could make direct loans only from the gold payments, the U.S. subscription and funds borrowed here, since it was not expected that European countries would permit the Bank to use their subscriptions or to borrow in their markets for the period in which they took advantage of the transitional provisions of the Fund Articles (XIV, 2) permitting them to restrict current transactions."

[49] The comparable provisions for the IBRD, IADB, and EBRD state where actions may be brought and exclude actions by members, but are not specific about immunity, though the intent was similar. EBRD Article 46; IADB Article XI, Section 3; and IBRD Article VII, Section 3.

[50] IBRD, as a UN Specialized Agency, provided comments on the draft AfDB Charter, including the suggestion to expressly limit the Bank's waiver of immunity to actions arising out of bond issues or guarantees, as had been the intent for IBRD but is not expressly stated in the IBRD Charter. Comments and Proposals Received by [from] the International Bank for Reconstruction and Development Concerning the Draft Agreement Establishing an African Development Bank, E/CN.14/FMAB/4/Add. 5, 16 July 1963, at 6.

[51] AsDB Article 50-1. *See* Krishnamurthi (1977) at 115–16: "In the Preparatory Committee, some delegations including the USA and Canada pointed out that the article as drafted departed from a similar provision in the IBRD charter and preferred the latter. It was pointed out by others that the ADB draft based primarily on the African Development Bank text, involved a fundamental difference from the IBRD provision.

the AfDB-AsDB formulation was followed for the Caribbean Development Bank in 1970, the Islamic Development Bank in 1974, the Black Sea Trade and Development Bank in 1994, and the New Development Bank in 2014,[52] while the IBRD formulation was maintained for EBRD in 1990.[53]

11.22 In those cases where there is an exception to AIIB's immunity, actions may be brought against AIIB only in a court of competent jurisdiction in the territory of a country in which AIIB has an office, or has appointed an agent for the purpose of accepting service or notice of process, or has issued or guaranteed securities.[54] Until there is a final judgment in such cases, AIIB's property and assets, wheresoever located and by whomsoever held, are immune from all forms of seizure, attachment, or execution.[55]

11.23 Members may not bring actions against AIIB, even where the exception to immunity applies as previously described (fundraising, guarantees, and certain securities transactions).[56] Rather, special provisions for controversies between AIIB and

The Consultative Committee had given careful consideration to whether the scope of the immunity should be broad (as in IBRD) or narrow and decided on a draft defining the circumstances in which the Bank shall not enjoy immunity from judicial proceedings. It was further pointed out, however, that the Bank's immunity involved two categories of activity; firstly, those relating to its borrowing activities in the capital markets; and, secondly, its other operations. While it was important that the Bank should not enjoy immunity in the former case lest its ability to raise money be impaired, it was however desirable in the latter case to provide it with an appropriate measure of immunity and thus prevent interference with its functions by, for example, 'nuisance suits'. It was noted that in any particular case, where the assertion of immunity would result in obvious unfairness, the Bank could waive its immunity." Krishnamurthi refers to the Report of the Preparatory Committee on the Draft Agreement [Establishing the Asian Development Bank], Bangkok, Thailand, 21 October to 1 November 1965, paragraph 73.

[52] CDB Charter 49-1; IsDB Charter 52-1; BSTDB Charter Article 45-1; NDB Charter Article 30 (a).

[53] The EBRD Chairman's Report of the negotiations provided: "Delegates noted that this Article was almost exactly the same as Section 3 of Article VII of the IBRD's Articles of Agreement. They hoped that courts construing it would draw on the jurisprudence that had evolved in connection with the IBRD's Articles." Chairman's Report on the Agreement Establishing the European Bank for Reconstruction and Development, May 1990, with respect to Article 46. A commentary on the EBRD Charter by the then-World Bank General Counsel noted: "This [statement in the Chairman's Report] would appear to be a reference to judicial precedents, in which U.S. courts concluded that they did not have jurisdiction over the IBRD in suits arising out of its employment relationship with its staff." Shihata (1990) at 93.

[54] AIIB Article 46-1. Through the AIIB Headquarters Agreement (Article 4-1), AIIB has further specified that it will not seek judicial immunity in certain cases in China, specifically: "(a) to the extent that the Bank shall have expressly waived any such immunity in any particular case or in any written document; (b) in respect of a civil action arising out of or in connection with its powers to raise funds, through borrowings or other means, to guarantee obligations, or to buy and sell or underwrite the sale of securities; (c) in respect of the enforcement of an arbitration award made against the Bank as a result of an express submission to arbitration by or on behalf of the Bank; (d) in respect of a civil action brought by a third party for damages arising from an accident in the People's Republic of China caused by a vehicle belonging to the Bank or operated on its behalf; or (e) in respect of any counter-claim directly connected with court proceedings initiated by the Bank." These clauses are nearly identical to Article 4-1 of the EBRD Headquarters Agreement, but do not include EBRD's express waiver of immunity from civil actions "relating to the death or personal injury caused by an act or omission in the United Kingdom." EBRD Headquarters Agreement Between the Government of the United Kingdom of Great Britain and Northern Ireland and the European Bank for Reconstruction and Development, April 15, 1991, Article 14-1 (d).

[55] AIIB Article 46-3.

[56] AIIB Article 46-2: "Notwithstanding the provisions of paragraph 1 of this Article, no action shall be brought against the Bank by any member, or by any agency or instrumentality of a member, or by any entity or person directly or indirectly acting for or deriving claims from a member or from any agency or instrumentality of a member."

its members are to be prescribed.[57] These provisions are nearly identical to other MDB Charters.[58] Where a member may have a dispute with AIIB related to an AIIB loan or guarantee, AIIB's General Conditions for Sovereign-backed Loans provide for arbitration to settle disputes.[59]

(3) Immunity of assets and archives

AIIB's property and assets, wheresoever located and by whomsoever held, are immune from search, requisition, confiscation, expropriation, or any other form of taking or foreclosure by executive or legislative action. AIIB's archives and documents are inviolable, wheresoever located and by whomsoever held.[60] This protection of AIIB's property and assets is nearly identical to the provisions in the other MDB Charters, as is the inviolability of archives.[61] The reference to inviolability of documents generally derives from the EBRD Charter. The reference to archives "wheresoever located and by whomsoever held" is unique to AIIB, bringing in language from the property and assets clause, and could, for example, clarify that AIIB documents stored electronically in "the cloud" should be treated the same as physical documents. **11.24**

(4) Freedom of assets from restrictions

AIIB's property and assets must be free from restrictions, regulations, controls, and moratoria of any nature, to the extent necessary to carry out AIIB's purpose and functions effectively, and subject to the provisions of the AIIB Charter.[62] These protections are nearly identical to the other MDB Charters.[63] **11.25**

[57] AIIB Article 46-2: "Members shall have recourse to such special procedures for the settlement of controversies between the Bank and its members as may be prescribed in this Agreement, in the by-laws and regulations of the Bank, or in the contracts entered into with the Bank." In addition, AIIB Article 55 provides for arbitration of disagreements between the Bank and a country which has ceased to be a member, or between the Bank and any member after adoption of a resolution to terminate the operations of the Bank.

[58] AfDB Article 52; AsDB Article 50; EBRD Article 46; IADB Article XI, Section 3; and IBRD Article VII, Section 3. The AsDB and IADB provisions also include the provision for special procedures for members, as seen in AIIB Article 46-2.

[59] AIIB's General Conditions for Sovereign-backed Loans (October 22, 2021) provide for arbitration to settle disputes under Section 8.04.

[60] AIIB Article 47.

[61] AfDB Article 53; AsDB Articles 51 and 53; EBRD Articles 47 and 48; IADB Article XI, Sections 4 and 5; and IBRD Article VII, Sections 4 and 5.

[62] AIIB Article 48.

[63] AfDB Article 54; AsDB Article 53; EBRD Article 49; IADB Article XI, Section 6; and IBRD Article VII, Section 6.

(5) Privilege for communications

11.26 AIIB's official communications are accorded by each member the same treatment that it accords to the official communications of any other member, a similar privilege as for other MDBs.[64]

(6) Immunities and privileges of officers and employees

11.27 AIIB's Governors, Directors, Alternates, the President, Vice-Presidents, and other AIIB officers and employees, including experts and consultants performing missions or services for AIIB, are provided specific privileges and immunities.[65] They are immune from legal process with respect to acts performed by them in their official capacity (except when AIIB waives the immunity)[66] and enjoy inviolability of all their official papers, documents, and records. Where they are not local citizens or nationals, they are accorded the same immunities from immigration restrictions, alien registration requirements, and national service obligations, and the same facilities as regards exchange regulations, as are accorded by members to the representatives, officials, and employees of comparable rank of other members. They are granted the same treatment in respect of traveling facilities as is accorded by members to representatives, officials, and employees of comparable rank of other members.

11.28 These privileges and immunities for connected persons are relatively consistent across the MDB Charters. The AIIB text includes the clarification that "employees" includes experts and consultants performing missions, or, in the updated wording, "services" for the Bank, as well as the inviolability of official papers, documents, and records found in the EBRD Charter.[67]

[64] AIIB Article 49. AfDB Article 55; AsDB Article 54; EBRD Article 50; IADB Article XI, Section 7; and IBRD Article VII, Section 7.

[65] AIIB Article 50.

[66] The AIIB Headquarters Agreement (Article 14-3 (a)) further specifies that, within China, these persons connected with AIIB (as defined therein) are "immune from jurisdiction and legal process, including arrest and detention, even after termination of their mission or service, in respect of words spoken or written and acts performed by them in their official capacity." There is a stated exception to this immunity, however, for civil liability only "either in case of damage from a road traffic accident, or in the case of other personal injury or death, if either is caused by an act of such person in the People's Republic of China." The comparable exception to immunity in the EBRD Headquarters Agreement (Article 15-2 (a)) refers to "civil liability in the case of damage arising from a road traffic accident caused by such person." Note that persons connected are only granted immunity in respect of official acts, so this waiver of immunity could apply only in cases where a person faces civil liability for damage, personal injury, or death caused by an act taken in China in his or her official capacity. Immunity would not apply in the first place for acts taken in a personal capacity.

[67] *See* AfDB Article 56; AsDB Article 55; EBRD Articles 51 and 52-1; IADB Article XI, Section 8; and IBRD Article VII, Section 8.

(7) Exemption from taxation

AIIB itself enjoys exemption from taxation. AIIB and its assets, property, income, and operations and transactions pursuant to the AIIB Charter are exempt from all taxation and from all customs duties. AIIB is also exempt from any obligation for the payment, withholding, or collection of any tax or duty.[68] These exemptions are generally consistent across the MDB Charters; among other reasons, this protection ensures that the Bank is not subject to tax by different members at the expense of the budget funded by all members.[69] **11.29**

Salaries, emoluments, and expenses paid by AIIB to officers and employees are also exempt from taxation.[70] However, a member can retain the right to tax salaries and emoluments paid to its citizens or nationals, but only if it does so at the time it joins AIIB,[71] meaning that tax treatment will not be uniform for all staff. Note that the AIIB Charter includes expenses paid to officers and staff within its exemption from tax, whereas other Charters are not explicit. A member country's taxation of AIIB payments of salaries and emoluments to its nationals is similarly permitted in AfDB, AsDB, EBRD, IADB, and IBRD, although the mechanisms differ.[72] **11.30**

There is also an exemption from taxes on obligations or securities issued by AIIB[73] or guaranteed by AIIB,[74] including dividends and interest on them, if the tax discriminates against the obligation or security solely because it is issued or guaranteed by AIIB, or because of the location of AIIB offices. The wording in the other MDB Charters is nearly identical, seemingly unchanged since the IBRD Charter was negotiated in 1944.[75] **11.31**

[68] AIIB Article 51-1.

[69] AfDB Article 57-1; AsDB Article 56; IADB Article XI, Section 9; and IBRD Article VII, Section 9. EBRD has a differently designed scheme in EBRD Article 53.

[70] AIIB Article 51-2. Directors and Alternate Directors are included in this provision, but it should be noted that, under AIIB Article 25-6, Directors and Alternate Directors serve without remuneration, unless the Board of Governors decides otherwise, but AIIB may pay them reasonable expenses incurred in attending meetings.

[71] Actions to reserve this right would normally be included with the registration of the AIIB Charter with the UN. In practice, while action to reserve this right is generally lodged with the depository for Signatories to the Charter, it is also provided to the Bank in respect to accession of new members.

[72] In the AfDB and AsDB Charters, the provisions are similar to the text used for the AIIB Charter, exempting salaries from tax but allowing a member to tax these payments to their own nationals if the member reserves the right to do so at the time of joining. AfDB Article 64-3 and AsDB Article 56-2. EBRD Article 53-7 is similar. In the IBRD, the Charter-based exemption from taxation on salaries and emoluments simply does not apply to those "who are local citizens, local subjects or other local nationals." IBRD Article VII, Section 9 (b). No action by the member country to retain the right to tax these local nationals is necessary. The formulation is similar in IADB Article XI, Section 9 (b).

[73] AIIB Article 51-3.

[74] AIIB Article 51-4.

[75] AfDB Article 57-3 and 57-4; AsDB Article 56-3 and 56-4; EBRD Article 53-9 and 53-10; IADB Article XI, Section 9 (c) and (d); and IBRD Article VII, Section 9 (c) and (d).

(8) Waivers

11.32 AIIB, at its discretion, may waive any of the privileges, immunities, and exemptions conferred under the AIIB Charter, "in any case or instance, in such manner and upon such conditions as it may determine to be appropriate in the best interests of the Bank."[76] AIIB's By-Laws authorize the Board of Directors to provide such waivers where the Board of Directors is of the opinion that the waiver would be appropriate in the best interests of AIIB.[77] Moreover, with respect to individuals, AIIB's By-Laws endow the President with the right—and the duty—to provide a waiver in respect of AIIB's officers, employees, experts, and consultants "where, in his opinion, the immunity, privilege or exemption would impede the course of justice and can be waived without prejudice to the interests of the Bank."[78] In the case of the President or the Vice-Presidents, the Board of Directors is authorized to provide such waivers, in similar circumstances and under the same conditions.[79] Similar provisions on waiver exist for AfDB, AsDB, and EBRD.[80]

(9) Privileges and immunities in non-member countries

11.33 AIIB's activities will not be restricted to member countries, including such activities as official travel, borrowing in non-member markets, and, exceptionally, financings in non-member territories. In these cases, AIIB's Charter-based privileges and immunities would not automatically apply. Rather, AIIB would be likely to conclude separate agreements or arrangements to ensure that its privileges and immunities will be observed, as other MDBs do in similar situations.

D. Administrative Framework

11.34 The AIIB Charter provides the basic legal framework for the administration of the Bank as an intergovernmental entity. This framework includes the relevant dimensions of AIIB's privileges and immunities summarized previously.

76 AIIB Article 52.
77 AIIB By-Laws, Section 7 (a).
78 AIIB By-Laws, Section 7 (b).
79 AIIB By-Laws, Section 7 (c).
80 The AIIB structure for waivers that couples a general clause in the charter with specific provisions in the By-Laws is directly derived from the AsDB. *See* AsDB Article 58. In the EBRD and AfDB, the details found in the AIIB By-Laws are included in the Charter. AfDB Article 59 and EBRD Article 55.

(1) Officers and employees

The President exercises the responsibility for the organization, appointment, and dismissal of officers and staff, in accordance with regulations adopted by the Board of Directors.[81] The Board of Directors appoints Vice-Presidents, on the recommendation of the President, on the basis of an open, transparent and merit-based process.[82] The AIIB Charter addresses the criteria for appointments, noting that "the President shall, subject to the paramount importance of securing the highest standards of efficiency and technical competence, pay due regard to the recruitment of personnel on as wide a regional geographical basis as possible."[83] Other MDBs have broadly similar provisions for the appointment, organization, and dismissal of staff.[84] All AIIB officers and employees, including the President and Vice-Presidents, are subject to the Code of Conduct for Bank Personnel, adopted by the Board of Governors at its Inaugural Meeting.[85] **11.35**

AIIB's Staff Regulations, approved by the Board of Directors in November 2016, include provisions on resolution of employment disputes.[86] The Staff Regulations establish a right to fair treatment in employment matters and provide for the establishment of a procedure for staff to challenge employment decisions that adversely affect them directly and personally. They also provide for a process to be put in place for appeals from that procedure to an independent administrative tribunal.[87] Many other MDBs have established their own independent administrative tribunals to hear such cases,[88] as the multilateral nature of the institutions and their privileges and immunities generally preclude access to national courts **11.36**

[81] AIIB Article 30-2. Staff Regulations of the Asian Infrastructure Investment Bank, approved November 2016.

[82] AIIB Article 30-1.

[83] AIIB Article 30-3. The reference to the wide regional geographical basis is identical to AsDB Article 34-6. Both AfDB and IADB Charters originally used the same broad wording as in the IBRD Charter: "as wide a geographical basis as possible." IBRD Article V, Section 5 (d). When non-regional membership was opened, reference to the regional character of the institution was added for AfDB (AfDB Article 37-5, where reference to an African preference was then deleted) and IADB (IADB Article VIII, Section 5 (e)).

[84] AfDB Article 37-2 and 37-5; AsDB Article 34-5 and 34-6; EBRD Article 30-5; and IBRD Article V, Sections 5 (b) and 5 (d). In IADB, the appointment provisions are similar, while the Board of Executive Directors is responsible for the basic organization of the Bank. IADB Article VIII, Sections 3 (i) and 5 (e).

[85] AIIB By-Laws Section 8. AIIB Board of Governors' Resolution No. 9, *Codes of Conduct*, adopted January 16, 2016.

[86] The Staff Regulations of the Asian Infrastructure Investment Bank, approved November 2016, Article 13.

[87] *See* Paper on the Oversight Mechanism, July 10, 2019 at paragraph 23: "As the Bank gains experience with the staff grievance procedure outlined above, an Independent Administrative Tribunal will be established in due time." The Paper also notes that a review of the Administrative Review Procedure would be carried out in three years: "This review is important input to implementation of Article 13(4) of the Staff Regulations, since the selection of an appropriate administrative tribunal should be made with a view to coherence with AIIB's internal procedures, settled after a period of testing."

[88] Reinisch (2008) at 285–6 summarizes the rationale for these administrative tribunals as being "established precisely for the purpose of settling disputes between international organizations and their employees in a predictable and coherent way. Litigation of staff disputes before national courts, perhaps even courts in different States, is thought to put uniform employment at risk and may lead to a fragmented and differentiated level of protection."

for employment disputes.[89] Some independent administrative tribunals are authorized to exercise jurisdiction over appeals for staff of other international organizations, under appropriate agreements between the host organization and the other organization.[90]

11.37 AIIB's staff has continued to grow since its inception. As of end 2024, AIIB had 633 professional staff members and 13 support staff from 73 economies, with 42% female representation.[91] AIIB's Staff Rules were most recently revised with effect from 2025. They cover routine employment matters (such as recruitment, appointment, leave, assignments, compensation, welfare) and also make provision for ethics investigations and misconduct procedures (Section 7) and dispute resolution and staff consultation mechanism (Section 8). Within that framework, AIIB's institutional structure for staff and workplace matters has continued to develop. In 2021, several new bodies were added:

- The Respectful Workplace Advisors (RWA) Program was launched as an informal service to foster a respectful workplace environment for all AIIB staff. The role of RWAs is to provide an informal, confidential, trustworthy, and readily accessible source for early assistance for staff who have concerns about a respectful workplace or who need information on how to seek assistance.[92]
- The Office of the Ombudsperson was established to facilitate informal resolution of workplace conflicts and problematic staff issues and concerns, identify and analyze systemic issues of AIIB policies, and recommend or alert senior management on such issues to improve the working environment and administer the Respectful Workplace Advisors Program.[93]
- The Staff Council (formerly Staff Consultative Mechanism) was established after elections in August 2021.[94] The Staff Council was intended as a constructive platform to facilitate an open dialogue between management and staff on a range of issues including working conditions, interactions between the staff and their supervisors, incentives and recognition of their performance, and general wellbeing.[95]

[89] The World Bank Administrative Tribunal was the first such MDB tribunal, set up in 1980, and since then, AfDB, AsDB, EBRD, and IADB have all set up similar bodies. Other international organizations, such as the UN and the International Labor Organization, have had such tribunals in place for many decades, even before the World Bank Administrative Tribunal came to be.

[90] *See, e.g.*, Statute of the Administrative Tribunal of the International Bank for Reconstruction and Development, International Development Association and International Finance Corporation (World Bank Administrative Tribunal), Article XV; Statute of the Administrative Tribunal of the International Monetary Fund, Article XXI; and Statute of the Administrative Tribunal of the International Labor Organization (ILO), Article II-5.

[91] AIIB Annual Report 2024 at 22, 97.

[92] AIIB Annual Report 2021 at 21, 22.

[93] AIIB Annual Report 2021 at 22.

[94] AIIB Annual Report 2024 at 97: "Through surveys and open communication channels, Management in 2024 worked closely with the Staff Council, an independent consultative mechanism composed of seven representatives elected by staff members, to better understand staff needs and priorities."

[95] AIIB Annual Report 2021 at 3, 81.

The AIIB Ethics Office publishes annual reports which offer a more detailed picture of how AIIB is developing as a place to work.[96] An Internal Management Review in 2023 also provided some recommendations in this area.[97]

(2) Ethics

AIIB has two ethics codes in place, one for Board officials and one for all staff and management. As noted earlier, both the Code of Conduct for Board Officials and the Code of Conduct for Bank Personnel were adopted by AIIB's highest authority, the Board of Governors, at its Inaugural Meeting.[98] The Board Code covers such areas as standard of conduct, disclosure of information, and conflicts of interest, and provides for implementation and sanctions. The Bank Personnel Code (which also covers the President and Vice-Presidents) covers core values, standards of conduct, external activities, conflicts of interest, financial matters, and use of information, as well as protection against retaliation. Both Codes include provisions for annual financial disclosures.[99] **11.38**

For the implementation of the Codes, there is a central role for AIIB's Chief Ethics Officer, shown on the AIIB Organizational Chart as reporting to the President. For the Board Code, the Budget and Human Resources Committee has been designated to serve co-extensively as the Ethics Committee under the Code that considers implementation, oversees annual financial disclosures, and handles allegations of misconduct, assisted by the Chief Ethics Officer.[100] For the Bank Personnel Code, the Board of Directors is directed to adopt implementing regulations, and the President is directed to issue necessary directives. **11.39**

[96] AIIB Ethics Office Annual Report 2024 at 30. About 80% of requests were advisory, mostly around potential conflicts of interest.

[97] Following an employee complaint in 2023 that was highly publicized, AIIB's Board of Directors oversaw an Internal Management Review to consider the circumstances of the complaint and the Bank's overall governance and culture. The Review considered AIIB's governance structure and decisions, and found no evidence to support the allegation by the former staff member that AIIB is unduly and improperly influenced by the Communist Party of China. (Executive Summary, paragraphs 3 through 11) The Review considered AIIB's workplace and procedures, and found no evidence of a "toxic culture" as alleged by the former staff member. However, the Review did highlight areas that require improvement, including fostering "a speaking-up and listening-up culture" and ensuring accountability across all levels. The Review also found that the particular issues that arose in the specific work unit showed that "the effectiveness and efficiency of the various staff grievance avenues and above all, the appropriate response time of these avenues, did not adequately respond to staff concerns." Executive Summary, paragraphs 12 and 13. The Review made recommendations to improve the integrity of AIIB's governance, Bank culture, Staff Grievance Avenues, and Human Resource (HR) Processes. Executive Summary, paragraph 15. AIIB (2023).

[98] The Code of Conduct for Bank Officials and the Code of Conduct for Bank Personnel were approved under Board of Governors' Resolution No. 9, *Codes of Conduct*, adopted January 16, 2016. The texts are available on AIIB's website.

[99] For Bank Personnel, annual financial disclosures are required at manager level and above. AIIB Code of Conduct for Bank Personnel, paragraph 31.

[100] The Rules of Procedure of the Ethics Committee were amended in 2025.

(3) Offices

11.40 The AIIB Charter establishes that AIIB's principal office is in Beijing, and authorizes the establishment of offices or agencies elsewhere.[101] AIIB's By-Laws further authorize the Board of Directors to decide on the establishment of AIIB agencies or offices elsewhere in the territories of any member, "whenever it is necessary to do so in order to facilitate the efficient conduct of the business of the Bank."[102] Other MDBs have similar provisions.[103] Wherever AIIB's offices may be located, the AIIB Charter is clear in stipulating that the working language is English.[104]

11.41 At its Inaugural Meeting, the Board of Governors approved AIIB's Headquarters Agreement with the People's Republic of China, which was signed on January 16, 2016.[105] Under the Headquarters Agreement, China agreed to arrange to build and furnish a suitable office building to serve as AIIB's permanent premises, and to provide temporary offices and facilities until the permanent offices are ready. (AIIB moved into its permanent headquarters in 2020.) The Headquarters Agreement also details the specific privileges and immunities of AIIB and its officers and staff in China, all consistent with the AIIB Charter. The headquarters agreements for other MDBs are similarly structured.

11.42 AIIB's Tianjin Office was set up in March 2021, as a backup office for business continuity and a venue for trainings, meetings, and other group activities. The Tianjin Office is about 180 km from the headquarters in Beijing.[106] The establishment of an Interim Operational Hub in Abu Dhabi was approved in 2022.[107] At a meeting in April 2024, the Board of Directors authorized the President to establish, in line with AIIB's By-Laws, a small number of multifunctional hub offices.[108] Press reports in June 2025 indicated that hubs would be opened in Hong Kong and Singapore, to get closer to markets.[109]

[101] AIIB Article 32.

[102] AIIB By-Laws, Section 1 (b).

[103] AfDB Article 39 and AfDB General Regulations Article 1; AsDB Article 37 and AsDB By-Laws Section 1; EBRD Article 33 and EBRD By-Laws Section 1; IADB Article XIV, Section 1 and IADB By-Laws Section 1; and IBRD Article V, Section 9 (a) and By-Laws Section 1.

[104] AIIB Article 34-1.

[105] AIIB Board of Governors' Resolution No. 7, *Headquarters Agreement between the Government of the People's Republic of China and the Bank*, adopted January 16, 2016. The text of the Headquarters Agreement is found on the AIIB website.

[106] AIIB Annual Report 2021 at 33.

[107] AIIB Annual Report 2024 at 103. "AIIB's Interim Operational Hub was inaugurated on Sept. 19, 2023 in Abu Dhabi, United Arab Emirates. Since its opening, it has supported the Bank in developing investments in line with the Bank's priorities and Corporate Strategy by enabling greater physical proximity to key clients, partners and stakeholders in the region."

[108] Minutes of the Meeting of the Board of Directors of the Asian Infrastructure Investment Bank, August 28, 2024, paragraph 1. The Minutes refer to the applicable criteria, Approach to AIIB's Global Presence, which is not publicly available.

[109] "AIIB mulls opening HK, S'pore offices' in biggest expansion yet," China Daily HK, May 28, 2025.

(4) Transparency and information

The AIIB Charter contains common provisions for the Bank to publish reports, including an annual report containing an audited statement of accounts.[110] Members are also obliged to furnish information to AIIB, in order to facilitate the performance of its functions. These provisions, too, are common to the other MDBs.[111] 11.43

In addition, the AIIB Charter contains an uncommon provision stipulating that AIIB establish a policy on disclosure of information "in order to promote transparency in its operations."[112] The Chief Negotiators' Report noted that the major policies under Article 26 should include disclosure.[113] The importance of transparency is also noted in the AIIB Charter among the principles for the design of the Oversight Mechanism to be established by the Board of Directors.[114] 11.44

The Board of Directors adopted a Public Information Interim Policy (the Interim Policy) at its Inaugural Meeting, in line with these stipulations. Under the Interim Policy, AIIB was committed to "enhancing transparency and accountability in all its activities so as to meet its purposes." The Interim Policy reflected the general approach of other MDBs, without providing all of the details that have evolved over time in their practices. Consequently, the Interim Policy provided for a public information policy review annually and for a comprehensive policy to be adopted by the Board of Directors in the future, in light of AIIB's early experience. 11.45

The AIIB Policy on Public Information was adopted by the Board of Directors in September 2018, to replace the Interim Policy. This Public Information Policy (2018) followed a review of the Interim Policy, "detailing and analyzing the Bank's early public disclosure experience, strategy, benchmarks and consultation."[115] Public consultations were also part of the policy development.[116] The Policy states AIIB's overarching intentions: proactive disclosure; maximum disclosure and transparency; and due regard for the efficiency of the Bank. Three governing principles apply for AIIB's disclosure of information to the public: (1) Presumption in Favor of Disclosure (disclosure unless there is an exception stated); (2) Duty 11.46

[110] AIIB Article 34.

[111] AfDB Article 41; AsDB Article 39; EBRD Article 35; IADB Article VIII, Section 6; and IBRD Article V, Section 13.

[112] AIIB Article 30-4. The Green Climate Fund instrument (paragraph 67) also requires that its operations be subject to an information disclosure policy developed by the Board. The NDB Charter provides that the Bank's proceedings should be transparent and requires provisions regarding access to documents. NDB Article 15.

[113] Representatives noted that major policies established by the Board of Directors under Article 26 (ii) would include such policies as environmental and social impact and procurement (Article 13) and disclosure (Article 34).

[114] AIIB Article 26 (iv).

[115] AIIB Policy on Public Information (2018) at paragraph 1.6.

[116] The presentation of the Policy on Public Information on AIIB's website includes a timeline of public consultations at https://www.aiib.org/en/policies-strategies/public-information/introduction/index.html (last visited July 14, 2025).

of Proactive Disclosure (e.g., financial events, institutional events, operational events); and (3) Non-Discrimination and Equal Treatment of Disclosure Requests.

11.47 Recognizing that legitimate interests may need to be protected in disclosure, the Policy sets out exceptions to disclosure of information that would: (1) compromise personal privacy, physical or mental safety of an individual; (2) compromise financial worth or competitiveness of a person, the Bank, or a corporate entity or assets; (3) compromise the Bank's administrative functions or deliberative and decision-making processes; (4) disclose information that is legally privileged or compromise integrity of inspection, investigation, legal proceedings, or audit involving the Bank; (5) compromise the Bank's creditworthiness or access to capital markets at prices the Bank deems reasonable; or (6) compromise the international character of the Bank (AIIB Article 31) or duty of due respect to national laws. The Policy also provides for the override of its exceptions and requirements (positive override by the President and negative override requiring the Board of Directors). Appeals of denial of disclosure go to the Managing Director (Complaints-resolution, Evaluation and Integrity Unit, CEIU), and overall administration is handled by the Head of the Communications Department.[117]

(5) Corporate Procurement Policy

11.48 AIIB's Corporate Procurement Policy (September 2018) sets out the objectives, key principles, and procedures for the procurement of goods, works, general services, and consulting services related to AIIB's operation as an institution. This policy applies to purchasing funded by AIIB's administrative budget or capital expenditure budget, and may be applied, by decision of the Board of Directors, to procurement funded from other sources. The investment operations carried out by recipients with AIIB financing are subject to AIIB's Procurement Policy.[118] Under the Corporate Procurement Policy, AIIB awards contracts taking into account "best value" as defined, most often after competitive procurement. Efficiency, transparency, integrity, and ethical standards, and environmental and social sustainability, are other relevant aspects.

[117] AIIB Annual Report 2024 at 83: "Almost all financial, institutional, and operational information was disclosed in a timely manner. The Bank processed 355 requests from the Public Information Request portal, down 16% from 2023 and equal to the number of requests received in 2022."

[118] *See* paragraphs 5.48–5.50 for a summary of the Procurement Policy applicable to AIIB-financed investment operations.

12

INNOVATIONS IN PRACTICE: AIIB's FIRST DECADE

AIIB's basic framework was established in the AIIB Charter, with its provisions for AIIB's mandate, operations, membership, finance, and governance. Previous chapters in these areas have described the Charter framework as it has developed in the nearly ten years since AIIB opened its doors. That framework echoed in large part the structures found in its comparator MDBs, dating back to IBRD, as outlined in Chapters 2 and 3, while AIIB's founders took the opportunity to introduce innovative features, as successive MDBs have innovated in turn.[1] **12.01**

This chapter begins with a description of how some of AIIB's special features have developed in practice: the non-resident Board of Directors; delegation of Board authority under AIIB's Accountability Framework; and Board supervision through AIIB's Oversight Mechanism that includes the novel Complaints-resolution, Evaluation and Integrity Unit (CEIU). Key developments during AIIB's first decade are then highlighted, including AIIB's response to the COVID-19 crisis and its broad support for international financial collaboration. Other developments, covered in other chapters, are summarized at the end. **12.02**

A. Non-Resident Board of Directors

AIIB's overall governance structure is largely based on the MDB model, as described in Chapters 3, 8, and 9. In brief, AIIB is governed by a Board of Governors, with one Governor representing each member, that meets annually, and a Board of Directors of twelve Directors, selected by the Governors, meeting regularly in person and virtually. The Board of Governors elects a President to serve a five-year term, who conducts the business of the Bank under the direction of the Board of Directors. **12.03**

The non-resident status of AIIB's Board of Directors is not unprecedented among MDBs.[2] AIIB's major comparators for this book (AfDB, AsDB, EBRD, IADB, IBRD) have resident Boards; other MDBs have non-resident Boards. For AIIB, innovation comes in how similar responsibilities can best be carried out with different **12.04**

[1] *See* paragraphs 3.47–3.53.
[2] *See* paragraphs 8.19–8.21.

modalities. (While the establishment of AIIB's non-resident Board predated the global pandemic in 2020, it calls to mind how organizations and individuals around the world experimented with a balance between remote work and in-person activities.)

12.05 To put the development of AIIB's non-resident board in context, this section starts with the history of resident Boards. Then, MDB Board practice is briefly surveyed.

(1) History

12.06 When IBRD and IMF were established in the 1940s, they instituted a governance model that included a resident Board of Directors. Those resident Boards were different from the more common corporate practice of non-resident Boards. The only international financial institution in operation at the time, the Bank for International Settlements (BIS), had a non-resident Board of Directors. Under the original BIS Statutes, the BIS Board of Directors met at least ten times per year and Directors were required to be ordinarily resident in Europe or in a position to attend Board meetings.[3] The BIS arrangement was noted favorably in the pre-Bretton Woods discussions, by a former BIS President:

> Some discussion took place on the question[s] whether Directors should devote their whole time to the work of the Fund and should reside at its headquarters. Mr. Beyen thought that such an arrangement would have very undesirable consequences. It would be impossible to find proper full-time work for 11 or 12 Directors; if they had to be brought into the machine, the business of management would become very cumbersome. There was also the danger that they would get out of touch with their own countries. He thought an arrangement on the lines of the BIS might work very well where under Directors met in Basle for three day[s] each month. Questions requiring quick decisions rarely arose out of the blue, and emergency meetings could, of course, be called as necessary.[4]

For the Inter-American Bank (IAB), agreed in 1940 but never established, the Board of Directors would also have been non-resident, intended to meet no less than four times a year.[5] Both BIS and IAB had provision for an optional Executive Committee of the Board to take actions between Board meetings.[6] The IAB Board

[3] BIS Statutes Articles 30 and 32, also providing that at least four meetings per year would be at the BIS office in Basel, Switzerland.

[4] Schuler and Canning (2019) at 362. Johan Beyen was the President of BIS from 1937–1939.

[5] IAB By-Laws Section 3B.

[6] BIS Statutes Article 43; IAB By-Laws Sections 3E. The debate in the BIS Organization Committee touched on points quite similar to the later debates about a resident board, including the difficulty of finding persons of sufficient stature who could decide on delicate matters and leave their normal place of business for a long period, as the Executive Committee would be present at the Bank, and the need to exclude sitting central bank governors. Baffi (2002) at 51. Toniolo (2005) at 43 also notes: "The French hostility to the executive committee derived from the desire to safeguard the prerogatives of the general manager, since their candidate

of Directors could have authorized the President or the Executive Committee to exercise any powers of the Board until the next meeting.[7]

How was the IBRD resident Board introduced? In retrospect, it appears to evolve from the Executive Committee option proposed for IAB and BIS. **12.07**

The first plans for IBRD, drawing on the IAB structure,[8] did not clearly require a resident Board of Directors. That Board of Directors was similar to the Board of Governors as it is known today: composed of one Director representing each member, and vested with the administration of the Bank, meeting periodically.[9] The requirement of a full-time body at headquarters exercising day-to-day management first appears for IMF, but still as optional for IBRD (in Harry Dexter White's first complete draft of 1941, circulated 1942): **12.08**

- The outline for the Fund proposes a Board of Directors that elects a chairman and a small operating committee. The chairman is chief of the operating committee, and the committee members "should devote full time to the management of the Fund, should be assisted by an appropriate technical staff, and should receive an adequate salary."[10]
- The outline for the Bank in the same document proposes a Board of Directors and an *optional* Executive Committee that could be authorized to exercise the powers of the Board.[11] The wording is taken directly from the IAB By-Laws (Section 3).
- The fuller description for the Bank for Reconstruction of the United Nations and Associates (Part III) is more expansive:

> As with the Fund, it would seem that the most efficient method of management is to have the administration of the Bank vested in the Board of Directors with an executive committee appointed by the Board of Directors and the President of the Bank elected by the directors . . . Also, *regulations should be such as to permit the Executive Board to conduct as much as possible of the day-to-day operations, without the necessity of referring to the larger Board for decisions* . . . To facilitate its operations, the Board should be able to grant to the executive committee authority to exercise any specified powers provided those powers are granted the committee by four-fifths majority vote . . . "[12] (emphasis added)

for the job (Pierre Quesnay, of the Bank of France) was waiting in the wings." This note highlights the tension between resident Board and President in later MDBs.

[7] IAB By-Laws Section 3E.
[8] *See* paragraphs 2.28–2.29.
[9] Oliver (1996) at 295.
[10] Oliver (1996) at 289.
[11] Oliver (1996) at 295.
[12] Oliver (1996) at 321. *See also* Shihata (2000) at 649–52.

The next year, the November 1943 Bank plan specifically required a resident Executive Committee: the Board of Directors would appoint an Executive Committee of not more than nine members, continuously available at the head office, to exercise authority delegated to it by the Board of Directors.[13]

12.09 In June 1944, the United Kingdom proposed that the Fund would be governed by a general body representing all members called a Governing Council (equivalent to White's Board of Directors) and a twelve-person Directorate (equivalent to White's Executive Committee), where the countries with the six largest quotas would each appoint a Director, and the remaining six Directors would be chosen by the other Councilors. The British proposal included both a Chairman of the Directorate and a General Manager (akin to the President and General Manager position at BIS at the time) and argued against a resident Board.[14] The issue was not resolved in the pre-negotiations at Atlantic City.[15] In the final negotiations at Bretton Woods, an Executive Committee continuously available at the head office became IBRD's resident Executive Directors (Executive Board for IMF) and the Board of Directors became the Board of Governors, meeting annually.

> [Some] countries, including the United Kingdom, felt that the Fund Executive Board should be essentially a consultative body which would meet infrequently. The United Kingdom thus proposed that Executive Directors should "meet no less than once every three months," and could delegate some of their functions to a Chairman. Others, including the United States, took the view that the Executive Directors should play a more direct and continuing role in the functioning of the institution. The United States prepared language which required the Executive Directors to exercise "all authority delegated to them by the Board of Governors" and "to be in continuous session at the principal office of the Fund for at least the first three years of operations." . . . The discussion appears to have been laborious and required the appointment of a special subcommittee to consider all proposals relative to the Executive Directors. The report of that subcommittee

[13] Preliminary Draft Outline Of a Proposal for A Bank for Reconstruction and Development of the United and Associated Nations, U.S. Treasury, November 24, 1943 (BWC1289-01), included in Schuler and Canning (2019) at 67–76. Section V (4) (BWC1289-09).

[14] Schuler and Canning (2019) at 475–9 (British Report on the International Monetary Fund, Annex E on Management and Inauguration, June 21, 1944). This Report considered the Fund "designed to be largely automatic, with defined obligations on both the Fund and the Members, thereby avoiding the need for frequent exercise of discretion or discrimination by the governing body. (*In this respect it differs essentially from the Reconstruction Bank, where a large element of discretion and judgment must, from the nature of the work, rest with the governing body.*) . . . the Fund also has important questions of discretion for the governing body, some of which arise at the beginning, and others occasionally.

But while these exercises of discretion involve large issues of judgment, it does not appear that the regular work of the Fund will call for frequent decisions on matters of policy, certainly not to the extent of requiring a very high-powered Directorate permanently in residence." Note the suggestion, with emphasis added, that IBRD's Board might need to exercise more discretion.

[15] Horsefield (1969) at 87: "The United States believed that the Executive Directors would have a fulltime duty, and should therefore be permanently available at the headquarters of the Fund. The Chinese delegate agreed with this view, at any rate as regards the first five years of the Fund's work. But the British delegate, with some support from the other members of the committee, strongly resisted this proposal, repeating the arguments set forth above. The controversy was unresolved when the Atlantic City conference ended."

> recommended the adoption of the provisions of the Fund Articles from which Section 4(a) and (e) of the Articles of the Bank are taken. These provisions contain elements of both the U.S. and the U.K. drafts and were agreed as a compromise.[16]

Even after the IMF and IBRD Charters had become effective, the practical meaning of residency was debated at the 1946 Inaugural Meeting of the IMF and IBRD Boards of Governors.[17]

Why did the US prefer a resident Board for IMF? One element was a difference in views on the automaticity of IMF lending: **12.10**

> The U.S. position was that the IMF would lend only upon approval by a resident board of directors. The British position was that lending should be automatic in response to legitimate requests from members.[18]

Other matters cited by the US delegation calling for prompt decisions were changes in the par values of currencies and borrowing by the Fund to replenish its resources.[19] Another aspect for the US was the view that Directors needed to be in continuous consultation, communicating the views of other Directors to influence their own governments. Continuous session was not favored by some 'smaller' countries that did not expect to be represented on the Board, and focused instead on access to the Board of Governors (such as the provision allowing five members or those representing one-fourth of the voting power to call for a meeting of the Board of Governors).[20] Overall, the preference for a resident IMF Board appears connected to prompt decisions on the use of Fund resources and par values, and more broadly on the Fund's role in the economic and financial policy of its members.[21]

[16] Shihata (2000) at 641.

[17] Bittermann (1971) at 87: "Keynes reopened the argument made at Atlantic City and Bretton Woods, that the directors should be men holding positions with their own governments, that they would be needed only occasionally to decide issues since the main work would be carried on by the Managing Director and President and their staffs. The U.S. representatives again urged that the directors and alternates would have to be available at all times for quick decisions, and that they could develop the information and judgment needed for the business through board discussions. Keynes also argued that 48 salaries [12 Executive Directors and 12 Alternates at each institution] would impose an excessive burden, and that that number of men could be employed more usefully in their own countries, and since both Executive Directors and alternates were not needed all the time, they could divide work and salaries."

Under the By-Laws as then agreed, continuous availability of either the Executive Director or his Alternate would suffice. Gold (1979) at 254.

[18] Boughton (2024) at 27.

[19] Gold (1979) at 249. Bittermann (1967) at 94–5 refers to differences of view on the degree of automaticity in Fund operations (British and Dutch favoring automaticity). He also recalls that the US pointed out some Fund decisions needing to be made quickly—decisions on changes in par value not exceeding 20% to be made within three days of application—a decision not to be left to the discretion of the Managing Director.

[20] Gold (1979) at 250. The provision mentioned was the original text of IMF Article XII, Section 2 (c).

[21] Horsefield (1969) at 138–9 recounts a draft in White's papers of the fifteen types of "judgments and decisions" which, in his view, the Executive Directors would be repeatedly called upon to make.

These included such difficult tasks as the following:

> Determine currently whether each member in its economic policies and practices is promoting exchange stability, maintaining an orderly exchange arrangement with others and avoiding competitive exchange alterations.

12.11 Like most of the institutional and management features of the IMF Charter, the same board configuration was applied in the IBRD Charter: a Board of Governors meeting annually and a resident Board (the Executive Directors). Observers have noted that this setup for the Bank was agreed to mirror the Fund, and not specifically tailored for the Bank.[22] The rationale at the Fund for prompt decisions and the role in influencing members' economic and financial decision-making does not translate easily to the decisions and role of the Bank Board.

12.12 Over the ensuing decades, whether or not to have a resident Board was discussed for later institutions. For instance, there was debate in the negotiations on the AfDB Charter (1963), AsDB Charter (1965), and EBRD Charter (1990), where the resident Board option was finally agreed.[23] On the other hand, other IFIs opted for non-resident Board mechanisms, including EIB, the Council of Europe Development Bank, CAF, CDB, NIB, ISDB, BSTDB, and the International Fund for Agricultural Development, and more recently, the European Stability Mechanism and NDB.[24] There is variation among MDBs, as IFIs have chosen resident or non-resident Boards to suit the needs and expectations of each institution and its members.

Determine when a member is using the resources of the Fund in a manner contrary to the purposes of the Fund, and, where desirable, recommend appropriate remedial steps.

Determine when any of the conditions under which a member may buy currencies from the Fund may be waived, and on what terms.

Determine when capital movements are not in accord with the purposes of the Fund. Advise a member when to place exchange controls over capital movements. Estimate the amount of capital transactions required for expansion of exports, or in ordinary course of trade, banking or other business.

... Mr. White continually stressed in oral exposition the importance and difficulty of the role of the Executive Directors in leading member countries toward the goal of monetary equilibrium.

22 Mason & Asher (1973) at 28–9 make this point, quoting an important US policymaker during the preparation of the Bank and Fund and the first US IBRD Executive Director, Emilio Collado, to the effect that the Bank organization mirrored that of the Fund, with no serious attempt to tailor it for the Bank. They also credit a key Dutch participant, later an IBRD Executive Director, Daniel Crena de Iongh, with noting in his oral history: "while in the light of history it was clear that the Fund needed a board of directors in continuous session, it might have been to the advantage of the Bank to have a board of directors composed of high officials of member governments who met in Washington every two months or so."

23 For AfDB, the issue of Board residency had been debated in the preparation of the institution, where some felt non-resident Directors "would facilitate the release by governments of people with requisite skills and also result in considerable savings." The Directors did not actually become resident until 1970. Gardiner and Pickett at 23.

For AsDB, during the negotiations on the Charter, cost-consciousness led to at least one proposal for a part-time Board. Wilson (1987) at 27.

For EBRD, a majority of the European Community countries originally favored a non-resident board in order to economize on cost, as in the EIB. Menkveld (1991) at 78. Apparently, the United States argued in favor of a resident board at EBRD to have a powerful voice in day-to-day functions, so as to assure that the vague compromises in negotiations would be implemented. Weber (1994) at 19.

24 One proposal to transform the World Bank Board from its resident, full-time status can be seen in the Report of the High-Level Commission on Modernization of World Bank Group Governance. Zedillo (2009) at Recommendation #2.

The choice of a non-resident Board for AIIB came with all of these considerations in the background, and a focus on the cost and footprint of a resident Board.[25] As this brief history indicates, the non-resident Board of Directors at AIIB is neither an innovation nor a rarity, yet it offered the opportunity to enhance Board effectiveness and take advantage of the technology and connectivity of the 21st century. These trends can be seen in the AIIB Charter, as it clearly establishes the Board's primary role in strategy and policy, emphasizes its oversight, and allows the Board to delegate policy implementation and operational decisions to the President. 12.13

(2) Board practice

How do non-resident and resident Boards differ in MDBs? The answers are no doubt as plentiful as the number of MDBs, and there is much commonality of functions and activities. An AfDB study summarized the differences: 12.14

> Each model has its pros and cons. The Resident Board encourages and allows for closer oversight and engagement by the Executive Directors. They typically serve on a full-time basis, are paid through the administrative budget of each organization, and have access to a larger staff and budget. The non-resident Board model, on the other hand, accepts a higher degree of delegation of the day-to-day operations and executive decisions to Management. This model allows for shareholders to nominate more senior officials who occupy line positions in government as Executive Directors; they remain a part of and thus closely connected with their capitals.
>
> Management widely perceives non-resident Boards to be more effective and efficient. The views of the Executive Directors are more divided; those serving on Resident Boards on balance favor that model. Regardless of the advantages and disadvantages of the two models, it is clear that once adopted, residency decisions of the Board have proven impossible to alter.[26]

AIIB has paired the non-resident Board with both enhanced delegation and enhanced oversight, as discussed in this chapter's Sections B (Accountability Framework and Delegation) and C (Oversight Mechanism and Supervision).

[25] Dollar (2015) at 163 notes the Zedillo criticism of the current World Bank arrangement of a resident board that approves all loans, and the point that the World Bank Group resident board "represents both a large financial cost to the bank ($70 million per year) and an extra layer of management that slows down project preparation and makes the bank less efficient." He also comments that slowness of project preparation is among the main client criticisms of MDBs.

In that period, some in the world of global international financial institutions were highlighting the importance of strengthening the Board's role in strategy as well as regularizing and lightening the Board's role in routine and operational decision-making. *See* paragraph 12.23.

[26] AfDB (2018) at 10.

BOARD FUNCTIONS (Statutory)	AfDB	AsDB	AIIB	EBRD	IADB	IBRD
Conduct/direct general operations of the Bank	✓	✓1	✓	✓	✓	✓
Take decisions concerning particular direct loans, guarantees, investments in equity capital, and borrowing	✓	✓	✓	✓	✓	✓
Take decisions concerning TA and other operations		✓	✓	✓	✓	2
Take decisions concerning business and country strategies	✓	3	✓	4	✓	5
Submit the accounts for approval to the Board of Governors	✓	✓	✓	✓	✓	✓
Submit an annual report for approval to the Board of Governors	✓	✓	✓	✓	✓	✓
Approve the budget	✓	✓	✓	✓	✓	✓
Approve the basic organization of the Bank	✓				✓	
Appoint Vice Presidents on recommendation of the President	✓		✓	✓	✓	
Prepare the work of the Board of Governors	✓	✓	✓	✓	✓	✓
Take decisions on Bank policy			✓	6		7
Take decisions on institutional borrowing	✓			✓		
Supervise management			✓			

Figure 12.1 Comparison of MDB Board of Directors Functions

[1] Provides strategic guidance only.

[2] Provides policy and strategic guidance only.

[3] Discusses but does not approve.

[4] Reviews (EBRD Article 11.2).

[5] Discusses but does not approve.

[6] Decides (EBRD Article 27 (ii)).

[7] President proposes and Board decides

Source: AfDB (2018) at 11, and Table A4.1 (Core Statutory Functions – Board of Directors).

(a) Functions

12.15 For many MDBs, the Board of Directors' primary responsibilities include a wide range of functions. Figure 12.1 summarizes the main statutory functions for AIIB and its primary comparators.

The common role and functions of the Board can be summarized, as in the Global Fund By-Laws, as strategy development, governance oversight, commitment of financial resources, assessment of organizational performance, and risk management.[27]

[27] Bylaws of the Global Fund to Fight Aids, Tuberculosis & Malaria (as amended through 2022) at 7.4. For the Global Fund Board, an additional function is Partnership Engagement, Resource Mobilization and Advocacy, relevant to the Global Fund's particular structure and functions.

Most MDB boards retain substantial if not complete authority to decide on the institution's financing operations. As one comparison of boards at international financial institutions (IFIs) notes: 12.16

> IFI boards do have significantly different mandates than private sector FIs [with] vastly more expansive authorities . . . [T]heir commercial counterparts that tend to delegate much more to professional management . . . [IFI Boards] typically retain most credit/financial decision-making authority, a function that has been delegated to management credit committees a long time ago. This has an important impact on the agendas of IFI boards that are disproportionately tilted towards operational decision making. This constraint seems even more counterproductive if one takes into consideration the profile of the large majority of IFI board members: civil servants with limited financial experience . . . Extensive retained authorities explain, at least partly, one more IFI characteristic: a significant majority of them are run by resident boards who meet much more often than private FI boards.[28]

Mechanisms to delegate that decision authority to management are increasingly being adopted, with a view to enhancing the board's focus on strategy and policy, among its other functions. AIIB has perhaps the clearest delegation under its Accountability Framework (Section B).

(b) Meetings

Resident or non-resident, Board members attend formal board meetings and also spend considerable time in other types of meetings and engagements. Much of the work of the Board takes place in its committees. The overall work of Directors includes a host of other functions beyond review and preparation of issues and documents, such as interactions with management, consultations with authorities and constituency matters. While these aspects play out differently when the Board is non-resident, they are part of the functioning of the Board. 12.17

Formal meetings of the Board are the easiest metric of Board activity, as they are usually documented by publicly available minutes. Figure 12.2 compares the frequency of Board meetings across selected IFIs. 12.18

The many other aspects of Board activities are harder to compare from the outside. A range of informal meetings, Board discussions without decision, committee meetings, and all sorts of interactions are likely featured at AIIB's counterparts.

[28] Nestor (2018) at 4.

IFI	Resident or Non-Resident Board	Number of Meetings
IBRD	Yes	>Twice/week
IMF	Yes	Several times/week
EIB	No	10/year
EBRD	Yes	2–3/month
IFAD	No	3/year
BSTDB	No	N/D
AsDB	Yes	Several times/month
AIIB	No	5/year*
AfDB	Yes	As often as required
IADB	Yes	1/week
NIB	No	8/year

Figure 12.2 Board Meeting Frequency in IFIs (Formal Board Meetings)
* *See* paragraph 12.19 for updated information.
Source: Nestor (2018) at 5 (Table 1).

(c) AIIB practice

12.19 At this early stage, AIIB's Annual Reports provide the outsider with some insight into the Board's activities each year.

- Formal Meetings. As a rule, AIIB's Board of Directors regularly meets in person four times a year and virtually as the work requires. Each in-person set of meetings covers several days. Many activities can be undertaken virtually, including formal board meetings. During the pandemic (2020–2022), AIIB's Board met virtually throughout the year, continuing its work.

  Prevented by COVID-19 from holding in-person meetings [2020–2021], the Board of Directors held more frequent virtual meetings, ensuring that it could continue to guide AIIB in deliberations over policies and strategies. AIIB was thus able to rapidly bring projects forward, particularly those under the COVID-19 Crisis Recovery Facility, for Board approval.[29]

  In 2022, the Board held 16 virtual meetings . . . In addition to project approvals, they discussed and approved several major policies and strategies, including the establishment of the Special Fund Window for Less Developed Members, AIIB's Approach to Global Presence, significant updates to the Energy Sector Strategy and the Operational Policy on Financing (OPF), and approval of the Board Efficiency and Governance Package.[30]

In-person formal board meetings resumed in 2023 and 2024.[31]

[29] AIIB Annual Report 2021 at 27–8.
[30] AIIB Annual Report 2022 at 37.
[31] AIIB Annual Report 2023 at 27; AIIB Annual Report 2024 at 75.

- Committee Meetings. The Committees of AIIB's Board[32] meet regularly formally and informally to discuss much of the work of the Board, especially non-project specific work on strategy, policy, and risk. The 2025 Annual Report of the Audit and Risk Committee, for instance, details the meetings, topics, and recommendations in 2024–2025, including a schedule of formal Committee meetings on a dozen or so days during the year.[33]
- Informal Meetings and Other Formats. A regular feature of the Board's work are the pre-Board project briefings (staff presentations and responses on operations before Board consideration), an important step in the Accountability Framework. The Directors also spend time in Board retreats and other briefings. In 2022, for instance, even during the pandemic:

  > To support the work of Directors and allow thorough review and discussions, 20 briefings were also organized. Additional events, such as dedicated Directors' Forums and roundtables, were organized to allow in-depth review of various issues including the Accountability Framework, the Performance Review of the President, and review of the Board Efficiency and Governance package.[34]

In 2024:

> Informal meetings held included Fireside Chats, and Board Briefings on the President Election Process and AIIB@10, the Investment Case for AIIB's Special Fund Window (SFW), Project Preparation Special Fund (PPSF), the AIIB Client Portal, Governance AIIB Partnership Development, and External Assessment of the Delegation of Project Approval and Board Efficiency Initiatives. Board Retreats were also held for the Corporate Strategy Midterm Review and PPM [Project-affected People's Mechanism], and two Board Seminars on Governance and the Asian Infrastructure Finance.[35]

Board group visits to AIIB projects are another opportunity to deepen the Board's understanding of AIIB's work.[36]

- Directors' Forum. The Board established a meeting form, called the Directors' Forum, for sharing information and exchanging views, including for performance review of the President; for meetings between the Board and the

[32] There are four Committees under the Board of Directors: the Audit and Risk Committee (ARC), the Budget and Human Resources Committee (BHRC), the Policy and Strategy Committee (PSC) and the Ethics Committee. *See* paragraph 8.29 and Figures 8.5 and 8.6.

[33] AIIB Audit and Risk Committee, Annual Report to the Board of Directors 2024–2025. *See also* AIIB Annual Report 2024 at 75–7.

[34] AIIB Annual Report 2022 at 37.

[35] AIIB Annual Report 2024 at 75.

[36] "The Board of Directors also participated in several visits, including a Project Visit to the Masdar Solar Power Plant in Samarkand, Uzbekistan, and Board group visits to projects in China, India, and Nepal. These visits allowed Board members to gain a deeper understanding of the Bank's operations and to further their insights on how to effectively guide the Bank in supporting our Members' development trajectory." AIIB Annual Report 2024 at 75.

Managing Director, CEIU; and for meetings among members of the Board. The Directors' Forum also serves to strengthen the independence of the CEIU, as the Managing Director, CEIU, can call for a Directors' Forum in addition to the quarterly meetings where the Managing Director reports to the Board.[37] To facilitate these meetings, the Board established the position of Dean of the Board, as the longest-serving Director of a nationality different from that of the President.[38]

- Supporting Mechanisms. Mechanisms to support the Directors in their AIIB roles have developed as AIIB has grown, for instance, to facilitate attendance by more Alternate Directors and other member representatives (especially helpful for lower-income members and larger constituencies).[39] Many of these avenues are common to resident MDB boards as well.[40] It is interesting to see how AIIB has taken up these tools from resident Boards and applied them towards deepening the role of its non-resident Board.

Both the mechanism of informal meetings among the Board and the position of Dean can be found in other MDBs,[41] while the Oversight Mechanism and its particular focus on supervision is novel.

B. Accountability Framework and Delegation

12.20 AIIB's mechanisms for delegation and supervision are newly designed, and part of defining and maintaining the role of the Board in the non-resident context. Delegation takes place under AIIB's Accountability Framework.

(1) Delegation of decisions on operations

12.21 Deciding on AIIB's financing operations is a specific function of the Board of Directors under the AIIB Charter.[42] Board decision on operations has been the practice in most of the comparator MDBs although it is not always spelled out in the Charter.[43] The IBRD Charter, for example, does not specify that loans are to be

[37] Sharif (2023) at 3.

[38] Paper on the Oversight Mechanism, July 10, 2019, paragraphs 38–43.

[39] AIIB Annual Report 2024 at 30: "To enhance governance and Board efficiency, the Bank introduced measures such as capacity support, on-demand briefings for projects and enhanced Management reporting."

[40] *See* AfDB (2018) at 34–5, highlighting that what they call social capital among Directors "is the oil that lubricates the complex machine."

[41] For example, the World Bank Group Board Manual FY22 (2021) at 7–10 lists the following engagements: Regular/Formal Meetings, Informal Meetings, Committee of the Whole, Executive/Restricted Executive Sessions, Technical Briefings, Executive Directors' Seminars, Dean's Teas, Executive Directors' Lunches, and Thematic Groups. The Manual states (at 16) that the position of the Dean is also traditionally held by the longest serving Executive Director.

[42] AIIB Article 26 (iii).

[43] *See* paragraph 8.25.

approved by the Executive Directors, yet that has been IBRD practice based on an early agreement between the President and the Executive Directors.[44]

The AIIB Charter is rare among MDB Charters in specifying that the Board of Directors may delegate this function to the President.[45] EIB and NIB have general provisions for delegation that would include decisions on financing.[46] Even without formal delegation of authority, the Board of Directors in some MDBs approves many operations without Board discussion, on a streamlined or absence of objection basis; in principle, these are still approvals by the Board, not delegated to the management.[47] A few MDBs have formally delegated decision authority for specific operations to management in the context of programs or similar umbrella initiatives approved by the Board:[48] **12.22**

- EBRD has had a delegated approval process since 1995 under which the Board approves a 'Framework' that sets an exposure limit and EBRD management approves individual projects within this framework.[49]
- Since 2017, IFC has increasingly used a 'platform' approach, under which the Board approves a ceiling exposure for categories of projects within which IFC management approves individual projects.[50]
- In 2015, AsDB adopted a framework for smaller non-sovereign transactions under which the Board delegates approval of transactions below certain limits

[44] Shihata (2000) at 649–52 (history) and 642–3 (practice).

[45] AIIB Article 26 (iii) allows the Board of Directors to delegate decisions on operations to the President by a majority representing not less than three-fourths of the total voting power. Early drafts of the IBRD Charter provided for delegation from the Board of Directors (non-resident) to an Executive Committee (resident) and in some cases, to the President, but these provisions were changed in later versions. Shihata (2000) at 649–52.

[46] The non-resident Board of Directors at the EIB is authorized to delegate some of its functions to the Management Committee, including decisions in respect of granting finance; decisions on such delegation require a qualified majority. EIB Article 9-1. In EIB, the Board of Directors approves all projects, some through written procedure. EIB (2015) at 6–7. The NIB's non-resident Board of Directors is generally authorized to delegate its powers to the extent considered appropriate. NIB Section 14.

[47] For the World Bank Group, streamlined approvals are not legally a delegation of approval authority but rather a simplified procedure for Board consideration. There have been some minor exceptions where grants or small loans have been approved by the President. Shihata (2000) at 646 discusses IBRD Learning and Innovation Lending and Adaptable Program Lending examples from the 1990s.

[48] AIIB CEIU (2024) at 6–7 (bullets added) and 15–16.

[49] *See* EBRD Evaluation Department, *Special Study: Delegated Authority*, EBRD, March 2019, Executive Summary, at ix, stating that "With over half of its projects approved by delegation, the EBRD is the IFI delegating the largest share of its approvals."

[50] *See* IEG (2025) at 3: "The International Finance Corporation (IFC) defines platforms as thematic interventions at a regional, global, or sectoral level designed to address a specific development challenge. Projects under each platform have clearly defined eligibility criteria and may use a range of IFC products (for example, loans, equity, and advisory services) to meet these thematic challenges. Platforms may benefit from delegation of authority—the transfer of project approval authority from the Board to management—in full or in part or may have no delegation of authority from the World Bank Group Board of Executive Directors (IFC 2022b). The Bank Group Board grants delegation of authority to IFC management to allow it to approve projects without a formal Board meeting decision (for example, without preparing a Board paper). This contrasts with a regular procedure of convening a formal Board meeting to decide on IFC's proposed investment or a streamlined absence of objection (AOB) procedure, in which IFC management is authorized to proceed with the proposed project on a closing date specified in the Board paper unless an executive director requests a full Board discussion."

to the President.[51] AsDB also created the multi-tranche financing facility (MFF) in 2005, as a modality to support large scale sovereign projects.[52]

The World Bank Group's "streamlined" approval process, under which some projects are approved by the Board on a "no-objection" basis without a formal discussion, is still considered a Board approval.[53]

12.23 The provision for formal delegation with specific contours was included in the AIIB Charter with an eye towards a clearer division of responsibilities between the Board and the President.[54] Subsequently, Board delegation was among the reforms to the global financial architecture recommended in 2018 by the G20 Eminent Persons Group on Global Financial Governance. That recommendation aimed at streamlining the roles of the Executive Board and Management to avoid overlaps and ensure clarity of responsibilities and accountability, and enhancing focus on strategic issues and directions.[55]

(2) AIIB's Accountability Framework

12.24 In 2018, AIIB's Board of Directors approved an overall Accountability Framework that supports the delegation of authority to the President to approve AIIB's financing operations within prescribed parameters.[56] The Accountability Framework has

[51] "In May 2022, the Board of Directors of the Asian Development Bank (ADB) approved the recommendation of the policy paper on the Enhanced Faster Approach to Small Nonsovereign Transactions (Enhanced FAST) framework. Enhanced FAST is the successor of the Faster Approach to Small Nonsovereign Transactions (FAST), a pilot framework approved by the Board in March 2015." Chair's Summary of AsDB Board Meeting on May 26, 2022.

[52] "The MFF is like a standby letter of credit. The Board approves a maximum amount for each MFF under specific terms and conditions. Based on the Board's approval, Management then converts this facility amount into a series of loans, guarantees, or credit lines as and when the investments are ready and the client requests financing." AsDB Policy Paper, Mainstreaming the Multitranche Financing Facility, June 2008 at paragraph 8.

[53] The World Bank Group Board Manual FY22 (2021) provides: "EDs [Executive Directors] approve all operations financed by the WBG (projects) with the exception of those approved by regional vice presidents (restructuring or small trust funds). Most proposals are considered on an "absence-of-objection" basis (i.e., without Board discussion), though EDs have the prerogative to request a discussion of any item through the Board Operations System (BOS). Board approved policies define criteria for the selection of operations for full Board discussion, based on four principles, namely: risk, innovation, areas of high interest to the Board, and operations that require Board approval of exceptions to policies (waivers)." These selection criteria for Board review are echoed in the categories reserved for Board decisions in AIIB. *See* paragraph 12.28.

[54] The Zedillo Report (Report of the High-Level Commission on Modernization of World Bank Group Governance) recommended that the IBRD Board delegate responsibility for the approval of all operations to management, in order to remove the co-managerial role and eliminate the conflict of interest, and to strengthen accountability. Zedillo (2009) at paragraph 128. An additional benefit suggested would be to free up more time for the Board's strategic and policy roles.

[55] The G20 Eminent Persons Group on Global Financial Governance recommended: "In keeping with this objective, consideration should be given to IMF, World Bank and other MDBs amending their Articles of Agreement where necessary, to allow for delegation of appropriate decision-making responsibilities to the Managements of the respective institutions. A practical and risk-based approach should form the basis for such delegation of responsibilities." G20 (2018) at 26 and 73–5, Proposals 20 and 21.

[56] AIIB (2018a) [Decision on Accountability Framework], AIIB (2018b) [Paper on Accountability Framework] and AIIB (2023a) [Regulation on Accountability Framework, as revised].

three phases: Strategy Setting, Delegation of Financing Decisions, and Presidential Accountability. The Accountability Framework goes hand in hand with Board supervision of the management and operation of AIIB and its establishment of an Oversight Mechanism for that purpose.[57] The Oversight Mechanism was formalized by the Board in 2019, underpinning its role under the Accountability Framework. (See Section C in this chapter.)

(a) Strategy setting

The Board of Directors approves AIIB strategies and policies, in line with its Charter-based powers.[58] AIIB's first Corporate Strategy was approved by the Board of Directors for the period 2021–2030, and an update was approved in 2025.[59] The Corporate Strategy, Financing Infrastructure for Tomorrow, sets AIIB's operational focus on green infrastructure, connectivity and regional cooperation, technology-enabled infrastructure, and private capital mobilization, and includes targets on climate financing for 2025 and cross-border connectivity and private sector financing for 2030. AIIB lists nine Strategies on its website.[60] AIIB also operates under several frameworks, such as the Environmental and Social Framework and Risk Management Framework. **12.25**

AIIB policies that apply to AIIB's financing operations are adopted by the Board of Directors. Among these are: AIIB's Operational Policy on Financing, Operational Policy on International Relations, Policy on Prohibited Practices, Policy on the Project-affected People's Mechanism, Procurement Policy for Projects, General Conditions for Sovereign-backed Loans, Sovereign-backed Loan and Guarantee Pricing (all discussed in Chapter 5). Importantly, the Board approves AIIB's Annual Business Plan and Budget. The Paper on the Accountability Framework identifies the Annual Business Plan and Budget as "the main instrument through which the Board directs the President in the operationalization of strategies and policies."[61] **12.26**

Board-approved strategies, policies, budgets, and annual plans provide the authorizing framework for the President's delegated decisions on AIIB financing operations. **12.27**

[57] AIIB Articles 26 (iii) [delegation], (iv) [oversight], and (v) [strategy].

[58] AIIB Article 26 (ii) and (v).

[59] AIIB Press Release, June 23, 2025, "AIIB Unveils Updated Growth-Focused Strategy to Tackle Global Challenges." "Following a comprehensive mid-term review, the updates ensure the strategy remains adaptive to a rapidly evolving global landscape, grounded in AIIB's growing operational experience, and aligned with the changing needs of its clients. The refresh also contains refinements to the Corporate Scorecard to align with AIIB's increased ambitions and enable more effective performance monitoring."

[60] AIIB website, How We Work, listing: Energy Sector Strategy: Sustainable Energy for Tomorrow; Strategy on Mobilizing Private Capital for Infrastructure; Strategy on Financing Operations in Non-Regional Members; Transport Sector Strategy; Sustainable Cities Strategy; Strategy on Investing in Equity; Water Sector Strategy; Digital Infrastructure Sector Strategy; and Health Strategy.

[61] AIIB (2018b) at paragraph 14.

(b) Delegation of financing decisions to the President

12.28 Decisions on AIIB financing operations are currently delegated to the President unless the operations fall within Board-determined exceptions that require Board approval. The Board has reserved its decision authority for four types of operations: large co-financings and three categories of projects.[62]

- Co-financing. The Board decides on financings over US$500 million that are co-financed with a lead partner MDB.[63]
- Precedent Setting (Category I). The Board decides on precedent-setting projects, including the first project in a member country; the first three projects under a Sector Strategy; and the first project involving a co-financier where co-financier policies would be applied.
- Significant Strategic and Policy Issues (Category II). The Board decides on projects with significant strategic and policy issues, including a project in a non-regional member country; a project where a Sector Strategy has not yet been approved; a project requiring derogation from a Sector Strategy, Policy, or Framework approved by the Board; and a project which directly implicates the Operational Policy on International Relations.
- Risk Tolerances (Category III). The Board decides on projects that exceed prescribed risk tolerances, including a project where the amount of AIIB's economic capital (as defined in the Regulation) is in excess of US$37.5 million; a project where the amount of AIIB financing exceeds US$300 million for Sovereign-backed financing or guarantees, US$150 million for Non-sovereign-backed financing or guarantees, or US$35 million for equity investments.[64]

Projects that fall outside these types of projects may be decided on by the President, in conformity with the Sector Strategies, Policies, Frameworks, and Annual Business Plan and Budget adopted by the Board of Directors.[65]

12.29 For any project, a Director can "call in" an operation for Board consideration. The President can also request Board consideration in lieu of his approval. For projects approved by the President, if later changes are proposed that would result in the project falling within the exceptions to delegation, the proposed changes should be referred to the Board for consideration.

[62] AIIB (2018a) and AIIB (2023a). *See also* paragraphs 9.24–9.27 and Figure 9.7.

[63] The Regulation on the Accountability Framework specifies: "These are cofinanced projects that apply the partner MDB's policies in lieu of the AIIB's Environmental and Social Framework and for which the partner MDB acknowledges the AIIB cofinancing in its documentation." AIIB (2023a).

[64] The Risk Tolerance limits were adjusted in the 2023 revision: economic capital was increased from US$25 million to US$37.5 million; Sovereign-backed financing was increased from US$200 million to US$300 million; and Non-sovereign-backed financing was increased from US$100 million to US$150 million. The limit for equity investment was unchanged at US$35 million.

[65] AIIB (2018a) [Decision on Accountability Framework], AIIB (2018b) [Paper on Accountability Framework], and AIIB (2023a) [Regulation on Accountability Framework, as revised].

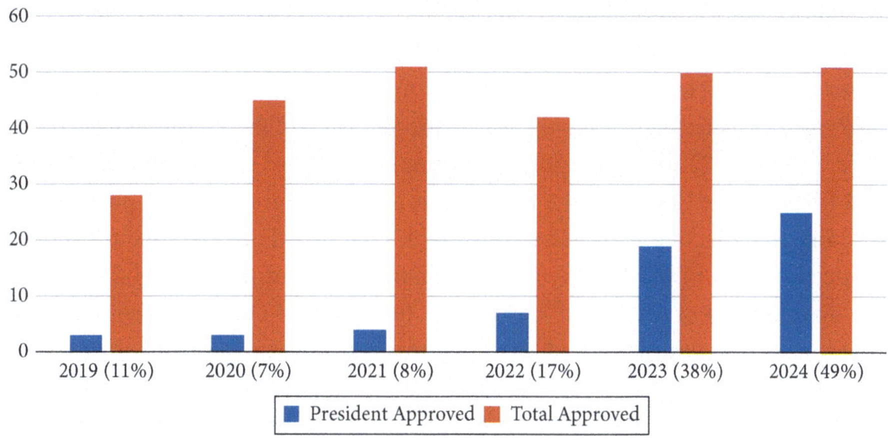

Figure 12.3 AIIB Projects Approved by the President

A 2024 assessment by AIIB's CEIU found that the use of delegated approvals had been generally consistent with the eligibility criteria for delegation. That review noted that eight projects had been called in and that the President had referred two projects back to the Board for approval, also envisaged under the Regulation.[66] Management also undertook its second Comprehensive Review of the Accountability Framework in March 2024, concluding that the provisions were being implemented as envisaged. As an input, an external assessment found that the agreed criteria for delegation were being applied appropriately and required reporting had been carried out through the investment approval process.[67] **12.30**

Since the delegations took effect in 2019, the majority of projects have continued to be approved by the Board, with an increasing proportion of projects approved by the President as AIIB's operations and strategies have developed.[68] Figure 12.3 illustrates this trend. **12.31**

For the 2024 fiscal year, the President approved just under half of AIIB projects.[69] The increasing percentage of delegated approvals follows the 2023 expanded delegation, and presumably also a decrease in the number of precedent setting projects that require Board decision, with fewer new borrowers, new strategies, and new co-financiers. It also reflects the end-2023 winding down of the AIIB COVID-19 Crisis Recovery Facility, that had required approvals by the Board of Facility financings.[70]

[66] AIIB CEIU (2024) at 18–20.

[67] AIIB Annual Report 2024 at 59.

[68] The proportion of projects approved by the President, and the names of the projects, can be found in AIIB's Annual Reports. AIIB Annual Report 2019 at 15, 30 (three of twenty-eight projects, 11%); AIIB Annual Report 2020 at 26 (three of forty-five projects, 7%); AIIB Annual Report 2021 at 28 (four out of fifty-one projects, 8%); AIIB Annual Report 2022 at 38 (seven of forty-two projects, 17%); AIIB Annual Report 2023 at 29 (nineteen of fifty projects, 38%); and AIIB Annual Report 2024 at 58 (twenty-five out of fifty-one projects, 49%).

[69] AIIB Annual Report 2024 at 30, 78 (twenty-five out of fifty-one projects, 49%).

[70] AIIB Annual Report 2023 at 67. The AIIB CEIU review of delegated authority notes that sixty-three Facility projects were approved by the Board and five by the President. AIIB CEIU (2024) at 28.

(c) President's accountability

12.32 In its 2018 Decision on the Accountability Framework, the Board of Directors resolved to approve terms of reference for an Annual Review of the Performance of the President. Since then, annual Performance Reviews of the President have taken place.[71] In the 2022 Annual Report, for example, the Board section notes: "The annual Performance Review of the President is a demonstration of our commitment to sound and effective governance and enables the Board of Directors to appraise the performance of the President in his chairmanship of the Board of Directors and management of the Bank."[72] That year, the Board of Directors also approved the scope and methodology of the Review.[73] An external assessment of AIIB's Performance Review process for the President was undertaken in 2023, concluding that the Bank was "at the forefront of leadership performance review practices among international financial institutions."[74]

12.33 Other MDBs have varied mechanisms for review and accountability of the President.[75]

C. Oversight Mechanism and Board Supervision

12.34 The AIIB Charter and Chief Negotiators' Report emphasize the Board's regular supervision of management and operations of AIIB, and require that the Board of Directors establish an Oversight Mechanism for this purpose.[76] AIIB's Board of Directors' 2019 Decision on the Oversight Mechanism set out the contours of the Oversight Mechanism, not as an integrated mechanism but rather as a collection of five components that support the Board's oversight of management.[77] The first three components are co-located under AIIB's independent CEIU: Project-Related Complaints, Evaluation, and Integrity. The fourth component is the External

[71] *See, e.g.*, AIIB Annual Report 2021 at 28, AIIB Annual Report 2022 at 39; AIIB Annual Report 2023 at 14; AIIB Annual Report 2024 at 75, 79.

[72] AIIB Annual Report 2022 at 39.

[73] AIIB Annual Report 2022 at 39: The Review "focused on six competencies—strategic vision and implementation, stakeholder and shareholder management, operational and administrative management, leadership behaviors and culture, governance and innovation . . . The findings of the Review, highlighted, among others, the President's strong leadership and sense of strategic vision, his ability to maintain relationships with different stakeholders and build consensus, his effective management of the Bank in a complex context marked by geopolitical challenges and the COVID-19 pandemic, and his commitment to innovation, all in the best interest of the Bank."

[74] AIIB Annual Report 2023 at 14; AIIB Annual Report 2024 at 79.

[75] AfDB (2018) at 21: "In 2011, the World Bank Board of Directors and Management adopted the principle of 'Dual Performance Feedback' (formerly called 'dual evaluation') whereby the President shares feedback of the Board's efficiency and effectiveness with the Dean (and co-Dean) in restricted session, while the Dean provides feedback to the President of the Executive Directors' view of his/her effectiveness."

[76] AIIB Article 26 (iv) requires that the Oversight Mechanism be in line with principles of transparency, openness, independence, and accountability. The Chief Negotiators' Report further provided that the Oversight Mechanism address areas such as audit, evaluation, fraud and corruption, project complaints, and staff grievances.

[77] Paper on the Oversight Mechanism, July 10, 2019 and Decision on the Oversight Mechanism, adopted on July 10, 2019, on AIIB website.

Audit function. The fifth component is AIIB's rules and process to address Staff Grievances. Separating out these functions for particular attention and periodic review reflects the importance of Board oversight for AIIB, as instilled by its founders.

The CEIU itself is an innovation at AIIB.[78] As summarized in the Paper on the Oversight Mechanism: 12.35

> The President has established CEIU that reports directly to the Board. CEIU combines three functions (evaluation, anti-fraud and corruption and complaints handling) traditionally carried out by different units at other MDBs. CEIU consolidates them under one roof. This allows for greater synergy between these functions (especially in deriving and sharing lessons learned) and supports the Board in its supervisory role. A key consideration in designing CEIU was to ensure it could exercise relevant functions independent of Management while ensuring that CEIU remains engaged with and contributes to the rest of AIIB.[79]

The arrangements and functions for the CEIU are set out in its terms of reference, which were revised in 2024 following the 2023 Review of the Oversight Mechanism. Changes included expansion of the CEIU's mandate to include an explicit role in conducting policy, strategy, and process evaluations.

(1) Project-related complaints

AIIB's independent accountability mechanism, approved in 2018, was envisaged under the AIIB Charter and AIIB's Environmental and Social Policy.[80] The Project-affected People's Mechanism (PPM), effective March 31, 2019, enables project-affected people to file submissions if they have been or are likely to be adversely affected by AIIB's failure to implement its Environmental and Social Policy, when their concerns cannot be addressed satisfactorily through Project-level grievance redress mechanisms or AIIB Management's processes.[81] 12.36

[78] The Inspectorate General (IG) at EIB has taken a gradual route to a similar structure. When first set up in 2005, IG consisted of two functions, Internal Audit and Operations Evaluation. By 2009, the Fraud Investigations Unit, initially under Internal Audit, became an IG Division tasked with detecting and investigating allegations of fraud and corruption in the EIB Group's operations and activities. In 2010, the Complaints Mechanism Division, established in 2008, was transferred from the Secretariat General to IG. In 2018, the Procurement Complaints Committee, chaired by the IG, an inter-services committee in charge of procurement complaints, was established with its Secretariat located within IG. In 2021, IG had three functions: Evaluation, Investigations, and Complaints Mechanism. A Coordination and Policy Unit, which also hosts the Secretariat of the Bank's Procurement Complaints Committee, supports the Directorate. EIB (2021) at 9.

[79] Paper on the Oversight Mechanism, July 10, 2019.

[80] AIIB Article 26 (iv) and Chief Negotiators' Report. Sharif (2023) at 4 points out that no member of the AIIB Board contested the need for the PPM, in contrast to acrimonious exchanges between developed and developing country members in other MDBs.

[81] AIIB, Project-Affected People's Mechanism, https://www.aiib.org/en/about-aiib/who-we-are/project-affected-peoples-mechanism/how-we-assist-you/index.html (last visited July 14, 2025). *See also* paragraphs 5.45–5.47 and Figure 5.1.

12.37 There are three functions under the PPM.

- Project Processing Queries. A Project Processing Query is designed to enable Project-affected people to obtain rapid resolution of their concerns about simple matters that arise during AIIB's environmental and social due diligence of a Project and do not require dispute resolution.
- Requests for Dispute Resolution. Requests for Dispute Resolution allow the PPM to seek to facilitate and coordinate the resolution of a dispute that has arisen over measures required to mitigate known and quantifiable, potential or actual material adverse environment and social impacts that arise during AIIB's due diligence of a Project or during Project implementation. The aim of this process is to reach a time-bound and monitorable dispute resolution agreement between the parties concerned on actions to mitigate these impacts.
- Requests for Compliance Review. The process under a Request for Compliance Review involves an investigation by the PPM of allegations by Project-affected people that AIIB has failed to comply with its obligations under the AIIB Environmental and Social Policy (ESP) in its environmental and social due diligence of a Project during Project preparation or its oversight of the Project during implementation, thereby causing or being likely to cause material adverse environmental or social impacts on the Project-affected people. If the allegations are substantiated, the process includes a review of any action plan proposed by Management to address these impacts. Unlike the two other processes, a Request for Compliance Review requires that the PPM assess whether AIIB is in compliance with its ESP.

The CEIU is responsible for PPM functioning through its Managing Director (MD-CEIU). As head of the PPM, the MD-CEIU reports directly to AIIB's Board of Directors and oversees the handling of submissions to the PPM; the issuance of PPM reports; and PPM's outreach, learning, and training activities.[82] The PPM is assisted by a Secretariat headed by a CEIU staff. The MD-CEIU supervises and provides guidance and direction to the Head-PPM Secretariat and PPM personnel.

12.38 As of June 2025, the PPM had received seven submissions, all of which have been deemed ineligible. Three were ineligible because the project applied a co-financier's policies, and the same webpage lists complaints regarding co-financed projects submitted under co-financier accountability mechanisms. Three were ineligible because the Requestor did not make good-faith efforts to resolve issues through

[82] Sharif (2023) at 3 points out from the vantage point of AIIB's Inaugural Managing Director, CEIU, that placing the PPM under the CEIU is unique "as it enables the MD-CEIU to directly influence policymaking relating to project-affected people, and directly liaise with the management and the board on matters of policy and practice through regular interaction. Ready access to the board without presence of management through the Directors' Forum is a check on any management non-cooperation or interference with CEIU's independence . . . Regular contact with management and the board also militates against the possibility that the [PPM] or other functions of the CEIU are shelved and forgotten."

project-level GRM and AIIB Management. One complaint was ineligible because the project was dropped from the AIIB pipeline.[83]

AIIB's CEIU commissioned an independent external review of the PPM in 2023–2024, as part of the five-year review envisaged at the time of approval.[84] In addition, the PPM Policy Review is scheduled for 2025. **12.39**

(2) Evaluation

The CEIU was initially called the Compliance, Effectiveness and Integrity Unit in the early phases. Effectiveness became the evaluation function, launched in 2019; AIIB's Learning and Evaluation Policy was adopted by the Board of Directors in 2021. The policy covers the purpose of learning and evaluation in the Bank and outlines the principles and internationally accepted criteria that underpin its learning and evaluation activities. As elaborated in the Policy, learning and evaluation under the Policy involve shared but distinct roles and responsibilities of the Board, CEIU, and Management. The Directive on the Learning and Evaluation Policy further elaborates on the role of Management. **12.40**

(3) Integrity

The integrity function under the CEIU oversees implementation of AIIB's Policy on Prohibited Practices.[85] **12.41**

That Policy seeks to enable AIIB and its clients to do business with trustworthy parties who adhere to the highest standards of integrity, and that, with respect to investment operations, its funds are used for the purposes intended. In line with the current practice at other MDBs, AIIB has established a regime for the sanctioning of firms and individuals that are found to have engaged in specified forms of fraud, corruption, and other prohibited practices in connection with AIIB-financed projects and AIIB's corporate procurement. **12.42**

As discussed in Chapter 5, AIIB has established a three-tiered process for enforcement of the Policy on Prohibited Practices, again in line with practice at Comparator Institutions: an Investigations Officer (in CEIU), a Sanctions Officer (to date, the Vice-President and Corporate Secretary) and a three-person Sanctions Panel to hear appeals (one internal and two external members.[86] A review of AIIB's **12.43**

[83] AIIB, Project-Affected People's Mechanism, https://www.aiib.org/en/about-aiib/who-we-are/project-affected-peoples-mechanism/how-we-assist-you/index.html (last visited July 14, 2025).

[84] Asian Infrastructure Investment Bank Project-Affected People's Mechanism, External Review, Dr. Zeinab Bashir Elbakri, May 2024.

[85] The Policy on Prohibited Practices is also discussed at paragraphs 5.51–5.54.

[86] AIIB Policy on Prohibited Practices, Sections III, IV, and V.

Annual Reports shows one integrity case handled in 2020.[87] In subsequent years, no cases have been reported as appealed to the Sanctions Panel, nor is there mention of investigations referred to the Sanctions Officer.[88]

12.44 AIIB's standards and setup for its anti-corruption function are quite similar to its counterparts, in an area where harmonization is key. As a new institution without an established system and track record for others to rely on, AIIB was not in position to join the 2010 Agreement for the Mutual Enforcement of Debarment Decisions (AMEDD) among AfDB, AsDB, EBRD, IADB, and World Bank, which would have required these institutions to accept AIIB debarment decisions.

12.45 There was no bar to AIIB accepting the debarment decisions of these institutions, however. Creatively, in December 2016, AIIB unilaterally debarred all entities already debarred by others under the AMEDD, through the AIIB Policy on Prohibited Practices.[89] AIIB's unilateral debarment is in line with the AMEDD, under which the Comparator Institutions undertook to recognize and enforce the principal sanctions decided by the others pursuant to their respective integrity procedures. Until AIIB is accepted by the Comparator Institutions as a party to the AMEDD, the Comparator Institutions are not obliged to cross-debar other entities debarred by AIIB itself.

12.46 Where AIIB co-finances an investment operation with one of the Comparator Institutions, AIIB may agree to apply the co-financier's sanctions policy and processes, and may agree to give full force and effect to the co-financier's sanctions decisions with respect to a joint co-financing.

(4) External audit

12.47 The Paper on the Oversight Mechanism that formed the basis for the Board's Decision on the Oversight Mechanism in 2019 outlined the role of the External Auditor for this purpose:

[87] "The remaining elements of the Policy on Prohibited Practices were put in place in 2020 by mobilizing the Sanctions Panel and inducting its newly appointed members. The importance of having a sanctions process was highlighted when the Complaints-resolution, Evaluation and Integrity Unit completed its first investigation. This led to the Bank's Sanctions Officer imposing sanctions on counterparties under a public-private partnership for the first time. No appeal was filed with the Sanctions Panel." Annual Report 2020 at 21.

[88] AIIB Annual Report 2023 at 30 notes that no investigations went to the Sanctions Officer, and no cases were filed for appeal to the Sanctions Panel. *See also* AIIB Annual Report 2022 at 40; AIIB Annual Report 2024 at 83.

[89] Additional AMEDD debarments have been added to the AIIB debarment list, as well as three AIIB debarments from 2020. AIIB website, Debarment List, https://www.aiib.org/en/about-aiib/who-we-are/debarment-list/index.html (last visited July 14, 2025).

See AIIB Annual Report 2024 at 83: "The Sanctions Officer, based on CEIU's review and recommendation, approved the inclusion of 341 entities (and removal of 166 entities) debarred by MDBs that are part of the AMEDD to its Debarment List. AIIB's Debarment List includes debarments based on AIIB's own investigation and the foregoing cross-debarred entities. As of Dec. 31, 2024, there were 1,155 entities in AIIB's Debarment List. Eighty-five percent of these debarments are related to Fraudulent Practices."

> External auditors reside outside any organization's structure, but perform an important role in the Bank's overall governance and control structure. The role of the external auditor is to independently assess financial reporting controls and audit financial statements. This, by nature, implies an assessment on part of the first, second and/or third LOD [line of defense], and thus plays an important role in providing assurances to the Board on the Bank's internal governance arrangements.
>
> The External Auditor is appointed by the Board, upon recommendation by the President through a competitive selection process. The work of the external auditor will be handled through the ARC [Audit and Risk Committee] of the Board, on which it will report annually to the Board.[90]

The 2023–2024 annual report of the Audit and Risk Committee summarized feedback and updates from the External Auditor (PricewaterhouseCoopers), and indicated that the Committee would participate in the next selection of an External Auditor in 2025.[91] The Committee's 2024–2025 annual report noted that the Committee would be monitoring preparations for the transition to a new external auditor in 2026.[92]

(5) Staff grievances

AIIB's Staff Regulations, approved by the Board of Directors in November 2016, **12.48** include provisions on resolution of employment disputes. The Staff Regulations establish a right to fair treatment in employment matters and provide for the establishment of a procedure for staff to challenge employment decisions that adversely affect them directly and personally. They also provide for a process to be put in place for appeals from that procedure to an independent administrative tribunal.[93]

D. COVID-19 Crisis Response

The worldwide COVID-19 crisis that began to unfold in early 2020 had an impact **12.49** on member countries of the MDBs as well as on the institutions themselves. The health crisis in countries and the economic crises that followed were addressed by many MDBs that year by expanding their assistance to members as rapidly as

[90] AIIB Paper on the Oversight Mechanism (2019), paragraphs 25–6.

[91] AIIB Board of Directors, Audit and Risk Committee Annual Report to the Board of Directors June 2023–May 2024, at 6. *See also* Audit and Risk Committee Annual Report to the Board of Directors 2024–2025.

[92] Audit and Risk Committee Annual Report to the Board of Directors 2024–2025 at 4.

[93] *See* paragraphs 11.36–11.37. The Paper on the Oversight Mechanism 2019 notes "since the selection of an appropriate administrative tribunal should be made with a view to coherence with AIIB's internal procedures, settled after a period of testing. Implementation of Article 13(4) of the Staff Regulations will be dealt with in a separate document discussed with, and authorized by, the Board, in due course."

possible. As international institutions, the MDBs also faced the challenges of staff affected by the spread of the disease, by travel limitations and shutdowns, and by introducing remote work around the globe. For those with resident Boards, there was also the need to find ways for governance structures to function in a novel environment.

12.50 AIIB and its members also faced these challenges, although its non-resident Board arrangement had already been operating for four years with experience in remote decision-making. By the time the World Health Organization declared COVID-19 a pandemic on March 11, 2020, AIIB's President and senior management had already been working out potential responses to the various dimensions of the crisis, briefing the Board of Directors in a March 16 Board meeting.[94] One month later, AIIB joined the coordinated international response as the Board of Directors approved on April 16 the launch of AIIB's COVID-19 Crisis Recovery Facility with an indicative financing envelope of US$5–10 billion over eighteen months. The Crisis Recovery Facility was eventually extended until end-2023 with an indicative financial envelope up to US$20 billion. The scope was narrowed in 2022 to cover co-financing of vaccines, co-financing of policy-based financing and financing of essential COVID-19 emergency healthcare or urgent expenditure needs, while liquidity support to infrastructure-related companies was mainstreamed into regular financing.[95]

12.51 In addition, the AIIB Board of Directors approved in May 2020 the carve out of US$30 million from AIIB's Project Preparation Special Fund to a Special Fund Window under the Facility. The Special Fund Window was a mechanism to lower the cost of AIIB's regular lending for lower income members, by providing grants to buy down up to 100 basis points on AIIB's interest rate. In 2021, the Board approved another carve out of up to US$25 million from the Project Preparation Special Fund to a Special Fund Window for vaccine financing under the Facility.[96]

12.52 The Crisis Recovery Facility was an umbrella initiative, covering all financings that AIIB undertook to assist its members in mitigating the impact of and recovery from COVID-19. Most projects were cofinanced, principally with AsDB and the World Bank Group. The Facility's scope and results are summarized in Figure 12.4.

12.53 The AIIB Final Report on the Facility highlighted several new mechanisms that were later introduced at AIIB based on experience with the Facility.[97]

- <u>Special Fund Window for Less Developed Members (SFW-LDM).</u> In March 2022, AIIB's Board of Directors approved the renaming of the Facility's Special

[94] Zaccaria (2024) at 432.
[95] AIIB (2024) [Review of the COVID-19 Crisis Recovery Facility] sets out a timeline for the CRF milestones on page 4.
[96] AIIB (2024) [Review of the COVID-19 Crisis Recovery Facility] at 4.
[97] AIIB (2024) [Review of the COVID-19 Crisis Recovery Facility] at 16.

SCOPE
- Sovereign and Non-sovereign financing
- New types of financing: immediate health sector needs, economic resilience, and liquidity
- Co-financing of quick disbursing instruments: World Bank Program-for-Results (PforR) and
- AsDB Results-based Lending (RBL)
- Regional and non-regional members eligible (all non-regional Projects approved by the Board of Directors)

RESULTS
- 68 projects in 26 member countries (US$18.48 billion)
- Financing approved for 21 regional countries (95% of financing) and 5 non-regional
- Low and lower-middle-income borrowers accounted for 65% of total approved financing
- Mostly sovereign borrowers (95%), reflecting the government role in crisis response
- Mostly co-financed (84%) with MDBs (AsDB 53%, World Bank Group 31%, and EBRD 0.4%)
- Projects addressed: policy-based financing (63%); public health, including vaccine financing
- (20%); financial intermediary/liquidity support (14%); and economic resilience (3%)

Figure 12.4 AIIB COVID-19 Crisis Recovery Facility
Source: AIIB (2024) [Review of the COVID-19 Crisis Recovery Facility], AIIB Final Report on the Crisis Response Facility.

Fund Window and turning it into a regular instrument, as the Special Fund Window for Less Developed Members (SFW-LDM) to serve the needs of less developed regional members.[98] The SFW-LDM was expected to serve a broadened scope with new contributions, providing interest rate buy-down to eligible sovereign borrowers aligned with AIIB's Corporate Strategy. As of end-2024, the SFW-LDM received a US$10 million contribution commitment from the Kingdom of Saudi Arabia, and a US$300 million contribution from China, and had made ten grants.

- AIIB's Approach to Emergency Response. The need to provide support to members to prepare for future crises was a lesson learned from the Facility. In June 2023, the Board approved AIIB's Approach to Emergency Response, which extends policy-based co-financing as part of AIIB's approach to help members respond to and recover from future eligible crises.[99]
- Results-based Financing (RBF). In 2023, with the approval of the Operational Policy on Financing Update, the Bank began offering Results-based Financing among its products for Sovereign-backed financing. This enables AIIB to provide standalone RBF support to investment programs with many small expenditures and activities with lower environmental and social risks.

[98] AIIB (2024) [Review of the COVID-19 Crisis Recovery Facility] at 10: "The SFW was instrumental to enable eligible debt-constrained AIIB Members to access AIIB financing by increasing the concessional element of their loan terms as required by the International Monetary Fund (IMF) and relevant WB policies. This relatively simple mechanism and its integration with the investment process ensured the swift utilization of the SFW... Following the successful rollout of SFW, the demand for its resources steadily increased, driven by the challenging external environment faced by less developed Members as well as AIIB's efforts to implement the Corporate Strategy to broaden its client base across the income spectrum. The SFW was later made permanent."

[99] Paper on AIIB's Approach to Emergency Response, June 13, 2023 and Decision to Support AIIB's Policy-based Cofinancing in Eligible Crises, adopted June 13, 2023.

The pandemic presented a challenge in particular to a young institution developing its operational pipeline and strengthening its institutional foundation. These lasting changes indicate that AIIB managed not only to weather this storm, but also to find ways to support its members in this crisis.[100]

12.54 Overall, the creation and implementation of AIIB's COVID-19 Crisis Recovery Facility highlighted AIIB's use of flexibility in its legal framework, in addition to making use of its capital base.[101] For instance, allowing for support for non-regional members under the existing strategy on non-regional operations made sense in light of the impact of a health and economic crisis that crossed regional lines and where non-regional impacts would also affect regional members.[102] Within that flexibility, the Board of Directors retained its power to approve all non-regional financing under the Facility, without delegation to the President that might otherwise have been authorized under the Accountability Framework. AIIB also piloted new types of operations (such as policy-based financing, results-based financing, and liquidity financing) in conjunction with co-financiers and applying their policies. The learning from these pilot operations for AIIB and its members supported later adoption of new types of lending.

12.55 The worldwide COVID-19 pandemic brought the need to utilize some of AIIB's institutional flexibility in other ways, as it did for other MDBs. Annual Meetings of the Board of Governors were held virtually,[103] as were meetings of the Board of Directors. The opening of an office in Abu Dhabi, which was to meet AIIB's business needs, can additionally be seen as a response to the challenges of travel and location during the pandemic.

E. Resource Mobilization Initiatives

(1) AIIB Special Funds and administration

12.56 Special Funds are separate funds put at AIIB's disposal to administer for purposes within its mandate. Contributions can come from outside sources, such as countries and other institutions; AIIB can also contribute to a Special Fund from its income or other sources. As described in Chapter 7, Special Funds are maintained separately from AIIB's own funds and its ordinary operations.[104]

[100] Zaccaria (2024) noting the challenges at 420 and the success of AIIB's leadership and its proactivity at 438.

[101] Standard and Poor's March 2025 Rating Report notes at 2: "AIIB had used its excess capacity to provide the pandemic package, demonstrating its ability to be a counter-cyclical lender."

[102] At completion, total financing (regular and Facility) in non-regional Members as a share of the Bank's total financing approved between December 31, 2020 and December 31, 2023 was 7.6%, far below the 15% ceiling set out in AIIB's Strategy on Financing Operations in Non-Regional Members. AIIB (2024) [Review of the COVID-19 Crisis Recovery Facility] at 7.

[103] The Annual Meetings of the AIIB Board of Governors were held virtually in 2020, 2021, and 2022. https://www.aiib.org/en/about-aiib/governance/board-governors/index.html (last visited July 14, 2025).

[104] *See* paragraphs 7.55–7.58.

AIIB has established several Special Funds, with various purposes and funding **12.57**
sources. As noted in paragraphs 7.55–7.58, AIIB has three internal Special Funds, established to receive and manage direct contributions from donors and governed by AIIB policies and decision-making bodies:[105]

- The Project Preparation Special Fund is a multi-donor facility to provide technical assistance grants to support the preparation of high-quality bankable projects for AIIB members, especially less developed members.
- The Special Fund Window for Less Developed Members (SFW) provides interest rate buy-down for eligible Sovereign-backed financing projects to make AIIB financing more affordable for its less developed members. As mentioned in paragraph 12.53, this Special Fund was inspired by AIIB's experience with the COVID-19 Crisis Recovery Facility.
- The Project Specific Window (PSW) is a special fund that allows AIIB to accept, manage, and disburse grant co-financings on behalf of contributors into eligible AIIB projects in AIIB members classified as either low- or middle-income or small island economies.[106]

In addition, three external Special Funds have been created within AIIB to receive and manage resources from facilities established by external parties for whom the Bank acts as one of several implementing entities. External Special Funds were established to channel resources from the Multilateral Cooperation Center for Development Finance (MCDF); the Global Infrastructure Facility (GIF); and the Pandemic Prevention, Preparedness and Response Financial Intermediary Fund (Pandemic Fund).[107] The MCDF platform extends beyond AIIB's Special Fund, as described in subsection (2).

(2) Multilateral Cooperation Center for Development Finance

The MCDF describes itself as a multilateral financial mechanism designed to pro- **12.58**
mote high-quality infrastructure and connectivity investments in developing countries through partnerships, committed to adopting IFI standards for projects. With its connection to the Belt and Road Initiative (BRI), the MCDF was established by China with collaboration from several MDBs.[108]

[105] Information here comes from the AIIB website, Special Funds Resources, https://www.aiib.org/en/how-we-work/partnerships/special-funds-resources/index.html (last visited July 14, 2025), supplemented by AIIB Annual Report 2023 at 74.

[106] AIIB website, Project Specific Window, https://www.aiib.org/en/what-we-do/special-funds/project-specific-window-fund/index.html (last visited July 14, 2025). Eligible projects also include projects that have been included in the Bank's Rolling Investment Pipeline prior to the consideration for PSW support.

[107] AIIB Annual Report 2023, at 74. *See* paragraph 7.58.

[108] Memorandum of Understanding on Collaboration on Matters to Establish the Multilateral Cooperation Center for Development Finance, March 25, 2019, MOF with AsDB, AIIB, CAF, EBRD, EIB, IADB, IFAD, and World Bank Group (WBG).

12.59 The MCDF is comprised of:

- An MCDF Collaboration Platform to promote communication and collaboration among the IFIs and other development partners regarding plans and activities relating to infrastructure and connectivity investments;
- An MCDF Finance Facility to provide grant resources to fund activities of the MCDF;
- An MCDF Administrator to provide administrative and financial services to the MCDF, including the establishment and hosting of the MCDF Secretariat; and
- An MCDF Secretariat to support the day to day operations of the MCDF.

In addition, the MCDF's governance structure includes guidance and oversight by two committees, the Governing Committee and the Coordination Committee.[109] IFI Implementing Partners are AIIB, AsDB, CAF, IFAD, IsDB, CDB, and African Finance Corporation, as of June 2025.[110]

12.60 AIIB has taken on several roles in support of the multifaceted MCDF. AIIB serves as the Administrator of the MCDF, hosts the MCDF Secretariat, and is one of the MDCF's Implementing Partners, receiving grants into AIIB's MCDF Special Fund. AIIB's support for the MCDF can be seen from the lens of AIIB's relationship with BRI as well as from the perspective of the many initiatives which other MDBs have supported by hosting secretariats, serving as administrator or trustee, and acting as an implementing partner.

12.61 This combination of functions that AIIB undertakes in the MCDF arrangements is comparable to the role of the World Bank with respect to the Global Environment Facility, and many other similar initiatives. In 2024, for instance, the World Bank supported some twenty-six financial intermediary funds (FIFs).

> Independent governing bodies set the strategic direction for FIFs, making funding decisions and selecting implementing entities, among other responsibilities. Projects funded by FIFs are implemented by multiple entities, including MDBs, UN agencies, and other organizations. The Bank Group has no decision-making

[109] Multilateral Cooperation Center for Development Finance (MCDF) website, https://www.themcdf.org/en/index.html, at Who We Are (last visited July 14, 2025). Governing Instrument of the Finance Facility of the Multilateral Cooperation Center for Development Finance.

> The Governing Committee is responsible for policy guidance and operational oversight to the MCDF Finance Facility. It includes Members (representatives of the contributors to the Finance Facility) and Observers (representatives of IFI Implementing Partners, the Administrator, and the CEO of the MCDF Secretariat).
>
> The Coordination Committee oversees and directs all activities undertaken by the Collaboration Platform. It includes representatives of IFIs who are parties to the Memorandum of Understanding (MoU) establishing MCDF, and the contributing members of the Finance Facility.

The donors to the MCDF Finance Facility that have given US$10 million or more for up to five years (China, Egypt, Hungary, Saudi Arabia) are voting members, and Cambodia, Lao PDR, and the Philippines are non-voting members.

[110] MCDF website, https://www.themcdf.org/en/what-we-do/index.html (last visited July 14, 2025).

> authority in FIFs. Instead, the World Bank provides services to 26 FIFs. It serves as trustee to all 26 FIFs and hosts the secretariat of 18 of them. The Bank is also an implementing entity for 20 of the FIFs . . . Each of these roles is distinct and performed by different units within the World Bank.[111]

Distinct from the FIFs, the World Bank Group administers a wide range of trust funds that are closer in function (but not legal structure) to AIIB's internal Special Funds.[112] World Bank Group trust funds enable one or more development partners to contribute money that is held in trust by the Bank Group, to achieve specific development objectives, under the World Bank Group's own policies and procedures.[113]

(3) Belt and Road Initiative (BRI)

AIIB's support of the MCDF, an outgrowth of China's BRI, brought forth the question of AIIB's relationship to BRI. While the BRI and AIIB came to the world's attention at the same time, they developed afterwards on separate paths with different phasing. Both the BRI and AIIB were proposed by China's President Xi Jinping in 2013, in the same speech in Indonesia in October that year, though the Silk Road Economic Belt component of the BRI had been announced in Almaty in September.[114] Both concepts had a much longer history behind the 2013 announcements. For the BRI: **12.62**

> Before 2013, when Xi Jinping first aired the concepts of a Silk Road Economic Belt across Eurasia and a 21st Century Maritime Silk Road linking Southeast Asia with Europe, several infrastructure projects to expand regional transportation networks had already been launched and partially completed. Through projects ranging from the oldest and most ambitious plan, led by the United Nations, to connect the entire Asian continent to Europe via road and rail, to the more recent and narrowly focused South Korean Iron Silk Road or U.S. New Silk Road initiative, transportation connectivity has been encouraged both by individual states and multilateral institutions.[115]

[111] World Bank Group 2024 Trust Fund Report at 8.

[112] IBRD and IDA do not have a legal mechanism for special funds, as was introduced first in the 1960s in the AfDB Charter and continued for later Charters. Legally, IBRD and IDA have trust funds that are used to support World Bank Group activities and financial intermediary funds, a form of trust fund with separate governance arrangements for which the World Bank provides tailored administrative, operational, legal, and financial services. The AIIB Charter provides for both Special Funds, which are the Bank's own resources, and Trust Funds, which are held in trust for a donor or donor(s). *See* paragraph 7.55 (Special Funds) and paragraph 7.59 (Trust Funds).

[113] World Bank Group 2024 Trust Fund Report at 4.

[114] Rolland (2017) at 45–6: "The Silk Road Economic Belt and the 21st Century Maritime Silk Road were both mentioned publicly for the first time by Xi, not together as 'One Belt, One Road,' but on two separate occasions. He announced the former during an address at Nazarbayev University in Astana on September 7, 2013, and the latter during a speech given in front of the Indonesian parliament in Jakarta on October 2, 2013." (Citations at Rolland, note 3.)

[115] *See* Rolland (2017) at 7, and the detailed discussion in Chapter 1, "Mapping the Silk Roads."

Similarly, as Chapter 3 details, the concept of an Asian investment/infrastructure bank had been floated in Asian discussions in the early 2000s, as regional financial institutions were being considered in the years following the 1997 Asian financial crisis. Earlier proposals included a 2005 report from the UN Economic and Social Commission for Asia and the Pacific that suggested the establishment of an Asian Investment Bank, adapted from the model of the European Investment Bank (EIB), to meet the region's infrastructure needs and promote regional development.[116] In 2009, a Chinese think tank suggested the formation of a new development bank focused on infrastructure.[117]

12.63 The AIIB proposal moved relatively swiftly for the setting up of a new international organization, with formal, visible steps involving other countries. China organized multilateral consultation meetings on AIIB with interested countries, starting in January 2014. By October 2014, one year after President Xi's announcement of the proposal, twenty-two regional countries signed a Memorandum of Understanding on Establishing the Asian Infrastructure Investment Bank in Beijing. A total of fifty-seven countries, regional and non-regional, joined the negotiations on setting up AIIB in meetings in January, March, April, and May 2015. The AIIB Charter was opened for signature at the end of June 2015 and AIIB formally opened its doors in January 2016.[118]

12.64 The BRI was under discussion internally in China during that period. It was not until March 2015 that a central leading small group for belt and road development was set up, and a founding document issued:

> With the release on March 28, 2015, of a document jointly issued by the NDRC, the Ministry of Foreign Affairs, and the Ministry of Commerce, the project was finally officially labeled the Belt and Road Initiative. Entitled "Vision and Actions on Jointly Building Silk Road Economic Belt and 21st-Century Maritime Silk Road," the document reads more like a general roadmap than a concrete and detailed proposal. While clearly an attempt to give some structure to the government's vision, it consists of a laundry list of ideas, mixing ends with means and sometimes putting together concepts that appear contradictory.[119]

By that time, the AIIB negotiations were well advanced, with many European and other developed countries having joined by the March 31, 2015 deadline. No wonder that the BRI was not featured in the AIIB negotiations. Even at AIIB's formal inauguration in January 2016, there was but one mention of the BRI in President Xi's speech: "And China continues to welcome AIIB and other international financial

[116] UN Economic and Social Commission for Asia and the Pacific (ESCAP) (2005) at 154.

[117] *See* Callaghan and Hubbard (2016) at 116, singling out the 2009 proposal by the China Center for International Economic Exchanges.

[118] *See* paragraphs 3.20–3.31.

[119] Rolland (2017) at 51.

institutions to take part in the building of the Silk Road Economic Belt and 21st Century Maritime Silk Road."[120]

While there are commonalities of purpose and geography across AIIB and BRI, there are also differences. As a former AIIB General Counsel explained in 2017: 12.65

> While the AIIB can and does finance infrastructure projects in Asia, it is not confined to doing so. Furthermore, the governance of the Bank means that investment policies are not necessarily those that drive the Belt and Road Initiative. Indeed, the 57 Signatories to the AIIB Charter made no mention of the Belt and Road Initiative in the Articles of Agreement. Similarly, there is no reference to the Belt and Road in any of the institutional rules or operational policies of the Bank. Conformity with Belt and Road objectives is not a consideration in AIIB's evaluation of investment proposals.
>
> The effect is that the AIIB finances projects both within and outside the places covered by the Belt and Road Initiative and its financing extends beyond infrastructure to include what, in undefined terms, the Charter calls "other productive sectors."[121]

In practice, India has received the largest share of AIIB financing, yet has not joined the BRI initiative.[122]

F. Other Developments

Transparency has been enhanced by the 2018 adoption of a full-blown Policy on Public Information, replacing the 2016 interim policy, and adding mechanisms for requesting information. Reports on policy implementation are available online. Also available online are regular reports on operational procurement, corporate procurement, PPM, and the CEIU overall, among others. Annual Reports on 12.66

[120] Full text of Chinese President Xi Jinping's address at AIIB inauguration ceremony, January 16, 2016, https://www.chinadaily.com.cn/business/2016-01/16/content_23116718.htm.

In Chinese Premier Li Qiang's address to the 10th Annual Meeting in June 2025, he encouraged AIIB to "strengthen synergy with the Belt and Road Initiative and the Global Development Initiative." "Li Qiang Attends and Addresses the Opening Ceremony of the 10th Annual Meeting of the Asian Infrastructure Investment Bank Board of Governors," Ministry of Foreign Affairs of the People's Republic of China press release, June 26, 2025,

https://www.fmprc.gov.cn/eng/xw/zyxw/202506/t20250627_11660565.html.

[121] Sanders (2017) at 368.

[122] Moody's Ratings, "Asian Infrastructure Investment Bank – Aaa stable, Recent update" at 7: "Membership in the bank can be seen as a financial investment that transcends related geopolitical considerations. Amid territorial disputes in the South China Sea, for example, borrowers such as Malaysia (A3 stable), the Philippines (Baa2 stable), and Vietnam (Ba2 stable) have retained their membership despite periodic bilateral tensions with China. Similarly, despite tensions related to projects under China's Belt and Road Initiative (BRI), Malaysia, the Maldives (Caa1 stable), and Sri Lanka have also continued to engage with AIIB. India, AIIB's largest borrower and its second-largest shareholder, has not joined the BRI, while many of the bank's non-borrowing members have been critical of the Chinese initiative." *See* Figure 5.5, AIIB Projects by Member.

AIIB's Sustainability Bonds and Partnerships, as well as from the AIIB Ethics Office allow for greater public awareness and scrutiny.

12.67 AIIB's Tianjin Office was set up in March 2021, as a backup office for business continuity and a venue for trainings, meetings, and other group activities. The Tianjin Office is about 180 km from the headquarters in Beijing. The establishment of an Interim Operational Hub in Abu Dhabi was approved in 2022, and the opening of offices in Hong Kong and Singapore were in the works in 2025.[123]

12.68 In 2025, AIIB was preparing for a seamless change in leadership, with the election of Madame Zou Jiayi at the 10th Annual Meeting of the Board of Governors. Her term would commence in January 2026, ten years after President Jin Liqun was elected to the first of his two terms permitted under the term limit in the AIIB Charter.[124]

[123] *See* paragraph 11.42.
[124] President Jin was re-elected for his second term in 2020. *See* paragraph 8.32.

13

REFLECTIONS REVISITED

The Asian Infrastructure Investment Bank (AIIB) Charter began with another Charter, which began with another Charter, and so on, stretching back nearly 100 years.[1] Those progenitors are identified throughout the pages of this book. The Charter comparisons tell us where the AIIB Charter came from, but they can't tell us where AIIB is going. AIIB's story has just begun; only its first phase is reflected in the chapters of this second edition. The stories of the multilateral development banks (MDBs) created by those other Charters, though, can help to identify factors that may influence the course of AIIB's future development. **13.01**

In looking back at others and looking forward for AIIB, it is prudent to start by noting the importance of unforeseen events. For an institution, responding to risks that were anticipated may be a lesser challenge than managing cataclysms never imagined. It is doubtful, for instance, that the end of the gold standard and fixed exchange rates was in the minds of the delegates at Bretton Woods, but those later events led to major adjustments for the World Bank (even more so for the International Monetary Fund (IMF)). On the other hand, the Bretton Woods drafters could have predicted that the Union of Soviet Socialist Republics would stay out of the World Bank, as negotiations had not been smooth;[2] it is unlikely, however, that they would have foreseen that a different country, Russia, would join the World Bank in 1992, alongside the fourteen other former republics of the Soviet Union. And they would probably not have predicted that the political changes in the Soviet Union, and contemporaneous changes in Central and Eastern Europe, would become the proximate cause for the establishment of the European Bank for Reconstruction and Development (EBRD) more than four decades after Bretton Woods. **13.02**

More recently, the world was surprised by the COVID-19 pandemic that began in 2020 and had an enormous impact on people, countries, and MDBs. Yet, AIIB's flexible framework, designed in 2015, prepared it to respond.[3] In 2025, countries and the international world are once more in an uncertain time, where it seems increasingly possible that old or new cataclysms may affect the future. **13.03**

[1] *See* Chapters 2 and 3.
[2] Conway (2014) at 273–80.
[3] *See* Chapter 12, Section D.

A. Themes from MDB History

13.04 What are some of the specific factors that have affected other MDBs and might affect AIIB? Let us consider a few that suggest themselves from MDB histories: overall economic and financial environment; international relations and politics; funding; membership changes; major shareholders; clients and operations; leadership and governance; and attitudes toward change.

(1) Economic and financial environment

13.05 For these institutions aimed at economic development, changes in the economies of countries, regions, and the world obviously have an impact on their work. Economic changes may prevent the success of an otherwise well-designed and implemented investment operation, or may transform the needs in a client country or region. Social and environmental phenomena can also have an impact on countries and regions—for example, pandemics, migration, droughts, and floods. (Again, the COVID-19 pandemic is a case in point.) Equally, economic and financial vicissitudes can change the equation for contributing countries, whether in a positive way (think petrodollars fueling the Venezuela Trust Fund at the Inter-American Development Bank (IADB) and the Nigeria Trust Fund at the African Development Bank (AfDB) in the 1970s) or a negative one (think reduction in foreign assistance in a domestic financial crunch or change of policy). These trends can have a profound effect on an institution, whether in its strategic directions or in its operations (such as breaks in concessional operations when a major donor's replenishment contributions are delayed).

13.06 Changes of the last ten years have affected AIIB, as one would imagine. Pandemic needs moved its assistance to members into the health sector and liquidity support, under AIIB's COVID-19 Crisis Recovery Facility (CRF), established in 2020. The CRF brought forward new types of policy-based financing, modalities for reducing interest rates for less developed members and a broader policy for emergency response more generally.[4] The vision of global interconnectedness that originally underpinned AIIB's goal of connectivity was brought home by the contagion of disease, making it clear in yet another way that pandemic support outside of Asia would benefit the health and countries of Asia. At the same time, economic connectivity was diminished by reduced travel and trade and a renewed attraction to self-reliance, affecting the economies of AIIB's members. At a strategic level, the changes of the last ten years have not diverted AIIB's focus on climate impact, regional cooperation and connectivity, and the mobilization of private finance, as laid out in AIIB's Corporate Strategy.[5]

[4] *See* Chapter 12, Section D.
[5] *See* paragraph 5.6.

(2) International relations and politics

As intergovernmental organizations, MDBs are created by countries to benefit countries and their people.[6] Relations with other countries are an important part of decisions to join or continue to support an MDB, or, as members, to come to a compromise on difficult policy choices or types of lending or recipients. The role of international relations in the founding of other MDBs illustrates this point; it also resonates with the account of AIIB's beginnings in Chapter 3.[7] 13.07

The creation of IADB in 1959, for instance, is a story that begins the century before, rooted in the economic and political history of Latin America as a region and its relations with its northern neighbor, the United States. As far back as 1890, there had been a regional impetus first for an "International American Bank" as a regional banking institution, and later for an intergovernmental financial institution, the Inter-American Bank, which nearly came to life in 1940. These regional forces renewed the push for a similar institution in the 1950s, when they found that the International Bank for Reconstruction and Development (IBRD) did not fully meet their needs in its early years.[8] A proposal for something very like the Asian Development Bank (AsDB) was not viewed favorably in Asia or elsewhere when floated quietly by Japan in the early 1960s, but later dovetailed with a movement of smaller Asian countries discussing a bank of their own at the UN Economic Commission for Asia and the Far East (ECAFE).[9] The United States was initially reluctant to throw its weight behind each of these proposed regional institutions, perhaps not so keenly aware of the gaps in assistance from the US-dominated World Bank perceived by regional developing countries. Only when faced with a need to improve its regional relations—with Latin America in the late 1950s, with Southeast Asia after the start of the US war against Vietnam—did the United States play a leading financial and political role in starting these regional banks,[10] remaining a major shareholder to this day. 13.08

For AfDB, regional economic history dating back to the 1880s underpinned the desire for an African financial institution in the post-colonial era. While the UN Economic Commission for Africa played a seminal role in AfDB's establishment (as ECAFE did for AsDB), it was the relations among different groups of African 13.09

[6] MDBs benefit the organizers as well as the recipients. *See* Bittermann (1967) at 1–2 on US motivations for IBRD: "The war was at its height, and war conditions in the United States released economic forces which doubled the G.N.P. between 1940 and 1945 (50 per cent increase in real terms). With the end of the war, not in sight in 1943, it was the view that this volume of production could be put to use for peaceful purposes, the reconstruction of war-torn countries and the development of the countries with lower incomes. The post-war revival of investment and trade could help in avoiding a big slump. The United States in helping other countries would help itself. This was understood by the other countries which realized that for some years to come they would have to depend on the U.S. for needed external capital."

[7] *See* Chapter 3, Section B.

[8] *See* Díaz-Bonilla and del Campo (2010) for an overall history, and at 58–9 on dissatisfaction with existing international financial institutions.

[9] Wilson (1987), Chapter 2, "The Birth of the Bank."

[10] Tussie (1995) at 18–19; Wilson (1987) at 12–13.

countries that determined the timing and contours of the bank that emerged. Relations with non-regional former colonial powers, such as France, had an impact on decisions to join the bank, and on forms of concessional financing, but non-regionals were not part of AfDB membership discussions until much later.[11]

13.10 EBRD was also a regional initiative, but one that responded to the abrupt appearance on the international agenda of aid to Central and Eastern Europe, rather than a longstanding dream of a regional bank. (A regional investment bank, the European Investment Bank (EIB), had been in operation since its establishment in 1958.) Politics was no less a part of EBRD's creation, reflecting differing views of key European protagonists (France, Germany, United Kingdom), European institutions (the EU and EIB were original EBRD members) and the United States and Japan. Domestic politics in recipient countries is expressly part of EBRD's purpose, aimed at the promotion of multiparty democracy and pluralism, along with market economics and private sector development. For both political and economic reasons, EBRD was established with a combination of regional and non-regional shareholders from the start.[12]

13.11 What is particularly striking in these origin stories is the role of politics. We saw in Chapter 11 that AIIB's provisions on political prohibitions and its independent character are common among the MDBs, with variations for EBRD and its explicit political mandate.[13] These lofty MDB Charter provisions—non-interference in domestic political matters, ignoring the political character of the member, only economic considerations to prevail—stand in contrast to the intense political jockeying exhibited in the negotiations that created them.[14] Looking back, politics has continued to have an impact on the life of these MDBs, whether influencing the types of projects or the recipients, as much as the institutions may strive to maintain their economic focus and to avoid political interference as mandated by their Charters.

13.12 A 1990 comparison of AfDB, AsDB, IADB, and the World Bank analyzed the ways in which politics affected these institutions, in such dimensions as policy changes, lending decisions, leadership selection, finance, and shareholding/voting power. In particular, hegemonic politics had a very significant effect in the World Bank and IADB (United States as hegemon) and a lesser but still noticeable effect in AsDB (Japan and United States). Without an acknowledged hegemon, AfDB was relatively insulated from this type of political influence. Yet, interorganizational and intraorganizational politics were found to be present in each one.[15]

[11] Gardiner and Pickett (1984) at 8–13.
[12] Weber (1994) at 13–23.
[13] *See* paragraphs 11.13–11.14.
[14] It has been suggested that the earliest version of these clauses (IBRD) was agreed at Bretton Woods to reassure the Soviet Union; even with this reassurance, the Soviet Union never joined the IBRD. Bittermann (1971) at 79.
[15] *See, generally*, Mingst (1990), Chapter 10, "Politics in the Multilateral Development Banks."

This older study reinforces the conclusion that geopolitical considerations are not just relevant in the beginning stage. Throughout the course of its existence, an MDB needs shareholder involvement and support for continued funding (capital increases and contributions for concessional finance), for decisions on strategic areas and for policy choices in new fields. How shareholders interact with each other, who leads and who follows and the tensions between developed and developing, regional and non-regional—these are all important elements. **13.13**

As AIIB's membership spans the globe, a broad range of regional and global frictions and friendships will doubtless influence its path forward. Now with 110 members, more than half non-regional, AIIB discussions will necessarily take on a more global outlook, notwithstanding that the balance of voting power remains decidedly regional (75%). Economic and political concerns from most regions of the world could play a role in AIIB's operations and decisions. In the increasing contention visible in 2025, with wars affecting AIIB members, it is difficult to expect that AIIB will be immune to these tensions.[16] **13.14**

(3) Funding

As financial institutions, MDBs require financial support from members to carry out their work. As we saw in Chapter 7,[17] the combination of market borrowing and callable capital can give the MDB considerable latitude in finding sources of finance, while financial ratios and structure can affect its leverage. At some point, a successful MDB may require more capital to finance the needs of its clients; in these circumstances, obtaining shareholders' agreement becomes crucial. Here, AIIB's ability to increase its lending limit to 250% of capital and reserves could provide additional headroom. The MDB reform discussions on capital adequacy are relevant for AIIB in its financial policies, although with this flexibility in its lending limit, Charter amendments have not been taken up for AIIB as they have been for AsDB, EBRD, EIB, and IBRD.[18] (Should major new shareholders come, the need for more than the remaining unallocated shares could mean some increase in capital to accommodate them.[19]) **13.15**

[16] One oft-cited example is AIIB's decision to put a hold on activities in Russia and Belarus as the war in Ukraine (not a member) unfolded. "AIIB Statement on war in Ukraine," AIIB Press Release, March 3, 2022.

Unrelated to this action, the war in Ukraine temporarily affected AIIB's borrowings along with the market, per S&P ("Asian Infrastructure Investment Bank 'AAA' Rating Affirmed; Outlook Stable," S&P Ratings Direct, March 13, 2025, at 3): "The early months of the Russia-Ukraine conflict, combined with overall complicated market dynamics, saw AIIB's spreads widen relative to peers. This led the bank then to rely more on private placements to reduce its overall funding cost. In line with our expectations, the impact was transitory and did not limit AIIB's ability to tap hard currency markets. From the start of 2024, bond spreads of the bank narrowed meaningfully and are now on par with much older 'AAA' rated institutions such as the International Bank for Reconstruction and Development and the Asian Development Bank."

[17] *See* paragraph 7.04.

[18] *See* paragraph 7.44.

[19] *See* Figure 7.2 for details on the allocation of shares since 2017, primarily to new members.

13.16 For those MDBs with concessional windows or entities, there is a constant need for replenishment of funds by donors. Concessional funds are provided for very long maturities at very low rates, so that the stream of reflows can be a trickle; grant funding means no reflows at all, so fresh donor funds are always needed. The cycle of regular replenishment negotiations opens up not just financial concerns, but has often provided an occasion for influencing major policy directions of the MDBs. The influence of International Development Association (IDA) replenishments on IBRD policy and operations is a well-known case in point.

13.17 The establishment of concessional funding windows also played a role in the history of other MDBs. IBRD did not have a soft loan window at the outset; rather than amending the IBRD Charter to create one within the IBRD, IDA was set up as a separate but affiliated institution. Around the same time IDA was agreed, the IADB was both fortunate and pioneering in starting out with its Fund for Special Operations as a separate concessional window *within* the bank and under its Charter, largely funded by the United States.[20] AsDB began with the legal structure permitting Special Funds, but the establishment and funding of its soft loan window (the Asian Development Fund) took several years more, in a different aid-giving climate.[21] The need for concessional funds was also key at AfDB, where it also took some time to set up a separate entity, the African Development Fund, that was necessary to bring in the needed finance from non-regional countries at a time when AfDB membership was open only to Africa.[22] EBRD has multiple Special Funds for special purposes, but does not provide soft loans.

13.18 At present, AIIB does not provide concessional finance for operations; AIIB's Special Funds have provided grants for project preparation and other purposes since the beginning. Starting under the CRF, AIIB has set up a Special Fund to cover an interest rate reduction on eligible sovereign-backed financing projects for its less developed members (Special Fund Window for Less Developed Members).[23] For the future, it is worth noting that, in more recent decades, specialized funds with innovative legal structures outside the MDBs have been more common, such as the Global Environment Facility; the Global Fund to Fight AIDS, Tuberculosis and Malaria; and the Green Climate Fund. In a way, AIIB's own establishment as a traditional international organization on the MDB model runs counter to that trend. Should concessional finance become necessary to meet AIIB's objectives, there would be many traditional and not-so-traditional options.

[20] White (1968) at 680.

[21] White (1968) at 682.

[22] White (1970) at 120–2. The AfDB Charter pioneered the provisions on Special Funds that are reflected in the Charters for AsDB, EBRD, and AIIB. The African Development Fund (AfDF) was originally set up as a special fund with AfDB funding, when the response of potential donors was not encouraging. By 1972, the AfDF was established as a separate international institution, by AfDB and non-regional donors. *See* Rigo Sureda (2004) at paragraphs 411–20.

[23] *See* paragraphs 12.53 and 12.57.

(4) Membership changes

Most of the MDBs surveyed here have added many members since their inception, as we saw in Chapter 6. In some cases, the arrival of new members required modifying the organization's character and its Charter: bringing in non-regional members and capital in IADB and AfDB, or adding Mongolia, then Southern and Eastern Mediterranean and then Sub-Saharan Africa and Iraq to EBRD's countries of operation.[24] In other cases, no outward revisions were needed, but major impacts were felt nonetheless. Here, one can think of the World Bank after the People's Republic of China took up China's seat in 1980, becoming the largest borrower for a long time (now the third largest shareholder), or in the 1990s, when Russia finally joined alongside many newly independent former members of the Soviet Union, changing the Bank's operations in Europe dramatically. 13.19

It may be some time before AIIB's flexibly designed Charter requires revision in this area, but significant changes in membership and power relationships can nonetheless affect an institution. The sheer number of AIIB members today (110) multiplies the efforts needed to maintain good country relationships, whether or not AIIB finance is involved.[25] It also adds new challenges to voice and representation within the institutional structure, as it has for AIIB's even larger counterpart, the World Bank, and its 189 members. As far as membership is concerned, it is often noted that the United States and Japan, two of the largest shareholders in other MDBs, such as AsDB, EBRD, and IBRD, are not members of AIIB. Should either one choose to join in some probably distant future, accommodating an appropriate shareholding based on economic weight within the 25% non-regional or 75% regional groups, respectively, would require some adjustment in voting power for other members. 13.20

(5) Major shareholders

Where one or two members hold a controlling share, the MDB's success can be closely tied to political, economic, and financial shifts in those countries. Controlling shareholders can push harder than others for policy changes and lending decisions, as well as protecting their strong interest in maintaining a controlling share.[26] Support for the MDB's overall mission can change, as countries often find themselves rebalancing their priorities between domestic and foreign 13.21

[24] *See* paragraph 6.29.

[25] Through 2024, AIIB has provided finance to thirty-eight members. "Annual Meeting Opening Remarks by AIIB President Jin Liqun, AIIB President and Chair of the Board of Directors, June 26, 2025," AIIB Press Release, July 4, 2025.

[26] *See* the detailed discussion in Mingst (1990) at 151–86 on how these hegemons influence specific policies and particular projects, and use financial tactics to do so. Where the hegemon holds enough voting power to prevent a quorum, such as the United States at the IADB Board of Governors, simply not attending a meeting can block a decision. IADB Article VIII, Section 2 (e) provides that a quorum requires the presence of Governors with 75% of the total voting power; the United States holds 30%.

needs at different times. Financial support can vary, too, depending on the major shareholders' needs.

13.22 AIIB has one shareholder, China, with around 26% of its voting power. The United States has also had a large share in IBRD (35% at the end of its first fiscal year in 1947, down to 23% in 1971 and around 16% in 2025) and in IADB (42% at its establishment, now required to be at least 30%). China's share in AIIB is slightly larger than the combined US and Japan share of 25% in AsDB. In their earliest years, both the IBRD and IADB in effect relied primarily on US financial support, borrowing principally against the US share of callable capital. When US finances and priorities changed, IBRD was able to fill the gap by expanding its borrowings into non-US markets, and the IADB embarked on a multi-year process to bring in new members and capital, eventually opening up to non-regional members and their contributions (initially Europe, Israel, and Japan).

13.23 Where there is no major shareholding country, there may be more democratic decision-making—such as the competition among regional shareholders in the selection of the AfDB President.[27] There is also the risk that it becomes difficult to garner sufficient support and attention for the bank from shareholders with dispersed interests.[28] Without one or two controlling shareholders, the required regional majorities are also influential, such as the European majority in the EBRD (including the EU and EIB) as well as the African majority in AfDB and the Asian majority in AsDB (both 60%).[29]

13.24 For the major decisions subject to qualified majorities as compared in Figure 9.4, large shareholders have a more obvious role. With decisions requiring a 75% or 85% majority, opposition by an individual shareholder or combination of shareholders with voting power of 25% or 15% can defeat a proposal, although it cannot assure passage without support from a considerable number of other shareholders. Thus, controlling majorities can have a substantial impact on an MDB's finances, policies and directions—indeed, they are designed to do just that. Most of the time, all of these majority requirements frame the options long before the matter is put to a vote, especially for institutions that often decide by seeking consensus rather than casting ballots.

13.25 China was the initiator of the AIIB proposal, and remains its largest shareholder. Its influence on AIIB is undeniable, and invites comparisons to the US influence on the World Bank—both have been the subject of considerable study, far beyond the focus of this book. In AIIB, China can block a list of important decisions (see

[27] There is still politics at play, among countries, but it is not in the form of hegemonic control. *See* Mingst (1990) at 19–24 for AfDB elections pre-1990.

[28] English and Mule (1996), at 2, noted that neither regionals nor non-regionals had given the AfDB priority: "This has been a mixed blessing. It has meant a relative freedom from attempts to influence lending policy, but also a low level of support from ministries back home and little involvement by governors." See Birdsall (2018) at 20, quoted in note 34 in this chapter.

[29] Paragraphs 6.31–6.32.

IBRD 6-26-25		AIIB 6-30-25	
Member	**Voting power %**	**Member**	**Voting power %**
US	15.79	China	26.52
Japan	7.00	India	7.57
China	5.85	Russia	5.95
Germany	4.16	Germany	4.14
France	3.82	Korea	3.48
UK	3.82	Australia	3.46
India	3.00	France	3.16
Russia	2.79	Indonesia	3.14
Saudi Arabia	2.71	UK	2.87
Italy	2.68	Türkiye	2.48
Canada	2.49	Italy	2.45
Brazil	1.89	Saudi Arabia	2.42

Figure 13.1 Comparison of Voting Power at IBRD and AIIB

Figure 9.2), including Charter amendments, changes in Board configuration, capital increases, and election of the President. The US can legally block one decision at IBRD (Charter amendment), and most likely block decisions on Board configuration and capital increases.[30] Neither the World Bank nor AIIB are controlled by the major shareholder, with the large block of voting power and influence held by other developed and developing countries leading to consensus decisions most of the time. Figure 13.1 compares the voting power of the twelve largest members in IBRD and AIIB.

In AIIB, the differences lie in the higher representation of developing countries in shareholding.

The balance of borrowing and non-borrowing shareholders is often considered relevant to how an MDB functions, notably when it comes to decisions on operational policies and particular projects. This, too, changes over time. At Bretton Woods, there were many potential borrowers among the forty-four negotiating teams, including much of Europe and twenty-eight countries from Latin America, Africa, and Asia.[31] Borrower perspectives influenced debates on some provisions, such as the proportion, timing, and use of hard currency paid-in capital. In fact, IBRD's first borrowers were France, the Netherlands, Denmark, and Luxembourg, before 13.26

[30] At IBRD, Charter amendment requires acceptance by three-fifths of the members holding an 85% majority of total voting power (IBRD Article VIII (a)). Capital increases require a 75% majority vote, and additions of Board seats require 80%. IBRD Article II, Section 2 (b). IBRD Article V, Section 4 (b). At IMF, there is a longer list of eleven decisions requiring an 85% majority vote, which the US can block. IMF Financial Operations 2018 at 161. US voting power in IBRD and IMF is around 16%.

[31] Helleiner (2014) at 13–14. The United Kingdom also borrowed but from the United States directly, on the eve of signing the IBRD Charter in 1945. Conway (2014) at 315, 323–33.

the US Marshall Plan (European Recovery Program) announced in 1947 gave much of Europe a better alternative.[32] Today, Europe and Japan (a significant IBRD borrower until 1966) have long since developed into principal financiers among IBRD shareholders; developing and transition countries (a proxy for borrowers) have held somewhat less than 50% of IBRD voting power.

13.27 IADB was initially known as the debtors' bank, starting as it did with nineteen Latin American countries and the United States; its early loans for social sectors contrasted with the operations of the World Bank at the time.[33] AfDB began with regional members only—most, if not all, with the potential to borrow. Its early struggles related to bringing in enough non-regional finance to meet their needs through concessional contributions, and eventually AfDB followed IADB in opening up to non-regional members and their capital. For each of them, the change took many years and involved significant effort to protect the regional nature of the institution, while bringing in non-regional funding and perspectives. For AfDB, the dominance of borrowing members has continued to have an effect on its financing.[34]

(6) Clients and operations

13.28 The development needs of an MDB's clients are fundamental to MDB operations. Changes in client needs, whether in financing terms, types of finance, priority sectors, or otherwise, have an impact on the MDB. Clients may also require advisory and other services beyond finance. Competition in the development field matters, too, as the lending terms and policy requirements of other sources of finance available to clients are highly relevant, whether public or private. For MDBs mandated to provide finance when private finance is not available on reasonable terms, that competition should be expected and welcomed.

13.29 The types of development finance can also change over time. IBRD, for instance, was set up principally to provide guarantees of loans by private investors, and only secondarily to provide direct loans to its borrowers, always with a government guarantee. Not only did the secondary purpose become its mainstay, but there was sufficient demand for loans without a government guarantee that an affiliate, the International Finance Corporation (IFC), was set up in 1956. Both IFC itself and later EIB subsequently added equity investment to their portfolio of permitted types of operation as well.[35] IADB also took the route of setting up an affiliate for

[32] Mason and Asher (1973) at 52, 150.
[33] Díaz-Bonilla and del Campo (2010) at 76, 81.
[34] Birdsall (2018) at 20 notes: "The dilemma of the African Development Bank is a structural one: its governance arrangements are not conducive to raising money to finance the Bank's activities. Borrowers have more votes on many operational decisions, and the presidency is held by a borrower; that makes it hard for the non-borrowers to take initiative on operational policies without working together; working together is hard because no single non-borrower or small group of non-borrowers has much skin in the game."
[35] *See* paragraph 5.17.

private sector finance, the Inter-American Investment Corporation (now known as IDB Invest).

For client needs that go beyond finance, IBRD over time set up two more affiliates to meet requests for additional support for members—within its mandate of promoting private foreign investment, but outside its particular functions. IBRD fostered the establishment of the International Centre for the Settlement of Investment Disputes (ICSID) in 1965 for investor-state dispute settlement, and the Multilateral Investment Guarantee Agency (MIGA) in 1988 for political risk insurance.[36] Together, IBRD and its separate affiliates (IDA, IFC, MIGA, and ICSID) function as the World Bank Group. **13.30**

AIIB has a built-in option to take on new types of development finance, in addition to its loans, guarantees, and equity operations. Nonetheless, changes in clients' financial needs and market financing trends can affect its future operations. **13.31**

(7) Leadership and governance

The histories of other MDBs also tell of the importance of leadership, particularly in the early years. For new MDBs, finding the right leadership and balance among the governing bodies has often taken some time. **13.32**

- IBRD had the most difficult task in many ways, being the first of its kind, and in a post-war situation. The first President (Eugene Meyer) was named only after the Inaugural Meeting of the Board of Governors and the first meetings of the Board of Executive Directors. He left after six months, frustrated with the unclear roles and tensions between the President and the Board. The next President (John J. McCloy) took up the position only after assurance that the President would have a clear and controlling hand in running the institution, yet resigned after two years. His successor (Eugene Black, the former US Executive Director) served for a continuous thirteen years, putting the leadership on a sound footing.[37]
- EBRD's first President (Jacques Attali) had been on board from his bank's inception and had served as its President-Designate. Yet his tenure too proved short and controversial, and he resigned some two years after the bank formally opened. His successor (Jacques de Larosière) put in place a foundation for less tumultuous and more productive decades to follow.[38]
- At AfDB, the first President elected in 1964 (Mamoun Beheiry) had been a leading member of the preparatory Committee of Nine, and thus was well

[36] For the establishment of ICSID, *see* Parra (2017). For the establishment of MIGA, *see* Shihata (1988).
[37] Mason and Asher (1973) at 40–52, 62–3.
[38] Erik Ipsen, "Criticism drives Attali from European Bank," *New York Times*, June 26, 1993 and Bronstone (1999) at 73–6 on de Larosière.

versed in the negotiating history and issues. Although re-elected in 1970, he resigned shortly thereafter, faced with a motion of censure by the Board of Directors. Controversies between the Board and the President and difficulties resolving the highly contested elections for President continued for some years thereafter.[39]

- For AsDB, familiarity with the institution proved beneficial: the first President (Takeshi Watanabe) had been among the leaders in its creation, and helped it to a fruitful beginning during his six-year tenure.[40]
- At IADB, the first President (Felipe Herrera), who led the bank from its start in 1959, had been involved in the negotiations as well. A long and highly positive tenure came to a close with his resignation in 1970 following his support for the socialist government elected in Chile, his home country—thus avoiding a Cold War conflict with the United States, the Bank's major shareholder.[41]

As discussed in more detail in Chapter 8,[42] geopolitics has played a role in leadership decisions, backed by the voting power of major shareholders. There has been an unwritten and unbroken tradition of US nationals serving as President of the World Bank, Europeans serving as IMF Managing Director, Japanese at the helm of the AsDB, and Europeans as President of EBRD. As of this writing, that tradition has persisted, even after the introduction of more competitive selection processes at IBRD, IMF, and EBRD; in AIIB, AfDB, and AsDB, the President must be a national of a regional member.

13.33 AIIB has had rather a calmer start than some, following the trend of having a President who played a key role in its development and served in management and governing bodies at other MDBs. As of mid-2025, AIIB was on the cusp of a leadership transition, as President Jin reaches the end of his two-term limit in January 2026. Madame Zou Jiayi was elected in June 2025 at AIIB's 10th Annual Meeting as the next AIIB President. Madame Zou, a former Chinese Vice-Minister of Finance, also played a role in AIIB's creation in 2014, and spent several years at the World Bank Board (including as Executive Director and Co-Dean of the Board). Her more recent positions have been at senior levels in Chinese government and political bodies (including anti-corruption).[43]

13.34 The other MDB experiences outlined above may still be instructive for AIIB in highlighting the centrality of productive governance relationships. Importantly, tensions between Board and management can plague an institution, as the IBRD

[39] English and Mule (1996) at 23–4.

[40] *See* Wilson (1987), throughout Chapter 2, "The Birth of the Bank" and Chapter 3, "The Family Doctor: The Watanabe Years 1966–72."

[41] Díaz-Bonilla and del Campo (2010) at 77 and 85.

[42] *See* paragraphs 8.31–8.33.

[43] "China Nominated Madam ZOU Jiayi as the Candidate for AIIB's Next President," Ministry of Finance of the People's Republic of China press release, March 31, 2025, https://www.mof.gov.cn/en/news/mn/202503/t20250331_3961143.htm.

story shows acutely and the AfDB tale obliquely. Here, AIIB's non-resident board structure may offer different advantages and disadvantages, as modern communications and ways of doing business have an impact on relationships and interactions.

(8) Attitudes toward change

Delving into MDB Charters reveals that there are different histories of Charter interpretation and amendment, which may reflect an organization's handling of change. **13.35**

- At IBRD, amendment is infrequent: three times in eighty years, to authorize lending to IFC, increase the majority for Charter amendment (maintaining the US veto), and increase basic votes. In 2025, a fourth amendment is in process to remove the statutory lending limit.
- At AsDB, amendment has never taken place. However, in 2025, an amendment is in process to remove the statutory lending limit.

In both cases, there is a premium on using interpretation to accommodate new directions and practices. IBRD has never amended its Charter to change outdated provisions, such as the Advisory Council or the 1944 gold dollar.[44]

- EBRD had three amendments in its first twenty-five years, all connected to the inclusion of new countries of operation. In 2025, two amendments took effect, one to expand countries of operation and the other to revise the statutory lending limit.[45]

While the wording changes brought in by the IBRD and EBRD amendments were limited, their significance was considerable.[46]

At the other end of the spectrum, we can see that IADB, AfDB, and IMF have had five or more Charter amendments throughout their history, some extensive.[47] In many cases these amendments brought far-reaching changes in the institution, such as the introduction of non-regional membership and capital into IADB and AfDB and the creation of the Special Drawing Right and the end of fixed exchange rates for IMF. Others appear less broad in impact, but reflected other laudable goals, such as AfDB's harmonization with other Charters. **13.36**

What accounts for the difference? True, some changes are impossible to achieve through interpretation, even though the Board of Directors' power of interpretation **13.37**

[44] *See* note 61 in Chapter 9 on the Advisory Council and paragraph 7.08 on the 1944 gold dollar.
[45] *See* paragraph 11.07.
[46] *See* paragraph 7.44 for the amendments pending in 2025.
[47] *See* paragraph 9.06.

is broad.[48] Perhaps it is simply that IBRD, AsDB, and EBRD have found other solutions in lieu of such changes (such as the creation of IFC and IDA as separate entities). Other factors discouraging amendments could be the difficulty of getting amendments agreed by shareholders through domestic approval processes, especially when there are clear veto holders. Perhaps another influence stems from the prevailing legal culture in each institution or its driving shareholders. Institutions with strong civil law traditions, such as in Latin America (IADB), parts of Africa (AfDB), and Europe (IMF), could favor amendment over expansive interpretation. The common law tradition of interpretation of precedents might, conversely, play a greater role in the Anglo-American influenced IBRD; AsDB seems to have followed that tradition.

13.38 The AIIB Charter exhibits the influence of perspectives from the World Bank and AsDB history, as evidenced by the numerous provisions that permit change without amendment. Rather than requiring creative lawyering to fit within a tight Charter, many AIIB clauses redirect the question to the shareholders, to decide whether the proposed change or exception is the right thing for AIIB to do considering its purpose and functions.[49] Whether AIIB makes use of this inherent flexibility or soon finds itself faced with Charter changes remains to be seen.

B. AIIB's Future

13.39 These themes from the experiences of other MDBs reflect particular combinations of parties and purposes, amply demonstrating that the same Charter provisions play out differently in different institutions. Moreover, some of these earlier experiences bespeak an MDB context of a different century, possibly worlds away from the times and places in which AIIB's future will be told.

13.40 What might AIIB's first decade portend for its future? Summing up, AIIB's development and results in a difficult time have been quite good. Indeed, the record is better than one might have anticipated in light of the perils faced by AIIB's predecessors in their early years, or concerns at its founding about a new MDB, with a new major shareholder.[50]

- Its investment operations have grown steadily, and reflect a mix of MDB co-financing as well as more innovative structures, including in private sector mobilization.

[48] Shihata (2000), at liii, attributes the introduction of changes at IMF through extensive formal amendments to its broad regulatory powers and the recognition of the impact of changes in its mandate or operations in the jurisdictions of its members.
[49] *See* paragraphs 3.52–3.53.
[50] *See* paragraphs 3.22–3.24.

- The near doubling of membership (now 110) indicates that countries perceive benefits from joining AIIB. Some may see economic benefits, as many of AIIB's new members since 2017 have been potential borrowers.[51] Others may attribute this growth to political factors, especially China's international influence. Some other MDBs have also been adding members in recent years, though not on the same scale.[52]
- AIIB's financial standing has been consistently strong. With its AAA ratings, AIIB has raised over US$54 billion in twenty currencies. Since 2022, operating income has covered administrative expenses, and in 2024, AIIB reported a profit of US$1.1 billion.[53]
- Institutionally, the step by step evolution of AIIB's governance framework has taken advantage of AIIB's unique combination of features (non-resident Board, Oversight Mechanism, delegation, and accountability). At the same time, these features call for continuous adaptation in ensuring that the non-resident Board continues to play its desired role as AIIB membership and operations expand.
- AIIB's 700 staff from more than seventy economies recall its Charter provision on employment, seeking the highest standards of efficiency and technical competence on as wide a geographical basis as possible.[54] Here, too, continuous adaptation will likely be needed to meet the challenges for staff and their families in AIIB's office locations, both Beijing and now other offices.

In short, the first decade should give AIIB a solid base as it moves forward.

Still, the lessons of history remain. Will the global economic environment favor multilateralism and infrastructure development, or make it more difficult? Will changes in membership come to change AIIB? Will AIIB client needs lead to financing structures yet unimagined? More broadly, how will the latest heir of that unique joint-stock company cum international organization created in 1930 (BIS) function one hundred years later? Where AIIB will end up in the history of international financial institutions is a story that is unfolding, and one that bears watching. **13.41**

[51] *See* note 17 in Chapter 6 listing non-regional developing country members.
[52] *See* paragraphs 6.41–6.43.
[53] "Annual Meeting Opening Remarks by AIIB President Jin Liqun, AIIB President and Chair of the Board of Directors, June 26, 2025," AIIB Press Release, July 4, 2025.
[54] AIIB Article 30-3.

APPENDIX 1

Articles of Agreement of the Asian Infrastructure Investment Bank

June 29, 2015

The countries on whose behalf the present Agreement is signed agree as follows:

CONSIDERING the importance of regional cooperation to sustain growth and promote economic and social development of the economies in Asia and thereby contribute to regional resilience against potential financial crises and other external shocks in the context of globalization;

ACKNOWLEDGING the significance of infrastructure development in expanding regional connectivity and improving regional integration, thereby promoting economic growth and sustaining social development for the people in Asia, and contributing to global economic dynamism;

REALIZING that the considerable long-term need for financing infrastructure development in Asia will be met more adequately by a partnership among existing multilateral development banks and the Asian Infrastructure Investment Bank (hereinafter referred to as the "Bank");

CONVINCED that the establishment of the Bank as a multilateral financial institution focused on infrastructure development will help to mobilize much needed additional resources from inside and outside Asia and to remove the financing bottlenecks faced by the individual economies in Asia, and will complement the existing multilateral development banks, to promote sustained and stable growth in Asia;

HAVE AGREED to establish the Bank, which shall operate in accordance with the following:

Chapter I Purpose, Functions and Membership

Article 1 Purpose

1. The purpose of the Bank shall be to: (i) foster sustainable economic development, create wealth and improve infrastructure connectivity in Asia by investing in infrastructure and other productive sectors; and (ii) promote regional cooperation and partnership in addressing development challenges by working in close collaboration with other multilateral and bilateral development institutions.
2. Wherever used in this Agreement, references to "Asia" and "region" shall include the geographical regions and composition classified as Asia and Oceania by the United Nations, except as otherwise decided by the Board of Governors.

Article 2 Functions

To implement its purpose, the Bank shall have the following functions:

(i) to promote investment in the region of public and private capital for development purposes, in particular for development of infrastructure and other productive sectors;
(ii) to utilize the resources at its disposal for financing such development in the region, including those projects and programs which will contribute most effectively to the

harmonious economic growth of the region as a whole and having special regard to the needs of less developed members in the region;

(iii) to encourage private investment in projects, enterprises and activities contributing to economic development in the region, in particular in infrastructure and other productive sectors, and to supplement private investment when private capital is not available on reasonable terms and conditions; and

(iv) to undertake such other activities and provide such other services as may further these functions.

Article 3 Membership

1. Membership in the Bank shall be open to members of the International Bank for Reconstruction and Development or the Asian Development Bank.
   (a) Regional members shall be those members listed in Part A of Schedule A and other members included in the Asia region in accordance with paragraph 2 of Article 1. All other members shall be non-regional members.
   (b) Founding Members shall be those members listed in Schedule A which, on or before the date specified in Article 57, shall have signed this Agreement and shall have fulfilled all other conditions of membership before the final date specified under paragraph 1 of Article 58.
2. Members of the International Bank for Reconstruction and Development or the Asian Development Bank which do not become members in accordance with Article 58 may be admitted, under such terms and conditions as the Bank shall determine, to membership in the Bank by a Special Majority vote of the Board of Governors as provided in Article 28.
3. In the case of an applicant which is not sovereign or not responsible for the conduct of its international relations, application for membership in the Bank shall be presented or agreed by the member of the Bank responsible for its international relations.

Chapter II Capital

Article 4 Authorized Capital

1. The authorized capital stock of the Bank shall be one hundred billion United States dollars ($100,000,000,000), divided into one million (1,000,000) shares having a par value of 100,000 dollars ($100,000) each, which shall be available for subscription only by members in accordance with the provisions of Article 5.
2. The original authorized capital stock shall be divided into paid-in shares and callable shares. Shares having an aggregate par value of twenty billion dollars ($20,000,000,000) shall be paid-in shares, and shares having an aggregate par value of eighty billion dollars ($80,000,000,000) shall be callable.
3. The authorized capital stock of the Bank may be increased by the Board of Governors by a Super Majority vote as provided in Article 28, at such time and under such terms and conditions as it may deem advisable, including the proportion between paid-in and callable shares.
4. The term "dollar" and the symbol "$" wherever used in this Agreement shall be understood as being the official currency of payment of the United States of America.

Article 5 Subscription of Shares

1. Each member shall subscribe to shares of the capital stock of the Bank. Each subscription to the original authorized capital stock shall be for paid-in shares and callable shares in the

proportion two (2) to eight (8). The initial number of shares available to be subscribed by countries which become members in accordance with Article 58 shall be that set forth in Schedule A.

2. The initial number of shares to be subscribed by countries which are admitted to membership in accordance with paragraph 2 of Article 3 shall be determined by the Board of Governors; provided, however, that no such subscription shall be authorized which would have the effect of reducing the percentage of capital stock held by regional members below seventy-five (75) per cent of the total subscribed capital stock, unless otherwise agreed by the Board of Governors by a Super Majority vote as provided in Article 28.
3. The Board of Governors may, at the request of a member, increase the subscription of such member on such terms and conditions as the Board may determine by a Super Majority vote as provided in Article 28; provided, however, that no such increase in the subscription of any member shall be authorized which would have the effect of reducing the percentage of capital stock held by regional members below seventy-five (75) per cent of the total subscribed capital stock, unless otherwise agreed by the Board of Governors by a Super Majority vote as provided in Article 28.
4. The Board of Governors shall at intervals of not more than five (5) years review the capital stock of the Bank. In case of an increase in the authorized capital stock, each member shall have a reasonable opportunity to subscribe, under such terms and conditions as the Board of Governors shall determine, to a proportion of the increase of stock equivalent to the proportion which its stock theretofore subscribed bears to the total subscribed capital stock immediately prior to such increase. No member shall be obligated to subscribe to any part of an increase of capital stock.

Article 6 Payment of Subscriptions

1. Payment of the amount initially subscribed by each Signatory to this Agreement which becomes a member in accordance with Article 58 to the paid-in capital stock of the Bank shall be made in five (5) installments, of twenty (20) per cent each of such amount, except as provided in paragraph 5 of this Article. The first installment shall be paid by each member within thirty (30) days after entry into force of this Agreement, or on or before the date of deposit on its behalf of its instrument of ratification, acceptance or approval in accordance with paragraph 1 of Article 58, whichever is later. The second installment shall become due one (1) year from the entry into force of this Agreement. The remaining three (3) installments shall become due successively one (1) year from the date on which the preceding installment becomes due.
2. Each installment of the payment of initial subscriptions to the original paid-in capital stock shall be paid in dollars or other convertible currency, except as provided in paragraph 5 of this Article. The Bank may at any time convert such payments into dollars. All rights, including voting rights, acquired in respect of paid-in and associated callable shares for which such payments are due but have not been received shall be suspended until full payment is received by the Bank.
3. Payment of the amount subscribed to the callable capital stock of the Bank shall be subject to call only as and when required by the Bank to meet its liabilities. In the event of such a call, payment may be made at the option of the member in dollars or in the currency required to discharge the obligations of the Bank for the purpose of which the call is made. Calls on unpaid subscriptions shall be uniform in percentage on all callable shares.
4. The Bank shall determine the place for any payment under this Article, provided that, until the inaugural meeting of the Board of Governors, the payment of the first installment referred to in paragraph 1 of this Article shall be made to the Government of the People's Republic of China, as Trustee for the Bank.

5. A member considered as a less developed country for purposes of this paragraph may pay its subscription under paragraphs 1 and 2 of this Article, as an alternative, either:
   (a) entirely in dollars or other convertible currency in up to ten (10) installments, with each such installment equal to ten (10) percent of the total amount, the first and second installments due as provided in paragraph 1, and the third through tenth installments due on the second and subsequent anniversary dates of the entry into force of this Agreement; or
   (b) with a portion in dollars or other convertible currency and a portion of up to fifty (50) per cent of each installment in the currency of the member, following the schedule of installments provided in paragraph 1 of this Article. The following provisions shall apply to payments under this sub-paragraph (b):
      (i) The member shall advise the Bank at the time of subscription under paragraph 1 of this Article of the proportion of payments to be made in its own currency.
      (ii) Each payment of a member in its own currency under this paragraph 5 shall be in such amount as the Bank determines to be equivalent to the full value in terms of dollars of the portion of the subscription being paid. The initial payment shall be in such amount as the member considers appropriate hereunder but shall be subject to such adjustment, to be effected within ninety (90) days of the date on which such payment was due, as the Bank shall determine to be necessary to constitute the full dollar equivalent of such payment.
      (iii) Whenever in the opinion of the Bank, the foreign exchange value of a member's currency has depreciated to a significant extent, that member shall pay to the Bank within a reasonable time an additional amount of its currency required to maintain the value of all such currency held by the Bank on account of its subscription.
      (iv) Whenever in the opinion of the Bank, the foreign exchange value of a member's currency has appreciated to a significant extent, the Bank shall pay to that member within a reasonable time an amount of that currency required to adjust the value of all such currency held by the Bank on account of its subscription.
      (v) The Bank may waive its rights to payment under sub-paragraph (iii) and the member may waive its rights to payment under sub-paragraph (iv).
6. The Bank shall accept from any member paying its subscription under sub-paragraph 5(b) of this Article promissory notes or other obligations issued by the Government of the member, or by the depository designated by such member, in lieu of the amount to be paid in the currency of the member, provided such amount is not required by the Bank for the conduct of its operations. Such notes or obligations shall be non-negotiable, non-interest-bearing, and payable to the Bank at par value upon demand.

Article 7 Terms of Shares

1. Shares of stock initially subscribed by members shall be issued at par. Other shares shall be issued at par unless the Board of Governors by a Special Majority vote as provided in Article 28 decides in special circumstances to issue them on other terms.
2. Shares of stock shall not be pledged or encumbered in any manner whatsoever, and they shall be transferable only to the Bank.
3. The liability of the members on shares shall be limited to the unpaid portion of their issue price.
4. No member shall be liable, by reason of its membership, for obligations of the Bank.

Article 8 Ordinary Resources

As used in this Agreement, the term "ordinary resources" of the Bank shall include the following:

(i) authorized capital stock of the Bank, including both paid-in and callable shares, subscribed pursuant to Article 5;
(ii) funds raised by the Bank by virtue of powers conferred by paragraph 1 of Article 16, to which the commitment to calls provided for in paragraph 3 of Article 6 is applicable;
(iii) funds received in repayment of loans or guarantees made with the resources indicated in sub-paragraphs (i) and (ii) of this Article or as returns on equity investments and other types of financing approved under sub-paragraph 2 (vi) of Article 11 made with such resources;
(iv) income derived from loans made from the aforementioned funds or from guarantees to which the commitment to calls set forth in paragraph 3 of Article 6 is applicable; and
(v) any other funds or income received by the Bank which do not form part of its Special Funds resources referred to in Article 17 of this Agreement.

Chapter III Operations of the Bank

Article 9 Use of Resources

The resources and facilities of the Bank shall be used exclusively to implement the purpose and functions set forth, respectively, in Articles 1 and 2, and in accordance with sound banking principles.

Article 10 Ordinary and Special Operations

1. The operations of the Bank shall consist of:
   (i) ordinary operations financed from the ordinary resources of the Bank, referred to in Article 8; and
   (ii) special operations financed from the Special Funds resources referred to in Article 17.

The two types of operations may separately finance elements of the same project or program.

2. The ordinary resources and the Special Funds resources of the Bank shall at all times and in all respects be held, used, committed, invested or otherwise disposed of entirely separately from each other. The financial statements of the Bank shall show the ordinary operations and special operations separately.
3. The ordinary resources of the Bank shall, under no circumstances, be charged with, or used to discharge, losses or liabilities arising out of special operations or other activities for which Special Funds resources were originally used or committed.
4. Expenses appertaining directly to ordinary operations shall be charged to the ordinary resources of the Bank. Expenses appertaining directly to special operations shall be charged to the Special Funds resources. Any other expenses shall be charged as the Bank shall determine.

Article 11 Recipients and Methods of Operation

1. (a) The Bank may provide or facilitate financing to any member, or any agency, instrumentality or political subdivision thereof, or any entity or enterprise operating in the territory of a member, as well as to international or regional agencies or entities concerned with economic development of the region.

(b) The Bank may, in special circumstances, provide assistance to a recipient not listed in sub-paragraph (a) above only if the Board of Governors, by a Super Majority vote as provided in Article 28: (i) shall have determined that such assistance is designed to serve the purpose and come within the functions of the Bank and is in the interest of the Bank's membership; and (ii) shall have specified the types of assistance under paragraph 2 of this Article that may be provided to such recipient.

2. The Bank may carry out its operations in any of the following ways:
   (i) by making, co-financing or participating in direct loans;
   (ii) by investment of funds in the equity capital of an institution or enterprise;
   (iii) by guaranteeing, whether as primary or secondary obligor, in whole or in part, loans for economic development;
   (iv) by deploying Special Funds resources in accordance with the agreements determining their use;
   (v) by providing technical assistance in accordance with Article 15; or
   (vi) through other types of financing as may be determined by the Board of Governors, by a Special Majority vote as provided in Article 28.

Article 12 Limitations on Ordinary Operations

1. The total amount outstanding of loans, equity investments, guarantees and other types of financing provided by the Bank in its ordinary operations under sub-paragraphs 2 (i), (ii), (iii) and (vi) of Article 11 shall not at any time be increased, if by such increase the total amount of its unimpaired subscribed capital, reserves and retained earnings included in its ordinary resources would be exceeded. Notwithstanding the provisions of the preceding sentence, the Board of Governors may, by a Super Majority vote as provided in Article 28, determine at any time that, based on the Bank's financial position and financial standing, the limitation under this paragraph may be increased, up to 250% of the Bank's unimpaired subscribed capital, reserves and retained earnings included in its ordinary resources.
2. The amount of the Bank's disbursed equity investments shall not at any time exceed an amount corresponding to its total unimpaired paid-in subscribed capital and general reserves.

Article 13 Operating Principles

The operations of the Bank shall be conducted in accordance with the principles set out below.

1. The Bank shall be guided by sound banking principles in its operations.
2. The operations of the Bank shall provide principally for the financing of specific projects or specific investment programs, for equity investment, and for technical assistance in accordance with Article 15.
3. The Bank shall not finance any undertaking in the territory of a member if that member objects to such financing.
4. The Bank shall ensure that each of its operations complies with the Bank's operational and financial policies, including without limitation, policies addressing environmental and social impacts.
5. In considering an application for financing, the Bank shall pay due regard to the ability of the recipient to obtain financing or facilities elsewhere on terms and conditions that the Bank considers reasonable for the recipient, taking into account all pertinent factors.
6. In providing or guaranteeing financing, the Bank shall pay due regard to the prospects that the recipient and guarantor, if any, will be in a position to meet their obligations under the financing contract.

7. In providing or guaranteeing financing, the financial terms, such as rate of interest and other charges and the schedule for repayment of principal shall be such as are, in the opinion of the Bank, appropriate for the financing concerned and the risk to the Bank.
8. The Bank shall place no restriction upon the procurement of goods and services from any country from the proceeds of any financing undertaken in the ordinary or special operations of the Bank.
9. The Bank shall take the necessary measures to ensure that the proceeds of any financing provided, guaranteed or participated in by the Bank are used only for the purposes for which the financing was granted and with due attention to considerations of economy and efficiency.
10. The Bank shall pay due regard to the desirability of avoiding a disproportionate amount of its resources being used for the benefit of any member.
11. The Bank shall seek to maintain reasonable diversification in its investments in equity capital. In its equity investments, the Bank shall not assume responsibility for managing any entity or enterprise in which it has an investment and shall not seek a controlling interest in the entity or enterprise concerned, except where necessary to safeguard the investment of the Bank.

Article 14 Terms and Conditions for Financing

1. In the case of loans made or participated in or loans guaranteed by the Bank, the contract shall establish, in conformity with the operating principles set forth in Article 13 and subject to the other provisions of this Agreement, the terms and conditions for the loan or the guarantee concerned. In setting such terms and conditions, the Bank shall take fully into account the need to safeguard its income and financial position.
2. Where the recipient of loans or guarantees of loans is not itself a member, the Bank may, when it deems it advisable, require that the member in whose territory the project concerned is to be carried out, or a public agency or any instrumentality of that member acceptable to the Bank, guarantee the repayment of the principal and the payment of interest and other charges on the loan in accordance with the terms thereof.
3. The amount of any equity investment shall not exceed such percentage of the equity capital of the entity or enterprise concerned as permitted under policies approved by the Board of Directors.
4. The Bank may provide financing in its operations in the currency of the country concerned, in accordance with policies that minimize currency risk.

Article 15 Technical Assistance

1. The Bank may provide technical advice and assistance and other similar forms of assistance which serve its purpose and come within its functions.
2. Where expenditures incurred in furnishing such services are not reimbursable, the Bank shall charge such expenditures to the income of the Bank.

Chapter IV Finances of the Bank

Article 16 General Powers

In addition to the powers specified elsewhere in this Agreement, the Bank shall have the powers set out below.

1. The Bank may raise funds, through borrowing or other means, in member countries or elsewhere, in accordance with the relevant legal provisions.

2. The Bank may buy and sell securities the Bank has issued or guaranteed or in which it has invested.
3. The Bank may guarantee securities in which it has invested in order to facilitate their sale.
4. The Bank may underwrite, or participate in the underwriting of, securities issued by any entity or enterprise for purposes consistent with the purpose of the Bank.
5. The Bank may invest or deposit funds not needed in its operations.
6. The Bank shall ensure that every security issued or guaranteed by the Bank shall bear on its face a conspicuous statement to the effect that it is not an obligation of any Government, unless it is in fact the obligation of a particular Government, in which case it shall so state.
7. The Bank may establish and administer funds held in trust for other parties, provided such trust funds are designed to serve the purpose and come within the functions of the Bank, under a trust fund framework which shall have been approved by the Board of Governors.
8. The Bank may establish subsidiary entities which are designed to serve the purpose and come within the functions of the Bank, only with the approval of the Board of Governors by a Special Majority vote as provided in Article 28.
9. The Bank may exercise such other powers and establish such rules and regulations as may be necessary or appropriate in furtherance of its purpose and functions, consistent with the provisions of this Agreement.

Article 17 Special Funds

1. The Bank may accept Special Funds which are designed to serve the purpose and come within the functions of the Bank; such Special Funds shall be resources of the Bank. The full cost of administering any Special Fund shall be charged to that Special Fund.
2. Special Funds accepted by the Bank may be used on terms and conditions consistent with the purpose and functions of the Bank and with the agreement relating to such Funds.
3. The Bank shall adopt such special rules and regulations as may be required for the establishment, administration and use of each Special Fund. Such rules and regulations shall be consistent with the provisions of this Agreement, except for those provisions expressly applicable only to ordinary operations of the Bank.
4. The term "Special Funds resources" shall refer to the resources of any Special Fund and shall include:
   (i) funds accepted by the Bank for inclusion in any Special Fund;
   (ii) funds received in respect of loans or guarantees, and the proceeds of any equity investments, financed from the resources of any Special Fund which, under the rules and regulations of the Bank governing that Special Fund, are received by such Special Fund;
   (iii) income derived from investment of Special Funds resources; and
   (iv) any other resources placed at the disposal of any Special Fund.

Article 18 Allocation and Distribution of Net Income

1. The Board of Governors shall determine at least annually what part of the net income of the Bank shall be allocated, after making provision for reserves, to retained earnings or other purposes and what part, if any, shall be distributed to the members. Any such decision on the allocation of the Bank's net income to other purposes shall be taken by a Super Majority vote as provided in Article 28.
2. The distribution referred to in the preceding paragraph shall be made in proportion to the number of shares held by each member, and payments shall be made in such manner and in such currency as the Board of Governors shall determine.

Article 19 Currencies

1. Members shall not impose any restrictions on currencies, including the receipt, holding, use or transfer by the Bank or by any recipient from the Bank, for payments in any country.
2. Whenever it shall become necessary under this Agreement to value any currency in terms of another or determine whether any currency is convertible, such valuation or determination shall be made by the Bank.

Article 20 Methods of Meeting Liabilities of the Bank

1. In the Bank's ordinary operations, in cases of arrears or default on loans made, participated in, or guaranteed by the Bank, and in cases of losses on equity investment or other types of financing under sub-paragraph 2 (vi) of Article 11, the Bank shall take such action as it deems appropriate. The Bank shall maintain appropriate provisions against possible losses.
2. Losses arising in the Bank's ordinary operations shall be charged:
   (i) first, to the provisions referred to in paragraph 1 above;
   (ii) second, to net income;
   (iii) third, against reserves and retained earnings;
   (iv) fourth, against unimpaired paid-in capital; and
   (v) last, against an appropriate amount of the uncalled subscribed callable capital which shall be called in accordance with the provisions of paragraph 3 of Article 6.

Chapter V Governance

Article 21 Structure

The Bank shall have a Board of Governors, a Board of Directors, a President, one or more Vice-Presidents, and such other officers and staff as may be considered necessary.

Article 22 Board of Governors: Composition

1. Each member shall be represented on the Board of Governors and shall appoint one Governor and one Alternate Governor. Each Governor and Alternate Governor shall serve at the pleasure of the appointing member. No Alternate Governor may vote except in the absence of his principal.
2. At each of its annual meetings, the Board shall elect one of the Governors as Chairman who shall hold office until the election of the next Chairman.
3. Governors and Alternate Governors shall serve as such without remuneration from the Bank, but the Bank may pay them reasonable expenses incurred in attending meetings.

Article 23 Board of Governors: Powers

1. All the powers of the Bank shall be vested in the Board of Governors.
2. The Board of Governors may delegate to the Board of Directors any or all its powers, except the power to:
   (i) admit new members and determine the conditions of their admission;
   (ii) increase or decrease the authorized capital stock of the Bank;
   (iii) suspend a member;

(iv) decide appeals from interpretations or applications of this Agreement given by the Board of Directors;
(v) elect the Directors of the Bank and determine the expenses to be paid for Directors and Alternate Directors and remuneration, if any, pursuant to paragraph 6 of Article 25;
(vi) elect the President, suspend or remove him from office, and determine his remuneration and other conditions of service;
(vii) approve, after reviewing the auditors' report, the general balance sheet and the statement of profit and loss of the Bank;
(viii) determine the reserves and the allocation and distribution of the net profits of the Bank;
(ix) amend this Agreement;
(x) decide to terminate the operations of the Bank and to distribute its assets; and
(xi) exercise such other powers as are expressly assigned to the Board of Governors in this Agreement.

3. The Board of Governors shall retain full power to exercise authority over any matter delegated to the Board of Directors under paragraph 2 of this Article.

Article 24 Board of Governors: Procedure

1. The Board of Governors shall hold an annual meeting and such other meetings as may be provided for by the Board of Governors or called by the Board of Directors. Meetings of the Board of Governors shall be called by the Board of Directors whenever requested by five (5) members of the Bank.
2. A majority of the Governors shall constitute a quorum for any meeting of the Board of Governors, provided such majority represents not less than two-thirds of the total voting power of the members.
3. The Board of Governors shall by regulation establish procedures whereby the Board of Directors may obtain a vote of the Governors on a specific question without a meeting and provide for electronic meetings of the Board of Governors in special circumstances.
4. The Board of Governors, and the Board of Directors to the extent authorized, may establish such subsidiary entities, and adopt such rules and regulations, as may be necessary or appropriate to conduct the business of the Bank.

Article 25 Board of Directors: Composition

1. The Board of Directors shall be composed of twelve (12) members who shall not be members of the Board of Governors, and of whom:
   (i) nine (9) shall be elected by the Governors representing regional members; and
   (ii) three (3) shall be elected by the Governors representing non-regional members.

Directors shall be persons of high competence in economic and financial matters and shall be elected in accordance with Schedule B. Directors shall represent members whose Governors have elected them as well as members whose Governors assign their votes to them.

2. The Board of Governors shall, from time to time, review the size and composition of the Board of Directors, and may increase or decrease the size or revise the composition as appropriate, by a Super Majority vote as provided in Article 28.
3. Each Director shall appoint an Alternate Director with full power to act for him when he is not present. The Board of Governors shall adopt rules enabling a Director elected by more than a specified number of members to appoint an additional Alternate Director.
4. Directors and Alternate Directors shall be nationals of member countries. No two or more Directors may be of the same nationality nor may any two or more Alternate Directors be of

the same nationality. Alternate Directors may participate in meetings of the Board but may vote only when the Alternate Director is acting in place of the Director.

5. Directors shall hold office for a term of two (2) years and may be re-elected.
   (a) Directors shall continue in office until their successors shall have been chosen and assumed office.
   (b) If the office of a Director becomes vacant more than one hundred and eighty (180) days before the end of his term, a successor shall be chosen in accordance with Schedule B, for the remainder of the term, by the Governors who elected the former Director. A majority of the votes cast by such Governors shall be required for such election. The Governors who elected a Director may similarly choose a successor if the office of a Director becomes vacant one hundred and eighty (180) days or less before the end of his term.
   (c) While the office of a Director remains vacant, an Alternate Director of the former Director shall exercise the powers of the latter, except that of appointing an Alternate Director.
6. Directors and Alternate Directors shall serve without remuneration from the Bank, unless the Board of Governors shall decide otherwise, but the Bank may pay them reasonable expenses incurred in attending meetings.

Article 26 Board of Directors: Powers

The Board of Directors shall be responsible for the direction of the general operations of the Bank and, for this purpose, shall, in addition to the powers assigned to it expressly by this Agreement, exercise all the powers delegated to it by the Board of Governors, and in particular:

(i) prepare the work of the Board of Governors;
(ii) establish the policies of the Bank, and, by a majority representing not less than three-fourths of the total voting power of the members, take decisions on major operational and financial policies and on delegation of authority to the President under Bank policies;
(iii) take decisions concerning operations of the Bank under paragraph 2 of Article 11, and, by a majority representing not less than three-fourths of the total voting power of the members, decide on the delegation of such authority to the President;
(iv) supervise the management and the operation of the Bank on a regular basis, and establish an oversight mechanism for that purpose, in line with principles of transparency, openness, independence and accountability;
(v) approve the strategy, annual plan and budget of the Bank;
(vi) appoint such committees as deemed advisable; and
(vii) submit the audited accounts for each financial year for approval of the Board of Governors.

Article 27 Board of Directors: Procedure

1. The Board of Directors shall meet as often as the business of the Bank may require, periodically throughout the year. The Board of Directors shall function on a non-resident basis except as otherwise decided by the Board of Governors by a Super Majority vote as provided in Article 28. Meetings may be called by the Chairman or whenever requested by three (3) Directors.
2. A majority of the Directors shall constitute a quorum for any meeting of the Board of Directors, provided such majority represents not less than two-thirds of the total voting power of the members.

3. The Board of Governors shall adopt regulations under which, if there is no Director of its nationality, a member may send a representative to attend, without right to vote, any meeting of the Board of Directors when a matter particularly affecting that member is under consideration.
4. The Board of Directors shall establish procedures whereby the Board can hold an electronic meeting or vote on a matter without holding a meeting.

Article 28 Voting

1. The total voting power of each member shall consist of the sum of its basic votes, share votes and, in the case of a Founding Member, its Founding Member votes.
   (i) The basic votes of each member shall be the number of votes that results from the equal distribution among all the members of twelve (12) per cent of the aggregate sum of the basic votes, share votes and Founding Member votes of all the members.
   (ii) The number of the share votes of each member shall be equal to the number of shares of the capital stock of the Bank held by that member.
   (iii) Each Founding Member shall be allocated six hundred (600) Founding Member votes.

In the event a member fails to pay any part of the amount due in respect of its obligations in relation to paid-in shares under Article 6, the number of share votes to be exercised by the member shall, as long as such failure continues, be reduced proportionately, by the percentage which the amount due and unpaid represents of the total par value of paid-in shares subscribed to by that member.

2. In voting in the Board of Governors, each Governor shall be entitled to cast the votes of the member he represents.
   (i) Except as otherwise expressly provided in this Agreement, all matters before the Board of Governors shall be decided by a majority of the votes cast.
   (ii) A Super Majority vote of the Board of Governors shall require an affirmative vote of two-thirds of the total number of Governors, representing not less than three-fourths of the total voting power of the members.
   (iii) A Special Majority vote of the Board of Governors shall require an affirmative vote of a majority of the total number of Governors, representing not less than a majority of the total voting power of the members.
3. In voting in the Board of Directors, each Director shall be entitled to cast the number of votes to which the Governors who elected him are entitled and those to which any Governors who have assigned their votes to him, pursuant to Schedule B, are entitled.
   (i) A Director entitled to cast the votes of more than one member may cast the votes for those members separately.
   (ii) Except as otherwise expressly provided in this Agreement, all matters before the Board of Directors shall be decided by a majority of the votes cast.

Article 29 The President

1. The Board of Governors, through an open, transparent and merit-based process, shall elect a president of the Bank by a Super Majority vote as provided in Article 28. He shall be a national of a regional member country. The President, while holding office, shall not be a Governor or a Director or an Alternate for either.
2. The term of office of the President shall be five (5) years. He may be re-elected once. The President may be suspended or removed from office when the Board of Governors so decides by a Super Majority vote as provided in Article 28.
   (a) If the office of the President for any reason becomes vacant during his term, the Board of Governors shall appoint an Acting President for a temporary period or elect a new President, in accordance with paragraph 1 of this Article.

3. The President shall be Chairman of the Board of Directors but shall have no vote, except a deciding vote in case of an equal division. He may participate in meetings of the Board of Governors but shall not vote.
4. The President shall be the legal representative of the Bank. He shall be chief of the staff of the Bank and shall conduct, under the direction of the Board of Directors, the current business of the Bank.

Article 30 Officers and Staff of the Bank

1. One or more Vice-Presidents shall be appointed by the Board of Directors on the recommendation of the President, on the basis of an open, transparent and merit-based process. A Vice-President shall hold office for such term, exercise such authority and perform such functions in the administration of the Bank, as may be determined by the Board of Directors. In the absence or incapacity of the President, a Vice-President shall exercise the authority and perform the functions of the President.
2. The President shall be responsible for the organization, appointment and dismissal of the officers and staff in accordance with regulations adopted by the Board of Directors, with the exception of Vice-Presidents to the extent provided in paragraph 1 above.
3. In appointing officers and staff and recommending Vice-Presidents, the President shall, subject to the paramount importance of securing the highest standards of efficiency and technical competence, pay due regard to the recruitment of personnel on as wide a regional geographical basis as possible.

Article 31 The International Character of the Bank

1. The Bank shall not accept Special Funds, loans or assistance that may in any way prejudice, limit, deflect or otherwise alter its purpose or functions.
2. The Bank, its President, officers and staff shall not interfere in the political affairs of any member, nor shall they be influenced in their decisions by the political character of the member concerned. Only economic considerations shall be relevant to their decisions. Such considerations shall be weighed impartially in order to achieve and carry out the purpose and functions of the Bank.
3. The President, officers and staff of the Bank, in the discharge of their offices, owe their duty entirely to the Bank and to no other authority. Each member of the Bank shall respect the international character of this duty and shall refrain from all attempts to influence any of them in the discharge of their duties.

Chapter VI General Provisions

Article 32 Offices of the Bank

1. The principal office of the Bank shall be located in Beijing, People's Republic of China.
2. The Bank may establish agencies or offices elsewhere.

Article 33 Channel of Communication; Depositories

1. Each member shall designate an appropriate official entity with which the Bank may communicate in connection with any matter arising under this Agreement.

2. Each member shall designate its central bank, or such other institution as may be agreed upon with the Bank, as a depository with which the Bank may keep its holdings of currency of that member as well as other assets of the Bank.
3. The Bank may hold its assets with such depositories as the Board of Directors shall determine.

Article 34 Reports and Information

1. The working language of the Bank shall be English, and the Bank shall rely on the English text of this Agreement for all decisions and for interpretations under Article 54.
2. Members shall furnish the Bank with such information it may reasonably request of them in order to facilitate the performance of its functions.
3. The Bank shall transmit to its members an annual report containing an audited statement of its accounts and shall publish such report. It shall also transmit quarterly to its members a summary statement of its financial position and a profit and loss statement showing the results of its operations.
4. The Bank shall establish a policy on the disclosure of information in order to promote transparency in its operations. The Bank may publish such reports as it deems desirable in the carrying out of its purpose and functions.

Article 35 Cooperation with Members and International Organizations

1. The Bank shall work in close cooperation with all its members, and, in such manner as it may deem appropriate within the terms of this Agreement, with other international financial institutions, and international organizations concerned with the economic development of the region or the Bank's operational areas.
2. The Bank may enter into arrangements with such organizations for purposes consistent with this Agreement, with the approval of the Board of Directors.

Article 36 References

1. References in this Agreement to Article or Schedule refer to Articles and Schedules of this Agreement, unless otherwise specified.
2. References in this Agreement to a specific gender shall be equally applicable to any gender.

Chapter VII Withdrawal and Suspension of Members

Article 37 Withdrawal of Membership

1. Any member may withdraw from the Bank at any time by delivering a notice in writing to the Bank at its principal office.
2. Withdrawal by a member shall become effective, and its membership shall cease, on the date specified in its notice but in no event less than six (6) months after the date that notice has been received by the Bank. However, at any time before the withdrawal becomes finally effective, the member may notify the Bank in writing of the cancellation of its notice of intention to withdraw.

3. A withdrawing member shall remain liable for all direct and contingent obligations to the Bank to which it was subject at the date of delivery of the withdrawal notice. If the withdrawal becomes finally effective, the member shall not incur any liability for obligations resulting from operations of the Bank effected after the date on which the withdrawal notice was received by the Bank.

Article 38 Suspension of Membership

1. If a member fails to fulfill any of its obligations to the Bank, the Board of Governors may suspend such member by a Super Majority vote as provided in Article 28.
2. The member so suspended shall automatically cease to be a member one (1) year from the date of its suspension, unless the Board of Governors decides by a Super Majority vote as provided in Article 28 to restore the member to good standing.
3. While under suspension, a member shall not be entitled to exercise any rights under this Agreement, except the right of withdrawal, but shall remain subject to all its obligations.

Article 39 Settlement of Accounts

1. After the date on which a country ceases to be a member, it shall remain liable for its direct obligations to the Bank and for its contingent liabilities to the Bank so long as any part of the loans, guarantees, equity investments or other forms of financing under paragraph 2 (vi) of Article 11 (hereinafter, other financing) contracted before it ceased to be a member is outstanding, but it shall not incur liabilities with respect to loans, guarantees, equity investments or other financing entered into thereafter by the Bank nor share either in the income or the expenses of the Bank.
2. At the time a country ceases to be a member, the Bank shall arrange for the repurchase of such country's shares by the Bank as a part of the settlement of accounts with such country in accordance with the provisions of paragraphs 3 and 4 of this Article. For this purpose, the repurchase price of the shares shall be the value shown by the books of the Bank on the date the country ceases to be a member.
3. The payment for shares repurchased by the Bank under this Article shall be governed by the following conditions:
   (i) Any amount due to the country concerned for its shares shall be withheld so long as that country, its central bank or any of its agencies, instrumentalities or political subdivisions remains liable, as borrower, guarantor or other contracting party with respect to equity investment or other financing, to the Bank and such amount may, at the option of the Bank, be applied on any such liability as it matures. No amount shall be withheld on account of the contingent liability of the country for future calls on its subscription for shares in accordance with paragraph 3 of Article 6. In any event, no amount due to a member for its shares shall be paid until six (6) months after the date on which the country ceases to be a member.
   (ii) Payments for shares may be made from time to time, upon surrender of the corresponding stock certificates by the country concerned, to the extent by which the amount due as the repurchase price in accordance with paragraph 2 of this Article exceeds the aggregate amount of liabilities, on loans, guarantees, equity investments and other financing referred to in sub-paragraph (i) of this paragraph, until the former member has received the full repurchase price.
   (iii) Payments shall be made in such available currencies as the Bank determines, taking into account its financial position.
   (iv) If losses are sustained by the Bank on any loans, guarantees, equity investments or other financing which were outstanding on the date when a country ceased to be a

member and the amount of such losses exceeds the amount of the reserve provided against losses on that date, the country concerned shall repay, upon demand, the amount by which the repurchase price of its shares would have been reduced if the losses had been taken into account when the repurchase price was determined. In addition, the former member shall remain liable on any call for unpaid subscriptions in accordance with paragraph 3 of Article 6, to the same extent that it would have been required to respond if the impairment of capital had occurred and the call had been made at the time the repurchase price of its shares was determined.

4. If the Bank terminates its operations pursuant to Article 41 within six (6) months of the date upon which any country ceases to be a member, all rights of the country concerned shall be determined in accordance with the provisions of Articles 41 to 43. Such country shall be considered as still a member for purposes of such Articles but shall have no voting rights.

Chapter VIII Suspension and Termination of Operations of the Bank

Article 40 Temporary Suspension of Operations

In an emergency, the Board of Directors may temporarily suspend operations in respect of new loans, guarantees, equity investment and other forms of financing under sub-paragraph 2 (vi) of Article 11, pending an opportunity for further consideration and action by the Board of Governors.

Article 41 Termination of Operations

1. The Bank may terminate its operations by a resolution of the Board of Governors approved by a Super Majority vote as provided in Article 28.
2. After such termination, the Bank shall forthwith cease all activities, except those incident to the orderly realization, conservation and preservation of its assets and settlement of its obligations.

Article 42 Liability of Members and Payments of Claims

1. In the event of termination of the operation of the Bank, the liability of all members for uncalled subscriptions to the capital stock of the Bank and in respect of the depreciation of their currencies shall continue until all claims of creditors, including all contingent claims, shall have been discharged.
2. All creditors holding direct claims shall first be paid out of the assets of the Bank and then out of payments to the Bank or unpaid or callable subscriptions. Before making any payments to creditors holding direct claims, the Board of Directors shall make such arrangements as are necessary, in its judgment, to ensure a pro rata distribution among holders of direct and contingent claims.

Article 43 Distribution of Assets

1. No distribution of assets shall be made to members on account of their subscriptions to the capital stock of the Bank until:
   (i) all liabilities to creditors have been discharged or provided for; and

(ii) the Board of Governors has decided, by a Super Majority vote as provided in Article 28, to make such distribution.

2. Any distribution of the assets of the Bank to the members shall be in proportion to the capital stock held by each member and shall be effected at such times and under such conditions as the Bank shall deem fair and equitable. The shares of assets distributed need not be uniform as to type of asset. No member shall be entitled to receive its share in such a distribution of assets until it has settled all of its obligations to the Bank.
3. Any member receiving assets distributed pursuant to this Article shall enjoy the same rights with respect to such assets as the Bank enjoyed prior to their distribution.

Chapter IX Status, Immunities, Privileges and Exemptions

Article 44 Purposes of Chapter

1. To enable the Bank to fulfill its purpose and carry out the functions entrusted to it, the status, immunities, privileges and exemptions set forth in this Chapter shall be accorded to the Bank in the territory of each member.
2. Each member shall promptly take such action as is necessary to make effective in its own territory the provisions set forth in this Chapter and shall inform the Bank of the action which it has taken.

Article 45 Status of the Bank

The Bank shall possess full juridical personality and, in particular, the full legal capacity:

(i) to contract;
(ii) to acquire, and dispose of, immovable and movable property;
(iii) to institute and respond to legal proceedings; and
(iv) to take such other action as may be necessary or useful for its purpose and activities.

Article 46 Immunity from Judicial Proceedings

1. The Bank shall enjoy immunity from every form of legal process, except in cases arising out of or in connection with the exercise of its powers to raise funds, through borrowings or other means, to guarantee obligations, or to buy and sell or underwrite the sale of securities, in which cases actions may be brought against the Bank only in a court of competent jurisdiction in the territory of a country in which the Bank has an office, or has appointed an agent for the purpose of accepting service or notice of process, or has issued or guaranteed securities.
2. Notwithstanding the provisions of paragraph 1 of this Article, no action shall be brought against the Bank by any member, or by any agency or instrumentality of a member, or by any entity or person directly or indirectly acting for or deriving claims from a member or from any agency or instrumentality of a member. Members shall have recourse to such special procedures for the settlement of controversies between the Bank and its members as may be prescribed in this Agreement, in the by-laws and regulations of the Bank, or in the contracts entered into with the Bank.
3. Property and assets of the Bank shall, wheresoever located and by whomsoever held, be immune from all forms of seizure, attachment or execution before the delivery of final judgment against the Bank.

Article 47 Immunity of Assets and Archives

1. Property and assets of the Bank, wheresoever located and by whomsoever held, shall be immune from search, requisition, confiscation, expropriation or any other form of taking or foreclosure by executive or legislative action.
2. The archives of the Bank, and, in general, all documents belonging to it, or held by it, shall be inviolable, wheresoever located and by whomsoever held.

Article 48 Freedom of Assets from Restrictions

To the extent necessary to carry out the purpose and functions of the Bank effectively, and subject to the provisions of this Agreement, all property and assets of the Bank shall be free from restrictions, regulations, controls and moratoria of any nature.

Article 49 Privilege for Communications

Official communications of the Bank shall be accorded by each member the same treatment that it accords to the official communications of any other member.

Article 50 Immunities and Privileges of Officers and Employees

All Governors, Directors, Alternates, the President, Vice-Presidents and other officers and employees of the Bank, including experts and consultants performing missions or services for the Bank:

(i) shall be immune from legal process with respect to acts performed by them in their official capacity, except when the Bank waives the immunity and shall enjoy inviolability of all their official papers, documents and records;
(ii) where they are not local citizens or nationals, shall be accorded the same immunities from immigration restrictions, alien registration requirements and national service obligations, and the same facilities as regards exchange regulations, as are accorded by members to the representatives, officials and employees of comparable rank of other members; and
(iii) shall be granted the same treatment in respect of travelling facilities as is accorded by members to representatives, officials and employees of comparable rank of other members.

Article 51 Exemption from Taxation

1. The Bank, its assets, property, income and its operations and transactions pursuant to this Agreement, shall be exempt from all taxation and from all customs duties. The Bank shall also be exempt from any obligation for the payment, withholding or collection of any tax or duty.
2. No tax of any kind shall be levied on or in respect of salaries, emoluments and expenses, as the case may be, paid by the Bank to Directors, Alternate Directors, the President, Vice-Presidents and other officers or employees of the Bank, including experts and consultants performing missions or services for the Bank, except where a member deposits with its instrument of ratification, acceptance, or approval a declaration that such member retains for

itself and its political subdivisions the right to tax salaries, and emoluments, as the case may be, paid by the Bank to citizens or nationals of such member.

3. No tax of any kind shall be levied on any obligation or security issued by the Bank, including any dividend or interest thereon, by whomsoever held:
   (i) which discriminates against such obligation or security solely because it is issued by the Bank; or
   (ii) if the sole jurisdictional basis for such taxation is the place or currency in which it is issued, made payable or paid, or the location of any office or place of business maintained by the Bank.
4. No tax of any kind shall be levied on any obligation or security guaranteed by the Bank, including any dividend or interest thereon, by whomsoever held:
   (i) which discriminates against such obligation or security solely because it is guaranteed by the Bank; or
   (ii) if the sole jurisdictional basis for such taxation is the location of any office or place of business maintained by the Bank.

Article 52 Waivers

1. The Bank at its discretion may waive any of the privileges, immunities and exemptions conferred under this Chapter in any case or instance, in such manner and upon such conditions as it may determine to be appropriate in the best interests of the Bank.

Chapter X Amendment, Interpretation and Arbitration

Article 53 Amendments

1. This Agreement may be amended only by a resolution of the Board of Governors approved by a Super Majority vote as provided in Article 28.
2. Notwithstanding the provisions of paragraph 1 of this Article, the unanimous agreement of the Board of Governors shall be required for the approval of any amendment modifying:
   (i) the right to withdraw from the Bank;
   (ii) the limitations on liability provided in paragraphs 3 and 4 of Article 7; and
   (iii) the rights pertaining to purchase of capital stock provided in paragraph 4 of Article 5.
3. Any proposal to amend this Agreement, whether emanating from a member or the Board of Directors, shall be communicated to the Chairman of the Board of Governors, who shall bring the proposal before the Board of Governors. When an amendment has been adopted, the Bank shall so certify in an official communication addressed to all members. Amendments shall enter into force for all members three (3) months after the date of the official communication unless the Board of Governors specifies therein a different period.

Article 54 Interpretation

1. Any question of interpretation or application of the provisions of this Agreement arising between any member and the Bank, or between two or more members of the Bank, shall be submitted to the Board of Directors for decision. If there is no Director of its nationality on that Board, a member particularly affected by the question under consideration shall be entitled to direct representation in the Board of Directors during such consideration; the representative of such member shall, however, have no vote. Such right of representation shall be regulated by the Board of Governors.

2. In any case where the Board of Directors has given a decision under paragraph 1 of this Article, any member may require that the question be referred to the Board of Governors, whose decision shall be final. Pending the decision of the Board of Governors, the Bank may, so far as it deems necessary, act on the basis of the decision of the Board of Directors.

Article 55 Arbitration

If a disagreement should arise between the Bank and a country which has ceased to be a member, or between the Bank and any member after adoption of a resolution to terminate the operations of the Bank, such disagreement shall be submitted to arbitration by a tribunal of three arbitrators. One of the arbitrators shall be appointed by the Bank, another by the country concerned, and the third, unless the parties otherwise agree, by the President of the International Court of Justice or such other authority as may have been prescribed by regulations adopted by the Board of Governors. A majority vote of the arbitrators shall be sufficient to reach a decision which shall be final and binding upon the parties. The third arbitrator shall be empowered to settle all questions of procedure in any case where the parties are in disagreement with respect thereto.

Article 56 Approval Deemed Given

Whenever the approval of any member is required before any act may be done by the Bank except under paragraph 2 of Article 53, approval shall be deemed to have been given unless the member presents an objection within such reasonable period as the Bank may fix in notifying the member of the proposed act.

Chapter XI Final Provisions

Article 57 Signature and Deposit

1. This Agreement, deposited with the Government of the People's Republic of China (hereinafter called the "Depository"), shall remain open until December 31, 2015 for signature by the Governments of countries whose names are set forth in Schedule A.
2. The Depository shall send certified copies of this Agreement to all the Signatories and other countries which become members of the Bank.

Article 58 Ratification, Acceptance or Approval

1. This Agreement shall be subject to ratification, acceptance or approval by the Signatories. Instruments of ratification, acceptance or approval shall be deposited with the Depository not later than December 31, 2016, or if necessary, until such later date as may be decided by the Board of Governors by a Special Majority vote as provided in Article 28. The Depository shall duly notify the other Signatories of each deposit and the date thereof.
2. A Signatory whose instrument of ratification, acceptance or approval is deposited before the date on which this Agreement enters into force, shall become a member of the Bank, on that date. Any other Signatory which complies with the provisions of the preceding paragraph, shall become a member of the Bank on the date on which its instrument of ratification, acceptance or approval is deposited.

Article 59 Entry into Force

This Agreement shall enter into force when instruments of ratification, acceptance or approval have been deposited by at least ten (10) Signatories whose initial subscriptions, as set forth in Schedule A to this Agreement, in the aggregate comprise not less than fifty (50) per cent of total of such subscriptions.

Article 60 Inaugural Meeting and Commencement of Operations

1. As soon as this Agreement enters into force, each member shall appoint a Governor, and the Depository shall call the inaugural meeting of the Board of Governors.
2. At its inaugural meeting, the Board of Governors:
   (i) shall elect the President;
   (ii) shall elect the Directors of the Bank in accordance with paragraph 1 of Article 25, provided that the Board of Governors may decide to elect fewer Directors for an initial period shorter than two years in consideration of the number of members and Signatories which have not yet become members;
   (iii) shall make arrangements for the determination of the date on which the Bank shall commence its operations; and
   (iv) shall make such other arrangements as necessary to prepare for the commencement of the Bank's operations.
3. The Bank shall notify its members of the date of the commencement of its operations.

DONE at Beijing, People's Republic of China on June 29, 2015, in a single original deposited in the archives of the Depository, whose English, Chinese and French texts are equally authentic.

SCHEDULE A

Initial Subscriptions to the Authorized Capital Stock for Countries Which May Become Members in accordance with Article 58

	Number of Shares	Capital Subscription (in million $)
PART A. REGIONAL MEMBERS		
Australia	36,912	3,691.2
Azerbaijan	2,541	254.1
Bangladesh	6,605	660.5
Brunei Darussalam	524	52.4
Cambodia	623	62.3
China	297,804	29,780.4
Georgia	539	53.9
India	83,673	8,367.3
Indonesia	33,607	3,360.7
Iran	15,808	1,580.8
Israel	7,499	749.9
Jordan	1,192	119.2
Kazakhstan	7,293	729.3
Korea	37,388	3,738.8
Kuwait	5,360	536.0
Kyrgyz Republic	268	26.8
Lao People's Democratic Republic	430	43.0
Malaysia	1,095	109.5

	Number of Shares	Capital Subscription (in million $)
Maldives	72	7.2
Mongolia	411	41.1
Myanmar	2,645	264.5
Nepal	809	80.9
New Zealand	4,615	461.5
Oman	2,592	259.2
Pakistan	10,341	1,034.1
Philippines	9,791	979.1
Qatar	6,044	604.4
Russia	65,362	6,536.2
Saudi Arabia	25,446	2,544.6
Singapore	2,500	250.0
Sri Lanka	2,690	269.0
Tajikistan	309	30.9
Thailand	14,275	1,427.5
Turkey	26,099	2,609.9
United Arab Emirates	11,857	1,185.7
Uzbekistan	2,198	219.8
Vietnam	6,633	663.3
Unallocated	16,150	1,615.0
TOTAL	750,000	75,000.0
PART B. NON-REGIONAL MEMBERS		
Austria	5,008	500.8
Brazil	31,810	3,181.0
Denmark	3,695	369.5
Egypt	6,505	650.5
Finland	3,103	310.3
France	33,756	3,375.6
Germany	44,842	4,484.2
Iceland	176	17.6
Italy	25,718	2,571.8
Luxembourg	697	69.7
Malta	136	13.6
Netherlands	10,313	1,031.3
Norway	5,506	550.6
Poland	8,318	831.8
Portugal	650	65.0
South Africa	5,905	590.5
Spain	17,615	1,761.5
Sweden	6,300	630.0
Switzerland	7,064	706.4
United Kingdom	30,547	3,054.7
Unallocated	2,336	233.6
TOTAL	250,000	25,000.0
GRAND TOTAL	**1,000,000**	**100,000.0**

Schedule B

Election of Directors

The Board of Governors shall prescribe rules for the conduct of each election of Directors, in accordance with the following provisions.

1. *Constituencies.* Each Director shall represent one or more members in a constituency. The total aggregate voting power of each constituency shall consist of the votes which the Director is entitled to cast under paragraph 3 of Article 28.
2. *Constituency Voting Power.* For each election, the Board of Governors shall establish a Minimum Percentage for constituency voting power for Directors to be elected by Governors representing regional members (Regional Directors) and a Minimum Percentage for constituency voting power for Directors to be elected by Governors representing non-regional members (Non-Regional Directors).
   (a) The Minimum Percentage for Regional Directors shall be set as a percentage of the total votes eligible to be cast in the election by the Governors representing regional members (Regional Governors). The initial Minimum Percentage for Regional Directors shall be 6%.
   (b) The Minimum Percentage for Non-Regional Directors shall be set as a percentage of the total votes eligible to be cast in the election by the Governors representing non-regional members (Non-Regional Governors). The initial Minimum Percentage for Non-Regional Directors shall be 15%.
3. *Adjustment Percentage.* In order to adjust voting power across constituencies when subsequent rounds of balloting are required under paragraph 7 below, the Board of Governors shall establish, for each election, an Adjustment Percentage for Regional Directors and an Adjustment Percentage for Non-Regional Directors. Each Adjustment Percentage shall be higher than the corresponding Minimum Percentage.
   (a) The Adjustment Percentage for Regional Directors shall be set as a percentage of the total votes eligible to be cast in the election by the Regional Governors. The initial Adjustment Percentage for Regional Directors shall be 15%.
   (b) The Adjustment Percentage for Non-Regional Directors shall be set as a percentage of the total votes eligible to be cast in the election by the Non-Regional Governors. The initial Adjustment Percentage for Non-Regional Directors shall be 60%.
4. *Number of Candidates.* For each election, the Board of Governors shall establish the number of Regional Directors and Non-Regional Directors to be elected, in light of its decisions on the size and composition of the Board of Directors pursuant to paragraph 2 of Article 25.
   (a) The initial number of Regional Directors shall be nine.
   (b) The initial number of Non-Regional Directors shall be three.
5. *Nominations.* Each Governor may only nominate one person. Candidates for the office of Regional Director shall be nominated by Regional Governors. Candidates for the office of Non-Regional Director shall be nominated by Non-Regional Governors.
6. *Voting.* Each Governor may vote for one candidate, casting all of the votes to which the member appointing him is entitled under paragraph 1 of Article 28. The election of Regional Directors shall be by ballot of Regional Governors. The election of Non-Regional Directors shall be by ballot of Non-Regional Governors.
7. *First Ballot.* On the first ballot, candidates receiving the highest number of votes, up to the number of Directors to be elected, shall be elected as Directors, provided that, to be elected, a candidate shall have received a sufficient number of votes to reach the applicable Minimum Percentage.
   (a) If the required number of Directors is not elected on the first ballot, and the number of candidates was the same as the number of Directors to be elected, the Board of Governors shall determine the subsequent actions to complete the election of Regional Directors or the election of Non-Regional Directors, as the case may be.

8. *Subsequent Ballots.* If the required number of Directors is not elected on the first ballot, and there were more candidates than the number of Directors to be elected on the ballot, there shall be subsequent ballots, as necessary. For subsequent ballots:
   (a) The candidate receiving the lowest number of votes in the preceding ballot shall not be a candidate in the next ballot.
   (b) Votes shall be cast only by: (i) Governors who voted in the preceding ballot for a candidate who was not elected; and (ii) Governors whose votes for a candidate who was elected are deemed to have raised the votes for that candidate above the applicable Adjustment Percentage under (c) below.
   (c) The votes of all the Governors who cast votes for each candidate shall be added in descending order of number, until the number of votes representing the applicable Adjustment Percentage has been exceeded. Governors whose votes were counted in that calculation shall be deemed to have cast all their votes for that Director, including the Governor whose votes brought the total over the Adjustment Percentage. The remaining Governors whose votes were not counted in that calculation shall be deemed to have raised the candidate's total votes above the Adjustment Percentage, and the votes of those Governors shall not count towards the election of that candidate. These remaining Governors may vote in the next ballot.
   (d) If in any subsequent ballot, only one Director remains to be elected, the Director may be elected by a simple majority of the remaining votes. All such remaining votes shall be deemed to have counted towards the election of the last Director.
9. *Assignment of Votes.* Any Governor who does not participate in voting for the election or whose votes do not contribute to the election of a Director may assign the votes to which he is entitled to an elected Director, provided that such Governor shall first have obtained the agreement of all those Governors who have elected that Director to such assignment.
10. *Founding Member Privileges.* The nomination and voting by Governors for Directors and the appointment of Alternate Directors by Directors shall respect the principle that each Founding Member shall have the privilege to designate the Director or an Alternate Director in its constituency permanently or on a rotating basis.

APPENDIX 2

Report on the Articles of Agreement of the Asian Infrastructure Investment Bank, Chief Negotiators for Establishing the Asian Infrastructure Investment Bank

Singapore May 22, 2015

Report on the Articles of Agreement of the Asian Infrastructure Investment Bank

The Asian Infrastructure Investment Bank (AIIB) stems from an initiative by China, joined by the parties to the Memorandum of Understanding of October 24, 2014 (MOU), recognizing the importance of infrastructure to the development of Asia and the need for considerable additional long-term financing for infrastructure in the region.

A Special Ministerial Meeting of the signatories to the MOU set up a forum to prepare the establishment of the AIIB, the Chief Negotiators' Meetings, joined by representatives of the parties to the MOU. These parties, having signed or later endorsed the MOU, are the Prospective Founding Members of the AIIB, to become Founding Members following their signature and ratification of the AIIB Articles of Agreement (the AIIB Articles).

The first Chief Negotiators' Meeting took place in Kunming, China in November 2014.[1] The second Chief Negotiators' Meeting took place in Mumbai, India in January 2015, co-chaired by India.[2] The third Chief Negotiators' Meeting took place in Almaty, Kazakhstan in March 2015, co-chaired by Kazakhstan.[3] The fourth Chief Negotiators' Meeting took place in Beijing, China in April 2015.[4] The fifth Chief Negotiators' Meeting took place in Singapore in May 2015, co-chaired by Singapore.[5] The final text of the Articles of Agreement of the Asian Infrastructure Investment Bank was adopted on May 22, 2015 at the Singapore meeting.

During the discussions on the draft AIIB Articles, the representatives came to the view that certain formulations in the text represented general understandings which needed to be recorded. It was therefore agreed that a report summarizing these understandings would form part of the AIIB's basic documents, for future reference in interpreting the AIIB Articles. The explanatory paragraphs attached to this introduction should be viewed against that background.

[1] Prospective Founding Members: Bangladesh, Brunei Darussalam, Cambodia, China, India, Indonesia, Kazakhstan, Kuwait, Lao PDR, Malaysia, Mongolia, Myanmar, Nepal, Oman, Pakistan, Philippines, Qatar, Singapore, Sri Lanka, Thailand, Uzbekistan and Vietnam.

[2] Maldives, New Zealand, Saudi Arabia and Tajikistan joined as Prospective Founding Members.

[3] Jordan, Luxembourg, Switzerland and the United Kingdom joined as Prospective Founding Members.

[4] Australia, Austria, Azerbaijan, Brazil, Denmark, Egypt, Finland, France, Georgia, Germany, Iceland, Iran, Israel, Italy, Korea, Kyrgyz Republic, Malta, Netherlands, Norway, Poland, Portugal, Russia, Spain, South Africa, Sweden, Turkey, and United Arab Emirates joined as Prospective Founding Members.

[5] Representatives from all Prospective Founding Members participated.

Chief Negotiators for Establishing the Asian Infrastructure Investment Bank Singapore May 22, 2015

Explanatory Notes

Preamble. Representatives highlighted that the Bank would be established as a multilateral financial institution to promote sustained and stable growth in Asia.

Article 1, paragraph 2. Representatives noted that the current geographical region and composition listing for Asia and Oceania by the United Nations for statistical purposes formed the basis for their consideration of "Asia" and "region". The listing can be found at http://unstats.un.org/unsd/methods/m49/m49regin.htm.

Representatives further noted that future decisions on regional classification, if needed, would be made by the Board of Governors under paragraph 2 of Article 1, and that decisions on new members would be made by the Board of Governors under paragraph 2 of Article 3.

Article 5, paragraphs 2 and 3. While representatives recognized that the Board of Governors might need to exercise some flexibility in the future that would reduce the regional shareholding percentage in paragraphs 2 and 3 below 75%, representatives agreed that a minimum of 70% regional shareholding would be important in preserving the regional character of the Bank. Representatives noted that, in Schedule A, unallocated shares had been shown for regional members (Part A) and non-regional members (Part B), respectively, in anticipation of additional members joining in each category.

Article 5, paragraph 4. Representatives noted that the basic parameter for allocation of capital stock to members would be the relative share of the global economy of members within the regional and non-regional groupings, respectively. Members' shares of the global economy would be measured by reference to Gross Domestic Product (GDP), with the understanding that GDP share would be indicative only for non-regional members.

Representatives further noted that reviews of capital stock by the Board of Governors need not result in a capital increase, and any such increase would require Board of Governors' approval in accordance with paragraph 3 of Article 4.

Article 6, paragraph 5. Representatives agreed that a member that is eligible to borrow from the International Development Association (but not from the International Bank for Reconstruction and Development) would be considered a less developed country for purposes of this paragraph.

Article 11, paragraph 1. Representatives noted that the Preamble and the functions and purposes of the Bank in Articles 1 and 2 focus on the economic development of the Asia region. To the extent permitted under its operational policies, the Bank could provide financing to recipients located outside the region under Article 11, paragraph 1, consistent with its purpose and functions.

Article 13, paragraph 4. Representatives emphasized that the operational and financial policies of the Bank, referred to in paragraph 4, would be subject to approval by the Board of Directors in accordance with Article 26 and should be based on international best practices. These policies would include, among others, environmental and social frameworks, disclosure, procurement, and debt sustainability. A policy on operations in disputed areas would provide that, for financing in a disputed area, member consent is obtained in accordance with paragraph 3, and the Bank does not take a position on territorial claims.

Article 15, paragraph 1. Representatives noted that the inclusion of "other similar forms of assistance" was intended to permit the possibility of investment grants and similar instruments commonly used in infrastructure financing by multilateral development banks and others. Project preparation support could also be provided under this paragraph.

Article 16, paragraph 1. Representatives noted that the reference to "relevant legal provisions" was not intended to restrict the Bank from the benefits of treatment commonly extended to multilateral development banks by member countries in their markets.

Article 16, paragraph 8. Representatives noted that this paragraph, together with paragraph 4 of Article 24, provided the framework for the establishment of subsidiary entities with the approval of the Board of Governors. The establishment of offices of the Bank under paragraph 2 of Article 32 would be regulated under the By-Laws of the Bank.

Article 25. Representatives noted that the Board of Governors would consider rules at its inaugural meeting to enable each Director in a constituency of more than a specified number of members to appoint an additional Alternate Director. Such rules would require a Director appointing an additional Alternate Director to designate which Alternate Director shall act for the Director: (i) in his absence; and (ii) when the office of the Director is vacant under sub-paragraph 5 (c).

Article 26. Representatives noted that major policies established by the Board of Directors under Article 26 (ii) would include such policies as environmental and social impact and procurement (Article 13) and disclosure (Article 34).

A higher three-quarters majority of total voting power would be required for decisions by the Board of Directors to approve major operational and financial policies, delegate authority to the President under Bank policies, and for decisions on delegation of the Board's authority to take decisions on operations.

Representatives agreed that the oversight mechanism to be established by the Board of Directors under Article 26 (iv) would be designed in line with the principles of transparency, openness, independence and accountability, and would address such areas as audit, evaluation, fraud and corruption, project complaints and staff grievances, and reflect the Bank's character as a multilateral financial institution focused on infrastructure development.

Article 60. Representatives agreed that, until the Articles of Agreement had entered into force, the Prospective Founding Members would continue to convene Chief Negotiators' Meetings to provide a broader consultation mechanism for the establishment of the AIIB. Once the Articles of Agreement had entered into force, and until the final date under Article 58, paragraph 1, Interim Arrangements would provide an opportunity for Prospective Founding Members to continue to participate in AIIB governance, pending their completion of the steps for membership. In that period, the Boards would accommodate non-voting representatives as follows, in order to ensure that major decisions will be supported by adequate consultation of all Signatories and reached by consensus to the maximum extent possible.

a. Board of Governors. Each Signatory that has not yet become a member could send a representative to attend meetings of the Board of Governors as an observer.
b. Board of Directors. Signatories could agree on notional constituency groupings, recognizing that actual constituencies would be formed when members' Governors cast their votes for or assign their votes to a Director. Based on these notional constituency groupings, each constituency would either be represented by a Director if one has been elected by a member or members in the constituency, or, if there is no Director yet for the constituency, by a special Constituency Representative selected by the constituency members through consultations. Constituency Representatives could participate in Board of Directors' meetings without voting. A Director would informally represent the Signatories in the constituency that had not yet become members, as well as formally representing the Governors who had cast their votes for or assigned their votes to the Director. Each constituency group would be represented by a Director or by a Constituency Representative, but not both.

Once the deadline has passed for Signatories to complete the steps for membership and become members under Article 58, the period to become Founding Members would end. At that point, all Founding Members would participate in AIIB governance under normal AIIB governance arrangements, and these Interim Arrangements would terminate.

REFERENCES

AIIB Website: Many of the sources cited are posted on the AIIB website, www.aiib.org. These include:
AIIB Annual Reports: cited by year.
AIIB Basic Documents:

- By-Laws (adopted January 16, 2016, amended December 19, 2017)
- Rules of Procedure of the Board of Governors (adopted January 16, 2016, amended December 19, 2017)
- Rules of Procedure of the Board of Directors (approved January 17, 2016, amended October 9, 2017 and July 10, 2019)
- Code of Conduct for Board Officials (adopted January 16, 2016)
- Code of Conduct for Bank Personnel (adopted January 16, 2016)
- Headquarters Agreement between the Government of the People's Republic of China and the Asian Infrastructure Investment Bank (January 16, 2016)
- Staff Regulations (November 11, 2016)

AIIB Board of Governors' Resolutions and summary proceedings of meetings.
AIIB Board of Directors' Minutes, Committees, and Composition.
AIIB Members (list of members and prospective members).
AIIB Policies, including:

- Corporate Procurement Policy (September 2018)
- Environmental and Social Policy (June 2024)
- General Conditions for Sovereign-backed Loans (October 22, 2021)
- Operational Policy on Financing (revised through November 26, 2024)
- Operational Policy on International Relations (March 21, 2017)
- Policy on Public Information (September 2018)
- Policy on Prohibited Practices (May 1, 2016, amended December 8, 2016)
- Procurement Policy (revised through June 26, 2024)
- Public Information Interim Policy (January 2016)
- Sovereign-backed Loan and Guarantee Pricing Decision (revised November 26, 2024)

AIIB Press Releases: cited by title and date.

AfDB (2018). AfDB Independent Development Evaluation, *Comparative Study of Board Processes, Procedures and Practices in International Financial Institutions.*

AIIB (2018a). AIIB Board of Directors Decision on the Accountability Framework, adopted April 11, 2018. [Decision on Accountability Framework].

AIIB (2018b). Paper on the Accountability Framework, issued for the Board discussion of April 11, 2018. [Paper on Accountability Framework].

AIIB (2023a). Regulation on the Accountability Framework, adopted April 11, 2018 (effective January 1, 2019) and revised with effect from April 1, 2023. [Regulation on Accountability Framework, as revised].

AIIB (2023b). *Internal Management Review Concerning the Departure of AIIB's Former Director General of the Communications Department, Report of Findings and Recommendations*, July 7, 2003.

AIIB (2024). *Final Review of the COVID-19 Crisis Recovery Facility*, prepared for the Board of Directors meeting on April 17, 2024. [Final Review of the COVID-19 Crisis Recovery Facility].

AIIB Complaints-resolution, Evaluation and Integrity Unit (CEIU) (2024). *Independent Review Of The Delegated Project Approval Process At The Asian Infrastructure Investment Bank.*

Baffi, Paolo (2002). *The Origins of Central Bank Coordination (the establishment of the Bank for International Settlements*). Historical Publications of the Bank of Italy, Editori Laterza.

Bhattacharyay, Biswa Nath (2012). "Modes of Asian Financial Integration: Financing Infrastructure," in *Infrastructure for Asian Connectivity*, edited by Bisa Nath Bhattacharyay, Mashiro Kawai and Rajat M. Nag, 349–401. Cheltenham, UK: Edward Elgar.

Birdsall, Nancy (2018). "The Dilemma of the African Development Bank: Does Governance Matter for the Long-Run Financing of the MDBs?" *Center For Global Development Working Paper 498*, November 2018.

Bittermann, Henry J. (1967). "The Negotiating History of the Bank." Unpublished manuscript on file with author.

Bittermann, Henry J. (1971). "Negotiation of the Articles of Agreement of the International Bank for Reconstruction and Development," *International Lawyer* 5, no. 1, 59–88.

Bordo, Michael D. (2007). "A Brief History of Central Banks." Federal Reserve Bank of Cleveland, Economic Commentary, 12/1/2007. https://www.clevelandfed.org/publications/economic-commentary/2007/ec-20071201-a-brief-history-of-central-banks.

Boughton, James (2024). "Interpreting and Amending the IMF Mandate, 1944-2011," Independent Evaluation Office of the International Monetary Fund, May 9, 2024 (BP/24-01/01).

Bretton Woods Conference Collection (BWC) in the IMF Archives online. https://archivescatalog.imf.org/Details/archive/110042780.

Bronstone, Adam (1999). *The European Bank for Reconstruction and Development: The Building of a Bank for East Central Europe*. Manchester, UK: Manchester University Press.

Cisse, Hassane (2012). "Should the Political Prohibition in Charters of International Financial Institutions Be Revisited? The Case of the World Bank," in *World Bank Legal Review, Volume 3, International Financial Institutions and Global Legal Governance*, edited by Hassane Cisse, Daniel D. Bradlow, and Benedict Kingsbury, 59–92. Washington, DC: World Bank.

Clement, Piet (2023). "Institutionalizing Central Bank Cooperation," in *The Spread of Modern Central Bank and Global Cooperation*, 1919–1939, edited by Barry Eichengreen and Andreas Kakridis, 80–102. Cambridge, UK: Cambridge University Press.

Cogan, Jacob Katz (2009). "Representation and Power in International Organization: The Operational Constitution and Its Critics," *American Journal of International Law* 103, no 2, 209–63 (April 2009).

Committee of Experts (1929). "Settlement of the Reparations Problem: Report of the Committee of Experts, Paris, June 7, 1929," *American Journal of International Law* 24, no. 2, 81–143. (Supplement: Official Documents (Apr. 1930)).

Conant, Charles A. (1910). *The National Bank of Belgium*. National Monetary Commission, United States Senate, 61st Congress, 2d Session, Document 400.

Conway, Ed (2014). *The Summit: Bretton Woods, 1944*. New York: Pegasus Books.

Delikanli, Ihsan, Dimitrov, Todor, and Agolli, Roena (2018). *Multilateral Development Banks, Governance and Finance*. London: Palgrave Macmillan e-book.

Dell, Sidney (1974). *The Inter-American Development Bank, A Study in Development Financing*. New York and London: Praeger Publishers.

Development Committee (formally known as the Joint Ministerial Committee of the Boards of Governors of the World Bank and International Monetary Fund on the Transfer of Real Resources to Developing Countries) (2007). "Voice and Participation in the World Bank: Legal Framework," found as Annex 1B to *Options Paper on Voice and Representation—Final Report*, DC2007-0009/1, April 6, 2007.

Development Committee (2008). *Enhancing Voice and Participation of Developing and Transition Countries in the World Bank Group: Options for Reform*, DC2008-0013, October 12, 2008.

Development Committee (2010). *World Bank Group Voice Reform: Enhancing Voice and Participation of Developing and Transition Countries in 2010 and Beyond*, DC2010-0006/1, April 25, 2010.

Development Committee (2011). *Strengthening Governance and Accountability: Shareholder Stewardship and Oversight*, Background Document, DC2011-0006, April 4, 2011, Annex 2.

Development Committee (2016). *Dynamic Formula—Report to the Governors, Annual Meetings 2016*, DC2016-0010, September 20, 2016.

Development Committee (2024). *Report to Governors at the 2024 Annual Meetings Technical Preparations for the 2025 Shareholding Review*, DC2024-0005, September 26, 2024.

Díaz-Bonilla, Eugenio and Maria Victoria del Campo (2010). *A Long and Winding Road: The Creation of the Inter American Development Bank*. Available via lulu.com.

Dollar, David (2015). "China's Rise as a Global and Regional Power," *Horizons*, Summer, no. 4, 162–72.

Dulles, Eleanor Lansing (1932). *The Bank for International Settlements At Work*. New York: The MacMillan Company.

Eichengreen, Barry (1992). *Golden Fetters, the Gold Standard and the Great Depression, 1919-1939*. New York and Oxford: Oxford University Press.

English, E. Philip and Harris M. Mule (1996). *The Multilateral Development Banks, Volume 1: The African Development Bank*. Boulder, CO: Lynne Rienner Publishers.

European Investment Bank (EIB) (2008). *The Bank of the European Union: The EIB, 1958–2008.* Luxembourg: European Investment Bank.
European Investment Bank (EIB) (2015). *European Investment Bank: The Governance.* Luxembourg: European Investment Bank.
European Investment Bank (EIB) (2021). *The European Investment Bank's Inspectorate General, From past to future.* Luxembourg European Investment Bank.
Fox, Grace (1950). "The Origins of UNRRA," *Political Science Quarterly* 65, 561–84.
G20 (Group of Twenty) Eminent Persons Group on Global Financial Governance (G20 2018). "Making the Global Financial System Work for All," October 2018, www.globalfinancialgovernance.org.
G20 (Group of Twenty) (2022). Boosting MDBs' investing capacity. (2022). An Independent Review of Multilateral Development Banks' Capital Adequacy Frameworks. Capital Adequacy Frameworks Panel Report. https://www.dt.mef.gov.it/export/sites/sitodt/modules/documenti_it/news/news/CAF-Review-Report.pdf.
Gardiner, Robert K.A. and James Pickett (1984). *The African Development Bank 1964–1984.* Abidjan, Cote d'Ivoire: The African Development Bank.
Giovanoli, Mario (1989). "The Role of the Bank for International Settlements in International Monetary Cooperation and Its Tasks Relating to the European Currency," *International Lawyer* 23, no. 4 (Winter 1989), 841–64.
Gold, Joseph (1979). *Legal and Institutional Aspects of the International Monetary System: Selected Essays*, edited by Jane B. Evensen and Jai Keun Oh. Washington, DC: International Monetary Fund.
Gold, Joseph (1974). *Membership and Nonmembership in the International Monetary Fund.* Washington, DC: International Monetary Fund.
Gutner, Tamar (2025). *The Asian Infrastructure Investment Bank, China's multilateral experiment.* Oxford: Oxford University Press.
He, Alex (2016). "China in the International Financial System: A Study of the NDB and the AIIB," *CIGI Papers*, no. 106 (June).
Helleiner, Eric (2014). *Forgotten Foundations of Bretton Woods: International Development and the Making of the Postwar Order.* Ithaca, NY: Cornell University Press.
Helleiner, Eric (2017). "The Latin American Origins of Bretton Woods," in *The Global Political Economy of Raúl Prebisch*, edited by Matias E. Margulis, 78–94. London: Routledge.
Helleiner, Eric (2017a). "What's Been Missing from Conventional Histories of Bretton Woods?" in *Global Perspectives on the Bretton Woods Conference and the Post-War World Order*, edited by Giles Scott-Smith and J. Simon Rofe, 17–34. London: Palgrave MacMillan.
Helleiner, Eric (2019). "Multilateral Development Finance in Non-Western Thought: From Before Bretton Woods to Beyond," *Development and Change* 50, no. 1, 144–163.
Herrera, Felipe (1960). "The Inter-American Development Bank," *Social Science* 35, no. 4, 216–21.
Horsefield, J. Keith (1969). *The International Monetary Fund 1945–1965, Twenty Years of International Monetary Cooperation Volume I: Chronicle.* International Monetary Fund.
Howland, Douglas (2015). "An alternative mode of international order: The international administrative union in the nineteenth century," *Review of International Studies* 41, no. 1, 161–83.
Huang, Po-wen, Jr. (1975). *The Asian Development Bank: Diplomacy and Development in Asia.* New York: Vantage Press.
Humphrey, Chris (2015a). "Developmental Revolution or Bretton Woods Revisited? The Prospects of the BRICS New Development Bank and the Asian Infrastructure Investment Bank," *Overseas Development Institute Working Paper* 418 (April 2015).
Humphrey, Chris (2015b). *Are Credit Rating Agencies Limiting the Operational Capacity of Multilateral Development Banks?* Intergovernmental Group of 24 (G-24), October 30, 2015.
Humphrey, Chris (2016). "The Invisible Hand: Financial Pressures and Organisational Convergence in Multilateral Development Banks," *Journal of Development Studies* 52, no. 1, 92–112.
Humphrey, Chris (2020). *Financing the Future.* New York: Oxford University Press.
Humphrey, Chris (2024), Chris McHugh, Eamonn White, and Bianca Getzel, "Maximising the developmental impact of MDB callable capital," ODI (Overseas Development Institute) Working Paper, April 2024. https://odi.org/en/about/our-work/maximising-the-developmental-value-of-mdb-callable-capital/.
Independent Evaluation Group (IEG) of the World Bank Group (2025). *Early-Stage Evaluation of International Finance Corporation Platforms Approach Addressing Development Challenges at Scale.*
International Bank for Reconstruction and Development (IBRD) (2024). *IBRD Information Statement*, September 19, 2024, filed with the U.S. Securities and Exchange Commission electronically through the EDGAR system and available at http://www.sec.gov/edgar.shtml.

Jin, Liqun (2015). "Financing for the Future—The Vision for the Asian Infrastructure Investment Bank," *Horizons*, Summer, no. 4, 54–61.
Kappagoda, Nihal (1995). *The Multilateral Development Banks, Volume 2: The Asian Development Bank.* Boulder, CO: Lynne Rienner Publishers.
Karns, Margaret P., Johnson, Tana, and Mingst, Karen A., (2024). *International Organizations, The Politics and Processes of Global Governance*, 4th edition. Boulder, CO: Lynne Rienner Publishers, Inc.
Krishnamurthi, R. (1977). *ADB-The Seeding Days*, Asian Development Bank.
Landmann, Julius (1910). *The Swiss Banking Law.* National Monetary Commission, United States Senate, 61st Congress, 2d Session, Document 401.
Lichtenstein, Natalie (2018). "Governance of the Asian Infrastructure Investment Bank in Comparative Context" in *Good Governance and Modern Financial Institutions, AIIB Yearbook of International Law, 2018*, edited by Peter Quayle and Xuan Gao, 50–67.
Luxford, Ansel F. (1961). Transcript of oral history interview with Ansel F. Luxford held on July 13, 1961 (English). World Bank Group Archives oral history program Washington, DC: World Bank. http://documents.worldbank.org/curated/en/910701468328808086.
Martinez-Diaz, Leonardo (2009). "Executive Boards in International Organizations," in *Studies of IMF Governance: A Compendium*, edited by Ruben Lamdany and Leonardo Martinez-Diaz, 82–126. Washington, DC: IMF International Evaluation Office.
Mason, Edward S. and Robert E. Asher (1973). *The World Bank Since Bretton Woods.* Washington, DC: The Brookings Institution.
Menkveld, Paul A. (1991). *Origin and Role of the European Bank for Reconstruction and Development.* London: Graham & Trotman.
Mingst, Karen A. (1990). *Politics and the African Development Bank.* Lexington, KY: The University Press of Kentucky.
Mistry, Percy (1995). *Multilateral Development Banks: An Assessment of Their Financial Policies, Structures and Practices.* The Hague: FONDAD.
Morris, Scott (2016). "Responding to AIIB: U.S. Leadership at the Multilateral Development Banks in a New Era," *Center for Global Development Policy Paper 091*, October 2016.
Nestor, Stilpon (2019). "Board Effectiveness in International Financial Institutions: A Comparative Perspective on the Effectiveness Drivers in Constituency Boards," in *Good Governance and Modern Financial Institutions, AIIB Yearbook of International Law, 2018*, edited by Peter Quayle and Xuan Gao, 4–28.
Oliver, Robert (1996). *International Economic Co-operation and the World Bank.* London: Macmillan.
Parra, Antonio R. (2017). *The History of ICSID* (second edition). Oxford: Oxford University Press.
Reinisch, August (2008). "The Immunity of International Organizations and the Jurisdiction of Their Administrative Tribunals," *Chinese Journal of International Law* 7, no. 2, 285–306.
Reinisch, August and Jakob Wurm (2010). "International Financial Institutions before National Courts," in *International Financial Institutions and International Law*, edited by Daniel Bradlow and David Hunter, 103–35. The Netherlands: Wolters Kluwer.
Reynolds, Jackson E. (1933). "The Legal Structure of the Bank for International Settlements," *American Bar Association Journal* 19 (May 1933), 289–93.
Rigo Sureda, Andres (2004). "The Law Applicable to the Activities of International Development Banks," in *Collected Courses of The Hague Academy of International Law*, 308. Boston, MA: Brill Nijhoff.
Rolland, Nadege (2017). *China's Eurasian Century? Political and Strategic Implications of the Belt and Road Initiative* (National Bureau of Asian Research).
Sanders, Gerard (2017a). "The Asian Infrastructure Investment Bank and the Belt and Road Initiative: Complementarities and Contrasts," *Chinese Journal of International Law* 16, no. 2, 367–71.
Sanders, Gerard (2017b). "Financing of Investment Projects at the AIIB: Institutional Set-Up and First Experiences," *Manchester Journal of International Economic Law* 14, no. 2, 262–65.
Sanders, Gerard (2022). "The Historical Roots of International Financial Institutions and their Impact on the Purposes and Governance of these Organizations," *Manchester Journal of International Economic Law* 19, no. 1, 2–36.
Schuler, Kurt and Gabrielle Canning (2019). *Just Before Bretton Woods, The Atlantic City Conference, June 1944.* Center for Financial Stability, online at www.centerforfinancialstability.org.
Sharif, Hamid (2023). "An Increased Normalization of IAMs Faces Ground Realities: Lack of Transparency Impedes Access to IAMs," Independent Accountability Mechanism Project, American University Washington College of Law, 1–12.

Shihata, Ibrahim F.I. (1988). *MIGA and Foreign Investment: Origins, Operations, Policies and Basic Documents of the Multilateral Investment Guarantee Agency.* Boston, MA: Martinus Nijhoff.
Shihata, Ibrahim F.I. (1990). *The European Bank for Reconstruction and Development: A Comparative Analysis of the Constituent Agreement.* London: Martinus Nijhoff.
Shihata, Ibrahim F.I. (1999). "The Creative Role of the Lawyer—Example: The Office of the World Bank's General Counsel," *Catholic University Law Review* 48, no. 4, 1041–53.
Shihata, Ibrahim F.I. (2000). *The World Bank Legal Papers.* The Hague: Martinus Nijhoff.
Simmons, Beth A. (1993). "Why Innovate? Founding the Bank for International Settlements," *World Politics* 45, no. 3 (Apr., 1993), 361–405.
Simpson, Seth (1944). "International Labor Conference: Twenty-sixth Session," American Journal of International Law 38, no. 4, 557–76 (October 1944).
Standard and Poor's (2015). Standard and Poor's Research Update: "Asian Infrastructure Investment Bank 'AAA' Rating Affirmed; Outlook Stable," March 13, 2025.
Sun, Yun (2015). "China and the Evolving Asian Infrastructure Investment Bank," in *Asian Infrastructure Investment Bank: China as Responsible Stakeholder*, edited by Daniel Bob, 27–41. Washington, DC: Sasakawa USA.
Thornton, Christy (2017). "Voice and Vote for the Weaker Nations: Mexico's Bretton Woods," in *Global Perspectives on the Bretton Woods Conference and the Post-War World Order*, edited by G. Scott-Smith and J.S. Rofe, 149–65. London: Palgrave Macmillan.
Thornton, Christy (2018). "Mexico Has the Theories: Latin America and the Interwar Origins of Development," in *The Development Century, A Global History*, edited by Stephen J. Macekura and Erez Manela, 263–82. Cambridge: Cambridge University Press.
Thornton, Christy (2021). *Revolution in Development, Mexico and the Governance of the Global Economy.* Oakland, CA: University of California Press.
Tussie, Diane (1995). *The Multilateral Development Banks, Volume 4: The Inter-American Development Bank.* Boulder, CO: Lynne Rienner Publishers.
UN Economic and Social Commission for Asia and the Pacific (ESCAP) (2005). *Implementing the Monterrey Consensus in the Asian and Pacific Region: Achieving Coherence and Consistency.* New York: United Nations.
US Department of State (1940). *United States Department of State Bulletin*, May 11, 1940, containing the text of the Convention for the Establishment of an Inter-American Bank (with attachments) at 512–25.
US Department of State (1948). *Proceedings and Documents of the United Nations Monetary and Financial Conference. Bretton Woods, New Hampshire, July 1–22, 1944. Vols. 1 and 2.*
US Department of Treasury Records. National Archives at College Park, MD. Record Group (RG) 56, General Records of the Treasury Department, Entry 67A1804 - Box 65, File 3: Inter-American Bank Memoranda, Vol. 1; [Merle] Cochran to [Harry Dexter] White, December 4, 1939 and [Simon] Hanson to [Harold] Glasser, "Organization of the Inter-American Bank," January 3, 1940.
US Department of Treasury (1944). "Questions and Answers on the Bank for Reconstruction and Development, June 10, 1944," mimeograph, Washington, DC, available as Center for Financial Stability, Paper in Financial History, *Questions and Answers on the Bank for Reconstruction and Development, June 10, 1944*, edited by Kurt Schuler and Dylan Schuler, August 14, 2013.
Wang, Hongying (2015). "The Asian Infrastructure Investment Bank: A New Bretton Woods Moment? A Total Chinese Triumph?" *CIGI Policy Brief*, no. 59, April 2015.
Wang, Hongying (2016). "New Multilateral Development Banks: Opportunities and Challenges for Global Governance," *Council on Foreign Relations Discussion Paper.*
Weber, Stephen (1994). "Origins of the European Bank for Reconstruction and Development," *International Organization* 48, no. 1, 1–38.
Weiss, Martin (2017). "Asian Infrastructure Investment Bank," *Congressional Research Service Research Report*, February 3, 2017.
White, John (1968). "The Asian Development Bank: A Question of Style," *International Affairs* 44, no. 4, 677–90.
White, John (1970). *Regional Development Banks: A Study of Institutional Style.* London: Overseas Development Institute.
Wihtol, Robert (2015). "Beijing's Challenge to the Global Financial Architecture," *Georgetown Journal of Asian Affairs*, Spring/Summer 2015, 7–15.
Williams, Sir John Fischer (1930). "The Legal Character of the Bank for International Settlements," *American Journal of International Law* 24, no. 4, 665–73 (October 1930).
Wilson, Dick (1987). *A Bank for Half the World: The Story of the Asian Development Bank 1966–86.* Manila, Philippines: Asian Development Bank.

World Bank Group 2024 Trust Fund Report.
Xi, Jinping (2013). "Deepen Reform and Opening Up and Work Together for a Better Asia Pacific," H.E. Xi Jinping, President of the People's Republic of China to the APEC CEO Summit, October 7, 2013, Bali, Indonesia, available at http://www.fmprc.gov.cn/mfa_eng/topics_665678/xjpfwynmlxycx21 apec_665682/t1088517.shtml.
Xu, Jiajun (2021). "The Asian Infrastructure Investment Bank: Its Birth, Mandates and Infrastructure Financing,' in *Regional Development Banks in the World Economy*, edited by Judith Clifton, Daniel Diaz-Fuentes, and David Howarth 195–220. Oxford: Oxford University Press.
Yago, Kazuhiko (2012). *The Financial History of the Bank for International Settlements*. London: Taylor & Francis Group.
Zaccaria, Giuseppe (2024). "Using COVID-19 as opportunity: the role of AIIB's leadership in its strategic adaptation to the pandemic," *The Pacific Review* 37, no. 2, 419–44.
Zedillo, Ernesto (2009). *Repowering the World Bank for the 21st Century: Report of the High-Level Commission on Modernization of World Bank Group Governance*. Washington, DC: World Bank.

INDEX

Figures are indicated by an italic *f* following the figure number.

The manufacturer's authorised representative in the EU for product safety is Oxford University Press España S.A. of El Parque Empresarial San Fernando de Henares, Avenida de Castilla, 2 - 28830 Madrid (www.oup.es/en or product.safety@oup.com). OUP España S.A. also acts as importer into Spain of products made by the manufacturer.
Printed and bound by CPI Group (UK) Ltd, Croydon, CR0 4YY
14/09/2026
02216285-0002